INTENSIVE BUI...

INTENSIVE BULGARIAN

A TEXTBOOK AND REFERENCE GRAMMAR

VOLUME 1

BY

RONELLE ALEXANDER

WITH THE ASSISTANCE OF OLGA M. MLADENOVA

THE UNIVERSITY OF WISCONSIN PRESS

The University of Wisconsin Press
1930 Monroe Street, 3rd floor
Madison, Wisconsin 53711-2059
uwpress.wisc.edu

3 Henrietta Street
London WC2E 8LU, England
eurospanbookstore.com

9   11   13   12   10

Printed in the United States of America

Library of Congress Cataloging-in-Publication Data

Alexander, Ronelle, with the assistance of Olga M. Mladenova
Intensive Bulgarian: A Textbook and Reference Grammar, Volumes 1 & 2
Volume 1 = 414 pp.   cm.; Volume 2 = 413 pp.   cm.
ISBN 0-299-16744-5 (Volume 1) (alk. paper)
ISBN 0-299-16754-2 (Volume 2) (alk. paper)
Bulgarian language Textbooks for foreign speakers–English.
I. Title.
PG839.5.E5A44 2000

491.8'082421–dc21 98-17528

Publication of this book has been made possible in part by
a grant from the Peter N. Kujachich Endowment in Balkan Studies
at the University of California-Berkeley.

ISBN-13: 978-0-299-16744-8 (Volume 1) (pbk.: alk. paper)
ISBN-13: 978-0-299-16754-7 (Volume 2) (pbk.: alk. paper)

DEDICATION

To the memory of two friends and colleagues who left us far too soon

Maksim Slavchev MLADENOV (1930-1992)

Mihaila Petkova STAINOVA (1940-1987)

Intensive Bulgarian audio tapes and CDs

Audio tapes and CDs that complement this textbook are available from the University of California-Berkeley Language Center. These tapes and CDs---one per volume---contain recordings of all the dialogues (both volumes), most of the sample sentences (volume 1 only), and certain readings (both volumes), as well as brief excerpts of Bulgarian folk music (both volumes).

To order, contact:

The University of California
Berkeley Language Center
Media Duplication Services
B-40 Dwinelle Hall #2640
Berkeley, CA 94720-2640

email: LL-dup@socrates.berkeley.edu
phone: (510) 642-0767, ext. 29
http://www.ITP.berkeley.edu/blc/mediaduplication.htm

CONTENTS

LESSON 2

LESSON 3

LESSON 4

LESSON 5

LESSON 6

LESSON 7

LESSON 8

LESSON 9

LESSON 10

LESSON 12

LESSON 13

LESSON 14

LESSON 15

INTRODUCTION

Bulgarian is the language of the Republic of Bulgaria, and as such is spoken by approximately ten million people. In global terms, this is a fairly small number. In geographical terms as well, Bulgaria is a relatively small country. It is thus unavoidable that both Bulgarians and those who teach and study Bulgarian become accustomed to thinking of it as a small or lesser-known language, since much of the world refers to it as such. It is clear to all who know it, however, that Bulgarian is an extremely fascinating and complex language, and that it carries in its expression a cultural heritage of long duration and great richness. Linguists have many different reasons to learn Bulgarian, for both its structure and its dialectal variation hold treasure stores of data yet to be mined and analyzed. Cultural historians also have many reasons to learn Bulgarian, for it covers a vast and important history. Finally, the people of modern Bulgaria are perhaps the best reason to learn Bulgarian. Communication is the purpose of language, after all, and they are a people eminently worth speaking with.

Intensive Bulgarian is designed to introduce the English-speaking student to the essentials of Bulgarian grammar. The text is presented in two volumes of 15 lessons each. Each lesson begins with a dialogue, which presents a segment of a continuing story told in contemporary colloquial spoken Bulgarian, focusing on the interaction between two visiting American students and several small groups of Bulgarians. Except for the review lesson at the end of Volume 1, each lesson concludes with a reading selection. Many of the reading selections also form part of a continuous narrative, presented as a series of letters between a Bulgarian family and an American family. Other reading selections are intended to expose the student to different styles of contemporary written Bulgarian. All but the final lessons in each volume also include drill and translation exercises, sample sentences (examples which illustrate usage to a greater extent possible than in the dialogue story script), and "Cultural commentary", containing brief explanatory notes about Bulgarian culture and society. Bulgarian-English glossaries are given at the end of each lesson, and are repeated in a cumulative glossary at the end of each volume. The Bulgarian-English glossary list in Volume 2 contains all words which occur in both volumes. Additionally, Volume 1 contains a brief English-Bulgarian glossary.

The central focus of both volumes is on the grammar explanations. As its subtitle indicates, *Intensive Bulgarian* is written with a dual intent. On the one hand, it is a textbook which gives a graded presentation of Bulgarian grammar that can be used either in the classroom or for self-study. Reflecting the fact that second-Slavic language classes are often a combination of undergraduates with no other exposure to foreign languages and graduates specializing either in Slavic languages or linguistics, the lessons are split into "Basic grammar" (designed for the first group) and "Additional grammar notes" (designed for the second group). Readings, sample sentences, substitution drills, and translation exercises complete the pedagogical side of *Intensive Bulgarian*. Audio tapes (also available in CD format), as a supplementary aid in the acquisition of pronunciation, may be purchased separately (see p. vi). These feature native speakers reading all the dialogues, most of the sample sentences, and selected readings from both volumes. The assumption throughout, exemplified in the primary focus on grammar, is that speaking will come on its own with practice (especially in a Bulgarian-speaking environment) once students have acquired a solid knowledge of grammatical structure. The presentation of grammar in Volume 2 continues in the same vein through the end of Lesson 23, after which the division between "Basic grammar" and "Additional grammar notes" is abandoned. Lessons 24-29 present the grammar in unified terms.

The other intent of *Intensive Bulgarian* is to serve as a reference grammar. To this end, the grammar explanations in Volume 1 have been made as thorough as possible while still remaining consistent with the textbook format. Additionally, Lesson 15 presents a concise synopsis of Bulgarian grammar, to which has been appended a full listing of all verbal paradigms (including those to be explicated in Volume 2) and a full presentation of all word order rules. A comprehensive index completes the presentation of Volume 1. Volume 2, while still maintaining the textbook format, goes into much further detail on analytic issues of Bulgarian grammar, and concludes with a new interpretation both of the Bulgarian conditional and of the entire Bulgarian tense-mood-aspect system.

Both volumes have been written in layman's language, on the assumption that complex grammatical issues can be made accessible to the intelligent layman if specialized jargon (or recourse to theories requiring special formalism) is avoided. During most of the writing of this book, the only other reference grammar available in English required knowledge of a specialized theory. As this book goes to press, however, other accessibly-written reference grammars have begun to appear. The contribution of *Intensive Bulgarian* to a suddenly enriched field lies in its unique dual focus: it is thorough enough to give the student and scholar not only linguistically sophisticated analyses accompanied by extensive examples and furnished with a full index, but it also offers the clarity and fullness of the pedagogical approach which includes lively speech, cultural notes, extensive glossaries and concise, accessible explanations, many of which make explicit reference to structural similarities and differences between Bulgarian and English.

 Intensive Bulgarian, therefore, provides a self-contained description of the Bulgarian language, written in textbook format but with a thoroughness approaching that of a reference grammar.

 As a textbook, *Intensive Bulgarian* is intended to aid students in acquiring communicative skills (via practice of the conversational phrases embedded in the dialogues, the letters, and included in certain of the sample sentences), structural comprehension (via study of the grammar explanations and the sample sentences), and ability in reading and writing. Language teachers and learners will find all the fundamental points of Bulgarian grammar in the "Basic" section of each lesson. Individual teachers (or self-study students) may choose to include some, all, or none of the more detailed information in the "Additional" notes which follow each "Basic" section. Most students, even those who know Russian and/or who are highly motivated and able to work intensively, will probably need three semesters to finish the book; others may require four semesters. Self-study is possible but (as in all language learning) success is more assured when the text is used in the classroom by an experienced teacher. The extent to which one (or more) of these skills are to be emphasized is at the discretion of the instructor. Students and instructors should both note that the glossary lists for each lesson are quite long, since they include all words encountered in all sections of each lesson, and that it is not expected that students attain active mastery of each lesson's vocabulary list before going on to the next lesson. It is suggested that each instructor select from the lists the words that are to be actively memorized for each lesson.

 As a reference grammar, *Intensive Bulgarian* offers a thorough account of Bulgarian morphology and syntax according to traditional models, while also introducing several innovations to descriptive Bulgarian grammar. These include:
 -- a new analysis of clitic ordering rules together with a new descriptive notation
(this presentation begins in Lesson 5, continues throughout Volume 1 to Lesson 13, and is summarized in schematic form in Lesson 15);
 -- a newly clarified schematic overview of the verbal system highlighting both the relationship between present and aorist forms (Lesson 12) and that between simplex and compound verb forms (Lesson 23 in Volume 2) and between tense and mood (Lesson 25 in Volume 2);
 -- new contributions to ongoing discussions of tense, mood and aspect (Lessons 28 and 29 in Volume 2); and, most notably,
 -- the addition of the "generalized past" to the roster of Bulgarian verbal paradigms (Lesson 29). Indeed, the major contribution of Volume 2 as a reference grammar is to demonstrate how a conventional description of the Bulgarian system of tense, aspect and mood leads naturally and inexorably to this innovative re-interpretation.

* * * * * * * *

 In writing this textbook, I have taken as authoritative sources the following standard dictionaries and grammars:
 Т. Атанасова и др., Българо-английски речник
 П. Пашов и Хр. Първев, Правоговорен речник на българския език
 Л. Андрейчин, Граматика на българския език
 Ю. Маслов, Грамматика болгарского языка

 Additionally, in an attempt to describe more accurately the language spoken by educated Bulgarians, I have introduced certain interpretations of my own. The data underlying all such interpretations have been checked extensively with university-educated native speakers of Bulgarian.

ACKNOWLEDGMENTS

The division of labor in the writing of this textbook has been as follows. The conception and organization of the book, and the grammatical interpretations, are my own. I have also written all the grammar sections, all the "Cultural Commentary" sections, dialogues 1-14, and dialogues 15-18 in collaboration with Olga Mladenova. The remaining dialogues (19-30), all the reading selections not otherwise identified, all the exercises, and all the sample sentences were composed by Olga Mladenova, who has also checked the earlier dialogues and all the example sentences in the text for accuracy, and has rendered me invaluable service as an informant, both in linguistic and cultural terms. Vladimir Zhobov has also contributed many hours as an informant, and has written the reading selections in Lessons 4, 8, 12 and 14. William S. Nickell gave invaluable help and moral support throughout earlier stages of work on this textbook, and especially in first-round compilations of the glossary lists. Milena Savova (together with Eve Sweetser) and Jonathan Barnes were also of great help in the earlier and later stages, respectively, of this project.

Several classes of students have given helpful feedback on the earlier versions of this textbook. I am grateful to them, and especially to their teachers, who include (in addition to myself) Jonathan Barnes, Grace Fielder, Robert Greenberg, Christina Kramer, John Leafgren, William Nickell, and Catherine Rudin. Others who have rendered aid of various sorts are Lauren Brody, Donald Dyer, Michael Holman, Katia McClain, Yves Moreau, Valentin Paunov, Maksim Stamenov, Andrei Stoevsky, and Maria Todorova. Photos which illustrate the text either were taken by me or were donated by Robin Brooks, Robert Greenberg, Michael Kuharski, Alex Madonick, Olga Mladenova, Dirk Morr, Milena Savova, Eve Sweetser, and Orna Weinroth, to whom I extend my gratitude collectively. Their photos appear on the following pages of this first volume:

Robin Brooks: p. 161
Robert Greenberg/Orna Weinroth: p. 167
Michael Kuharski: pp. 52, 59, 280
Alex Madonick: p. 244
Olga Mladenova: pp. 67, 263, 304
Dirk Morr: pp. 45, 73
Milena Savova: pp. 79, 99, 193
Eve Sweetser: pp. 214, 216, 269

The University of Wisconsin Press has produced a beautiful volume, and Steve Salemson has been an ideal editor, without whose efforts the book would not have come to light in its present elegant manner (and with whom it has been a great pleasure to work). Cynthia Ramsey was of great assistance in the final stages of text output.

For having been allowed entry into the world of Koprivshtitsa, the inspiration of which is seen throughout both volumes of the book, I am indebted to Petăr and Vasil Petrov (and most of all to the late Mihaila Stainova); I likewise extend my gratitude to the many Bulgarian friends through whom I came to love this beautiful country and its language, especially my linguist colleagues and friends among whom stand out Tanja Behar, Todor Boyadzhiev, Georgi Kolev, Darina Mladenova, Olga Mladenova, Babina Pavlova, Vasil Vasilev, Doryana Velcheva, Vladimir Zhobov, and most of all the late Maksim Mladenov. Finally, I am grateful to family members and friends in California for their patience and unflagging support through the years it took for this work to come to fruition.

INTENSIVE BULGARIAN

LESSON A

Learning to read Bulgarian

Bulgarian is written in the Cyrillic alphabet, the same alphabet in which Russian is written. The correspondence between letters and sounds in Bulgarian is very close to that of Russian, but not identical. Once students who know Russian have adjusted to the minor differences, they will find Bulgarian very easy to read.

Students who are encountering the Cyrillic alphabet for the first time should not despair -- it is not as hard as it looks. Indeed, it will be considerably easier to learn to read Bulgarian than it was to learn to read English. One of the reasons for this is that, with very few exceptions, every Bulgarian letter always stands for the same sound. Furthermore, every sound is always rendered by the same Bulgarian letter. Once the correspondence between letter and sound is learned, therefore, one is able to read (and to write) Bulgarian. The few exceptions to the "one letter = one sound" rule will be detailed in Lesson C.

The letters of the Bulgarian alphabet are presented below in four different groups. The full Bulgarian alphabet is given at the end of Lesson A.

Letter and sound found in English, letter-sound correspondence as in English

Letter	sound	as in
a	a	father
e	e	bet
к	k	skin, score
м	m	mall, mix
т	t	stiff

Note that -т- and -к- are pronounced *without* the puff of breath that normally accompanies them in English. Pronounce "kin" holding your hand in front of your mouth; now pronounce "skin". You will note that the "k" in "skin" lacks the puff of breath that is present when you say "kin". *All* instances of -к- (and of -т-) in Bulgarian should be pronounced in this second way, without the puff of breath.

Letter and sound found in English, letter-sound correspondence not as in English

Letter	sound	as in
в	v	video, evidence
н	n	noise, instance
о	o	or
р	r	[trilled -r-] *
с	s	sister, center
у	u	boot
х	ch	[velar -ch-] **

* found in many European languages
** as in Scottish *loch* or German *Bach*

The sounds represented by -p- and -x- exist in English only as an imitation of the native pronunciation of certain European speakers. These sounds are quite common, however, especially in certain intellectual environments.

The sounds represented by -o- and -y- are very close to those of English -o- and -u-. The difference is that the Bulgarian vowel sounds are pronounced without the offglide (the slight "w" sound at the end) that accompanies them in English. Pronounce "boat" and "boot" very slowly and listen for the point at which each vowel glides down into a hint of "w". To pronounce the Bulgarian sound correctly, stop *before* the English -o- or -oo- sound moves to the "w" stage.

Sound found in English, letter not found in English

Letter	sound	as in
б	b	boy, abide
г	g	girl, again
д	d	doll, add
ж	zh	pleasure
з	z	zebra, to use
и	ee	feet
й	y	yard, bayou
л	l	less, alive
п	p	spin
ф	f	feature, tough
ц	ts	cats, tsetse
ч	ch	church
ш	sh	shift, sugar
щ	sht	ashtray
ъ	[a] *	sofa

* English unstressed [a]

4

Bulgarian -п- is pronounced like English -p- in "spin" (that is, without the puff of breath that accompanies the English -p- in "pin"; see the note above for -т- and -к-). Bulgarian -и- is pronounced without the final glide into "y" (see the note above for -o- and -y-).

The other sound-letter correspondences may seem strange, but will be acquired with practice. Pronounce the English words given above and listen for the sound. Take care to differentiate between the sounds -ц- and -с-, and between -и- and -й-. Students who know Russian should take additional care to note that -щ- signifies both the sounds -sh- and -t- together, and that -ъ- represents a fully stressable vowel.

Neither sound nor letter found in English

The letters in the final group function to distinguish hard from soft consonants. To learn the hard/soft distinction, compare the pronunciation of the middle consonant in the following pairs of English words:

hard	*soft*
canon	canyon
willow	William

Most consonants in Bulgarian are hard. Soft consonants are possible only before the vowels -o-, -y-, -a- and -ъ-, and are signaled by *vowel* letters, as follows:

Letter	*meaning*
ь	found only in the sequence -ьо-, signifies that the preceding consonant is soft
ю	signifies sequence of soft consonant + -y-
я	signifies sequence of soft consonant + -a-, or soft consonant + -ъ

Here are examples of soft consonants in Bulgarian, and of their expression in writing:

hard	*meaning*	*soft*	*meaning*	*contrast*
синове́	sons	си́ньо	blue	[hard vs. soft -н-]
бала́да	ballad	бя́ла	white	[hard vs. soft -б-]
лу́да	crazy	любо́в	love	[hard vs. soft -л-]

The letter -я- is also written for the sounds [-a-] and [-ъ-] when they occur after the letter -и-. Both the sequences и + a and и + ъ are written -ия. When the letters -ю- and -я- occur in initial position or after a vowel, they represent a complex of sounds, as follows:

letter	meaning	written example	meaning	pronounced as
ю	й + у	уютен	comfortable	[уйу́тен]
я	й + а	я́бълка	apple	[йа́бълка]

Remember that the letters -ю- and -я- always signify a vowel sound *plus* something else: either the softening of a preceding consonant, or the presence of a preceding "y" glide.

The Bulgarian alphabet

The names of the Cyrillic vowel letters are as they are pronounced, while the names of the consonant letters are pronounced with a following -ъ (а, бъ, въ, гъ, дъ, etc.). The name of the letter -й- is и кра́тко, the name of the letter -ъ- is ер голя́м, and the name of the letter -ь- is ер ма́лък.

Students learning Cyrillic for the first time must devote some attention to learning the alphabet sequence, as one cannot use a dictionary effectively without knowing alphabetical order. The order of letters in the Bulgarian alphabet is as in English in certain sequences, but quite different in others. For instance:

Similar to English

a-b	d-e	i-j-k-l-m-n-o-p	r-s-t-u
а-б	д-е	и-й-к-л-м-н-о-п	р-с-т-у

Different from English

b-d-e-f-g-h-i	f .. u-v-w-x	(end of alphabet)
б-в-г-д-ж-з-и	у-ф-х	ц-ч-ш-щ-ъ-ь-ю-я

The full Bulgarian alphabet is given on the following pages. Both upper and lower case letters are given, alongside with the Latin letters which are usually used when Bulgarian words are transliterated (rendered in the Latin alphabet).

Two different transliteration possibilities are given, the so-called "academic" transliteration, and the several transliterations used in more popular writings.

In this book, Bulgarian is transliterated as little as possible. In the few cases where it is necessary, a mixed system has been used: the "academic" version of the last four letters and the "popular" version of the others.

THE BULGARIAN ALPHABET

CYRILLIC		TRANSLITERATED	
upper case	*lower case*	*academic*	*popular*
А	а	a	a
Б	б	b	b
В	в	v	v
Г	г	g	g
Д	д	d	d
Е	е	e	e
Ж	ж	ž	zh
З	з	z	z
И	и	i	i
Й	й	j	i
К	к	k	k
Л	л	l	l
М	м	m	m
Н	н	n	n
О	о	o	o
П	п	p	p
Р	р	r	r
С	с	s	s (ss)
Т	т	t	t
У	у	u	u (ou)
Ф	ф	f	f
Х	х	x	h (kh)
Ц	ц	c	ts
Ч	ч	č	ch
Ш	ш	š	sh
Щ	щ	št	sht
Ъ	ъ	ǎ	u
	ь	'	
Ю	ю	ju	iu (yu)
Я	я	ja	ia (ya)

LESSON B

Learning to write Bulgarian

It is best to learn to write Cyrillic by practicing on lined paper. Write the letters double height at the beginning, so as to learn which ones extend above (or below) the line and which ones remain the same height. The handwritten words on the following pages illustrate the formation of capital and lower case letters at the beginning of a word, and of lower case letters in the middle of a word. The student should be able to guess the meanings of most of these words.

It is advisable to learn to write Bulgarian letters correctly at the outset. It is much harder to unlearn mistakes once they have become set into habit.

Height of the letters

All capital letters extend to the full height. Of the lower case letters, only б, в and ф are written as high as capital letters (in the scheme as given below, only they extend above the line). All others are written at the same height (the height of the space between the two middle lines). Pay particular attention to this in the case of к and л: they do not reach the same height as their English counterparts.

Depth of the letters

The letters д, р, у, ц and щ extend below the line. This will seem natural for д and у, but it must be learned especially for the others. For ц and щ, the portion that extends below the line is the loop at the lower right corner.

Diacritics and other distinguishing marks

The breve mark *must* be written over the letter й, in order to distinguish it from the letter и. Indeed, there are two words which consist only of the letter и. The one which means "her" is written with a grave accent mark (ѝ) in order to distinguish it from the one which means "and" (и).

The letters л, м and я are written with a small hook at the beginning, which *must* be there in order to distinguish them from other letters.

Examples of Bulgarian handwriting

А, а	Америка	аспирин	пират

Б, б	България	бар	орбита

В, в	Виетнам	виза	овал

Г, г	Гренландия	гангстер	диалог

Д, д	Дания	дилър	шоколад

Е, е	Европа	екватор	диета

Ж, ж	Дон Жуан	жокей	имидж

З, з	Нова Зеландия	зона	дизайн

Зз   Нова Зеландия   зона   дизайн

И, и	Италия	илюстрация	стил

Ии   Италия   илюстрация   стил

Й, й	Йордания	йерархия	май

Йй   Йордания   йерархия   май

К, к	Канада	кабина	рефлекс

Кк   Канада   кабина   рефлекс

Л, л	Лондон	лазер	култ

Лл   Лондон   лазер   култ

М, м	Мексико	мемоар	компютър

Мм   Мексико   мемоар   компютър

Н, н	Норвегия	номер	секунда

Нн   Норвегия   номер   секунда

О, о	Осло	орбита	маратон

П, п	Пловдив	пакт	апатия

Р, р	Русия	ромб	метър

С, с	София	саксофон	маска

Т, т	Турция	трилър	рекет

У, у	Унгария	утопия	стимул

Ф, ф	Франция	фарс	графика

Х, х	Хелзинки	хаос	щрих

Ц, ц	Цейлон	церемония	танц

Ч, ч	Чикаго	чинчила	сандвич

Ш, ш	Шотландия	шанс	туш

Щ, щ	Щраус	щат	мащаб

Ъ, ъ	ъперкът	спектакъл	сър

ь	Кьолн	шофьор	импортьор

Ю, ю	Югославия	юни	илюзия

Я, я	Япония	яхта	батерия

LESSON C

Learning to pronounce Bulgarian

The best way to learn to pronounce Bulgarian correctly is, of course, to listen regularly and carefully to native speakers of Bulgarian (or to tapes of them) and to imitate them. The following comments are only a guide: the way to success is constant and consistent practice.

Word accent

Word accent in Bulgarian is similar to that of English in a number of ways. First, the syllable of the word which is accented is pronounced louder and with more emphasis than the other syllables of the word. Second, one cannot predict which syllable of the word is accented but must learn it for each word. Third, the syllable which is accented is pronounced clearly as it is written, but the syllables which are unaccented are often pronounced with less enunciation. As an example, divide the English words "initiation" and "stationary" into their separate syllables:

i - ni - ti -á - tion   stá - tio - na - ry

In "initiation", the fourth syllable is accented, and in "stationary", the first syllable is accented. In each case the accented "a" sound is clearer, stronger, and somewhat longer than the other sounds. To pronounce these words correctly, one must know precisely which syllable to accent in each word. Unfortunately, the spelling of English does not provide this information.

Bulgarian is similar: one must know the place of accent in order to pronounce the word correctly, and Bulgarian spelling does not provide this information. As a guide to learning, therefore, all Bulgarian words in this textbook will be accented. The student should memorize the place of accent when learning each word, and read and speak aloud as much as possible so that the place of accent will begin to sound right to the ear.

Another similarity between Bulgarian and English concerns unaccented words and particles. Take as an example the English sentence "I'll see you." Although it is composed of four meaningful chunks, only two bear clear stress (and in fast speech, only one does). These four chunks are

I	'll	see	you
+	-	++	-

The words marked with a hyphen are written as separate components and have separate meaning. In terms of accent, however, they must lean on the neighboring word in order for the sentence to be pronounced correctly.

Bulgarian has a number of small words of this sort, called "clitics". They have no accent of their own, and obey strict word order rules. Learning to produce them in the proper order while still not accenting them takes considerable practice. Once achieved, however, it is a major step towards the acquisition of a real Bulgarian "accent".

One accentual property of Bulgarian which is not shared by English is the fact that Bulgarian can shift accent between certain forms of the same word (such as singular vs. plural). Such changes of accent must also be learned with each word.

Unstressed vowels

Syllables which are not accented are pronounced with less enunciation than those which are; this phenomenon is sometimes called "vowel reduction". The degree and manner of this reduction vary in different areas of Bulgaria, but the following description is characteristic of most speakers in the capital area, Sofia. (Throughout this textbook, letters written within brackets represent the *sound* of a word and not its spelling.)

letter	sound when accented	sound when unaccented
о	[о]	[у] *
а	[а]	[ъ]
я	[я]	[йъ]

* or sometimes like a mix between [о] and [у].

Unstressed -и-, -у- and -е- usually do not change their pronunciation. To illustrate vowel reduction, here is the spelling, and the most frequent pronunciation by Bulgarians, of three sample words:

spelling	pronunciation	(meaning)
ня́колко	[ня́кулку]	several
по́щата	[по́щътъ]	post office
ютия́	[йути́йъ]	iron [for clothing]

This incomplete correspondence of sound and letter can give the student some difficulty at the beginning. With attention, it is relatively easy to get used to.

Voicing assimilation

Most Bulgarian consonants exist in pairs, according to a phenomenon called "voicing". The terms ("voiced" vs. "unvoiced") are not important to learn, but the relationship is. This is because when certain consonants are pronounced together, the first will adjust its degree of voicing to the second, in a process called voicing assimilation.

"Voicing" refers to a relatively stronger vibration of the vocal cords. To hear voicing in English, hold your hand on your throat and say first "bin", then "pin". The vibration which distinguishes the sound -b- from the sound -p- is called voicing.

The Bulgarian consonants for which this distinction is important are the following:

(voiced)	б	д	г	з	ж	дж	в
(unvoiced)	п	т	к	с	ш	ч	ф

When a voiced consonant occurs immediately before an unvoiced one, it is pronounced as its unvoiced partner (the one immediately below it in the chart); and when an unvoiced consonant occurs immediately before a voiced one, it is pronounced as its voiced partner (the one immediately above it in the chart). When voiced consonants occur at the end of the word, they are pronounced like their unvoiced partners. Here are examples of voicing assimilation in Bulgarian:

written form	*spoken form*	*assimilation process*
изпу́скам	[испу́скам]	voiced › unvoiced before unvoiced (-з- › -с- before -п-)
отби́вам	[одби́вам]	unvoiced › voiced before voiced (-т- › -д- before -б-)
гра́д	[гра́т]	voiced › unvoiced at end of word

"Grammatical" pronunciation

There is a striking non-correspondence between letter and sound in the case of three different grammatical categories. In these instances, sounds that are *written* as -a or -я are always *pronounced* as [-ъ] or [-йъ]. When the vowel is unstressed, the difference is minimal, as unstressed -a and -я are usually pronounced as [-ъ] / [-йъ] anyway. When the vowel is stressed, however, the difference is very noticeable.

This phenomenon occurs in the 1st singular and 3rd plural present of verbs, and the definite form of masculine nouns. In the following examples, the apostrophe indicates that the preceding consonant is soft.

	spelling	pronunciation	meaning
1ˢᵗ singular	четá	[четъ́]	I read
	вървя́	[върв'ъ́]	I walk
3ʳᵈ plural	четáт	[четъ́т]	they read
	вървя́т	[върв'ъ́т]	they walk
masculine definite	в градá	[в градъ́]	in the city
	деня́т	[ден'ъ́т]	the day
	през деня́	[през ден'ъ́]	during the day

Holiday sign in downtown Sofia, late December 1990

LESSON 1

DIALOGUE

От Ва́рна за Со́фия

// Миле́на, Дими́тър, А́нгел, Де́йвид и Джу́ли пъту́ват за Со́фия от Ва́рна. //

Милена: Тръ́гваме! На́й-по́сле!

Ангел: Ви́е за къде́ пъту́вате?

Димитър: За Со́фия. А ви́е?

Ангел: И а́з пъту́вам за Со́фия. Ка́к се ка́звате?

Димитър: А́з се ка́звам Дими́тър Сто́йков. А тя́...

Милена: Ка́звам се Миле́на! Миле́на Сто́йкова!

Ангел: Откъде́ сте? От Ва́рна ли сте?

Димитър: Да́. Ни́е сме от Ва́рна.

Ангел: А ви́е, госпо́жице?

Джули: А́з се ка́звам Джу́ли Бе́йкър. Студе́нтка съм, от Аме́рика.

Дейвид: И а́з съм студе́нт, съ́що от Аме́рика. Ка́звам се Де́йвид Бо́йд.

Ангел: От Аме́рика ли сте? Студе́нти? Мно́го интере́сно!

Милена: Е́й! Откъде́ ду́ха? Ста́ва тече́ние!

Джули: Какво́ е "тече́ние"?

BASIC GRAMMAR

1.1. Gender of nouns

Nouns in Bulgarian are either masculine, feminine or neuter. Practically all masculine nouns end in a consonant, and most feminine nouns end in **-a**. This includes most personal names. Here are some examples of masculine and feminine nouns:

masculine	*feminine*
Дими́тър	Миле́на
Сто́йков	Сто́йкова
А́нгел	госпо́жица
студе́нт	студе́нтка

Nouns referring to profession or role are usually masculine. They can refer either to a male person, or to the category in general. The same noun with **-ка** added refers only to a female person.

1.2. Vocative form of nouns

When a person or object is being addressed, a special form, called the vocative, is used. The endings are **-e** for masculine nouns and **-o** (or **-e**) for feminine nouns. Here are examples of the most frequently used vocative forms, those for the nouns meaning "Mr.", "Mrs." and "Miss". Note that the accent changes place in the vocative of госпожа́ (Госпо́жо!).

neutral form	*vocative form*	*(meaning)*
господи́н	господи́н-е	Mr.
госпожа́	госпож-о	Mrs.
госпо́жица	госпо́жиц-е	Miss

1.3. Plural of nouns

Most masculine nouns, and practically all feminine nouns, form the plural by adding **-и**. Masculine nouns add this ending directly to the singular form, while feminine nouns replace the singular ending **-a** by the ending **-и**. For example:

	singular	plural
masculine	студе́нт	студе́нт-и
feminine	студе́нтк-а	студе́нтк-и

The noun госпожа́ shifts stress in the plural (госпо́жи). Such stress shifts are very exceptional.

1.4. Personal pronouns: the verb "be"

Following is the conjugation of the verb "be" in the present tense. It is given together with the personal pronouns.

	singular		plural	
1st person	а́з съм	I am	ни́е сме	we are
2nd person	ти́ си	you are *	ви́е сте	you are **
3rd person	то́й е	he is	те́ са	they are
	тя́ е	she is		

* (single person / familiar)   ** (single person / formal, or more than one person)

The 3rd plural form ca is pronounced [съ].

1.5. Present tense of verbs

All verbs have six forms in the present tense. The subject of the verb determines which form is to be used. Here is the present tense conjugation of the verb пъту́вам "go, travel". Many other Bulgarian verbs are conjugated according to this same pattern.

	singular	plural
1st person	пъту́в-ам	пъту́в-аме
2nd person	пъту́в-аш	пъту́в-ате
3rd person	пъту́в-а	пъту́в-ат

Because the ending of the verb always specifies the verb's subject, personal pronouns are optional in Bulgarian. The phrases "I am a student" and "I am traveling to Sofia" can be expressed both with and without the pronoun "I". For example:

Пъту́вам за Со́фия.	I am traveling to Sofia.
А́з пъту́вам за Со́фия.	*[same]*
Студе́нт съм.	I am a student.
А́з съм студе́нт.	*[same]*

1.6. Questions

Questions in Bulgarian, as in English, are of two types. One type includes a word such as "why?", "who?", and "where?". This type of question requests specific information. The other kind simply asks whether a particular statement is true or not, and expects yes or no as an answer. In Bulgarian, as in English, each type of question has specific word-order rules associated with it.

If a question word such as "where?" is present, it always comes right before the verb. Thus, if a subject is present, the word order will be different from that of English. For example:

	За къде́	пъту́вате?	Where are you going?
Ви́е	за къде́	пъту́вате?	*[same]*

The word order in a yes-no question changes only if the verb is **съм**. In these sentences the verb is placed at the end. Otherwise the word order stays the same. All yes-no questions, however, must contain the particle **ли**. This particle is placed right *before* a form of the verb **съм**, and right *after* all other verb forms. For example:

Ви́е	пъту́вате		дне́с.	You are traveling today.
Ви́е	пъту́вате	ли	дне́с?	Are you traveling today?
Ви́е	сте	студе́нт.		You are a student.
Ви́е		студе́нт	ли сте?	Are you a student?

1.7. Prepositions

The usage of prepositions in Bulgarian (as in English) is highly idiomatic. Most prepositions have a basic meaning, but all have numerous additional meanings which are not directly predictable from the basic meaning.

(a)   The basic meaning of the preposition **от** is that of English "from". This meaning is also present in the compound question word **откъде́**.

А́з съм от Ва́рна.	I am from Varna.
Откъде́ ду́ха?	Where is it blowing from?

(b)   The basic meaning of the preposition **за** is that of English "for". When referring to a travel goal, it is usually translated "to". The English expressions "Where are you headed for?" or "I'm leaving for Europe" may help the student to remember this usage of **за**.

Пъту́ваме за Со́фия.	We are traveling to Sofia.
За къде́ пъту́вате?	Where are you traveling to?

1.8.   Clitics and word order

Bulgarian includes a number of small, unaccented words called clitics. Among the most frequent clitics are the forms of the verb **съм,** and the particle **се**. Clitics must obey special word order rules, the most important of which is that they cannot begin a sentence or phrase. In addition, the particle **се** must always occur next to the verb it accompanies (and directly before it if possible). Likewise, a form of **съм** must always occur next to a predicate noun or adjective (and directly before it if possible). Here are examples:

А́з се ка́звам Де́йвид Бо́йд.	My name is David Boyd.
Ка́звам се Де́йвид Бо́йд.	*[same]*
А́з съм студе́нт.	I am a student.
Студе́нт съм.	*[same]*

1.9.   The conjunction "and"

There are two different ways to express the idea "and" in Bulgarian. If the two things joined are considered to be equivalent, the conjunction **и** is used; but if there is some sort of contrast, Bulgarians use the conjunction **а**. For example:

Миле́на и Дими́тър пъту́ват за Со́фия.	Milena and Dimitri are traveling to Sofia.
Миле́на пъту́ва за Со́фия, а Весели́н пъту́ва за Га́брово.	Milena is traveling to Sofia, and Veselin is traveling to Gabrovo.

EXERCISES

I. Write the questions to which the following are answers:

1. Ни́е пъту́ваме за Ва́рна.
2. Да́, те́ са студе́нти.
3. Да́, то́й е ле́кар.
4. От Со́фия съм.
5. То́й е от Со́фия, а тя́ е от Ва́рна.
6. Ка́звам се Миле́на.
7. То́й се ка́зва Ма́ксим.

II. Fill in the blanks with the correct verb form.

1. А́нгел _____ от Со́фия.
2. Миле́на и Дими́тър _____ от Ва́рна.
3. А́з отъде́ _____?
4. Ви́е от Аме́рика ли _____?
5. Ти́ студе́нт ли _____?
6. Ни́е _____ студе́нтки.
7. Те́ от Со́фия ли _____?

III. Choose the correct conjunction.

1. А́з се ка́звам Ива́н _____ ви́е ка́к се ка́звате?
2. Ни́е сме от Ва́рна _____ те́ са от Га́брово.
3. Джу́ли _____ Де́йвид са студе́нти от Аме́рика. _____ А́нгел не е́ студе́нт.
4. Ива́н _____ Ко́ста са ле́кари.
5. Ива́н е ле́кар _____ Ко́ста е ле́кар.
6. Ива́н е ле́кар _____ Дими́тър не е́.
7. А́з се ка́звам Мари́я, _____ тя́ се ка́зва Мари́я.

ADDITIONAL GRAMMAR NOTES

1.1a. **Gender of nouns**

Both first and last names in Bulgarian usually mark gender. Thus, male members of a family will have surnames ending in a consonant (Стóйков), while female members will have surnames ending in -a (Стóйкова).

Foreign names are spelled as they are pronounced:

Джýли Бéйкър	Julie Baker
Дéйвид Бóйд	David Boyd

Masculine nouns referring to a profession or role cover a broad range of meaning: they can mean the category in general, a specific male person who is a member of that category, or (in the plural) a mixed group at least one of which is male. The same noun with the suffix -ка refers exclusively to a specific female person who belongs to that category. Compare the following possible translations:

Тé са студéнти.   They are students.

    a) "they" = a group of male students
    b) "they" = a group of male and female students
    c) "they" = general (gender not important)

Тé са студéнтки.   They are students.

        "they" = a group of female students

When Bulgarians choose to focus more on the fact of a profession than on the sex of its practitioner, they may also use the masculine form to refer to a woman representative of that profession:

Тя́ е лéкар.   She is a doctor.

For many nouns such as студéнт and лéкар, there also exist the suffixed nouns студéнтка and лéкарка. In all cases the non-suffixed noun refers either to males specifically or to the category in general, and the suffixed noun refers exclusively to females. Glossary lists in this textbook will designate nouns of this sort as follows:

    Glossary listing: студéнт (ка)   student

1.3a. Vocative form of nouns

The title **господи́н** is used in the vocative when it stands alone, but when it appears with a surname, the neutral form is used.

Господи́не!	Sir!
Господи́н Атана́сов!	Mr. Atanasov!

Certain masculine nouns add **-ю** in the vocative. Among these are **друга́р** "comrade" and **прия́тел** "friend". The vocative forms of **друга́р** and **друга́рка** are **друга́рю** (both with and without a surname) and **друга́рко**. The vocative forms of personal names will be learned in Lesson 2.

1.4a. Personal pronouns; the verb "be"

As in most European languages (other than English), Bulgarian has two different words meaning "you". The singular form **ти́** is used to address children, animals, God, and close friends. The plural form **ви́е** is used to address people one does not know well and wishes to treat with courtesy, or those who are elders or people of higher rank. In this meaning, the pronoun **ви́е** refers to a single person. When it is written in a letter, it is usually capitalized. The pronoun **ви́е** (non-capitalized) is also the only form one can use to address a group of people.

In English, one must always use a subject pronoun. One cannot, for instance, say * "Am a student", but must rather say "I am a student". (The asterisk means that a phrase or sentence is ungrammatical.) In Bulgarian, however, subject pronouns are optional. They are used when the person is identified for the first time, or when one wishes to emphasize the identity of the subject. Otherwise, they are omitted.

Third person singular pronouns are **то́й** (masculine), **тя́** (feminine) and **то́** (neuter). Although most nouns designating human beings are either masculine or feminine, there are a few neuter nouns which also refer to humans (such as **дете́** "child", **момче́** "boy" and **моми́че** "girl"). The neuter pronoun is used to refer to these nouns.

1.6a. Questions

Both Bulgarian and English have specific word order rules for the formation of questions. Furthermore, both languages have different rules for yes-no questions and for Q-word questions (those containing a question word such as "who", "what", or the like).

Q-word questions in English must reverse the order of subject and auxiliary verb. In the following, for example, the subject, "you", and the auxiliary verb, "are", switch places:

		You	are		going.
(statement)		You	are		going.
(question)	Where		are	you	going?

To form correct Q-word questions in Bulgarian, one must remember both that the word order does *not* shift, and that the Q-word itself must always precede the verb directly. Thus:

(statement)	Вие		пътувате.
(question)	Вие	за къде́	пътувате?
		За къде́	пътувате?

Yes-no questions in English are formed by changing the order of subject and verb and adding rising intonation. Note the difference between the statement and the question in the following:

Statement

	word order	*sentence intonation*
You are a student.	[subject - verb]	*falling*

Question

	word order	*sentence intonation*
Are you a student?	[verb - subject]	*rising*

In Bulgarian, the word order changes only if the verb is съм; otherwise it remains the same. The particle ли is always added, however. It carries no stress of its own, but causes a strong high-pitched stress on the immediately preceding word. Study the following contrasts between statement and question:

Statement

	meaning	*intonation*
Ви́е пъту́вате дне́с.	You are traveling today.	*sentence: falling*
Ви́е сте студе́нт.	You are a student.	*sentence: falling*

Question

	meaning	*intonation*
Ви́е пъту́вате ли дне́с?	Are you traveling today?	*verb: high* *sentence: falling*
Ви́е студе́нт ли сте?	Are you a student?	*predicate: high* *sentence: falling*

1.7a. Prepositions

Monosyllabic prepositions are pronounced together with their objects as one word. Each of the following phrases, therefore, has only one accent:

от Ва́рна	from Varna
за Со́фия	to Sofia

Students who know other Slavic languages must pay especial attention to the usage of prepositional phrases in Bulgarian. This is because nouns in Bulgarian, unlike those in other Slavic languages, do not have case endings. Relationships between nouns are expressed exclusively by prepositional phrases, and the same preposition can have a number of different meanings depending on the context. One example is the preposition **на**, which has at least three basic meanings:

Meaning	*Corresponding case form in other Slavic languages*
on	Locative (sometimes called prepositional)
to	Dative
of	Genitive

1.8a. Clitics: the particle ce

The particle **ce** occurs together with a number of verbs. This particle has several meanings, the most general of which is to make a verb intransitive. When **ce** accompanies a verb, it is an integral part of that verb and must appear with every instance of the verb. Although some verbs do not even exist without **ce**, most verbs exist in two variants -- with and without **ce**. For these verbs, it is important to note that the presence or absence of **ce** changes the meaning. For instance, **ка́звам** (without **ce**) means "say", but **ка́звам ce** means "to be called":

Ка́звам се Джу́ли Бе́йкър.	My name is Julie Baker.

1.9a. The conjunction "and"

The contrast in meaning between the conjunctions **a** and **и** is much greater when they are used at the beginning of a sentence. In these cases, **и** is usually translated as "also", while **a** continues to be translated as "and". For example:

И а́з пъту́вам за Со́фия.	I'm also traveling to Sofia.
А ви́е, госпо́жице?	And you, miss?

SAMPLE SENTENCES

1. -- Лékар ли сте?
   -- Дá, а вие?
   -- И áз.

2. -- За къдé пъту́вате днéс?
   -- За Вáрна. И вие ли?
   -- И áз.

3. -- Елéна и Лиля́на са студéнтки. А Мари́я и Иˊскра?
   -- И Мари́я е студéнтка. А Иˊскра не é студéнтка. Тя́ е преподавáтелка.

4. Áз кáзвам: "Кáк се кáзвате?"
   Тóй кáзва: "Кáзвам се Áнгел. А вие?"
   Áз кáзвам: "И áз се кáзвам Áнгел."

5. -- Каквó кáзваш?
   -- Кáзвам и́стината.

   -- Кáк се кáзваш?
   -- Кáзвам се Ивáн.

SENTENCES FOR TRANSLATION

1. Are you a teacher, Miss?

2. Are you from Varna? We are going to Varna soon.

3. His name is Angel. He is a physician. He is from Plovdiv.

4. Does he know Mrs. Antonova? She is also from Plovdiv.

5. The Stoykovs are traveling to Sofia today. They are teachers.

6. Where are you from, sir? And where are you going?

7. Lilyana and Milena are friends. David and Julie are also friends.

READING SELECTION

<u>Кореспонде́нция - (1)</u>

Бо́йко Атана́сов е ле́кар. Кали́на Атана́сова е учи́телка. Те́ са от Со́фия.
И Бо́б Ми́чел е ле́кар. То́й е от Са́н Франци́ско, а сега́ пъту́ва за Со́фия.

---

15 ма́рт, Са́н Франци́ско

Господи́н Атана́сов,

    Аз се ка́звам Ро́берт Ми́чел. Ле́кар съм. Прия́тел съм на Джо́н
Гри́йн. То́й е учи́тел в Со́фия. Позна́ва госпожа́ Атана́сова.
    Ско́ро пъту́вам за Со́фия. Ви́е сега́ в Со́фия ли сте? И ви́е, ка́зва
Джо́н, сте ле́кар. Зна́чи, ни́е сме ле́кари. Мно́го интере́сно! За съжале́ние
аз разби́рам са́мо ма́лко бъ́лгарски.

Ро́берт Ми́чел

Alexander Nevsky Cathedral, Sofia (detail of dome)

28

GLOSSARY

а	and
а ви́е, госпо́жице?	and you, miss?
а́з	I
а́з се ка́звам	my name is
ба́й	uncle, old man (term of address)
бъ́лгарски	Bulgarian (language)
в	in
ви́е	you (pl.)
ви́е	you (sg., polite)
господи́н	Sir, Mr.
госпожа́ (pl. госпо́жи)	Ma'am, Mrs.
госпо́жица	Miss
да́	yes
дете́	child
дне́с	today
друга́р (ка)	comrade
ду́ха	it's blowing
е	is (3sg.)
е́й!	hey!
ефе́нди	effendi, sir (archaic term of address)
за	for, to
за къде́ пъту́вате?	where are you going?
за съжале́ние	unfortunately
зна́чи	that means, so, thus
и	and, also
и а́з	me too
и ви́е ли?	and you as well?
интере́сно	interesting
и́стина	truth
и́стината	the truth
ка́зва	s/he says
ка́зва се	his/her name is
ка́звам	I say, I tell
ка́звам се	my name is
ка́зваш	you say (familiar)
ка́к	how
ка́к се ка́звате?	what is your name? (polite)

ка́к се ка́зваш?	what is your name? (familiar)
какво́	what
какво́ е "тече́ние"?	what's a "тече́ние"? / what does течение mean?
ки́р	sir (archaic term of address)
ки́ра	ma'am (archaic term of address)
къде́	where
ле́кар (ка)	doctor, physician
ли	(question particle)
ма́лко	a little
ма́рт	March
мно́го	very
мно́го интере́сно	that's very interesting
моми́че	girl
момче́	boy
на	of
на́й-по́сле	finally
не	not
ни́е	we
от	from
от Аме́рика ли сте?	are you from America?
откъде́	whence, from where
откъде́ сте?	where are you from?
позна́ва	s/he knows, is acquainted with
преподава́тел (ка)	teacher (university level)
прия́тел (ка)	friend
пъту́вам	travel, am traveling (1sg.)
пъту́ват	travel, are traveling (3pl.)
пъту́вате	travel, are traveling (2pl.)
разби́рам	understand (1sg)
са	are (3pl)
СА́Щ = Съедине́ните америка́нски ща́ти	USA (United States of America)
са́мо	only
се	verbal particle

29

сега́	now	тече́ние	current, draft
секрета́р (ка)	secretary	ти́	you *(sg., familiar)*
си	are *(2sg.)*	то́	it *(rarely:* he, she)
ско́ро	soon	то́й	he, it
сме	are *(1pl.)*	тръ́гваме	[we're] leaving
ста́ва	there's getting to be	тя́	she, it
ста́ва тече́ние	there's a draft	тя́ се ка́зва	her name is
сте	are *(2pl.)*		
студе́нт (ка)	university student	учи́тел (ка)	teacher (up to
съжале́ние	pity		12th grade)
съм	am *(1sg.)*		
съ́що	also	ща́т	state
		Ща́тите	the States
те́	they		

CULTURAL COMMENTARY

Reference to the U.S.

As do many elsewhere in the world, Bulgarians use the term Аме́рика colloquially to refer to the U.S. The official term for the U.S. is САЩ (Съедине́ните америка́нски ща́ти), pronounced as one word [са́щ]. Some also refer to the U.S. colloquially as Ща́тите ("the States").

Traveling: air currents

As in certain other countries, Bulgarians are very sensitive to currents of air, especially when traveling. The belief is that exposure to such currents will cause illness, especially in children.

Forms of address: Mr., Ms., etc.; professional titles

The term госпожа́ is used in the manner of English "Ms.", when one can not (or does not wish to) specify the marital status of the woman concerned. If the woman is known to be single but is middle-aged or older, it is also considered more polite to refer to her as госпожа́.

The terms господи́н, госпожа́ and госпо́жица are now the neutral forms of address. They were introduced into Bulgaria in the late 19th century to replace the old terms of address ефе́нди, ки́р (ки́ра) and ба́й (the latter used only for older men). During the socialist regime (1944-1989) they were used only to address foreigners from the west; in Bulgaria at that time one used друга́р and друга́рка. The term ба́й is still used familiarly to refer to older people.

For certain high-prestige professions, it is considered derogatory to use the form ending in -ка to refer to a woman practitioner of that profession. For instance, one would not refer to a woman Secretary-General of the U.N. as секрета́рка unless one wanted to imply disrespect.

Letter writing

When Bulgarians write dates, they put the date first and then the month (similar to English "the fifteenth of March"). A letter is headed with the date and the place of its writing.

School systems

As in other countries, there is one system of schooling that takes the student from the elementary grades through graduation from high school, and another that is concerned with university education. Bulgarian extends this difference even to the words for "teacher": учи́тел refers exclusively to a teacher in elementary or high school, and преподава́тел exclusively to a teacher at university level. Similarly, the term студе́нт refers only to university students.

There is an English language high school in Sofia, which for many years has employed British and American teachers. Although the students are Bulgarian, all instruction is in English. Admission to the school is highly competitive. There are similar schools with instruction in French, German, Spanish, and Russian. An American university (also with English language instruction) was opened in Bulgaria in 1991. It is located in the southwestern Bulgarian city of Blagoevgrad.

LESSON 2

DIALOGUE

Пътуват с влак

// Димѝтър, Милѐна, А́нгел, Джу́ли, Дѐйвид (и дру́ги) пъту́ват с вла́к от Ва́рна за Со́фия. Вла́кът е мно́го дъ́лъг. Тѐ са в купѐ № 7 (но́мер сѐдем). Купѐто е тя́сно. Коридо́рът съ́що е тѐсен. Врата́та на купѐто е затво́рена. Та́ня отва́ря врата́та. //

Таня: Извинѐте, къдѐ е мя́сто № 1 (но́мер едно́)?

Ангел: То́ е до врата́та. Мя́стото е свобо́дно.

Камен: А нѝе, ма́мо?

Таня: Вѝе сте ту́ка. Ка́мене, ти́ си на № 2 (но́мер двѐ), а На́дка е на № 3 (но́мер трѝ).

Ангел: Ѐто, госпо́жо, мя́сто № 2 е съ́що до врата́та, а мя́сто № 3 е в средата́. Ѝмате ли бага́ж?

Таня: Благодаря́, мно́го сте любѐзен. Ѐто, ча́нта и ку́фар. Ча́нтата е ма́лка, но тѐжка. Ку́фарът е голя́м, но не ѐ тѐжък.

Камен: Ма́мо, какво́ ѝма в ча́нтата? Гла́ден съм. И жа́ден. И На́дка е жа́дна! Нѝе сме жа́дни!

Таня: По́сле, Ка́мене.

Камен: Какво́ ѝма в ча́нтата? Това́ не ѐ ли шишѐ?

Таня: Да́, това́ е шишѐ, но....

Камен: Какво́ ѝма в шишѐто?

Таня: Ракѝя. От сѐло.

Ангел: Ракѝя ли? Това́ е чудѐсно! Добрѐ дошлѝ, госпо́жо!

BASIC GRAMMAR

2.1. Gender of nouns

Every noun in Bulgarian belongs to one of three genders: masculine, feminine or neuter. Because pronouns, adjectives and articles all have different forms depending on the gender of the noun they refer to, it is extremely important to know the gender of every noun.

The gender of a noun can usually be inferred from its ending. Since endings by definition contain a vowel, masculine nouns (which end in a consonant) are said to have a "zero" ending. Neuter nouns end in -o or -e, and feminine nouns usually end in the sound [a], which can be written either -a or -я. For example:

masculine	feminine	neuter
багáж	врат-á	куп-é
влáк	госпож-á	мя́ст-о
коридóр	раки́-я	течéни-е

2.2. Pronoun agreement

Every pronoun which refers to a singular noun must agree with that noun in gender. There is only one plural pronoun. Here are the forms, followed by examples of usage in sentences:

masculine	feminine	neuter	plural
ТÓЙ	ТЯ́	ТÓ	ТÉ

masculine: Товá е влак.   That's a train.
              Тóй е дъ́лъг.   It is long.

feminine: Товá е раки́я.   This is rakia.
             Тя́ е си́лна.   It is strong.

neuter: Éто сéло.   Here's a village.
           Тó е мáлко.   It is small.

plural: Дéйвид и Джу́ли са студéнти.   David and Julie are students.
           Тé са от Амéрика.   They are from America.

          Éто, чáнта и ку́фар.   Here, a bag and a suitcase.
          Тé са тéжки.   They are heavy.

2.3. Definite articles

Bulgarian has a definite article, similar in usage to English "the". The Bulgarian definite article is added after the ending of the noun, and must agree with it in gender. Here are the forms of the article, followed by examples of usage in sentences.

masculine	feminine	neuter	plural
-ът	-та	-то	-те

masculine:	Товá е влак.	That's a train.
	Влáкът е дъ̀лъг.	The train is long.
feminine:	Товá е ракѝя.	This is rakia.
	Ракѝята е сѝлна.	The rakia is strong.
neuter:	Éто сéло.	Here's a village.
	Сéлото е мáлко.	The village is small.
plural:	Товá са студéнти.	These are students.
	Студéнтите са от Амéрика.	The students are from America.
	Éто чáнти и кýфари.	Here are bags and a suitcases.
	Чáнтите са тéжки,	The bags are heavy,
	а кýфарите не сá тéжки.	but the suitcases are not heavy.

The masculine definite article is always pronounced as [-ът]. After nouns ending in -тел, -ар, and -й, it is written -ят. Nouns ending in -й drop the -й before adding the definite article. For example:

indefinite form	студéнт	лéкар	приятел	трамвáй
definite form	студéнт-ът	лéкар-ят	приятел-ят	трамвá-ят

2.4. Adjective agreement

Adjectives in Bulgarian must also agree with the nouns they modify. There are three endings in the singular, corresponding to the three genders, and one in the plural. Here are the endings, followed by examples of usage.

masculine	feminine	neuter	plural
(zero)	-a	-o	-и

masculine	Кýфарът е тéжък.	The suitcase is heavy.
feminine	Чáнтата е тéжка.	The bag is heavy.
neuter	Мя̀стото е свобóдно.	The seat is empty.
plural	Студéнтите са свобóдни.	The students are free. [= not busy]

These agreement patterns follow a "rhyming principle", whereby nouns, definite articles and adjectives often repeat the same sound. This principle is especially clear in feminine and neuter nouns:

Ча́нт<u>ата</u> е голя́м<u>а</u> и те́жк<u>а</u>.   The bag is big and heavy.

Се́л<u>ото</u> е ма́лк<u>о</u> и ху́бав<u>о</u>.   The village is small and pretty.

2.5. Fleeting vowels in adjectives

Feminine, neuter and plural nouns and adjectives end in a vowel. Masculine nouns and adjectives usually end in a consonant. Frequently, this consonant is preceded by the vowel -ъ- or -e-, which drops out in other forms of the adjectives (and is therefore called "fleeting"). For example:

masculine	*feminine*	*neuter*	*plural*
доб-ъ́-р	доб-ра́	доб-ро́	доб-ри́
те́ж-ъ-к	те́ж-ка	те́ж-ко	те́ж-ки
гла́д-е-н	гла́д-на	гла́д-но	гла́д-ни
свобо́д-е-н	свобо́д-на	свобо́д-но	свобо́д-ни

2.6. Alternating vowels in adjectives

A number of adjectives occur with -я- in the singular and -e- in the plural. Certain of these adjectives have -e- in the masculine form as well. For example:

masculine		*feminine*	*neuter*		*plural*
гол<u>я</u>м		гол<u>я</u>ма	гол<u>я</u>мо	*vs.*	гол<u>е</u>ми
б<u>я</u>л		б<u>я</u>ла	б<u>я</u>ло	*vs.*	б<u>е</u>ли
т<u>е</u>сен	*vs.*	т<u>я</u>сна	т<u>я</u>сно	*vs.*	т<u>е</u>сни

2.7. Vocative of personal names

The vocative of masculine names ends in -e. If the neutral form of the name ends in -ър, this -ъ- is lost before the vocative ending.

	neutral form	*vocative form*
masculine	Ка́мен	Ка́мене
	Дими́тър	Дими́тре
	Пе́тър	Пе́тре
	господи́н	господи́не

The vocative of feminine names ends in **-о** or **-е**. If the neutral form of the name ends in **-ца**, **-га** or **-ка**, the ending **-е** is added. In other nouns, the ending **-о** is used.

	neutral form	*vocative form*
feminine	ма́ма	ма́мо
	госпожа́	госпо́жо
	На́дка	На́дке
	О́лга	О́лге
	Роси́ца	Роси́це

2.8. Имам vs. има

The verb **и́мам** means "have", and corresponds in usage to English "have".

И́мате ли бага́ж?	Do you have [any] baggage?

The 3rd singular form **и́ма** is also used in the general meaning "there is" or "there are". This form of the verb is unchanging regardless of whether the subject is singular or plural. For example:

И́ма ли ту́ка свобо́дно мя́сто?	Is there an empty seat here?
Какво́ и́ма в ча́нтата?	What is [there] in the bag?

В ча́нтата и́ма интере́сни книги.	There are [some] interesting books in the bag.

2.9. Negation

Verbs are negated by placing the particle **не** immediately before the verb. Although this particle is not accented, it causes the following word to receive a strong accent, *even if this word is a clitic*. For example:

Ни́е не пъту́ваме дне́с.	We are not traveling today.
Не съм учи́тел.	I am not a teacher.
Не е́ студе́нтка.	She is not a student.

Negation of the verb **и́мам** is an exception. Here, one must use a different verb, **ня́мам**. For example:

-- **И́маш ли един мо́лив?**	"Do you have a pencil?"
-- **Ня́мам мо́лив.**	"I don't have a pencil."

2.10. Position of ли

The question particle **ли** usually occurs right after the verb. Exceptions are the verb **съм**, and a conscious intent to focus one's question on something other than the verb. In the case of **съм**, the particle **ли** occurs immediately before the verb, unless the verb is negated, in which case **ли** occurs immediately after the verb.

Тóй студéнт ли е?	Is he a student?
Тóй не é ли студéнт?	Isn't he a student?

In the case of special focus, the particle **ли** is placed after the word in question. When question focus changes, word order often changes as well. For example:

Ракúя ли?	Is it rakia [you've got there]?
Кáмен ли пътýва днéс?	Is it Kamen who's traveling today?
Кáмен днéс ли пътýва?	Is it today that Kamen is traveling?
Днéс ли пътýва Кáмен?	*[same]*

2.11. Prepositions

(a)   The basic meaning of the preposition **в** is "in" (or "into", depending on the context). The sense "within a closed or defined space" is usually implied. Thus:

Тé са в купé № 7.	They are in compartment No. 7.
Тú си в средáта.	You are in the middle [of the row].

It can also mean "within the confines of" in a less literal sense, as in the idiomatic expression **в óтпуска** "on leave, on a break, on vacation"; one could think of this as "within the time frame allowed to one to be absent from work".

(b)   The basic meaning of the preposition **до** is "next to", "by" (or "up to"). The general idea is that of approaching a limit.

Мя́стото е до вратáта.	The seat is next to the door.
Коридóрът е до купéто.	The corridor is by the compartment.

(c)   The preposition **на** has a number of different meanings. The first (seen already in Lesson 1) is that of possession. For example:

Вратáта на купéто е затвóрена.	The door of the compartment is closed.
Прия́тел съм на Джóн Грúйн.	I am a friend of John Green's.
Кнúгата е на Нáдка.	The book is Nadka's.

In another meaning, **на** is closely related to **в**, and is often translated "on", "at" or "in". In the following example, for instance, the reference is not to being physically *in* the seat, but to having the ticket for that seat:

Ти́ си на но́мер две́, а тя́ е на но́мер три́.   You're in seat no. 2, and she's in no. 3.

(d)   The basic meaning of the preposition **с** is "with". When referring to means of conveyance, it is translated idiomatically as "by". For example:

Те́ пъту́ват с вла́к, а тя́ пъту́ва с автобу́с.   They are traveling by train and she is traveling by bus.

Windmill at the entrance to Nesebăr, near Burgas

EXERCISES

I. Fill in the blanks with the appropriate pronoun.

1. Откъде́ е раки́ята? _____ е от се́ло.
2. За къде́ пъту́ва вла́кът? _____ пъту́ва за Со́фия.
3. Къде́ е се́лото? _____ е до Со́фия.
4. Откъде́ са Дими́тър и Миле́на? _____ са от Ва́рна.
5. Къде́ са ку́фарите? _____ са в купе́то.
6. Врата́та отво́рена ли е? Не́, _____ е затво́рена.
7. Къде́ е Дими́тър? _____ е в о́тпуска.

II. Complete each sentence with the article and the appropriate form one of the following adjectives: дома́шен, чуде́сен, ма́лък, голя́м, дъ́лъг, те́жък, затво́рен.

1. Къ́ща_____ е _____.
2. Врата́_____ е _____.
3. Ку́фари_____ са _____.
4. Автобу́с_____ е _____.
5. Раки́я_____ е _____.
6. Ви́но_____ е _____.
7. Ча́нти_____ са _____.

III. How many different questions can you make out of the following sentences by using the particle ли *in different positions?*

1. То́й пъту́ва с вла́к.
2. Купе́то е тя́сно.
3. Мя́стото е свобо́дно.
4. Ка́мен е гла́ден и жа́ден.
5. В шише́то и́ма раки́я.
6. Та́ня отва́ря врата́та.
7. Мя́сто но́мер две́ е до врата́та.

ADDITIONAL GRAMMAR NOTES

2.1a. Gender of nouns

The great majority of masculine nouns end in a consonant; that is, their ending is the "zero" ending. Certain masculine nouns referring to persons, however, end in a vowel. Most feminine nouns end in the vowel -a, but there are a sizable number of feminine nouns with a zero ending. The forms of these irregular nouns will be learned later.

2.2a. Pronoun agreement

Pronoun agreement in Bulgarian differs considerably from that of English. With certain idiomatic exceptions, the English pronouns "he" and "she" refer only to male and female persons. Otherwise the pronoun "it" is used.

In Bulgarian, however, it is the grammatical gender of a noun which determines the form of the pronoun. English speakers would refer to a train or a door as "it", but Bulgarian must refer to a train (вла́к) as то́й, and a door (врата́) as тя́. In the plural, however, English and Bulgarian are similar: the pronouns "they" and те́ are used regardless of the meaning of the noun.

2.3a. Definite articles

The forms of the definite article in Bulgarian are unchanging. Every feminine noun takes the article -та no matter what its form, and every neuter noun takes the article -то. Most plural nouns take the article -те, and the great majority of masculine nouns take the article -ът / -ят. The spelling -ят occurs in a number of masculine nouns. In masculine nouns which end in -ар or -тел or in the consonant -й, this spelling is predictable. In others, it must be learned. The definite forms of the latter type of nouns will be noted in vocabulary lists.

The usage of definite articles in Bulgarian is generally similar to that of English: when a noun has been specified or "defined" in a conversation, subsequent mentions of that noun are usually accompanied by the definite article. There are differences, however. One of these concerns reference to family members. When the relationship is a direct one and is clear from the context, Bulgarian uses the article where English would use "my", "your" or the like. For example:

<table>
<tr><td>Пра́щам с братовче́дката
   Кръсти́на едно́ шише́
   дома́шна раки́я.</td><td>I am sending with my cousin Krăstina
   a bottle of homemade rakia.</td></tr>
</table>

39

2.5a. Fleeting vowels in adjectives

The stem of an adjective is found by dropping the vowel ending from the feminine or neuter form. Thus the stem of the adjective **тѐжка** is **тежк-**, the stem of the adjective **добра́** is **добр-**, and the stem of the adjective **гла́дна** is **гладн-**. When the stem of an adjective ends in two consonants, the masculine form usually inserts a vowel between these two consonants. This vowel is called "fleeting" because it disappears in all other forms of the adjectives. Fleeting vowels can be either **-ъ-** or **-е-**. That in stems whose final consonant is **-н-** will often be **-е-**; and for stems whose final consonant is **-к**, it will often be **-ъ-**.

Adjectives are listed in dictionaries in the masculine singular form. While it is not possible to predict with certainty which vowels will "fleet" and which will remain, the general rule is that **-ъ-** and *unstressed* **-е-** will disappear. Thus, one should assume that the feminine forms of **бо́лен** and **дъ́лъг** are **бо́лна** and **дъ́лга**, respectively. Exceptions to this rule will be noted in vocabulary lists. If you encounter an adjective in a non-masculine form and have trouble finding it in the dictionary, try predicting a masculine form with an inserted vowel.

2.6a. Alternating root vowels

A number of Bulgarian words occur with **-я-** in some forms of the word, and **-е-** in others. The rule governing the alternation is as follows: If the vowel is stressed, **-е-** occurs if there is **-е-** or **-и-** in the following syllable; otherwise **-я-** occurs. If the vowel is unstressed, it is always **-е-**. Adjectives learned in this lesson exemplify the first half of this rule. Examples of the second half will be seen later.

2.7a. Vocative of personal names

The regular vocative ending for masculine personal names, and for feminine personal names in **-ка**, **-га** or **-ца**, is **-е**. The ending **-о**, however, is used regularly only with those feminine nouns which refer to relationships (e.g. **госпожа́**, **ма́ма**). In personal names, this vocative ending is used more and more rarely (and, for some speakers, carries a tinge of unfriendliness). Students are advised to avoid it.

The ending **-о** in **друга́рко** is an anomaly: since the neutral form of the noun ends in **-ка**, one would expect the ending **-е**.

2.8a. Имам vs. има

The impersonal meaning of **и́ма** is largely the same as that of French *il y a,* and Russian *есть* (and is similar to that of German *es gibt*). Similarly, the impersonal meaning of **ня́ма** is like that of French *il n'y a pas de* and Russian *нет* (and is similar to that of German *es gibt kein*).

2.12. "Presentative" това

The word **товá** is used in connection with the verb **съм** to introduce persons or topics. Although it can be translated with English "this", "that", "these" or "those", its form in Bulgarian is unchanging. Its order in the sentence is likewise unchanging: it always comes at the beginning. Students must pay attention to this word order rule when **товá** occurs in a question. Thus:

Товá е кни́га.	This/that is a book.
Товá са кни́ги.	These/those are books.
Товá кни́ги ли са?	Are these/those books?
Товá не é ли шишé?	Isn't that a bottle?

2.13. Agreement with вие

When the plural pronoun **ви́е** refers to a single person, the verb continues to be plural. Adjectives, however, are usually in the singular. For instance:

Ви́е сте мнóго любéзен.	You are very kind.

2.14. The conjunction "but"

The conjunction **но** implies strong contrast and is always translated "but". There is a gradation between the three conjunctions **и**, **а** and **но** which is schematized in the chart below and illustrated by the examples following.

conjunction	translation	meaning
и	and	equivalence
а	and	comparison
но	but	contrast

Ча́нтата е голя́ма и тéжка.	The bag is big and heavy.
Ча́нтата е ма́лка, а ку́фарът е голя́м.	The bag is small and the suitcase is big.
Ча́нтата е ма́лка, но е тéжка.	The bag is small, but it is heavy.

SAMPLE SENTENCES

1. Ма́йка пъту́ва ли?

2. Ма́йка ли пъту́ва?

3. Ка́мен е гла́ден.

4. Ка́мен гла́ден ли е?

5. Ка́мен ли е гла́ден?

6. Раки́ята е от се́ло.

7. Раки́ята от се́ло ли е?

8. Това́ раки́я от се́ло ли е?

9. Еле́на и Лиля́на са прия́телки.

10. Еле́на и Лиля́на прия́телки ли са?

11. Еле́на и Лиля́на ли са прия́телки?

12. Ка́мен и На́дка са гла́дни. А А́нгел е жа́ден, но не е́ гла́ден.

13. Ча́нтата е голя́ма и те́жка. А ку́фарът е голя́м, но не е́ те́жък.

SENTENCES FOR TRANSLATION

1. Rositsa, is there a good lawyer here in Sofia?

2. Mladen, do you have a manual for the TOEFL test?

3. The corridors are very narrow, and the compartment is also cramped.

4. There are hungry students in the compartment. They are also thirsty.

5. Where are there houses with large doors and entryways? In Plovdiv, Mladen's house is small, but it has a large entryway. In Sofia, Stoyan's house is large, but it has a small entryway.

6. The wind is very strong. Where is it blowing from?

7. Is the suitcase heavy? No, it isn't heavy. But the bag is very heavy.

READING SELECTION

Кореспонде́нция - (2)

Сега́ Бо́йко и Бо́б са прия́тели. Бо́б отно́во е в Са́н Франци́ско. Бо́йко е в Со́фия. Кали́на изуча́ва англи́йски.

---

              1 юли, Со́фия

Дра́ги Бо́б,

Сърде́чни по́здрави от Со́фия! Пра́щам с братовче́дката Кръсти́на едно шише́ дома́шна раки́я за здра́ве. Гро́здова е, от се́ло.
Ни́е сме здра́ви. Вре́мето е то́пло, но и́ма си́лен вя́тър. Аз съм в о́тпуска и ремонти́рам къ́щата. И́мам о́ще мно́го ра́бота, а ма́лко вре́ме. Ви́е ка́к сте? Здра́ви ли сте?

Вси́чко ху́баво,

              Бо́йко

Патри́ша Ми́чел е адвока́тка. Жена́ е на Ро́берт Ми́чел.

---

              4 юли, Са́н Франци́ско

Дра́ги Бо́йко и Кали́на,

Благодаря́ за раки́ята. Тя́ е мно́го си́лна! Ни́е в Калифо́рния обикнове́но не оби́чаме мно́го си́лен алкохо́л. Но оби́чаме раки́ята. Тя́ найстина е мно́го ху́бава.
Ни́е не сме́ мно́го добре́. Бо́б е ма́лко бо́лен. И́ма просту́да. Какво́ ремонти́ра Бо́йко в къ́щата?

По́здрави,

              Патри́ша

P.S. Отде́лно пра́щам за Кали́на уче́бник за **TOEFL**.

43

GLOSSARY

автобу́с	bus	и́ма си́лен вя́тър	it's very windy
адвока́т (ка)	lawyer	и́ма	s/he has
алкохо́л	alcohol	и́мате	you have *(polite)*
англи́йски	English (language)	и́мате ли бага́ж?	do you have [any] luggage?
бага́ж	baggage, luggage	и́маш	you have *(familiar)*
благодаря́	thank you	интере́сен	interesting
бо́лен	sick		
братовче́д (ка)	cousin	какво́ и́ма	what is there in the bag?
бя́л *(pl.* бе́ли*)*	white	в ча́нтата?	
		кни́га	book
в о́тпуска	on a break, vacation	коридо́р	corridor, entryway
ви́но	wine	коридо́рът е те́сен	the passageway is narrow
вла́к	train	купе́	compartment
врата́	door	купе́ № 7	compartment No. 7
вре́ме	time; weather	купе́то е тя́сно	the compartment is cramped
вси́чко	all, everything		
вси́чко ху́баво	all the best	ку́фар	suitcase
вя́тър	wind	къ́ща	house
гла́ден	hungry	любе́зен	kind
голя́м *(pl.* голе́ми*)*	large, big		
гро́здов	[made] of grapes	ма́йка	mother
		ма́лко	a little, [very] little
две́	two (in counting)	ма́лко вре́ме	not much time
до	by, near, next to	ма́лко бо́лен е	he's under the weather
добре́	well, fine	ма́лък	small
добре́ дошли́!	welcome!	ма́ма	Mom
добъ́р	good	ма́мо	Mom! *(vocative)*
дома́шен	homemade	мно́го	much
дра́ги	dear *(masc. plural)*	мно́го ра́бота	a lot of work
дру́г	other, another	мо́лив	pencil
дъ́лъг	long	мя́сто	place, seat
		мя́стото е свобо́дно	the seat is not taken
еди́н	one, a *(masculine)*		
едно́	one (in counting)	на	in, on, at
е́то	here *(pointing)*	на № 2 си	you've got No. 2
		наи́стина	really, truly
жа́ден	thirsty	но	but
жена́	woman, wife	но́мер	number
		ну́жда	need
затво́рен, -ена	closed	ня́ма	there isn't/aren't any
здра́в	healthy	ня́ма ну́жда	there's no need, it's not necessary
здра́ве	health		
		ня́мам	I don't have
и́ма	there is, there are	ня́маме	we don't have
и́ма о́ще мно́го ра́бота	there's still a lot of work [to do]	обикнове́но	usually
и́ма ма́лко вре́ме	there's not much time	оби́чаме	we like

отва́ря	s/he opens	се́дем	seven
отво́рен, -ена	open	се́ло	village
отде́лно	separately, under separate cover	си́лен	strong
		среда́	middle
отно́во	again, once more	сърде́чен	hearty
о́тпуска	break, time off, vacation		
		те́жък	heavy
о́ще	still, yet	те́сен, тя́сна	tight, cramped, narrow
о́ще мно́го	a lot more yet	то́ е до врата́та	it's by the door
		това́	that, this
по́здрав	greeting	това́ не é ли шише́?	isn't that a bottle?
по́сле	later, afterwards		
пра́щам	I am sending, I send	TOEFL	Test Of English as a Foreign Language
просту́да	cold (illness)		
пъту́ва	s/he travels, is traveling	то́пъл	warm
		трамва́й	tram
пъту́ваме	we travel, are traveling	три́	three
		ту́ка	here (location); also ту́к
пъту́вам с вла́к	travel by train		
		уче́бник	textbook, manual
ра́бота	work		
раки́я	rakia (strong fruit brandy)	ху́бав	fine, nice, beautiful, pretty
ремонти́рам	I redo, make repairs		
ремонти́ра	s/he redoes, makes repairs	ча́нта	bag, briefcase
		чуде́сен	marvelous, wonderful
с	with	шише́	bottle
свобо́ден	free, not occupied		
свобо́ден съм сега́	I'm not busy now	ю́ли	July

Rotunda "St. George", downtown Sofia

CULTURAL COMMENTARY

Traveling: trains

Trains are a very common means of travel in Bulgaria. Each car of the train is divided into a number of compartments. After climbing up into the train, one walks along the narrow corridor which runs the length of the car, and enters a compartment by sliding a door aside. Within the compartment are two rows of seats facing each other, stretching from the single large window to the compartment door. Second-class compartments have four seats on each side.

Food and drink: rakia

Rakia (ракия), which is a strong, double-distilled brandy, is in a sense the national drink. It is normally made from grapes, but can be made from any fruit; plums or apricots can also serve as the base. The best is that which is home-made, outside the city. The drinking of rakia in moderate quantities is considered to be good for one's health, both physical and emotional. Indeed, for many Bulgarians, drinking rakia together is an important friendship ritual.

City and country

A very large part of Bulgarian society is still rural, focused on the village (сéло); and practically everyone who lives in the city still has some sort of connection with a village, usually through family.

Gifts

Bulgarians consider that the most appropriate (and the most certain) way to send someone a gift over a long distance is to send it with a person. The person to whom the gift is entrusted is under a strong obligation to deliver it, even if s/he does not know the recipient. The recipient, in turn, is usually obliged to entertain the person acting as go-between, at least briefly; and (naturally) to send a gift in return.

Vacation

"Vacation" is a complex concept in Bulgaria. The majority of time off from work is spent not on holiday but in taking care of the business of daily life. One often hears Bulgarians say, only partly in jest, that they need to go back to work in order to get some rest.

Learning English

Learning English is extremely popular among Bulgarians now. Some learn English because it has become the fashionable second language, but most learn it in order to have a salable skill. Passing the standardized TOEFL test certifies that one possesses this skill. One sees in Sofia now countless small agencies that offer crash courses in English that claim to prepare one for the TOEFL (pronounced тóйфъл).

Body language

The head movements accompanying the Bulgarian words for "yes" and "no" are the *opposite* of those used in English (and most other Western languages). To signify "yes", Bulgarians move their heads from side to side, with a slight rocking movement. To signify "no", they move their heads up and down; this gesture always begins with a sharp upward movement.

LESSON 3

DIALOGUE

Какво́ пра́виш?

Надка: Ма́мо, какво́ пра́ви ле́лята?

Таня: Нали́ ви́ждаш? Чете́. Чете́ кни́га.

Надка: И а́з чета́! А́з пра́вя като ле́лята!

Камен: Не́, ти́ не чете́ш, ти́ са́мо отва́ряш и затва́ряш кни́гите.

Таня: Ка́мене! Ня́ма ну́жда! Ти́ си голя́м, а На́дка е о́ще ма́лка. Тя́ о́ще не
чете́, но рису́ва мно́го добре́. На́дке, е́то един ху́бав мо́лив. Добре́ ли си
сега́?

Джули: Какво́ рису́ваш? Къ́ща ли?

Надка: Да́, това́ е къ́ща.

Джули: Каква́ ху́бава къ́ща!

Надка: Разби́ра се, че е ху́бава.

Джули: Какво́ е това́, ту́ка в среда́та на къ́щата?

Надка: Това́ е врата́та на къ́щата. Та́зи къ́ща и́ма мно́го прозо́рци, но са́мо
една́ врата́. А́з мно́го оби́чам прозо́рци. От прозо́рците ви́ждам
гради́ната.

Дейвид: И ту́ка в купе́то и́ма един прозо́рец. То́й е голя́м, нали́?

Надка: Да́, но ня́ма гради́на. Не оби́чам то́зи прозо́рец!

Милена: И а́з не оби́чам то́зи прозо́рец, защо́то е отво́рен. Ста́ва тече́ние!
Това́ е мно́го ло́шо!

Ангел: Сти́га с то́зи прозо́рец! Госпо́жо, нали́ и́мате едно шише́? Къде́ е
това́ шише́? Ха́йде по една́ глъ́тка!

BASIC GRAMMAR

3.1. Present tense

There are three present-tense conjugations in Bulgarian. They are named after the vowel of the 3rd singular ending: the **a**-conjugation, the **и**-conjugation, and the **e**-conjugation. Here are examples of the three conjugations:

a-conjugation

	singular	*plural*	*singular*	*plural*
1st person	пъту́в-ам	пъту́в-аме	затва́р-ям	затва́р-яме
2nd person	пъту́в-аш	пъту́в-ате	затва́р-яш	затва́р-яте
3rd person	пъту́в-а	пъту́в-ат	затва́р-я	затва́р-ят

Verbs whose 3rd singular is in **-я** also belong to this conjugation; the **-я-** is consistent throughout the conjugation. All verbs of this conjugation are accented on the syllable immediately preceding the ending.

и-conjugation

	singular	*plural*	*singular*	*plural*
1st person	пра́в-я	пра́в-им	бро-я́	бро-и́м
2nd person	пра́в-иш	пра́в-ите	бро-и́ш	бро-и́те
3rd person	пра́в-и	пра́в-ят	бро-и́	бро-я́т

Verbs of this conjugation can be accented on either the stem (as **пра́в-я**) or the ending (as **бро-я́**). The place of accent must be learned with each verb.

e-conjugation

	singular	*plural*	*singular*	*plural*
1st person	пи́ш-а	пи́ш-ем	чет-а́	чет-е́м
2nd person	пи́ш-еш	пи́ш-ете	чет-е́ш	чет-е́те
3rd person	пи́ш-е	пи́ш-ат	чет-е́	чет-а́т

	singular	*plural*	*singular*	*plural*
1st person	пи́-я	пи́-ем	живе́-я	живе́-ем
2nd person	пи́-еш	пи́-ете	живе́-еш	живе́-ете
3rd person	пи́-е	пи́-ят	живе́-е	живе́-ят

In the e-conjugation, the 1st singular and 3rd plural can end either in **-а/-ат** or **-я/-ят**. Verbs in the latter group always accent the syllable immediately before the ending. Those in the former group are accented either on the stem or the ending; the accent must be learned with each verb. When the 1st singular and 3rd plural forms are accented on the ending (-á, -áт or -я́, -я́т), these endings are pronounced as if the vowel in each case were [-ъ].

Bulgarian has no infinitive. One can predict the conjugation type from the dictionary form of a verb, the 1st singular form. Verbs in **-ам** or **-ям** belong to the **a**-conjugation, and verbs in **-я** preceded by a consonant or the vowel **-o-** belong to the **и**-conjugation. All others (including verbs in **-я** preceded by any other vowel) belong to the e-conjugation. In certain instances, primarily verbs ending in **-ча**, **-ша** or **-жа,** one cannot tell whether a verb belongs to the e-conjugation or the **и**-conjugation. For such verbs, the conjugation type must be learned. For these verbs, 2nd singular forms are regularly given in glossary listings, as follows:

> пи́ша (-еш)

3.2. Demonstrative pronouns

The word for "this / these" agrees in gender with the noun it modifies.

masculine	*feminine*	*neuter*	*plural*
то́зи	та́зи	това́	те́зи

When the neuter form **това́** precedes the verb forms **e** or **са**, it can also mean "that" or "it". In this meaning, **това́** is unchanging, even if the verb is plural.

-- Какво́ рису́ваш? Къ́ща ли?	"What are you drawing? A house?"
-- Да́, това́ е къ́ща.	"Yes, it's a house.
А това́ е врата́та на къ́щата.	And this is the door of the house."
Това́ са Миле́на и Дими́тър Сто́йкови.	This is Milena and Dimitri Stoykov.
Това́ е мно́го интере́сно!	That's very interesting!

3.3. Indefinite article

The Bulgarian indefinite article is similar in usage to English "a, an". Like the definite article, the indefinite article also agrees with its noun in gender. Here are examples, with the definite article given for comparison:

	indefinite	*definite*	*meaning*
masculine	един прозо́рец	прозо́рец-ът	a/the window
feminine	една врата́	врата́-та	a/the door
neuter	едно шише́	шише́-то	a/the bottle

Bulgarians use the definite article in roughly the same contexts as English. For Bulgarians, however, the indefinite article is optional. Either of the following is possible, and there is no essential difference in meaning:

Чета́	**една**	**интере́сна кни́га.**	I'm reading an interesting book.
Чета́		**интере́сна кни́га.**	*[same]*

In the plural, **едни** is used to mean "some [unspecified]". The same meaning can be conveyed without the article.

Чета́	**едни**	**интере́сни кни́ги.**	I'm reading some interesting books.
Чета́		**интере́сни кни́ги.**	*[same]*

3.4. Adjectives vs. adverbs; какъв vs. какво

In most cases, adverbs are identical to the neuter form of adjectives. The adverb **добре́**, however, has a different form. Compare the following:

ADJECTIVE (*masculine, neuter*)	**ADVERB**	**Meaning** *adjective*	*adverb*
съ́щ, съ́що	съ́що	same	also
търпели́в, търпели́во	търпели́во	patient	patiently
ху́бав, ху́баво	ху́баво	nice	nicely, well
отде́лен, отде́лно	отде́лно	separate	separately
че́ст, че́сто	че́сто	frequent	often
добъ́р, добро́	добре́	good	fine, well, OK

The relationship between the question word **какво́** and the adjectival pronoun **какъ́в** is similar to that between adverb and adjective. **Какво́** is unchanging and always asks the question "what?". **Какъ́в** changes to modify a noun, and has several meanings, all of which are usually translated as "what". It can express an emotion such as surprise, it can ask a question about descriptive detail, or it can ask about professional or work identity. For example:

question word

Какво́ пра́виш?	What are you doing?
Какво́ е това́?	What is that?

pronominal adjective

Каква́ ху́бава къ́ща!	What a nice house!
Каква́ е та́зи кни́га?	What [sort of] book is that?
-- Какъ́в е то́й?	"What does he do?"
-- То́й е ле́кар.	"He's a doctor."

3.5. Fleeting vowels in nouns: the suffix -ец

Certain masculine nouns contain a fleeting vowel, which drops out when the plural ending -и is added. The vowel in the frequently occurring suffix -ец is an example. In the examples below, the suffix is separated from the root by hyphens. When followed by the "zero" ending, the suffix is -ец, but when followed by the plural ending, it is simply -ц. For example:

singular	*plural*	*meaning*
прозо́р-ец	прозо́р-ц-и	window
америка́н-ец	америка́н-ц-и	American
чужден-е́ц	чужден-ц-и́	foreigner, stranger

All nouns in -ец which do not drop this vowel in other forms will be noted in the glossary. Thus, the simple listing **вегетериа́нец** presumes the plural **вегетериа́нци**.

3.6. Plural of masculine nouns in -к or -г

Masculine nouns ending in -к or -г in the singular replace these consonants by -ц and -з, respectively, in the plural.

singular	*plural*	*meaning*
ези́к	ези́ц-и	language
уче́бник	уче́бниц-и	textbook
археоло́г	археоло́з-и	archaeologist
съпру́г	съпру́з-и	spouse

3.7. Prepositions

(a)   The basic meaning of the preposition **като** is "as, like". For example:

бя́л като сня́г   as white as snow

(b)   The basic meaning of the preposition по is "along, by"; this usage will be learned in Lesson 5. One of the idiomatic meanings of this preposition is the distributive one, which is best translated by English "each". For example:

Хáйде по еднá глъ́тка!	Let's each have a drink [= a swallow]!
Студéнтите четáт по сéдем стрáници.	The students read seven pages each. [= The students (each) read seven pages at a time.]

(c)   The basic meaning of the preposition под is "under". For example:

Обу́вките на Пéтър са под пéйката.	Peter's shoes are under the bench.

Man in traditional folk costume, Koprivshtitsa folk festival

EXERCISES

I. Fill in the blanks with the appropriate form of one of the following verbs: пи́ша, ви́ждам, вървя́, пра́вя, чета́, зна́я.

1. Я́на _____ ка́ртичката с мо́лив.
2. Ти́ какво́ _____? Кни́га ли _____?
3. Багажъ́т на Дими́тър е те́жък. Дими́тър _____ мно́го ба́вно.
4. А́з не _____ къ́щата. Къде́ е тя́?
5. Миле́на и Лиля́на _____ гре́шки.
6. Та́зи кни́га е на бъ́лгарски. _____ ли бъ́лгарски?
7. А́з не _____ гре́шки.

II. Fill in the blanks with the correct form of the demonstrative pronoun:

1. _____ е мно́го инте́ресно.
2. _____ врата́ отво́рена ли е?
3. _____ ку́фар е те́жък.
4. _____ са Миле́на и Дими́тър.
5. Защо́ _____ прозо́рци са отво́рени?
6. Какво́ и́ма в _____ е́зеро?
7. _____ америка́нци са студе́нти.

III. Fill in the correct preposition.

1. На́дка рису́ва _____ мо́лив.
2. _____ Та́ня и́ма свобо́дно мя́сто.
3. А́нгел отва́ря врата́та _____ купе́то.
4. Миле́на и Дими́тър пи́ят _____ една́ ча́ша ви́но.
5. Ива́н и Я́на живе́ят _____ Со́фия.
6. _____ прозо́рците _____ къ́щата и́ма пе́йка.
7. И а́з съм жа́ден _____ На́дка.

ADDITIONAL GRAMMAR NOTES

3.1a. Present tense

The characteristic vowel of a conjugation -- the vowel which appears alone in the 3rd singular -- is called the theme vowel. The theme vowel of the **a**-conjugation, **-а-**, can also occur as **-я-**.

In the **a**-conjugation, all six forms contain the theme vowel. In the other two conjugations, the theme vowel is present only in four out of six forms (2-3sg and 1-2pl). The remaining two forms, the 1st singular and 3rd plural, always end in the sound [-ъ]. This sound is never written as **-ъ-**, but always as **-а-** or **-я-**. In this case sound and letter are not predictable from each other, even when this ending is accented. The words written **четá** and **четáт** must be pronounced [четъ́] and [четъ́т]; and the spoken forms [върв'ъ́] and [върв'ъ́т], in which the apostrophe signals softening of the preceding consonant, must be written **вървя́** and **вървя́т**.

Note also that in the **a**-conjugation the 1st singular ends in **-м**, and the 1st plural ends in **-ме**. In the **e**- and **и**-conjugations, however, the 1st singular ends in a vowel and the 1st plural ends in **-м**. Care must be taken to interpret correctly the meaning (and conjugation) of verbal forms ending in **-м**.

Although the great majority of verbs whose 1st singular ends in **-я** preceded by a consonant belong to the **и**-conjugation, a few of them belong to the **e**-conjugation. The most common of these is **къ́пя** (**къ́пеш**, etc.) "bathe".

3.2a. Demonstrative pronouns

The forms of the demonstrative pronouns are very similar to those of the personal pronouns; this similarity should be exploited in learning them. Here are the two sets of pronouns listed together:

masculine	feminine	neuter	plural	Type
тóзи	тáзи	товá	тéзи	Demonstrative
тóй	тя́	тó	тé	Personal

3.3a. Indefinite article

English has both a definite and an indefinite article, italicized in the following examples. Note that English must place one of these two articles before a singular noun. The third example on the following page is incorrect English.

I am reading *an* interesting book.
I am reading *the* interesting book [I mentioned to you before].
* I am reading interesting book.

Bulgarian differs from English in that only the definite article is obligatory when the meaning "definite" is present. To express the meaning "indefinite", Bulgarians have an option: sometimes they use the word for "one" and sometimes they use nothing.

Most standard Bulgarian grammars do not yet recognize a separate category of "indefinite article". The existence of a frequent accentual difference between the meanings "one" [as opposed to more than one] and "a" [the indefinite article], however, indicates that most Bulgarians do in fact distinguish these two meanings. When един, една, едно means "a", Bulgarians tend to pronounce it with a much weaker accent than when it means "one". In this book, един with the meaning "indefinite article" will not be accented.

3.4a. Adjectives vs. adverbs

Adverbs are used either as predicates (after the verb съм) or as attributes (adding information about a verbal state or action). Note the difference, especially in the case of добър, between the predicative usage of an adverb (the first two examples) and of an adjective (the third example):

Predicative

| -- Добре́ ли си сега́? | "Are you OK now?" |
| -- Да́, добре́ съм. | "Yes, I'm fine." |

Той е мно́го добъ́р.   He's very good [= a very good person].

Attributive

На́дка рису́ва мно́го добре́.   Nadka draws very nicely.

3.5a. The suffixes -ец, -ин and -ски

In nouns referring to persons, the suffix -ец usually indicates origin (or membership in a particular group). Another suffix designating origin is -ин (which is historically related to English "one [of]"). In the plural, this suffix is dropped. When referring to origin, both these suffixes are frequently preceded by the suffix -ан-. Note that the noun господи́н "Mr." also contains the suffix -ин-, and that its plural (usually translated as "Gentlemen") is irregular.

singular	*plural*	*meaning*
бъ́лгар-ин	бъ́лгар-и	Bulgarian
англич-а́н-ин	англич-а́н-и	Englishman
госпо́д-и́н	госпо́д-а́	Mr. (*plural:* Gentlemen)

The suffixes **-ец** and **-ин** form nouns of origin which refer either to a male (singular and plural usages) or to the generalized category (plural usage only). By contrast, the suffix **-к-** designates a specifically female representative of each category (since this suffix is always followed by the feminine noun ending **-а**, it is frequently referred to as **-ка**). These three suffixes are discussed in much greater detail in Lesson 23.

singular/general	*specifically female*	*meaning*
америк-а́н-ец	америк-а́н-ка	American
англич-а́н-ин	англич-а́н-ка	English[wo]man
бъ́лгар-ин	бъ́лгар-ка	Bulgarian
чужд-ен-е́ц	чужд-ен-ка́	foreigner, stranger
вегетери-а́н-ец	вегетери-а́н-ка	vegetarian

The above forms are nouns. Adjectives indicating origin are formed with the suffix **-ск-**. When the masculine form of such an adjective is used alone, the noun "language" is understood, as in English. For example:

Разби́рам са́мо ма́лко бъ́лгарски.	I understand only a little Bulgarian.
Разби́рате ли англи́йски?	Do you understand English?

This suffix forms adjectives of numerous sorts. The form of the root to which the suffix is added is not always predictable. For example:

national name [masculine]	*stem*	*derived adjective*
бъ́лгар-ин	бъ́лгар-	бъ́лгар-ски
англи-ча́нин	англи́й-	англи́й-ски

In the masculine, these adjectives always end in **-и**. Other forms are regular:

masculine	бъ́лгарск-и	ези́к		англи́йск-и	рома́н
feminine	бъ́лгарск-а	раки́я		англи́йск-а	къ́ща
neuter	бъ́лгарск-о	ви́но		англи́йск-о	се́ло
plural	бъ́лгарск-и	студе́нти		англи́йск-и	студе́нти

3.8. Нали

The question word **нали́** can appear either at the beginning or at the end of a sentence. It signifies that the speaker expects a positive answer to the question. Its most frequent translation is as the so-called tag question ("isn't it?", "aren't you?", or the like). For instance:

Нали́ ви́ждаш?	Don't you see?
Нали́ и́мате мо́лив?	You have a pencil, don't you?
То́й е голя́м, нали́?	It's big, isn't it?
Къ́ща рису́ваш, нали́?	You're drawing a house, aren't you?

3.9. Definite forms of plurals in -a

A few masculine nouns, and all neuter nouns, form their plural in -a. The rules for forming these plurals will be learned in later lessons. For now, note the fact that *any* noun which ends in -a, no matter what its number or gender, takes the definite article -та.

Here are two examples. The plural of the masculine noun **нóмер** "number" is **номерá**, and the plural of the neuter noun **детé** "child" is the slightly irregular **децá**. The definite forms of these nouns are:

gender	*singular*	*plural*
masculine	**нóмерът**	**номерáта**
neuter	**детéто**	**децáта**

The easiest way to remember the forms of these plural articles is as follows:

**Nouns ending in -a take a rhyming form of the article,
no matter what they mean.**

Thus: книгата   децáта
          (feminine singular)   *(neuter plural)*

❖   ❖   ❖   ❖   ❖

SAMPLE SENTENCES

1. А́з и́мам (са́мо) еди́н прия́тел.

2. Един прия́тел пъту́ва за Аме́рика.

3. А́з и́мам едно́ дете́.

4. Едно дете́ отва́ря врата́та.

5. Това́ са студе́нти от Аме́рика.

6. Това́ са цве́тни мо́ливи. Това́ са кни́ги.

7. Каква́ е та́зи кни́га? Това́ е рома́н.

8. Ко́й отва́ря врата́та? Едно дете́. Какво́ е то́? Ма́лко или голя́мо?

9. Ка́мен и На́дка зна́ят по едно́ стихотворе́ние.

10. Студе́нтите но́сят по еди́н ку́фар.

SENTENCES FOR TRANSLATION

1. What lovely windows there are in this house! Do you see these windows?

2. What are Kamen and Nadka doing? They are counting pencils. Now what are they drawing? Kamen is drawing a pond next to a house, and Nadka is drawing a mountain.

3. Unfortunately I know very little Bulgarian because I am a foreigner. We, as foreigners, read slowly.

4. Americans and English speak English. This Englishwoman also speaks Bulgarian. Do the American women speak Bulgarian?

5. Is there a post office in this village? No, there isn't, because this is a small village.

6. What's this under the bench? Are these shoes? What large shoes they are!

7. Bulgarians like books. They read books often, and not only in Bulgarian. Does this Bulgarian woman read English?

READING SELECTION

<u>Кореспонде́нция - (3)</u>

20 ю́ли, Со́фия

Дра́га Патри́ша,

Пóщата е мнóго бáвна, но и́ма óще мнóго врéме. Ня́ма мя́сто за па́ника. Чáкам търпели́во кни́гата. Четá уси́лено дрýги кни́ги. Вéче разби́рам мáлко англи́йски, но óще не говóря.

Интерéсно, ти́ кáк си? Добрé ли си? Бóб здрáв ли е вéче?

Бóйко ремонти́ра бáнята. Смéня плóчките. Остáва óще мáлко. Обикновéно ни́е почи́ваме в Копри́вщица, но тáзи годи́на врéме за почи́вка ня́ма. Децáта са на сéло в Родóпите -- нали́ знáеш, че áз съм оттáм.

Копри́вщица е мнóго хýбаво мя́сто. Оттáм прáвим и́злети в планини́те. Съби́раме мали́ни и вари́м слáдко. В Копри́вщица и́ма типи́чна бъ́лгарска атмосфéра -- кри́ви тéсни ýлици и бéли къ́щи с червéни пóкриви.

Нали́ знáеш, Я́на рисýва мнóго хýбаво. Прáщам тáзи рисýнка за Мáйкъл. Товá е цъ́рквата Алексáндър Нéвски. Планинáта отзáд е Ви́тоша. На пéйката до цъ́рквата сме Я́на и áз. Идили́чен пейзáж, нали́?

Сърдéчни пóздрави

Кали́на

Street scene in Koprivshtitsa

GLOSSARY

америка́нец	American (male)	идили́чен	idyllic
америка́нка	American (female)	и́злет	excursion
англича́нин	Englishman, English person	или	or
		интере́сно, ти́ ка́к си?	I wonder how you are?
англича́нка	Englishwoman		
археоло́г	archaeologist		
атмосфе́ра	atmosphere	каква́ ху́бава къ́ща!	what a nice house!
		какво́ е това́?	what's this?
ба́вен	slow	какъ́в	what kind of, what
ба́ня	bath, bathroom	какъ́в е то́й?	what [work] does he do?
броя́	count	ка́ртичка	postcard
бъ́лгарин	Bulgarian (male)	като	like, as
бъ́лгарка	Bulgarian (female)	класи́чески	classical
		ко́й	who (see Lesson 5)
варя́	boil, cook	кри́в	crooked
вегетериа́нец	vegetarian (male)	къ́пя, -еш	bathe
вегетериа́нка	vegetarian (female)		
ве́че	already, by now	ле́ля	aunt (father's sister); "auntie"
ви́ждам	see		
вървя́	walk, move, go	ло́ш	bad
гимна́зия	academically oriented high school	мали́на	raspberry
глъ́тка	swallow	на	in, at
гово́ря	speak, talk	на бъ́лгарски	[written or spoken] in Bulgarian
годи́на	year		
гора́	woods, forest	на село́	[staying] in the village
господа́	gentlemen	нали́	isn't it? aren't there? doesn't she? (etc.)
гради́на	garden		
гре́шка	mistake	нали́ ви́ждаш?	don't you see?
		нали́ е голя́м?	it's big, isn't it?
да́ма	lady		
да́ми и господа́	ladies and gentlemen	нали́ зна́еш, че а́з съм...	you know, don't you, that I'm...
деца́ (pl. of дете́)	children		
добре́ ли си сега́?	are you O.K. now?	нача́лен	beginning, elementary
дра́г	dear	нача́лно образова́ние	elementary education
еди́н	one (masculine)	не́	no
една́	one (feminine)	но́мер (pl. номера́)	number
едно́	one (neuter)	но́ся	carry, wear
е́зеро	lake, pond	ня́ма мя́сто за па́ника	there's no need to worry
живе́я	live		
		оби́чам	like, love
защо́	why	образова́ние	education
защо́то	because	обу́вка	shoe
затва́рям	close	оста́вам	remain, stay
зна́я	know	оста́ва о́ще ма́лко	there's still a bit left

отва́рям	open	сняг	snow
отде́лен	separate	сре́ден	middle (adj.)
отза́д	in back, behind	сти́га	[that's] enough
о́ще не говоря́	I can't speak yet	сти́га с то́зи прозо́рец	enough about that window
о́ще не чете́	s/he doesn't [know how to] read yet	стихотворе́ние	poem
		страни́ца	page
па́ника	panic, worry	съби́рам	gather, collect
пейза́ж	landscape, scene from nature	съпру́г	husband, spouse
		същ	same
пе́йка	bench		
пи́ша (-еш)	write	та́зи	this (feminine)
пи́я	drink	те́зи	these
планина́	mountain	те́хникум	technical high school
пло́чка	tile	типи́чен	typical
по	each (distributive)	това́	this (neuter)
под	under, below	то́зи	this (masculine)
позна́вам	know, be acquainted with	търпели́в	patient (adj.)
по́крив	roof	у́лица	street
почи́вам	rest, go on holiday	уси́лено	intensively
почи́вка	vacation trip, rest		
по́ща	mail, post office	ха́йде	come on, let's
пра́вя	do, make	ха́йде по една́ глъ́тка!	[come on,] let's each have a drink!
пра́вя и́злет	go on an excursion		
пра́щам	send		
прозо́рец (pl. прозо́рци)	window	цве́тен	colored
		цъ́рква	church
пъту́вам	travel		
		ча́кам	await, wait, wait for
разби́ра се	of course	ча́ша	glass, cup
разби́рам	understand	че	that (conjunction)
рису́вам	draw	черве́н	red
рису́нка	drawing	че́ст	frequent
рома́н	novel	че́сто	often
		чета́	read
сла́дко	thick sweet preserves	чуждене́ц	foreigner, stranger (male)
сла́дък	sweet	чужденка́	foreigner, stranger (female)
сме́ням	change, replace		

CULTURAL COMMENTARY

Forms of address

Bulgarian children often refer to strangers by kinship terms such as "aunt", "uncle", "grandma", "grandpa", depending on the sex and the (relative) age of the stranger. A young (to middle-aged) woman could thus be referred to by a child as "lelya" (ле́ля).

School systems: levels

As in America, Bulgarian children begin school at age 6 or 7. After completing the four grades of elementary school (нача́лно образова́ние), they move to the three grades of middle school (прогимна́зия), and then to one of several higher educational schools. These are of two types: the academically oriented (гимназия) and the technically oriented (техникум). By law Bulgarian children must complete at least one year of higher education (that is, through eight grades of school). Among the most prestigious of the academically oriented schools is the "classical" high school (Класическата гимназия). Students are admitted to university by a very rigorous series of examinations.

Home life: repairs

Home repairs, such as replacing the tiles in the bathroom, are almost always done by individual homeowners. Most Bulgarians learn to do these jobs out of necessity.

Geography: Koprivshtitsa

The picturesque town of Koprivshtitsa (Копривщица) is located to the east of Sofia, in the foothills of the mountain range called Sredna Gora (Средна гора). The town has been designated a "museum-city", and many of the houses in it have been given the protective status of "historical monument". The houses are all of the old, Ottoman-inspired style, with overhanging balconies and dark red-tiled roofs. The streets are narrow and cobblestoned. Koprivshtitsa was the site of the initial Bulgarian uprising against the Ottomans; the homes of several of the famous revolutionaries have been converted into museums.

Geography: the Rhodopes

The Rhodope mountains (Родопите) are situated in the south of Bulgaria. The region is known for its physical beauty and for its characteristic traditional handicrafts, music and speech.

Geography: Sofia

One of the most striking sights in Sofia is the cathedral dedicated to Alexander Nevski (Александър Невски), built in honor of the Russian armies who liberated Bulgaria from the Ottoman overlordship in the late 19th century. Its golden dome is visible from a great distance, and its massive interior, crypt treasury and excellent choir make for a memorable visit. There is a large open square in front of the church where Sofia residents stroll and often have their pictures taken. Many street vendors have set up business there in recent years.

Geography: Vitosha

Directly to the south of Sofia is Vitosha mountain (Витоша) at 7,506 feet. It is a favorite spot for excursions. On Sundays it is filled with Sofia residents picnicking and hiking; regularly scheduled city buses travel there.

City and country

Connections to one's rural roots are generally valued in Bulgaria. Those who still have relatives "in the village" (i.e. in a particular rural settlement) try to visit in the summers or at least to send their children there. These visits are not only for the rural experience, but also to maintain contact with one's extended family.

Food and drink: sladko

Bulgarians enjoy sweets, and particularly the thick, sweet home-cooked preserves called "sladko" (сладко). This can be made from any fruit, but it is commonly made from berries or plums, preferably freshly gathered. A combination of fruit, water and sugar is brought to the boil and then simmered for several hours. The resulting sweet is served to guests on small saucers when they first arrive, together with a glass of cold water or a small cup of Turkish coffee.

LESSON   4

Затворе́те прозо́реца, мо́ля!

Милена: Мо́ля ви се, господи́не, затворе́те прозо́реца!

Дейвид: Защо́? Заду́шно е. И́маме ну́жда от въ́здух! Не затва́ряйте прозо́реца, мо́ля.

Милена: Не зна́ете ли? Тече́нието е мно́го опа́сно за ма́лките. Нали́ ви́ждате? Деца́та седя́т на тече́ние! Ми́тко, ведна́га затвори́ прозо́реца!

Димитър: Добре́, ми́ло. Затва́рям.

Ангел: Седне́те, господи́не. А́з съм до прозо́реца, сега́ затва́рям.

Таня: На́дке, вземи́ мо́ливите от по́да.

Надка: Защо́, ма́мо?

Таня: Не пи́тай, са́мо слу́шай. Сложи́ мо́ливите в ча́нтата. Къде́ е ча́нтата? Ка́мене, зна́еш ли къде́ е ча́нтата?

Камен: Да́, зна́я. Сега́ сла́гам вси́чко в ча́нтата.

Таня: Благодаря́, Ка́мене, добро́ момче́.

Ангел: Пу́шите ли? И́мате ли една́ цига́ра?

Дейвид: Не́, ни́е не пу́шим. Нали́ зна́ете, димъ́т е мно́го опа́сен за ма́лките.

Джули: И за голе́мите. Ви́е, ако пу́шите, изле́зте в коридо́ра, мо́ля.

Ангел: Добре́, госпо́жице. Сега́ изли́зам.

BASIC GRAMMAR

4.1. Aspect

Nearly every verbal idea in Bulgarian is expressed by two different verbs, each of which conveys a different point of view, or "aspect". One of these views the action as general, basic and unbounded, and is called "imperfective". The other views the action as bounded in some way or another, and is called "perfective".

The combination of the two verbs is called an "aspect pair". Dictionaries usually list the two together, with the imperfective form first. When one knows only the perfective, one must predict (or guess) the imperfective form in order to look up the meaning of the verb in the dictionary. For this reason, it is best to learn both members of an aspect pair at the same time.

All glossary listings from now on will be in this format; the glossary to this lesson repeats all verbs learned up to this point, now in the form of aspect pairs. Following are examples, always listed with imperfective preceding perfective.

Imperfective / Perfective	*meaning*
влѝзам / вля́за	enter, go in
вѝждам / вѝдя	see
затва́рям / затво́ря	close
ка́звам / ка́жа	say
оста́вам / оста́на	stay, remain
отва́рям / отво́ря	open
пра́щам / пра́тя	send
сла́гам / сло́жа	put
трѐгвам / трѐгна	leave, set out

Perfective verbs most frequently refer to a single instance of completed action. Imperfective verbs usually describe an action in progress, refer to the general idea of an action, or suggest multiple, repeated instances of a single action. Because of the nature of their meaning, verbs such as съм "be" and и́мам "have" exist only in the imperfective aspect.

4.2. Imperative

There are two sets of imperative endings in Bulgarian. These are:

	singular	plural
Type 1	-й	-йте
Type 2	-ѝ	-е́те

Singular forms are used when addressing a person one speaks to as **ти**, and plural forms are used either with a group or when addressing a person one speaks to as **вие**.

To form the imperative, drop the final letter of the 1st singular present form. Add Type 1 endings to verbs of the **a**-conjugation or verbs whose 1st singular ends in **-я** preceded by a vowel. Add Type 2 endings to all other verbs, and shift the accent to the ending.

	1st sg. present	*sg. imperative*	*pl. imperative*
Type 1	затва́р-ям	затва́р-яй!	затва́р-яйте!
	пи́-я	пи́-й!	пи́-йте!
	бро́-я	бро́-й!	бро́-йте!
	зна́-я	зна́-й!	зна́-йте!
Type 2	пи́ш-а	пиш-и́!	пиш-е́те!
	върв-я́	върв-и́!	върв-е́те!
	затво́р-я	затвор-и́!	затвор-е́те!
	чет-а́	чет-и́!	чет-е́те!

Some verbs have irregular imperatives. Among the most common of these are:

	1st sg. present	*sg. imperative*	*pl. imperative*
(irregular)	ви́дя	ви́ж!	ви́жте!
	вля́за	вле́з!	вле́зте!
	изля́за	изле́з!	изле́зте!

Positive commands are usually formed from perfective verbs. This is because the focus is on the speaker's desire that an action be performed once and completed. Negative commands are normally formed from imperfective verbs. This is because the focus is on the speaker's desire that the process of an action not be undertaken. Below are two examples:

perfective

      Затвори́ врата́та!   Close the door!

imperfective

      Не затва́ряй врата́та!   Don't close the door!

4.3. Masculine definite objects

When masculine definite nouns are used as the object of a verb or preposition, the final **-т** of the article is lost, and the article is written **-а.** Nouns whose article is written **-ят** simply drop the **-т.** Here are examples:

subject

Прозо́рецът е голя́м.	The window is big.
Ка́к се ка́зва ле́карят?	What is the doctor's name?

object

То́й седи́ до прозо́реца.	He is sitting by the window.
Това́ шише́ е на ле́каря.	This bottle belongs to the doctor.

4.4. Verbs of body position

Bulgarian has two different verbs each for the concepts "sit", "stand" or "lie". One means to assume the position (as in "sit down, stand up, lie down") while the other means to be in the position (as in "be seated, be standing, be lying down"). By the nature of their meaning, verbs of the second group exist only in the imperfective aspect.

ASSUME a position		BE in a position	
imperfective	*perfective*	*imperfective*	
ся́дам	се́дна	седя́	*SIT*
ста́вам	ста́на	стоя́	*STAND*
ля́гам	ле́гна	лежа́	*LIE*

4.5. Embedded questions

When a question is integrated into another sentence, usually as the object of a verb, it is said to be "embedded". In English, such questions shift the word order of the original question. In Bulgarian, however, the word order remains unchanged. Note that in all three of the examples below, the Bulgarian question къде е чантата ("where is the bag") maintains the same word order, while the English question does not. Note too that the sentence in which a question is embedded does not have to be a question itself.

	Къде́ е ча́нтата?	Where is the bag?
Зна́еш ли	къде́ е ча́нтата?	Do you know where the bag is?
Не́, не зна́я	къде́ е ча́нтата.	No, I don't know where the bag is.

4.6. Prepositions

The preposition в means either "in" or "into" depending on the context.

Мо́ливите са в ча́нтата.	The pencils are in the bag.
Сега́ сла́гам вси́чко в ча́нтата.	Now I'm putting everything into the bag.

4.7. Subjectless sentences

Bulgarian sentences which describe general conditions do not have a subject. English, by contrast, must use the subject "it". For example:

Тýка е задýшно. Задýшно е тýк.	It's stuffy in here.
Днéс е тóпло. Тóпло е днéс.	It is warm today.

In order to translate correctly from English to Bulgarian, this "it" (which linguists call the "dummy it") must be distinguished from the "it" that refers to something in particular, as in "It's a house." Do not use товá in Bulgarian unless the "it" is of this second sort.

Synagogue, downtown Sofia

EXERCISES

I. Fill in the blanks with the appropriate form of the article.

1. Дете____ е мно́го голя́мо. Ви́ждаш ли дете́____?
2. Коридо́р___ на вла́к____ е те́сен. Те́ защо́ стоя́т в коридо́р____?
3. Къде́ са мо́ливи____? В ча́нта____ или в ку́фар____?
4. Къде́ е трамва́____ ? И́ма ли мя́сто в трамва́____?
5. Обу́вки____ са под пейка____. Ви́ждаш ли обу́вки____?
6. Дим_____ е мно́го опа́сен. Седя́ дале́че от дим____.
7. Вле́зте в кабине́т____ на ле́кар____. Ле́кар____ е ту́ка.

II. Fill in the blanks with the appropriate form of one of the following verbs: затва́рям / затво́ря; вли́зам / вля́за; оста́вам / оста́на; тръ́гвам / тръ́гна; ка́звам / ка́жа; ся́дам / се́дна.

1. Не _____ в купе́то, ня́ма мя́сто.
2. Мо́ля ви се, _____ врата́та, ста́ва тече́ние.
3. _____ ту́ка о́ще ма́лко, не _____!
4. _____ и́стината.
5. Не _____ това́, ако не е́ и́стина.
6. Защо́ стои́ш до врата́та? _____, _____ на пе́йката!
7. Не _____ на та́зи пе́йка, не е́ чи́ста.

III. Fill in the blanks with the appropriate verb of body position.

1. Ка́мен и На́дка пъту́ват за Со́фия. Те́ _____ до прозо́реца.
2. Ка́мене, _____ на сто́ла!
3. Ка́мене, _____ от сто́ла!
4. В коридо́ра на вла́ка и́ма мно́го хо́ра. Те́ _____ прави.
5. Ку́чето спи́. То́ _____ под пе́йката.
6. _____, Ка́мене. Мно́го е къ́сно.
7. За момче́то ня́ма мя́сто. То́ _____ на по́да. А́нгел ка́зва:
   "_____! По́дът не е́ чи́ст."

ADDITIONAL GRAMMAR NOTES

4.1a. Aspect

Perfective verbs imply a meaning of boundedness and imperfective verbs imply the absence of such a meaning. The most frequent sort of boundedness is that of a single instance of an action, usually with a view to its completion. Present tense verb forms are normally used in the perfective only after various conjunctions or particles which signify boundedness. Examples will be seen in the next lesson.

Because of the non-bounded meaning of the imperfective aspect, present tense verb forms are used very frequently in the imperfective. Here are examples of the three primary meanings of the present imperfective:

action in progress

Какво́ рису́ваш? Къ́ща ли?	What are you drawing? A house?
Та́ня отва́ря врата́та.	Tanya opens the door.

generic idea of action

Пу́шите ли?	Do you smoke?
На́дка рису́ва мно́го добре́.	Nadka draws very well.

habitual, repeated action

Обикнове́но почи́ваме в Копри́вщица.	Usually we go to Koprivshtitsa for our vacation.
Чета́ уси́лено дру́ги кни́ги.	I've been reading other books in a concentrated fashion.

The perfective aspect can also be used to describe habitual actions in a more vivid, immediate manner. Students are advised to avoid this usage for the present. It takes time, and exposure to the language, to learn the proper emotional contexts for such usage. For example:

Се́днем в кола́та и сме та́м.	[All we have to do is] get into the car and there we are!

Bulgarian dictionaries list many verbs only in the imperfective aspect. Sometimes this is because the meaning of the verb is not compatible with the idea of boundedness (e.g. и́мам, съм). More frequently, it is because Bulgarians often consider the basic idea of a verb to be imperfective. Examples of such verbs, which are called "simplex verbs", are пи́ша "write", чета́ "read", пи́я "drink".

69

The perfective forms of these verbs are created by adding a prefix to them. Several types of prefixes can be added to these verbs; in each case, the prefix adds a particular sort of bounded meaning to the verb. Bulgarians consider that the addition of a prefix *always* changes the meaning of the verb -- sometimes slightly, sometimes radically. For this reason, every prefixed verb has a separate imperfective verb associated with it, and correspondingly, a separate listing in the dictionary. Here is an example of a "basic" verb, and of an aspect pair related to it by prefixation:

Simplex *(imperfective only)*		**Aspect pair** *(perfective / imperfective)*	
Verb	*meaning*	Verb pair	*meaning*
гле́дам	look	разгле́ждам / разгле́дам	study, examine

The perfective forms of these basic verbs, and this general type of aspect relationship, will be discussed in Lessons 7, 18 and 26. At this point, the student should focus on learning aspect pairs of the sort ка́звам / ка́жа.

4.2a. Imperative

Affirmative commands are usually given in the perfective aspect and negative commands in the imperfective aspect. The imperfective imperative can be also used to convey repeated commands, or greater abruptness and a more insistent (and consequently less polite) command. These usages will be studied in later lessons.

Type 1 endings are also added to the irregular verb да́м "give", whose present tense conjugation will be learned in Lesson 9. Its imperative is:

present	*singular imperative*	*plural imperative*
да́м	да́й!	да́йте!

4.3a. Masculine definite objects

Although the object form of definite masculine nouns is written **-a**, its *sound* remains [-ъ-]. That is, although it has lost the final **-т** of the subject article, both in writing and in pronunciation, it retains the same vowel *sound*. The object form of the article in **-ят** keeps the same vowel letter in the written form, **-я**, although the vowel in all four of these article forms is pronounced as if written [-ъ]. This pronunciation is especially clear when the article is accented. For example (the apostrophe denotes softening of the preceding consonant):

Димъ́т е мно́го опа́сен за ма́лките.	[димъ́т]	Smoke is very dangerous for children.
Те́ седя́т дале́че от дима́.	[димъ́]	They are sitting away from the smoke.
Деня́т е ху́бав.	[ден'ъ́т]	It's a nice day.
Рабо́ти през деня́.	[ден'ъ́]	He works during the day.

Most Bulgarians do not distinguish definite subjects from objects when speaking, and will often pronounce the subject form without the final -т. The distinction must be made in writing, however.

4.4a. Verbs of body position

The structural similarities between the three different sets of verbs for body position can help the student remember them. These similarities are described below for each of the three types, listed by column number.

(1)	(2)		(3)		
imperfective	*perfective*		*imperfective*		
ся́дам	се́дна		седя́		*SIT*
ста́вам	ста́на		стоя́		*STAND*
ля́гам	ле́гна		лежа́		*LIE*

(1) Paired imperfective verbs indicating a change of position all belong to the a-conjugation and all have the sound [a] in the root.

(2) Paired perfective verbs indicating a change of position all belong to the e-conjugation, all have the consonant -н- in them, and all are accented on the stem.

(3) Unpaired imperfective verbs denoting a state all belong to the и-conjugation, and all are accented on the ending.

Two of these verbs have additional meanings: ста́вам (perfective ста́на) also means "get up [in the morning]", "become" and "happen"; and ля́гам (perfective ле́гна) also means "go to bed".

4.6a. Prepositions

(a) The preposition от is used to indicate the basic ingredients or material of which something is made. If the ingredient is an added one, the preposition с is used. Both these meanings are usually rendered in English by an adjective.

сала́та от зе́ле и мо́ркови	carrot and cabbage salad
омле́т с гъ́би	mushroom omelet

(b)   The basic meaning of the preposition **освéн** is "except [for]". The idiomatic expression **освéн товá** means "in addition, besides".

4.8. Shifting vowels in verb roots

The **е/я** vowel shift, seen earlier in **голя́м / голéми**, can also occur in accented verb roots. Two very common such verbs are the perfectives **изля́за** "go out" and **вля́за** "enter, come in". Here is the conjugation of **изля́за**, with the shifting vowels underlined:

	singular	*plural*
1st person	изля́за	излéзем
2nd person	излéзеш	излéзете
3rd person	излéзе	изля́зат
imperative	излéз!	излéзте!

The rule governing the alternation is the same as with adjectives: if -**е**- or -**и**- occurs in the following syllable, the alternant -**е**- is used; otherwise the alternant -**я**- is used. In conjugation, present tense forms with the theme vowel -**е**- have the root vowel -**е**-, while the 1st singular and 3rd plural have the root vowel -**я**-.

The fact that the alternant -**е**- occurs in the imperative of this verb must be learned separately.

4.9. Generic definiteness

Bulgarian uses definite articles in a number of instances where English does not. One of the commonest of these is in referring to general categories. Consider the following sentence, and the several possible English translations:

Течéнието е мнóго опáсно за мáлките.

> Drafts are very dangerous for children.
> A draft is a very dangerous thing for children.
> A draft is a very dangerous thing for any small person.

Here, the noun **течéние** refers both to the generic category "draft" and to any one specific instance of this category. Normal English usage is either without an article or with the indefinite article. Bulgarian, however, must use the definite article. Similarly, when the adjectives **мáлък** and **голя́м** are used in the definite plural, they can refer both to the generic categories "children" and "adults" and to any particular representatives of these categories. (The neutral words for children and adults are **децá** and **възрастни**, respectively.)

The Bulgarian generic use of the definite article is similar to that found in French and German. English speakers must pay attention to learn this usage.

72

4.10. Third-plural passives

As in English, third person plural verb forms often convey the idea of the passive mood. The subject is "they", but the persons to whom the pronoun "they" refers are unspecified. Examples:

Не знам какво сервират.
I don't know what they serve here.
I don't know what is served here.

Тук всичко готвят добре.
They cook everything well here.
Here everything is cooked well.

4.11. Alternate verb forms

Many people in the capital city of Sofia say both зная and знам in the 1st singular of the verb meaning "know". Both variants are considered correct.

Mosque, downtown Sofia

73

SAMPLE SENTENCES

1. Децáта обúчат слáдко.

2. Пýшенето е опáсно за здрáвето.

3. Бъ́лгарите пúят червéно вúно.

4. Човéкът е смъ́ртен.

5. -- Вúе кóй сте?
   -- Áз съм Бóйко Атанáсов.
   -- Какъ́в сте?
   -- Лéкар съм.

6. Кóй съм áз? Знáеш ли кóй съм áз?

7. Какъ́в съм áз? Знáеш ли какъ́в съм áз?

8. Кáк се кáзваш?

9. Кажéте кáк се кáзвате!

10. Закъдé пътýвате? Тóй пúта закъдé пътýвате.

11. Милéна стоú прáва. Димúтър кáзва: "Мóля, седнú. Úма свобóдно мя́сто до прозóреца." Милéна ся́да до прозóреца. В купéто влúзат Тáня и Нáдка. Милéна седú до прозóреца. Тя́ стáва и кáзва: "Мóля седнéте. Вúе сте с мáлко детé."

12. Лéкарят кáзва: "Легнéте, úмате нýжда от прéглед". Тóй излúза от кабинéта. Пациéнтът ля́га. Лéкарят влúза. Пациéнтът лежú на леглóто.

SENTENCES FOR TRANSLATION

1. "See what there is here?! Beer and rakia! Have [= drink] a beer!"
   "No, this beer seems warm. I don't like warm beer."

2. We're going out for a bit, because we're getting hungry. Are you hungry too?

3. "Wait a minute! Don't shut the door! I'm coming in also."
   "Hurry up! We don't have much time."

4. Don't sit in the draft! Don't you know that drafts are dangerous?

5. "Ask the waiter where the menu is."
   "I don't need a menu. I know what they serve."
   "Are you saying you know the menu by heart?"

6. Please put the salad and the rakia here. But don't put the omelet here now.
   We're not in a hurry.

7. Please put the drawings and the pencil in separate bags. And don't put the book
   in the bag. I'm reading that book.

8. Come into the water, the lake is very warm today. The children are also coming
   in.

9. Children, don't come into the house that way! See, this house has a door!

10. Take the bus! Don't take the tram, it's very slow.

READING SELECTION

<u>В ресторанта</u>

Марин: Гла́ден ли си? Изгле́ждаш неспоко́ен.

Пламен: Ве́че огладня́вам. Осве́н това́ следо́бед съм на ра́бота и ня́мам мно́го вре́ме. Ви́ждаш ли сервитьо́ра набли́зо?

Марин: Ча́кай ма́лко. За пъ́рви път съм ту́ка. Не зна́м какво́ серви́рат. О́ще разгле́ждам ли́ста.

Пламен: А́з зна́м меню́то наизу́ст. Поръ́чвам пържо́ла с гарниту́ра и шо́пска сала́та. Ти́ какво́ предпочи́таш? Какво́ гле́даш то́лкова в меню́то, не зна́еш ли бъ́лгарски? Поръ́чай съ́щото.

Марин: Ти́ бъ́рзаш, но а́з не бъ́рзам. Ви́наги изби́рам ба́вно. Осве́н това́ съм вегетериа́нец. Ако оби́чате!

Сервитьо́рът: Мо́ля!

Марин: И́мате ли омле́т?

Сервитьо́рът: Да́, разби́ра се.

Марин: А ко́лко стру́ва?

Сервитьо́рът: Омле́тът с шу́нка стру́ва 150 ле́ва, омле́тът с гъ́би 130 ле́ва, а омле́тът с кашкава́л 120 ле́ва.

Марин: А какви́ сала́ти и́мате?

Сервитьо́рът: Сала́та от зе́ле и мо́ркови и шо́пска сала́та.

Марин: Пла́мене, ту́к добре́ ли пра́вят омле́та?

Пламен: Ту́к вси́чко го́твят добре́. И напи́тките са ви́наги студе́ни.

Марин: Това́ ме подсе́ща. И една́ ма́лка раки́я. С ху́бава сала́та ви́наги пи́я раки́я. А ти́?

Пламен: Зна́еш, че съм на ра́бота. Не мо́га.

Марин: Пи́й една би́ра тога́ва. А́з пла́щам.

Пламен: Би́ра мо́же. У́тре че́рпя а́з.

GLOSSARY

ако	if
ако оби́чате	if you please
би́ра	beer
бъ̀рзам	hurry, be in a hurry
ведна́га	immediately, at once
вземи́ мо́ливите!	pick up the pencils!
взи́мам (*or* взе́мам) / взе́ма	take
ви́ждам / ви́дя	see
ви́наги	always
вли́зам / вля́за	enter, go in
вода́	water
въ̀здух	air
въ̀зрастен	adult
въ̀зрастни	grownups
гарниту́ра	garnish
гле́дам	look at
голе́мите	big ones, adults
го́твя	prepare, cook
гъ̀ба	mushroom
да́й, да́йте!	give! *(see L. 9 for conjugation)*
дале́че	far, far away
де́н, -я́т (*pl.* дни́)	day
ди́м, -ъ̀т	smoke
заду́шен	stuffy
затва́рям / затво́ря	close
зе́ле	cabbage
зна́м = зна́я	know
изби́рам / избера́	choose, select
изгле́ждам	look, appear, seem
изли́зам / изля́за	leave, go out
изуча́вам / изу́ча (-иш)	study, make a study of
и́мам ну́жда от	need, have need of
кабине́т	office (e.g. doctor's)
ка́звам / ка́жа (-еш)	say
какво́	what for, why
какво́ гле́даш то́лкова в	why are you so absorbed in
кашкава́л	kashkaval (yellow cheese)
кола́	car, automobile
ко́лко	how much, how many
ко́лко стру́ва?	how much does it cost?
ку́че	dog
къ̀сен	late
ле́в	lev (Bulgarian currency)
120 ле́ва	120 levs / leva *(see L. 6 for ending)*
легло́	bed
ле́гна *see* ля́гам	
лежа́ (-и́ш)	lie, be lying
ли́ст	sheet of paper
ля́гам / ле́гна	lie down, go to bed
ма́лките	small ones, children
ме	me *(see L. 5)*
меню́ *(neuter)*	menu
ми́л	dear
ми́ло	darling *(vocative)*
мо́га	can, be able *(see L. 5)*
мо́же	possible, OK
мо́ля	please
мо́ля ви се, господи́не	if you please, sir
мо́ля!	at your service
мо́рков	carrot
на ра́бота съм	be at work, be on the job
набли́зо	nearby
наизу́ст	by heart, verbatim
напи́тка	beverage, drink
неспоко́ен	uneasy, restless
огладня́вам / огладне́я	get hungry
омле́т	omelet
омле́т с гъ̀би	mushroom omelet
омле́т с кашкава́л	cheese omelet
омле́т с шу́нка	ham omelet
опа́сен	dangerous
осве́н	except [for]
осве́н това́	besides, in addition
оста́вам / оста́на	remain, stay
от	[made] of
отва́рям / отво́ря	open
пацие́нт (ка)	patient (medical)

пи́там	ask	слу́шам	listen, obey
пла́щам / пла́тя	pay	сме́ням / сменя́	change, replace
по́д	floor	смъ́ртен	mortal
подсе́щам / подсе́тя	remind, call to mind	спя́	sleep
поръ́чвам / поръ́чам	order	ста́вам / ста́на	get up, stand up, become, happen
почи́вам / почи́на	rest, go on holiday		
пра́в	straight, upright	сто́л	chair
пра́щам / пра́тя	send	стоя́	stand, be standing
пре́глед	examination (medical)	стоя́ пра́в	stand, remain standing
предпочи́там / предпочета́	prefer	стру́вам	cost
през	during (see L. 9)	студе́н	cold
пу́ша (-иш)	smoke	съби́рам / събера́	gather
пу́шене	smoking	съ́щото	the same thing
пъ́рви	first	ся́дам / се́дна	sit down, take a seat
пържо́ла	chop, steak		
пържо́ла с гарниту́ра	steak with the trimmings	тaка́	that way, like that
		та́м	there
пъ́т	time (instance)	това́ ме подсе́ща	that reminds me
		тога́ва	then, in that case
ра́бота	work, job	то́лкова	so much, so many, to such a degree
рабо́тя	work		
разби́рам / разбера́	understand	тръ́гвам / тръ́гна	set out, leave
разгле́ждам / разгле́дам	examine, study		
		у́тре	tomorrow
рестора́нт	restaurant	у́тре че́рпя а́з	it's my treat tomorrow
сала́та	salad	хо́ра	people
сала́та от зе́ле	cabbage salad		
сала́та от мо́ркови	carrot salad	цига́ра	cigarette
сега́ изли́зам	I'll go out right away		
се́дна see ся́дам		че́рпя	treat [someone]
седне́те, господи́не!	have a seat, sir!	чи́ст	clean
седя́	sit, be seated	чове́к	man, person
седя́ на тече́ние	sit in a drafty place		
серви́рам	serve, have available	шо́пска сала́та	"Shope salad"
сервитьо́р (ка)	waiter	шо́пски	pertaining to the "Shope" area near Sofia
сла́гам / сло́жа (-иш)	put		
следо́бед	afternoon	шу́нка	ham
следо́бед съм на ра́бота	I have to work this afternoon		

78

CULTURAL COMMENTARY

Forms of address: nicknames

Nicknames are very common in Bulgaria, and often end in **-ко** or **-че**. The nickname **Мѝтко** is formed from the second syllable of **Дими́тър** plus **-ко**.

Families

Bulgarians are extremely fond of children. They will usually make special efforts to help pregnant women or mothers with small children.

Food and drink: restaurants; vegetables; Shopska salata; drinks with meals

The range of available options in Bulgarian restaurants is often quite predictable, although in recent years there has been an increase in variety. Meat is normally available. A fried or grilled chop (**пържо́ла**), usually of pork, is a frequent choice. When the menu specifies "garnish" (**гарниту́ра**), the main portion of meat will be served together with various accompaniments, usually fried potatoes and/or rice, and stewed or pickled vegetables.

Vegetarianism is not unknown in Bulgaria, although it is not yet common. In the months when fresh fruits and vegetables are readily available, the cuisine centers around them, and in winter months, cheese and eggs are staples.

Salads are very popular in Bulgaria. An especial favorite is "shopska salata" (**шо́пска сала́та**), which is composed of chopped cucumber, tomato, onion, and pepper, and is topped with grated feta cheese. It is a particular Bulgarian custom to eat this salad (or at least some of its components) as an accompaniment to a pre-dinner rakia. Bulgarians find incomprehensible the Western custom of eating nuts, pretzels, or popcorn as an accompaniment to alcoholic drinks.

In many parts of Bulgaria, the drinking of rakia is limited to the appetizer portion of the meal; beer or wine are drunk with the main meal. Some Bulgarians will drink rakia throughout, however. Formerly, all drinks were served at room temperature, but in recent years it has become fashionable to drink beer and soft drinks cold. Hospitality decrees that friends should take turns treating each other to drinks. Most drinks come in standard portions. The request of **една́ ма́лка** (or **една́ голя́ма**) **раки́я** will bring a standard sized drink.

Refectory, Troyan Monastery (north-central Bulgaria)

LESSON 5

DIALOGUE

<u>Йдва един висóк човéк</u>

// Áнгел стои́ в коридóра и пýши. Йдва един висóк човéк. Нóси фотоапарáт, касетофóн, и видеокáмера. Áнгел го глéда и ми́сли. Какъ́в ли е тóзи човéк? Йска да го пи́та, но не знáе кáк. //

Веселин: Извинéте, и́скам да ми́на.

Ангел: Заповя́дайте, минéте.

Веселин: Не мóга, ня́ма мя́сто.

Ангел: Защó нóсите тóлкова мнóго? Глéдам ви и се чýдя. Каквó рабóтите?

Веселин: Журнали́ст съм.

Ангел: А-á! Журнали́ст! За къдé пътýвате?

Веселин: Оти́вам в Гáброво, на фестивáла.

Ангел: На кóй фестивáл?

Веселин: На фестивáла на хýмора и сáтирата, разби́ра се.

Ангел: Ахá, затовá нóсиш тéзи апарáти! Не сá ли тéжки?

Веселин: Тéжки са, разби́ра се.

Ангел: Сложи́ ги на пóда тогáва! А нé, нé в коридóра. Елá да влéзем в купéто. Хáйде да изпи́ем по еднá раки́я.

Веселин: Не мóга да вля́за. Йскам да намéря свобóдно мя́сто. Товá купé е пъ́лно, нали́?

Ангел: Дá, пъ́лно е, но децáта мóгат да сéднат зáедно.

// Весели́н и́ска да продължи́ по коридóра, но в тóзи момéнт забеля́зва Джýли, и си кáзва -- Коя́ ли е тáзи хубави́ца? //

Веселин: Добрé, хáйде да влéзем!

80

BASIC GRAMMAR

5.1. Infinitive replacements

Where other languages use infinitives, Bulgarian uses a phrase composed of да + the present tense form of the verb. Such "да-phrases" have a number of uses in Bulgarian, but the most common is in this function of infinitive meaning.

Verbs used in да-phrases must have the proper personal ending. Because subject pronouns are often omitted in Bulgarian, it is especially crucial to have the right verb ending. In many cases, the verb of the да-phrase has the same ending as the verb upon which it depends. In these instances, the English translation uses a simple infinitive. For example:

Искам	да	намеря	свободно място.
I want	to	find	an empty seat.
Искам	да	мина.	
I want	to	pass by.	

Децата	искат	да	седнат заедно.
The children	want	to	sit together.

In the above sentences, the one who wants the action performed is the same as the one who would perform it: both verbs have the same subject.

It is often the case, however, that the two verbs do not have the same subject. In these instances, the English translation must name the second subject. Furthermore, the identity of the Bulgarian *subject* is named by an English *object* pronoun. Care must therefore be taken both to get the right ending on the Bulgarian verb in the да-phrase, and not to be confused by the structure of the corresponding English sentence. In the following example, the meaning of the English pronoun "them" must be expressed by the 3rd plural ending on the Bulgarian verb дойдат.

Искаме		да	дойдат	и този път.
We want	them	to	come	this time too.

Not every Bulgarian да-phrase corresponds to an infinitive in English. After the verb "can", for instance, English adds the verb directly. But Bulgarian treats this sequence of two verbs as any other infinitive replacement. (Thinking of the verb "can" as "be able" may help the student produce the correct construction in Bulgarian.) For example:

81

Не и́скам	да	вля́за.
I don't want	to	come in.

Не мо́га	да	вля́за.
I can't		come in.
I'm not able	to	come in.

Infinitive replacements are also common after the word ха́йде. This word, which is unchanging in form, usually refers to a group of which the speaker considers himself a member. The verb following it, therefore, is usually 1st plural. Ха́йде can also be used without a verb; in these cases a verb must be understood.

Ха́йде да вле́зем.	Let's go in.
Ха́йде да изпи́ем по една́ раки́я!	Let's each drink a rakia!
Ха́йде по една́ глъ́тка!	Let's each [have] a drink!

5.2. The verb мога

The conjugation of the verb мо́га "can, be able" is slightly irregular, in that the stem-final consonant -г- shifts to -ж- before the theme vowel -е-.

	singular	*plural*
1st person	мо́г-а	мо́ж-ем
2nd person	мо́ж-еш	мо́ж-ете
3rd person	мо́ж-е	мо́г-ат

5.3. Aspect choice in да-phrases

Perfective verbs signify an action which is bounded in some way. Infinitive replacement phrases often suggest this boundedness, and for this reason perfective verbs are very common after да.

The boundedness meaning is usually that of completion. When a speaker expresses her desire *to do* something, or exhorts someone else *to do* something, her focus is usually on the successful completion of a particular action. Compare the following, in which all the verbs following да are perfective:

И́скам да ми́на.	I want to get by.
И́скам да наме́ря свобо́дно мя́сто.	I want to find an empty seat.
Ха́йде да вле́зем!	Let's go in.
Ха́йде да изпи́ем по една́ би́ра.	Let's each have a beer.

Likewise, the verb мо́га "can" is almost always followed by a perfective verb, since the essential focus is on the desired completion of an action. This is the case whether or not the particular action is seen as possible or impossible.

Imperfective verbs can appear after да if the specific meaning of boundedness is absent. The first of the two examples below, for instance, describes the speaker's state of wishing he could ask for more information but not being able to do so. Since no boundedness is implied, the imperfective verb пи́там is used.

The second describes a speaker's state after the doctor has told him he must stay inside the house for an extended period of time. Since the "going out" is not bounded to any single conceivable instance but rather covers the whole span of many possible instances, the imperfective verb изли́зам is used.

Йска да го пи́та, но не зна́е ка́к.	He wants to ask him, but doesn't know how [to go about it].
Не мо́га да изли́зам -- бо́лен съм.	I can't go out -- I'm sick.

5.4. Direct object pronouns

Bulgarian distinguishes three cases in personal pronouns: subject, direct object and indirect object. Subject pronouns were learned in Lesson 1. This lesson presents direct object pronouns. Indirect object pronouns will be learned in Lesson 7.

In the following chart, direct object pronouns are given alongside subject pronouns, for ease of comparison:

	subject	*direct object*
1st singular	а́з	ме
2nd singular	ти́	те
reflexive		се
3rd singular		
feminine	тя́	я
masculine	то́й	го
neuter	то́	го
1st plural	ни́е	ни
2nd plural	ви́е	ви
3rd plural	те́	ги

The particle **се** is included in this chart under the category "reflexive", which is the traditional name given by Bulgarian grammarians to it. Its range of usage is much wider, however.

Subject pronouns are fully accented words and may stand in any position in the sentence. Object pronouns are clitics, and obey the word order rules given in Lesson 1. That is, they may not occur at the beginning of a sentence or phrase, and they must occur adjacent to the verb on which they depend. In essence, this means that object pronouns precede the verb directly unless the verb stands at the beginning, in which case they follow the verb directly. The following two examples demonstrate this rule. In the first, the object pronoun stands directly in front of the verb it depends on. In the second, however, the verb begins the sentence, and the object pronoun must come directly after it.

Áнгел го глéда и мúсли.	Angel is looking at him and thinking.
Сложú ги на пóда!	Put them on the floor!

5.5. Usage of direct objects

The meaning of "direct object" in Bulgarian is the same as in English: the person or object which is most directly affected by the action of the verb. In Bulgarian, as in English, direct objects follow the verb directly, without an intervening preposition. For instance:

Put	the books	on the floor.
Сложú	кнúгите	на пóда!
verb	*direct object*	*prepositional phrase*

You	are carrying	a lot of baggage.
(Тú)	нóсиш	мнóго багáж.
subject	*verb*	*direct object*

Bulgarian and English usage happen to coincide in the case of the above two verbs. In a number of other instances, however, what is a direct object in Bulgarian will be expressed by a prepositional phrases in English. For instance:

Áнгел	глéда	човéка.
subject	*verb*	*direct object*

Angel	looks	at the man.
subject	*verb*	*prepositional phrase*

One must be wary of literal translation in such instances. The usage of a verb is part of its overall meaning, and needs to be learned along with that meaning.

Direct object pronouns are used after the impersonal expression ня́ма "there isn't" and the pointing word е́то.

Къде́ е Ива́н?	Where is Ivan?
Не зна́я. Ня́ма го ту́к.	I don't know. There's no sign of him.
Къде́ е та́зи кни́га?	Where is that book?
Не зна́я. А, е́то я.	I don't know. Oh, here it is.

5.6. Interrogative pronouns

Like other pronouns, the interrogative pronoun "who, which" expresses gender and number. Here are the forms:

masculine	*feminine*	*neuter*	*plural*
ко́й	коя́	кое́	кои́

The neutral question word for "who" is ко́й. That is, if nothing is known of the sex of the person queried about, the masculine form ко́й is used.

| Ко́й седи́ на това́ мя́сто? | Who (*unspecified*) is sitting in this seat? |

If the sex is known, however, the appropriate form is used:

| Веселѝн забеля́зва Джу́ли и си ка́зва -- Коя́ е та́зи хубави́ца? | Veselin sees Julie and says to himself, "Who (*feminine*) is this beauty?" |

When the interrogative pronoun modifies a noun, it agrees with its noun and has the meaning "which". For example:

| -- На ко́й фестива́л? | "To which (*masculine*) festival?" |
| -- На фестива́ла на ху́мора и са́тирата, разби́ра се. | "To the festival of humor and satire, of course." |

5.7. Motion verbs

The basic verbs for "come" and "go" in Bulgarian are

	imperfective	*perfective*
come	и́дв-ам	до́йд-а
go	оти́в-ам	оти́д-а

Both verbs carry within them the meaning of directedness; that is, of someone coming or going *towards* a particular end-point (even if that end-point is not explicitly specified). The idea of directedness is reinforced by the presence of от- and до- in certain of these verbs. The similarity to the prepositions meaning "from" and "to" can help remind the student of the "directed" meaning of these verbs.

By contrast, the verb вървя́ (which, with rare exceptions, exists only in the imperfective aspect) implies the absence of any direction. For this reason, it is usually translated "walk". It can also, however, be translated "go", "come", "move", or any of a number of verbs signifying locomotion. The primary difference between вървя́ and the other verbs is the factor of directedness. For example:

и́двам

А́нгел стои́ в коридо́ра.	Angel is standing in the corridor.
И́два еди́н висо́к чове́к.	A tall man comes [towards him].

оти́вам

-- За къде́ пъту́вате?	"Where are you headed for?"
-- Оти́вам в Га́брово, на фестива́ла.	"I'm going to Gabrovo, to the festival."

вървя́

Весели́н върви́ по коридо́ра.	Veselin walks down the corridor.
Вла́кът върви́ мно́го ба́вно.	The train is going very slowly.

In the first two sets of examples, an end-point of the movement is either implied or stated directly. Those in the last set, however, explicitly avoid mention of an end-point.

5.8. Double interrogatives

Normally, questions have either a question word or the question particle ли. When a question has both of these, the meaning "I wonder..." is added.

Какъ́в ли е то́зи чове́к?	I wonder what kind of a man this is?

5.9. Prepositions

(a)   Both в and на can mean "to". While many of the specific differences are idiomatic, there is a tendency for в to refer to specific physical locations which one can enter, while на is more likely to refer to abstract ideas, events, general locales, or places conceived of as surfaces rather than enclosures. Consider the following examples:

Отивам	в Габрово,	на фестивала.
I'm going	to Gabrovo,	to the festival.
	[a city one can enter]	*[an event]*

Сложи ги	на пода.	А не,	не в коридора.
Put them down	on the floor.	Ah, no,	not in the corridor.
	[onto a surface]		*[within the enclosure of a space]*

The student is advised to watch the usage of **в** and **на**, and learn examples idiomatically until s/he gets a feel for it.

The preposition **на** can also mean possession. For example, the first **на** in the following sentence means "to", while the second **на** signifies possession:

Отивам на фестивала на хумора и сатирата, разбира се.	I'm going to the festival of humor and satire, of course.

(b)   The basic meaning of **по** is "along, down". For example:

Веселин иска да продължи по коридора, но в този момент....	Veselin intends to continue down the corridor, but at that instant...

По also has many other meanings, however. One of these is "according to, of, in the manner of". For example:

Искам да ги посрещна по български.	I want to entertain them in the Bulgarian manner. *[à la bulgare]*
учебник по български	a Bulgarian textbook *[textbook of the Bulgarian language]*
преподавател по български	Bulgarian teacher *[a teacher who teaches Bulgarian]*

EXERCISES

I. Fill in the blanks with the appropriate personal endings.

1. Йскам да намéр____ шáпката на Андрéй.
2. Йскам и Тáня да вúд____ шáпката на Андрéй.
3. Мóля, идéте да посрéщн_____ Джýли на гáрата.
4. Съвéтвам Áнгел да слýш____ каквó кáзвате.
5. Седнú! Йскаш ли áз да свáр_____ едно кафé?
6. Не мóга да разбéр_____ каквó кáзваш.
7. Джýли продължáва да ýч____ бългáрски.

II. Fill in the blanks with the appropriate form of the interrogative pronoun (кóй, коя́, коé, кой).

1. _____ от тéзи женú е кондýкторка?
2. От _____ шоколáд úскаш да кýпим?
3. Áз говóря бългáрски и англúйски. На _____ езúк úскаш да говóрим?
4. _____ детé мóже да брóй до стó?
5. _____ е на телефóна?
6. _____ кнúги врúщаш в библиотéката?
7. _____ е тáзи непознáта женá?

III. Rewrite the following sentences, replacing the underlined nouns with the correct pronouns.

1. Тáня познáва Ивáн добрé.
2. Димúтър úска да вúди тéзи студéнти.
3. Джýли и Дéйвид не пúят ракúя.
4. Кóста не мóже да намéри сéлото на кáртата.
5. Веселúн за съжалéние не познáва тáзи хубавúца.
6. Къдé отúва момчéто? Не вúждам товá момчé.
7. Кóй знáе тóзи урóк? Кóй мóже да вúрне тéзи кнúги в библиотéката?

ADDITIONAL GRAMMAR NOTES

5.1a. Infinitive replacements

Sentences such as "I want them to come" are notably difficult for English speakers to translate into Bulgarian. This is partly because in such sentences the English *object* pronoun (here, "them") denotes *subject* meaning (in this case, "they" are the ones who "will come"). In a neutral meaning, the Bulgarian translation of this sentence does not use a pronoun at all. If emphasis is intended, however, the subject pronoun (in this case, тé "they") will be used:

> **Ѝскам и тé да дóйдат.**   I want *them* to come as well.

The problem is further complicated by the fact that in such sentences an English object pronoun can sometimes also correspond to a Bulgarian object pronoun:

Áз	те	съвéтвам	да дóйдеш.	I advise you to come.
	2sg object		*2sg verb*	

Ѝскам	тѝ		да дóйдеш.	I want *you* to come.
	2sg subject		*2sg verb*	

In both sentences, the subject of the verb дóйдеш "come" is the second person singular тѝ "you". It is explicitly stated in the second sentence, but only because the meaning is emphatic. It is omitted from the first sentence because its meaning has already been introduced by the object pronoun те (which is the object of the verb съвéтвам "advise").

The contrast is seen more clearly when the verbs and pronouns are third person singular, where there is a more marked difference between subject and object pronouns.

Áз	я	съвéтвам	да дóйде.	I advise her to come.
	3sg object		*3sg verb*	

Ѝскам	тя́		да дóйде.	I want *her* to come.
	3sg subject		*3sg verb*	

In order to translate these sentences correctly into Bulgarian, one must determine the relationship between the verb preceding да in Bulgarian and the pronoun which always appears as an English object (e.g. "her" in the English sentences above). If the verb takes a pronoun object, then the correct pronoun in Bulgarian is the object one. But if the verb takes an entire phrase as its object, then the correct pronoun in Bulgarian is the subject one. This can be represented schematically as follows:

89

| Áз я съвéтвам да дóйде. | (a) | I advise | her | |
| | (b) | | she | [is] to come |

| Ѝскам тя́ да дóйде. | (a) | I want | | |
| | (b) | | she | [is] to come |

Each of these sentences can be broken down into two components, which are represented above as (a) and (b). The (a) portion of each sentence is what comes before the да, and the (b) portion is what comes after it. In the first example, the "she" of part (b) simply disappears into the "her" of part (a). In the second example, however, the "she" of part (b) must move up into part (a). In English it turns into an object when it moves up, but in Bulgarian it remains a subject.

5.4a. Object pronouns and word order

Word order rules involving verbal clitics are quite complex in Bulgarian, and for this reason they will be learned gradually. Since clitics are unaccented, they are spoken quickly and are often hard to hear. Special care must be taken, therefore, to learn the rules governing their placement.

To help the student become aware of these rules, examples will be given using a notation developed for this purpose. All rules learned in this book are given according to this notational format, together with a full list of abbreviations used, in Lesson 15. Within lessons, word order rules are explained and illustrated with examples in which the relevant words are identified notationally. Sentences are given either in complete form, or with sufficient grammar to illustrate the context; only the portion of each sentence relevant to the word order rule being learned, however, is specifically analyzed.

According to this notational analysis, abbreviations identifying clitics are written entirely in capital letters, those identifying fully-accented words (upon which clitics can depend) are written entirely in lower-case letters, and those identifying conjunctions which are unstressed but which may begin a sentence (and therefore are not clitics) are written with a capital letter. The following examples illustrate this notation.

(1) | Ѝска | да | го | пѝта | но... |
| *verb* | *Cnj.* | *DIR* | *verb* | |

He wants to ask him but...

(2) | Глéдам | ви | и | се | чýдя. |
| *verb* | *DIR* | *Cnj.* | *DIR* | *verb* |

I look at you and am amazed.

Placement of object pronouns

The basic rule is that a pronoun verbal object must be directly adjacent to the verb it depends on, and that it must follow at least one accented word.

(3)

Ангел	го	гле́да	и ми́сли.
subj.	DIR	verb	

> Angel looks at him and thinks.

(4)

Сложи́	ги	на по́да.
verb	DIR	

> Put them on the floor.

Conjunctions and negation

The conjunction да occupies a special position in this schema: it has no accent of its own, but it is not a clitic. This means that it (like other conjunctions) can function as an accented word for purposes of clitic placement. The word order of да-phrases is very rigid: the verb must follow да directly unless the verb has a pronoun object. In this case the pronoun object *must* come directly between да and the verb. Example (1) above illustrates this rule.

For word order purposes, the negative particle не acts like the conjunction да, requiring clitics to follow it directly. Remember that a clitic following the negative particle is accented.

(5) Ангел

не	го́	гле́да.
Neg.	DIR	verb

> Angel does not look at him.

(6)

Не	ги	сла́гай	на по́да.
Neg.	DIR	verb	

> Don't put them on the floor!

The question particle

In a neutral question, the interrogative particle ли always follows the verb, and must come between the verb and any pronoun object. (It follows from this that clitics can never precede the verb in this type of question.) If both negative and interrogative particles are present, the pronoun object comes between them.

(7) Ангел

гле́да	ли	го?
verb	INT	DIR

> Is Angel looking at him?

(8)

Сла́гаш	ли	ги	на по́да?
verb	INT	DIR	

> Are you putting them on the floor?

(9)

Не	ги́	ли	сла́гаш	на по́да?
Neg.	DIR	INT	verb	

> Aren't you putting them on the floor?

5.4b. Predicates and word order

When present tense forms of the verb **съм** are used to connect a subject and a predicate noun or adjective, they function as the copula of the sentence. These copula forms are clitics, and follow rules very similar to those formulated above for object pronouns. They cannot stand in initial position, they always occur adjacent to the predicate noun or adjective, and they must follow the negative or interrogative particle directly.

When both negative and interrogative particles are present, the copula is placed between them. This is the only time when the copula does not occur directly adjacent to the predicate noun or adjective. Here are examples, with numbering consecutive across lessons:

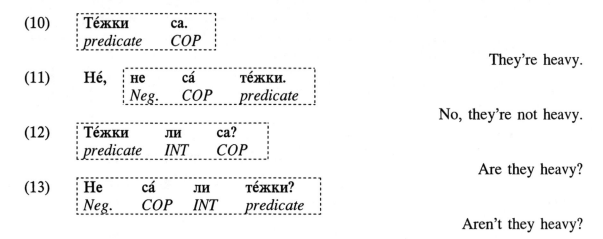

(10) | Тѐжки са.
      | *predicate* *COP*

They're heavy.

(11) Нѐ, | не сѐ тѐжки.
         | *Neg.* *COP* *predicate*

No, they're not heavy.

(12) | Тѐжки ли са?
      | *predicate* *INT* *COP*

Are they heavy?

(13) | Не сѐ ли тѐжки?
      | *Neg.* *COP* *INT* *predicate*

Aren't they heavy?

All of the above word order patterns will be drilled in later lessons.

5.7a. Motion verbs

The **от-** and the **до-** in the motion verbs **отѝвам**, **отѝда** and **дойда** are called prefixes. Prefixes are similar to, but not identical with, prepositions; this relationship will be discussed later. All four directional motion verbs contain the same root, **-ид-**, although its form is slightly obscured in **отѝвам** (compare **ѝдвам**, where the **-д-** has been retained before the suffix **-вам**) and in **дойда** (where the **-и-** has shifted to **-й-**).

This bare root is found in the verb **ѝда**, which can be used in place of **отѝда**. There is no essential difference in meaning. **Ѝда** is especially frequent in the imperative:

Идѝ в магазѝна!   Go to the store!

The imperative form of **дойда** is a Greek borrowing, completely unrelated to it in form. The imperative of **ѝдвам** is regular, however.

indicative	imperative	
	singular	plural
дойда	ела́	ела́те
и́двам	не и́двай	не и́двайте

Bulgarians use **и́двам** and **дойда** as any other aspect pair. Bulgarian dictionaries, however, list them as two separate verbs. Officially, the imperfective of **дойда** is the rarely used **дохо́ждам**.

5.10. Contrastive negation

When it negates a verb, the negative particle **не** is unstressed. When it is used contrastively, to negate another part of speech or when standing alone, it bears accent. For example:

А не́, не́ в коридо́ра.   Oh no, not in the corridor.

-- Дете́то гово́ри ли?   "Does the child talk?"
-- О́ще не́.   "Not yet."

Professor Stayko Kabasanov with traditional Rhodope bagpipe player and singer

SAMPLE SENTENCES

1. Той и́ска да чете́ кни́ги. Той и́ска да прочете́ та́зи кни́га.

2. Обикнове́но сла́гам кни́гите в ча́нтата. Сега́ не и́скам да ги сло́жа в ча́нтата.

3. Лиля́на пи́ше (едно) писмо́. Йска да го напи́ше.

4. -- Оти́вам с Весели́н на ки́но. Ела́ и ти́!
   -- Йскам да до́йда, но не мо́га.

5. -- Иди́ за хля́б.
   -- Не зна́я къде́ е магази́нът.
   -- И а́з и́двам тога́ва.

6. Заду́шно е, отва́рям врата́та. Та́ня я затва́ря.

7. Бо́б е бо́лен. Сла́гам го да ле́гне.

8. Ти́ ме пи́таш ка́к се ка́звам.

9. А́з те ви́ждам отту́ка.

10. Той ви́наги ка́зва и́стината.

11. Бо́йко оби́ча деца́та. И Бо́б ги оби́ча.

Ruins of Byzantine basilica, Nesebăr

94

SENTENCES FOR TRANSLATION

1. Look, here comes Lilyana! Do you see her? Why is she walking so slowly?

2. Don't you want to come to the movies today? Let's go! Ivan is at the theater already, and he wants us to meet him there.

3. The Bulgarian teacher advises you to go to the library often. She wants you to go there now. She wants us to study these lessons well. Of course, we also want to know them.

4. I need this book. Are you reading it? If you are not reading it, please put it on the table. Then I can read it. Or do you want me to return it to the library?

5. We are going to the station now. Milena is coming from Gabrovo and we want to meet her. Do you want to come too? Come on, let's go!

6. Who is calling? Do you want to speak with Tanya? She can't come to the phone right now. She is with the children. She is putting them to bed.

7. Which book do you advise me to read? I don't want to read a textbook, I want to read a novel. Which Bulgarian novels are good? Can you read them?

8. "Ivo can't open the window, he is [too] small. Can you open it, please?"
"Which window do you want me to open? But then let's close the door. Can you close it, please?"

READING SELECTION

Кореспонде́нция - (4)

---

31 а́вгуст, Со́фия

Дра́га Патри́ша,

    И́мам една ра́достна новина́, бъ́рзам да я съобща́. Седя́ дне́с в ку́хнята и чета́. Изведнъ́ж звъне́цът звъни́. Ста́вам, отва́рям врата́та и какво́ ви́ждам? Едно непозна́то моми́че. Откъде́ и́два? От по́щата! Но́си съобще́ние за коле́т. От Аме́рика! Взе́мам ча́нтата и тръ́гвам за по́щата.
    Мно́го благодаря́ за уче́бника, Патри́ша! То́й и́два съвсе́м навре́ме. Подгото́вката върви́ идеа́лно. И́зпитът, ка́зват, не е́ мно́го тру́ден.
    Пиши́ от какво́ и́маш ну́жда? А́з мо́га ли с не́що да се реванши́рам?

Целу́вам те,

Кали́на

---

14 септе́мври, Сан Франци́ско

Дра́га Кали́на,

    Зна́чи уче́бникът е ве́че в Со́фия. Ра́двам се. Успе́х на и́зпита!
    Ни́е сме добре́. Е́мили тръ́гва отно́во на учи́лище. Бо́б рабо́ти, а Ма́йкъл игра́е с деца́та на съсе́дите.
    Ско́ро Бо́б и́ма рожде́н де́н. Ви́наги и́дват на го́сти прия́тели. И́скаме да до́йдат и то́зи пъ́т. И́мам една страхо́тна иде́я. И́скам да ги посре́щнем екзоти́чно, по бъ́лгарски. И́маме бъ́лгарска наро́дна му́зика. Ту́ка в магази́ните и́ма бъ́лгарско ви́но. Мо́га да сго́твя бъ́лгарски го́зби. Какво́ ме съве́тваш да сго́твя? И́скам не́що типи́чно, ефе́ктно, но не́ мно́го сло́жно.

Пиши́!

Патри́ша

GLOSSARY

а́вгуст	August	иди́ за хля́б!	go buy some bread
апара́т	apparatus, equipment	изведнъ́ж	suddenly
аха́	aha	извиня́вам /	pardon, excuse
		извиня́	
библиоте́ка	library	изпи́вам / изпи́я	drink up
		и́зпит	exam, test
в то́зи моме́нт	then, at that point	и́скам	want
	in time		
ви	you (*object pronoun*)	какво́ рабо́тите?	what [kind of] work
видеока́мера	video camera		do you do?
висо́к	tall, high	какъ́в ли е то́й?	what's he like, I wonder?
връ́щам / въ́рна	return	ка́рта	card, map
		касетофо́н	cassette player
га́ра	Station (bus, train)	кафе́	coffee, cup of coffee
ги	them (*object pronoun*)	ки́но	cinema, movies
го	him, it (*obj. pronoun*)	ко́й, коя́, кое́, кои́	who, which
го́зба	dish	коле́т	parcel, package
го́ст	guest	конду́ктор (ка)	conductor
		купу́вам / ку́пя	buy, purchase
да	(*subordinating	ку́хня	kitchen
	conjunction*)		
и́скам да до́йда	I want to come	ли	(*question particle*)
не мо́га да до́йда	I can't come		
до	[up] to	магази́н	store
дохо́ждам / до́йда	come, arrive (*5.7a*)	ме	me (*object pronoun*)
		мина́вам / ми́на	pass
екзоти́чен	exotic	ми́сля	think
ела́	come!	моме́нт	moment
елега́нтен	elegant	му́зика	music
ефе́ктен	effective		
		на телефо́на съм	be (talking) on the phone
журнали́ст (ка)	journalist	навре́ме	on time
		нами́рам / наме́ря	find
забеля́звам /		напи́свам /	write, write down, finish
забеле́жа (-иш)	notice, spot	напи́ша (-еш)	writing
за́едно	together	наро́ден	national, folk
заповя́дай	help yourself!	не́	(*contrastive negation*)
заповя́двам /		не́ та́м	not there [but elsewhere]
заповя́дам	command, order	непозна́т	unknown
затова́	therefore, thus	не́що	something
звъне́ц	bell	ни	us (*object pronoun*)
звъня́	ring	новина́	[a piece of] news
игра́я	play	оти́вам / оти́да	go
и́да	come, go	отту́ка	from here
и́двам	come	о́ще не́	not yet
и́двам на го́сти	come/go to visit		
идеа́лен	ideal	по	along, down
иде́я	idea	по	according to, in the
			manner of

подготóвка	preparation	съвсéм наврéме	at exactly the right moment
подготóвката върви́	the preparation's coming along	съобщáвам / съобщя́	announce, inform
посрéщам / посрéщна	meet, greet, entertain	съобщéние	announcement
преподавáтел по бъ́лгарски	teacher of Bulgarian	съобщéние за колéт	postal notice for a package
продължáвам / продължá (-и́ш)	continue	съсéд (ка)	neighbor
прочи́там / прочетá	read (to completion)	те	you (object pronoun)
пъ́лен	full	телефóн	telephone
		трýден	difficult
рáдвам се	rejoice, be happy	тръ́гвам на учи́лище	start school
рáдостен	happy, joyful		
реванши́рам се	make up, return a favor	урóк	lesson
		успéх	success
реванши́рам се с нéщо	make [it] up by doing something	успéх на и́зпита	good luck on the test
рождéн	birth (adj.)	ýча (-иш)	learn, teach
рождéн дéн	birthday	учи́лище	school
сáтира	satire	фестивáл	festival
сваря́вам / сваря́	cook, boil	фотоапарáт	camera
сгóтвям / сгóтвя	cook, make		
се	oneself (object pronoun)	хля́б	bread
		хубави́ца	beauty
септéмври	September	хýмор	humor
си	to oneself (see L. 7)		
слáгам да лéгне	put [someone] to bed	целýвам / целýна	kiss
слóжен	difficult, complex		
стó	[a] hundred	чýдя се	wonder
страхóтен	horrible, dreadful, terrifying	шáпка	hat
страхóтна идéя	[a] terrific idea	шоколáд	chocolate
съвéтвам	advise		
съвсéм	completely	я	her (object pronoun)

CULTURAL COMMENTARY

Geography: Gabrovo

Gabrovo (**Гáброво**) is a town in north central Bulgaria. The residents of this town are known for their sense of humor, and for the jokes they tell about themselves. Most of these jokes turn on their sense of "economy", and are similar to the jokes Scotsmen tell about themselves. These jokes have become so famous that the town of Gabrovo now holds an annual week-long "festival of humor". It is a very popular tourist event, for which tickets are hard to obtain.

Families

Bulgarians have a highly developed sense of family. Sometimes this sense of "family" extends even into public space. Some Bulgarian parents might feel it an intrusion that an adult they do not know would make decisions about their children (such as deciding the children can share a seat in the train), but others would accept it in the sense of "temporary family".

Hospitality

Hospitality towards a guest is a central feature of Bulgarian society. Many sacrifices will be made (willingly) in service of the "guest-host" relationship.

Forms of address: ти vs. вие

Most urban Bulgarians will address a stranger as **вие** out of politeness. Two people making each other's acquaintance will only switch to **ти** upon mutual agreement. A number of Bulgarians, however, especially those from rural environments, will either address anyone they meet in unofficial circumstances as **ти** from the very outset, or will move to **ти** extremely quickly (and without the formality of a mutual agreement).

Postal system

Traditionally, Bulgarians have had low confidence in the mail service, considering it to be slow at best and generally untrustworthy. This is at least partly due to memories of the Communist regime, when everything that came through the mails was subject to search; in more recent years such fears have been replaced by fears of theft. The distrust of the mails is thus especially great when it comes to packages (or anything that could conceivably contain valuables).

Troyan Monastery (north-central Bulgaria)

LESSON 6

DIALOGUE

<u>Къдé бéше досегá?</u>

Веселин: Дóбър дéн.

Ангел: Децá, я́ напрáвете мя́сто на тóзи човéк да сéдне. Кáк се кáзваш бе, прия́тел?

Веселин: Кáзвам се Веселúн Хрúстов.

Ангел: Áз съм Áнгел, от Балчúк. А товá са Милéна и Димúтър от Вáрна, Тáня от .... откъдé си, Тáня?

Таня: От Сóфия.

Ангел: А товá са Джýли и Дéйвид от Амéрика.

Веселин: А вúе, децá, кáк се кáзвате?

Камен: Кáмен.

Надка: Нáдка.

Веселин: На кóлко сте годúни?

Камен: Áз съм на сéдем годúни, а Нáдка е на пéт.

Веселин: На сéдем годúни ли? Хóдиш ли на учúлище? Знáеш ли да броúш?

Камен: Знáя, разбúра се. Отдáвна вéче. Като бя́х на трú годúни пúтах мáйка...

Веселин: Пребро́й кóлко местá úма в купéто.

Камен: Еднó, двé, трú, чéтири, пéт, шéст, сéдем, óсем.

Милена: А кóлко дýши сме? Пътýваме от едúн чáс сáмо, а úмаме óще шéст чáса пъ́т. Мнóго дъ́лъг пъ́т!

Надка: Чúчко, тú къдé бéше досегá?

Веселин: Бях в коридóра. Пътýвах прáв. Глéдах през прозóреца.

Надка: Мáмо, когá пристúгаме в Шýмен? Áз съм глáдна. Úскам едно кебáпче.

Камен: Áз úскам двé кебáпчета.

Таня: Пристúгаме в двá часá. Знáчи, след петнáйсет минýти.

Камен: Знáчи, всúчко трú кебáпчета.

Надка: Нé! Чéтири!

Веселин: Позволéте, госпóжо, да почéрпя всúчки в купéто с по двé кебáпчета. Госпóжице Джýли, знáете ли каквó е кебáпче?

Джули: Знáя, но áз за съжалéние съм вегетериáнка.

Надка: Мáмо, каквó е вегетериáнка?

Traditional Bulgarian pottery

101

BASIC GRAMMAR

6.1. Past tense

The simple past tense in Bulgarian is called the aorist. It corresponds to the English simple past ("I came", "you saw", "he did"). The conjugation is the same for all verbs: there is no ending in the 2nd and 3rd singular, and other endings contain the consonant **-х-**. These endings are:

	singular	plural
1st person	-х-	-х-ме
2nd person	-	-х-те
3rd person	-	-х-а

Preceding these endings is the aorist tense theme vowel. For **a**-conjugation verbs, this vowel is the same as in the present tense -- either **-а-** or **-я-**.

For comparison, here are both present and aorist tense forms of the verbs **пи́там** and **отва́рям**. (Aorist forms of the other conjugations will be learned later.)

	PRESENT	AORIST	PRESENT	AORIST
1st singular	пи́т-ам	пи́т-ах	отва́р-ям	отва́р-ях
2nd singular	пи́т-аш	пи́т-а	отва́р-яш	отва́р-я
3rd singular	пи́т-а	пи́т-а	отва́р-я	отва́р-я
1st plural	пи́т-аме	пи́т-ахме	отва́р-яме	отва́р-яхме
2nd plural	пи́т-ате	пи́т-ахте	отва́р-яте	отва́р-яхте
3rd plural	пи́т-ат	пи́т-аха	отва́р-ят	отва́р-яха

The past tense conjugation of the verb **съм** is somewhat irregular. It is as follows:

	PRESENT	AORIST
1st singular	съм	бях
2nd singular	си	бе́ше
3rd singular	е	бе́ше
1st plural	сме	бя́хме
2nd plural	сте	бя́хте
3rd plural	са	бя́ха

The meaning corresponds to English "was" or "were" used as a simple past. The form **бé** can be used in place of **бéше** with no change in meaning. For example:

Къдé бéше досегá?	Where were you before?
Бя́х в коридóра.	I was in the corridor.
Бя́хте ли на морéто?	Were you at the seaside?
Не бéше мнóго интерéсно.	It wasn't very interesting.
Тóй бé тáм досегá.	He was there until now.
Пи́тах мáйка....	I asked my mother....

6.2. Plural of neuter nouns

The plural of neuter nouns is **-a**, which appears in several different forms. If the singular ends in **-o**, then the plural usually ends in **-a**. If the singular ends in **-e**, then the plural usually ends in **-ета**. If the singular ends in **-e** preceded by **-и-**, then the plural ending is written **-я**. Neuter nouns ending in **-e** keep the accent on the same syllable in both singular and plural.

The simple ending **-a** is almost always accented, regardless of the accent in the singular. The **-e-** of the ending **-ета** is accented only if the singular ending **-e** is accented, and the ending **-я** is never accented. The definite article is **-та** (obeying the rule requiring all noun forms ending in **-a** to take a rhyming article). Here are examples:

Type sg / pl	singular	plural	definite plural
-o / -a	мя́сто	местá	местáта
	éзеро	езерá	езерáта
	сéло	селá	селáта
-e / -ета	кебáпче	кебáпчета	кебáпчетата
	купé	купéта	купéтата
	моми́че	моми́чета	моми́четата
	момчé	момчéта	момчéтата
-ие / -ия	течéние	течéния	течéнията

Plurals of all neuter nouns which cannot be predicted from the above rules will be noted in the glossary. Certain common ones are:

singular	plural
врéме	временá
и́ме	именá
учи́лище	учи́лища
цвéте	цветя́

The plural ending on all adjectives continues to be **-и**. Therefore, adjectives modifying plural neuter nouns have the same ending as adjectives modifying all other plural nouns.

6.3. Numbers

The number 1 is identical with the indefinite article except that it is always accented. It changes form according to the gender of the noun counted: **еди́н** (masculine), **една́** (feminine), **едно́** (neuter).

There are two forms for the number 2: **два́** for masculine nouns, and **две́** for feminine and neuter nouns. The remaining numbers do not change form. Here are the numbers from 3-100:

		11	едина́йсет				
		12	двана́йсет	20	два́йсет		
3	три́	13	трина́йсет	30	три́йсет		
4	че́тири	14	четирина́йсет	40	чети́ридесет		
5	пе́т	15	петна́йсет	50	петдесе́т		
6	ше́ст	16	шестна́йсет	60	шестдесе́т		
7	се́дем	17	седемна́йсет	70	седемдесе́т		
8	о́сем	18	осемна́йсет	80	осемдесе́т		
9	де́вет	19	деветна́йсет	90	деветдесе́т		
10	де́сет					100	сто́

Compound numbers are formed by addition. The conjunction **и** must be both written and spoken. For example:

21	(= 20 + 1)	два́йсет и едно́
32	(= 30 + 2)	три́йсет и две́
89	(= 80 + 9)	осемдесе́т и де́вет

6.4. Masculine nouns after numbers

Nouns which appear after numbers are said to be "quantified". For feminine and neuter nouns, the quantified forms are exactly the same as the plural forms, but for masculine nouns the quantified form is different from the plural. Its ending is similar to that of the definite object form (**-a** if the article is **-ът**, and **-я** if the article is **-ят**), but with a potential accentual difference. This is because the definite article can sometimes be accented, but the quantified ending can *never* be accented.

The quantified form of masculine nouns is used after *all* numbers, after **ко́лко** "how many", "how much" and **ня́колко** "some, several". After **мно́го** "many", however, the *plural* form is used. The chart below summarizes the non-plural forms of masculine nouns:

	SINGULAR		QUANTIFIED
indefinite	*definite (subject)*	*definite (object)*	
мо́лив	мо́ливът	мо́лива	два́ мо́лива
трамва́й	трамва́ят	трамва́я	два́ трамва́я
гра́д	градъ́т	града́	два́ гра́да
ча́с	часъ́т	часа́	два́ ча́са

Fleeting vowels lost in the plural are retained before the quantified ending.

singular	*quantified*	*plural*
прозо́р-ец	прозо́р-ец-а	прозо́р-ц-и

The word **чове́к** "man, person" exists only in the singular. The form **ду́ши** is used for the quantified meaning, and the form **хо́ра** for the plural meaning. Note that **хо́ра**, like all plurals ending in **-a**, takes a rhyming article. For example:

-- Ко́лко ду́ши и́ма в купе́то?	"How many people are in the compartment?"
-- Са́мо еди́н чове́к.	"Only one person."
Мно́го хо́ра пъту́ват с то́зи вла́к.	Many people are [traveling] on this train.
Ту́ка хо́рата живе́ят добре́.	People live well here.

6.5. Masculine numbers

The numbers from 2 to 6 have a special form before masculine nouns referring to human beings. The nouns themselves are in the plural. For example:

еди́н ле́кар	one doctor
два́ма ле́кари	two doctors
три́ма ле́кари	three doctors

The masculine quantifier forms for 4, 5 and 6 are **четири́ма** (or **чети́рма**), **пети́ма**, **шести́ма**. For larger quantities, the regular numbers are used. The noun remains in the plural. "Masculine" numbers are always used before the noun **ду́ши**, regardless of the sex of the persons counted.

6.6. Motion verbs, continued

The verb **хо́дя** means "go". It is like **оти́вам** (perfective **оти́да**) in that an end-point is implied. Its meaning is broader, however: it can refer to a round-trip movement, a repeated movement, or to the general idea of going somewhere without reference to any one specific trip. Here are examples:

Хо́диш ли на учи́лище?	Do you go to school?
А́з хо́дя че́сто на теа́тър.	I go to the theater often.
Хо́дим на Ви́тоша вся́ка неде́ля.	We go to Vitosha every Sunday.
Ха́йде да хо́дим на ци́рк!	Let's go to the circus!

6.7. Telling time

The definite form of the noun **ча́с** "hour" is used to tell time. The subject form refers to time at the moment of speech, and the object form (which occurs only after a preposition) refers to any other time. In this usage, **часа́** corresponds to the English "o'clock", and is often abbreviated **ч.**

The definite form of **ча́с** is always accented on the article (which is always pronounced as if written [-ъ́]). The preposition **в** corresponds to English "at" in time expressions. Here are examples of both subject and object usage:

Ко́лко е часъ́т?	What time is it?
В ко́лко часа́?	At what time?
Часъ́т е еди́н.	It's one o'clock.
В еди́н часа́. (в 1 ч.)	At one o'clock.
Часъ́т е ше́ст.	It's six o'clock.
В ше́ст часа́. (в 6 ч.)	At six o'clock.

One can also identify the hour without the noun (as in English).

-- В ко́лко часа́?	"When?" [= At what time?]
-- В два́.	"At two."

The prepositions **от** and **до** refer to the starting point and the ending point, respectively, of a time period, while the prepositions **след** and **преди́** refer respectively to periods following or preceding a particular point in time.

То́й рабо́ти все́ки де́н от 9 до 5.	He works daily from 9 to 5.
Ела́ след два́ часа́, но преди́ пе́т!	Come after 2 o'clock, but before 5.

От ко́лко часа́ и́маш ле́кции?	When do your classes start? [= From when do you have lectures?]
До ко́лко часа́ и́маш ле́кции?	When are your classes done? [= Until when do you have lectures?]

Time after the hour is expressed by the conjunction **и**. To say "half past" the hour, Bulgarians use the word **полови́на**. For example:

Сега́ е три́ и два́йсет	It's 3:20.
Ела́ в ше́ст и полови́на!	Come at 6:30 [at half past six].

Time before the hour is expressed by the preposition **без**:

-- Ко́лко е часъ́т?	"What time is it?"
-- Едина́йсет без два́йсет.	"It's twenty to eleven [10:40]."
Сега́ е без де́сет.	It's ten of.
Ела́ в три́ без петна́йсет!	Come at 2:45 [at a quarter of three].

In certain official contexts, the time is expressed using the 24-hour clock:

Вла́кът трѣ́гва в 19 часа́.	The train leaves at 7 p.m.

6.8. Time as duration

The indefinite form of the noun **ча́с** refers to a period of 60 minutes' duration. The form after numerals other than 1 is the quantified form. The accentual difference between the definite object form and the quantified form is very important in distinguishing these two meanings. In addition, the two different meanings of the preposition **преди** are distinguished by accent. For example:

Това́ бе́ше преди́ два́ часа́.	That was before 2:00.
Това́ бе́ше преди два́ ча́са.	That was two hours ago.
Ела́ след три́ часа́.	Come after 3:00.
Ела́ след три́ ча́са.	Come in three hours. [= 3 hrs. from now]
А́з ча́кам ту́ка от три́ часа́.	I've been waiting here since 3:00.
А́з ча́кам ту́ка [от] три́ ча́са.	I've been waiting here for three hours.

When the English preposition "for" refers to immediately past duration which extends into the present (as in the above example), it can be translated either by **от** or by the absence of a preposition altogether. The student must avoid using the preposition **за** in this meaning. This preposition refers only to a closed sequence of time, as in the following examples:

Оти́вам на море́то за две́ се́дмици.	I'm going to the seacoast for two weeks.
Обикнове́но прочи́там една кни́га за два́ де́на.	I usually read a book in two days.

6.9. Prepositions

Following is a recapitulation of the usage of prepositions in time expressions.

Preposition	(meaning)	Example	(meaning)
в	at	в 2 часа́	at 2:00
без	to, till, of	в 5 без 10	at 10 to 5 (4:50)
на	...old	на 10 годи́ни	10 years old
от	from	от 9 до 5	from 9 to 5
	since, for	от 7 годи́ни	for 7 years
до	to, until	от 9 до 5	from 9 to 5
	up to, until	до преди 3 годи́ни	until 3 years ago
преди́	before	преди́ 6 часа́	before 6:00
преди	ago	преди 3 годи́ни	3 years ago
след	after	след 10 часа́	after 10:00
	in	след 10 мину́ти	in 10 minutes
за	in	за 2 де́на	[with]in 2 days
	for	за 2 се́дмици	for 2 weeks

Remember that **преди́** in the meaning "before" carries stress, to differentiate it from **преди** in the meaning "ago", which is unstressed.

EXERCISES

I. Rewrite the following sentences in the past tense, replacing всéки дéн, чéсто *or* днéс *with* вчéра.

1. Всéки дéн тú глéдаш телевúзия от 1 до 2.
2. Днéс врéмето не é хýбаво.
3. Нúе пúтаме всéки дéн за новинú от Бълга́рия.
4. Днéс вúе пътýвате с дрýг вла́к.
5. Тé ка́рат кола́ всéки дéн.
6. А́з чéсто сънýвам кошма́ри.
7. Нúе сме вкъ́щи, а тé не са́.

II. Write the numerals out in words, and fill in the blanks with the appropriate ending.

1. В ча́нтата úма 1 я́бълк___, 2 мóлив____, и 5 кнúг____.
2. Та́ня úма 2 съсéдк_____, а позна́ва са́мо една́.
3. Тóй купýва 2 вéстник____ всéки дéн.
4. Úма 3 пра́зни куп_____ в тóзи вагóн, а 2 лéкар____ стоя́т в коридóра и пýшат.
5. В ня́колко сел____ úма са́мо 1 училищ____ и 1 бóлниц_____, а в дрýги сел____ úма по 2 училищ____ и 2 бóлниц_____.
6. А́нгел úма 32 зъ́б____ а Веселúн са́мо 26.
7. Всéки дéн 48 трамва́____ мина́ват по мóста.

III. Place the proper accent mark on the word часа *in each of the following.*

1. А́з рабóтя до 2 часа. Ела́ в 3 часа ако úскаш да ме вúдиш.
2. Сега́ е 4 часа. Ела́ в 6 часа, зна́чи след 2 часа.
3. Мнóго е къ́сно! Ча́кам те вéче 3 часа!
4. Кóлко часа рабóтиш днéс? В кóлко часа úскаш да дóйда?
5. Тóй ка́ра кола́ вéче 4 часа.
6. Учúлище запóчва в 7 часа и свъ́ршва в 12 часа.
7. Рестора́нтите не рабóтят след 11 часа.

ADDITIONAL GRAMMAR NOTES

6.1a. Word order and the past tense of съм

The verb **съм** is a copula, joining a subject and a predicate noun or adjective. In the present tense, **съм** is also a clitic, and can therefore never begin a sentence. The past tense copula is not a clitic, however. It is a fully stressed verb, and can occur in any position in the sentence. For example:

Вака́нцията бе́ше ху́бава.	[Our] vacation was good.
Бе́ше ху́баво на море́то.	It was very nice at the seashore.

6.2a. Plural of neuter nouns

Neuter nouns in **-o** usually shift the stress to the ending in the plural. If the noun in question contains an alternating root vowel, this causes the **-я-** to shift to **-e-** (because the **-e-** *always* appears when the vowel is unstressed, regardless of the vowel in the following syllable). Examples:

singular	*plural*
мя́ст-о	мест-а́
мля́к-о	млек-а́

In the capital city of Sofia, one often hears the singular forms **место́** and **млеко́**. These are now accepted as alternate pronunciations.

The word **не́що** is both a pronoun meaning "something" and a noun meaning "thing". Only the noun has a plural: **неща́** means "things".

6.3a. Numbers

Students who know Russian should take care to remember that **два́** is used *only* with masculine nouns, and **две́** with both feminine *and* neuter nouns. When counting or naming something by number, one uses the neuter forms:

едно́, две́, три́...

№ 1 [но́мер едно́],   № 2 [но́мер две́],   № 3 [но́мер три́]...

Numbers for the teens (11 - 19) are formed with the suffix **-на́йсет**. Numbers for four of the decades (20, 30, 40 and 60) are formed with the suffix **-йсет**. The historical source of these suffixes may help the student remember which is which.

Teens (11 - 19)

The sequence -найсет is historically a contraction of на + десет. The number дванайсет (12) therefore is "two on ten" (2 +10). One can also express the teens in uncontracted fashion, e.g. единадесет, дванадесет, тринадесет, четиринадесет, etc., but these forms are considered bookish and are encountered rarely in speech.

Decades (20, 30, 40, 50, 60, 70, 80, 90)

The suffix -йсет is historically a contraction of десет. The number двайсет (20) is therefore "two tens" (2 x 10). Uncontracted forms of 20 and 30 also exist -- двадесет, тридесет, as do contracted forms of the numbers 40 and 60 -- четирийсет and шейсет. All are used frequently, although the contracted forms are more common in speech, and the uncontracted ones more common in writing. Indeed, for the numbers 50, 70, 80 and 90, only the uncontracted forms are used.

The accent is on the first part of the number in 20, 30, 40, but on the end in the remaining forms. Care must be taken to remember to write the middle -т in петдесет and деветдесет, since it is not heard in speech. The pronunciation of these forms is: [педесет, деведесет].

6.4a. Masculine nouns, review

A masculine noun has five possible forms, three in the singular (indefinite, definite subject and definite object), one non-singular form used after numerals, and one plural form. Do not confuse the quantified form with the definite object form, even though in many nouns they look and sound alike. Their meanings are quite different. The definite object is a singular noun, while the quantified noun conveys the meaning of "a specific countable amount of more than one". Plural carries the meaning of "more than one, non-counted". For example:

quantified

Колко молива има в чантата?	How many pencils are in the bag?
В чантата има шест молива.	There are six pencils in the bag.
В чантата има няколко молива.	There are several pencils in the bag.

plural

| Има много моливи в чантата. | There are lots of pencils in the bag. |

Another difference is that certain masculine nouns shift the accent in the ending in the definite form. In these nouns, the definite object forms and the quantified forms are distinguished by accent placement. While other forms may have end stress, the quantified form never shifts stress onto the ending. For example:

indefinite	*definite subject*	*definite object*	*quantified*
(един) ден	денят	деня	два дена
(един) час	часът	часа	два часа
(един) град	градът	града	два града

111

6.5a. Masculine numbers

The numbers **двама, трима**, etc. are used with masculine personal nouns in both the "specifically male" and the "general category" meanings. Thus, **трима студенти** can mean either "three male students" or "three students, at least one of whom is male". Only in the case of **души** (where no other number is possible) can **двама, трима**, etc., refer to nouns denoting specifically non-masculine persons.

6.6a. Motion verbs, continued

The following summarizes the Bulgarian motion-verb system:

Category	verbs	meaning
Directional, single one-way trip	отивам / отида	go
	идвам / дойда	come
Directional, unrestricted	ходя	go
Non-directional	вървя	walk, go, move

The first two verbs (**отивам** and **идвам**) refer to a single, one-way movement in space towards a specified end-point (either explicitly mentioned or implied). The third, **ходя,** refers to movement in space towards a specific end-point without restriction as to numbers of trips. When reference is to a single trip, it implies round trip movement. The last verb in the list, **вървя**, refers to the idea of locomotion without a specified end-point.

Only the two unidirectional verbs exist in aspect pairs. The other two, **ходя** and **вървя,** are either imperfective or perfective, depending on the context.

6.7a. Tense and time expressions

The fact that Bulgarian uses the present tense with a broader scope of meaning than in English is particularly relevant in time expressions. If a time period which began at some clearly defined point in the past continues into the present, Bulgarians speak of it with the present tense. In such instances, English must use the progressive form of the present perfect tense in order to express this broader scope. Students must take care not to transfer English usage into Bulgarian or vice versa. For example:

Аз те чакам от три часа!	I have been expecting you for three hours!
От колко време живеете в Америка?	How long have you been living in America?

By contrast, both English and Bulgarian can use the present tense to denote a period which also includes the future. In English this occurs primarily with motion verbs, while in Bulgarian it can be used with other verbs as well. For example:

Ча́кам до три́ часа́, а по́сле тръ́гвам.	I'll wait until 3:00, but then I'm leaving.

6.9a. Prepositions

(a)   The preposition **на** has three very distinct meanings, detailed below. Context is usually sufficient to distinguish among these meanings.

1.	*possession*	Това́ е врата́та на къ́щата.	This is the door of the house.
2.	*direction location*	Оти́вам на фестива́ла. Ча́нтата е на по́да.	I'm going to the festival. The bag is on the floor.
3.	*indirect object*	Направе́те мя́сто на то́зи чове́к! Подна́сям кафе́то на го́стите.	Make space for this man. I'm offering the guests coffee.

Indirect object constructions will be studied in detail in the next lesson.

(b)   Bulgarian, like English, often has more than one preposition in a row. In this case the object of the first preposition is the phrase including the second one.

до [преди 3 годи́ни]	up to [3 years ago]
поче́рпя с [по две́ я́бълки]	treat to [2 apples each]

(c)   The preposition **без** means "without".

Не мо́жем без прия́тели.	We can't [live] without friends.

6.10. "All, every"

The pronominal adjective **все́ки, вся́ка, вся́ко** means "each, every". Grammatically, it is an adjective: it changes in form to agree with the noun it refers to, and can only be used with a noun following. In form, it is noteworthy for the я/е alternation, and because the masculine form ends in **-и**. Its plural form is **вси́чки**.

The pronoun **вси́чко** means "all, everything". It is grammatically an adverb: it is used alone (it cannot be used with a noun following), and it has only one form in the singular. Its plural form, which means "everyone", is also **вси́чки**. Here are examples of usage:

| Нали́ вся́ко дете́ ту́к оби́ча сладоле́д? | Every child here likes ice cream, yes? |
| Да́, вси́чки деца́ оби́чат сладоле́д. | Yes, all children like ice cream. |

Вси́чко ху́баво!	All the best!
Зна́чи, вси́чко три́ кеба́пчета.	That means three kebabs in all.
Йскам да поче́рпя вси́чки в купе́то.	I want to treat everyone in the compartment.

6.11. The particles я and бе

The particle я́ is frequently used before imperative forms, where it functions to soften the force of the order somewhat. In this way, the command is transformed more into an invitation or a prompt. The meaning is hard to translate exactly, and depends upon the context; often the most correct translation is to ignore the particle altogether.

Я́ направе́те мя́сто на то́зи чове́к да се́дне!

Why not make a place for this man to sit down?

How about making a place for this man to sit down?

Make a place for this man to sit down!

In terms of word order, the particle я́ is classed with the conjunction да and the negative marker не, and follows the rules outlined in Lesson 5. It must precede the verb form directly, and any pronoun object must be placed directly between я́ and the imperative form. For example (numbering of word order examples is cumulative across lessons):

(14)
Я́	напра́ви	мя́сто!
Part.	*verb*	

How about making a place?

(15)
Я́	го	сложи́	на по́да!
Part.	*DIR*	*verb*	

Come on, put it on the floor!

The particle бе is used as a vocative of sorts. It adds a tone of familiarity to the conversation, indicating that the speaker feels on colloquially casual terms with the person s/he is speaking to. Formerly (and still, in rural contexts) it was used only to address men. In modern urban contexts, the use of this particle in modern urban contexts is now non-differentiated as to sex.

| Ка́к се ка́зваш бе, прия́тел? | What's your name, friend? |

114

SAMPLE SENTENCES

1. В трамва́я и́ма мно́го хо́ра. Ей, внима́вайте, бу́тате чове́ка!

2. Ста́вам в ше́ст часа́. В о́сем часа́ оти́вам на учи́лище.

3. -- На ко́лко годи́ни сте?
   -- На осемна́йсет.
   -- А а́з съм на деветна́йсет годи́ни.

4. Рабо́тното вре́ме на магази́на е от о́сем до осемна́йсет часа́.

5. От три́ годи́ни не съ́м в Бълга́рия.

6. Мо́ля, не вди́гайте шу́м след де́сет часа́.

7. Ела́ ту́ка след еди́н ча́с.

8. Вла́кът тръ́гва в двана́йсет без пе́т.

9. -- Ко́лко е часъ́т?
   -- Часъ́т е три́ без петна́йсет.
   -- Часъ́т е три́ и петна́йсет.

10. Не и́скаш ли да хо́дим на ки́но? Ти́ хо́диш са́мо на ле́кции!

11. Не́ вся́ка жена́ рабо́ти са́мо вкъ́щи.

12. Вси́чко е гото́во.

13. Поръ́чахме са́мо десе́рт, защо́то не бя́хме мно́го гла́дни.

14. То́й бе́ше за пъ́рви пъ́т в града́ и мно́го пъ́ти пи́та за посо́ката.

15. -- Къде́ ли са сни́мките?
    -- Не зна́м. Ня́ма ги.
    -- А ту́ка гле́дахте ли?
    -- Да, Лиля́на ве́че отва́ря то́зи шка́ф.

SENTENCES FOR TRANSLATION

1. How many tomatoes do you have? Do you want me to put the tomatoes into the pot?

2. Do you know where we were until now? We were looking out the window for three hours. To tell the truth, it wasn't very interesting.

3. "Did you ask Lilyana why she isn't coming today?"
   "Why do you want to know?"
   "Because she wasn't here yesterday, and I dreamed that she was in the hospital, and that three doctors were looking at her."
   "Do you often dream about doctors and hospitals?

4. What time does Ivan come home from work? How many hours does he work each day?

5. "When do you want me to come?"
   "Come quickly! Can you come in fifteen minutes? I have many things to say. And all these things are interesting."

6. "Where are those two students?"
   "They were here ten minutes ago but I don't know where they are now."

7. We are going to the circus with three Greeks, five Turks, and six Bulgarians. And you are going to the movies with two children.

8. These children don't go to school yet. They are still very little. Boris is three years old and Marina is four. But Kamen goes to school every day: he is seven.

9. Do all students study every Sunday? Not all -- some of them go to the sea and others watch television.

10. "Did you watch television at home yesterday?"
    "No, I was in the library. I watched a video there."

READING SELECTION

<u>Кореспонде́нция - (5)</u>

29 септе́мври, Со́фия

Здраве́й Патри́ша,

За го́стите мо́жеш да сго́твиш сарми́. А́з ги го́твя така́.
Взи́мам листа́ от лоза́, ори́з, лу́к, полови́н килогра́м кайма́, три́ лъжи́ци о́лио, и подпра́вки. Пъ́ржа лу́ка, ори́за и кайма́та в о́лиото. Сла́гам в среда́та на все́ки ли́ст по една́ лъжи́ца от това́, и го зави́вам от вси́чки страни́. Наре́ждам сарми́те в те́нджера и ги варя́ полови́н ча́с. Серви́рам ги то́пли с ки́село мля́ко. Ако не прода́ват листа́ в Са́н Франци́ско, мо́жеш вкъщи да ги консерви́раш. А́з ве́че консерви́рах ня́колко бурка́на и съм мно́го дово́лна.
По то́зи на́чин пра́вя и сарми́ с ки́село зе́ле. Мо́га да пъ́лня съ́що чу́шки и дома́ти. За вегетериа́нци, мо́жеш да го́твиш те́зи го́зби и без месо́.
Мо́га да те нау́ча да пра́виш и сала́ти, ако и́скаш.

Сърде́чни по́здрави,

Кали́на

12 окто́мври, Са́н Франци́ско

Дра́га Кали́на,

Бъ́лгарите, изгле́жда, го́твят като гъ́рците и ту́рците. Си́гурна съм, че в Са́н Франци́ско мо́га да наме́ря консерви́рани ло́зови листа́.
Бо́б ка́зва, че тарато́рът по бъ́лгарски е мно́го вку́сен и ста́ва бъ́рзо. Тарато́ра пра́вят от ки́село мля́ко с кра́ставица, ко́пър, че́сън, о́рехи и о́лио, нали́? Пи́тах Бо́б за реце́птата, но то́й не зна́е то́чно.
Предпочи́там ле́сни реце́пти, защо́то рабо́тя до 6 часа́ и ня́мам мно́го вре́ме да го́твя.
Пиши́ ка́к са деца́та.

Вси́чко ху́баво,

Патри́ша

117

GLOSSARY

бе	(vocative particle)	домáт	tomato
без	without	досегá	until now
бéше	was (2sg., 3sg.)	дýши	people (counting form)
бóлница	hospital		
буркáн	jar, can	единáйсет	eleven
бýтам	push, shove		
бъ́рз	fast, quick	за	[with]in, for
бя́х	was (1sg.)	за двé сéдмици	for two weeks
бя́ха	were (3pl.)	завúвам / завúя	turn, bend, wrap
бя́хме	were (1pl.)	запóчвам /	begin
бя́хте	were (2pl.)	запóчна	
		здравéй	hi
в кóлко часá?	at what time?	зъб	tooth
в послéдно врéме	lately		
вагóн	wagon, car	изглéжда	it seems
вакáнция	vacation	úме (pl. именá)	name
вдúгам / вдúгна	raise, lift		
вдúгам шýм	make noise	каймá	ground meat
вéстник	newspaper	кáрам	drive, ride, push
вкýсен	tasty, delicious	кáрам колá	drive a car
вкъщи	home, at home	като	like, as; when
внимáвайте, бýтате	careful, you're	като бя́х	when I was
човéка	pushing someone	кафéен, -éйна	coffee (adj.)
внимáвам	pay attention	кафéна лъжúчка	coffee spoon
всéки, вся́ка, вся́ко	every	кебáпче	kebab
всéки момéнт	any minute	килогрáм	kilogram
всúчко шéст	six in all	кúсел	sour
		кúсело зéле	sauerkraut
готóв	prepared, ready	кúсело мля́ко	yogurt
грáд, -ъ́т (pl. in L. 7)	town, city	когá	when
гъ́рци (sg. in L. 23)	Greeks	кóлко дýши сме?	how many of us are there?
двá	two (masculine)	кóлко е часъ́т?	what time is it?
двáйсет	twenty	консервúрам	preserve, can
двáма	two (masculine animate)	консервúран	preserved, canned
		кóпър	dill
дванáйсет	twelve	кошмáр	nightmare
двé	two (feminine, neuter)	крáставица	cucumber
дéвет	nine	лéкция	lecture, class
деветдесéт	ninety	лéсен	easy
деветнáйсет	nineteen	лúст (pl. листá)	leaf
дéн, -я́т (pl. днú, 2 дéна / дéня)	day	лозá	vine
		лóзов	grape, vine (adj.)
десéрт	dessert	лóзови листá	grape leaves
дéсет	ten	лýк (pl. in L. 7)	onion
до	until (time)	лъжúца	spoon, spoonful
дóбър дéн	hello, good day	лъжúчка	teaspoon, teaspoonful
довóлен	pleased, satisfied		

118

месо́	meat	преди	ago
места́	places	през	through
мину́та	minute	присти́гам /	arrive
мля́ко (*pl.* млека́)	milk	присти́гна	
море́	sea	прода́вам / прода́м	sell
мо́ст (*pl. in L. 7*)	bridge	(*conj. in L. 9*)	
		пъ́лня	fill
на 10 годи́ни	10 years old	пъ́ржа (-еш)	fry
на ко́лко сте годи́ни?	how old are you?	пъ́т (*pl. in L. 8*)	way, road
		пъ́т (*pl.* пъ́ти)	time, instance
на море́то	at the seaside		
напра́вям / напра́вя	do, make	рабо́тен	work (*adj.*)
наре́ждам / наредя́	set up, arrange	рабо́тно вре́ме	office hours, hours of operation
науча́вам / нау́ча (-иш)	teach	реце́пта	recipe
на́чин	way, manner		
неде́ля	Sunday	сарми́	stuffed cabbage or grape leaves
ня́колко	several		
		свъ́ршвам / свъ́рша (-иш)	complete, finish
окто́мври	October		
о́лио	cooking oil	седемдесе́т	seventy
о́рех	walnut	седемна́йсет	seventeen
ори́з	rice	се́дмица	week
о́сем	eight	си́гурен	sure, certain
осемдесе́т	eighty	сладоле́д	ice cream
осемна́йсет	eighteen	след	after
от	since (time)	след 15 мину́ти	in 15 minutes
от вси́чки страни́	from / on all sides	сни́мка	photograph
от еди́н ча́с	for an hour	ста́ва бъ́рзо	it goes quickly
отда́вна	long ago	страна́	side
отда́вна ве́че	for a long time now	съну́вам	dream
		съну́вам кошма́ри	have nightmares
пе́т	five		
пе́т без де́сет	ten of five (o'clock)	тарато́р	yogurt and cucumber soup
петдесе́т	fifty		
пети́ма	five (*masculine animate*)	теа́тър	theater
		телеви́зия	television
петна́йсет	fifteen	те́нджера	(cooking) pot
пи́там за посо́ката	ask directions	то́чен	exact, precise
по то́зи на́чин	in this way	то́чно	exactly
подна́сям / поднеса́	present, offer, serve	три́йсет	thirty
подпра́вка	spice	три́ма	three (*masculine animate*)
позволя́вам / позволя́	allow	трина́йсет	thirteen
полови́н(а)	half	ту́рци (*sg. in L. 23*)	Turks
по́сле	then, next		
после́ден	last	учи́лище (*pl.* учи́лища)	school
посо́ка	direction		
почерп́вам / поче́рпя	treat someone to		
пра́зен	empty	хо́дя	go
преброя́вам / преброя́	count out	хо́дя на ки́но	go to the movies
		хо́дя на учи́лище	go to school
преди́	before	цве́те (*pl.* цветя́)	flower

119

цирк *(pl. in L. 7)*	circus	шест	six
		шестдесет *or*	sixty
час, -ът, 2 часа	hour	шейсет	
(pl. in L. 7)		шестима	six *(masculine*
чесън	garlic		*animate)*
четири	four	шестнайсет	sixteen
четиринайсет	fourteen	шкаф *(pl. in L. 7)*	cupboard
четиридесет *or*	forty	шум	noise
четирийсет			
четирима	four *(masculine*	я	*(imperative particle)*
	animate)	я направете място	come on, make space
чичко	uncle *(affectionate)*	ябълка	apple
чушка	pepper (vegetable)		

CULTURAL COMMENTARY

Geography: Varna and Balchik

One of the main train lines in Bulgaria runs through northern Bulgaria from Varna to Sofia. Varna, on the Black Sea coast, is a major seaport and tourist center, and is the third largest city in Bulgaria. Balchik (**Балчик**) is a small town to the north of Varna.

Traveling: eating in trains

Although there are restaurant cars on certain Bulgarian trains, Bulgarians tend not to patronize them. Instead, travelers either come laden with food, or buy snacks from platform vendors during scheduled stops.

Food and drink: general; kebaches; yogurt

Bulgaria's cuisine is a generally Balkan one; its cuisine is similar to that found in Greece and Turkey. Grilled meats and stuffed vegetable dishes are favorites. In its cultural function the Bulgarian kebabche (**кебапче**) is roughly equivalent to the Western hamburger. The formal differences are that the ground meat is generally more spicy, and that it is formed into small sausage-shaped meatballs which are then either grilled on a skewer or fried.

Bulgarian **кисело мляко** (literally, "sour milk") is yogurt. Yogurt is a mainstay in Bulgarian cuisine. It is eaten alone, served with many dishes, and forms the basis of other dishes, such as the cold yogurt soup called **таратор**. Bulgarian yogurt is famous for its high quality; in fact the Latin name of the yogurt culture is *bacillus bulgaricus*. Yogurt can be made from cow's milk, sheep's milk, and even from the milk of the water buffalo. The latter is a rarity and therefore considered a delicacy.

Weights and measures

Bulgarians measure weight in grams and kilograms ("kilo" for short). A pound is roughly half a kilo. Spoons are of three sizes. The largest, called **лъжица**, is served with meals and is roughly the size of a soup-spoon. In recipes it is equivalent to a tablespoon. The medium-sized one, called **лъжичка**, is served with tea or Western-style coffee, and is the size of a regular spoon. In recipes, it is equivalent to a teaspoon. The smallest, called **кафена лъжичка**, is served with Turkish or espresso coffee. Cooking heats, both in the oven and atop the stove, are "low", "medium" and "high".

LESSON 7

DIALOGUE

<u>На перо́на в га́рата</u>

Надка: Ма́мо, ви́ж, присти́гаме! Éто я га́рата! Éто ги кеба́пчетата на перо́на!
Éто я продава́чката!

Веселин: Да́, сега́ сли́зам да ви ку́пя кеба́пчета. О́сем пъ́тника в купе́то --
зна́чи, шестна́йсет кеба́пчета. А на Джу́ли, какво́ да й ку́пя? Джу́ли, да
сле́зем ли да потъ́рсим не́що? Ха́йде да сле́зем!

Милена: Не забра́вяйте, че и́мате са́мо де́сет мину́ти. Коли́чката с
кеба́пчетата е в кра́я на перо́на!

Димитър: А́з веднъ́ж така́ купу́вах кеба́пчета, и вла́кът отпъту́ва. Прека́рах 5
ча́са на една́ пе́йка на га́рата. Бе́ше еди́н сту́д...

// На перо́на, при коли́чката с кеба́пчетата //

Веселин: Да́йте ми шестна́йсет кеба́пчета, мо́ля.

Продавачката: С хля́б или без хля́б?

Джули: Бе́з, защо́то аз и́мам два́ хля́ба във вла́ка.

Веселин: И́мате ли не́що безме́сно? Госпо́жицата е вегетериа́нка.

Продавачката: Ами́-и... ня́ма мно́го. И́мам са́мо кашкава́л и си́рене. И
плодове́.

Веселин: Какво́ жела́ете, Джу́ли?

Джули: Предпочи́там кашкава́л.

Веселин: Добре́, на госпо́жицата кашкава́л.

Продавачката: Éто ви, госпо́жице, една́ по́рция кашкава́л. А ви́е, господи́не,
ще поча́кате ма́лко за кеба́пчетата.

Децата (от прозо́реца): Ха́йде, бъ́рзайте! Вла́кът ще тръ́гне!

Веселин: Каче́те се, Джу́ли. А́з ще взе́ма кеба́пчетата.

Джули: Но ако изпу́снете вла́ка...

Веселин: Не се́ притесня́вайте, вси́чко е наре́д. Ня́ма да изпу́сна вла́ка!

BASIC GRAMMAR

7.1. Future tense

To form the future tense in Bulgarian, place the particle ще (or the phrase няма да) before the present tense form. The meaning of the future tense is as in English, "I will/won't + *verb*". Here are the affirmative and negative future conjugations of the verb четá:

FUTURE TENSE

	affirmative	*negative*
1ˢᵗ singular	ще чет-á	няма да чет-á
2ⁿᵈ singular	ще чет-éш	няма да чет-éш
3ʳᵈ singular	ще чет-é	няма да чет-é
1ˢᵗ plural	ще чет-éм	няма да чет-éм
2ⁿᵈ plural	ще чет-éте	няма да чет-éте
3ʳᵈ plural	ще чет-áт	няма да чет-áт

The future marker (ще or няма да) does not change, but the verb following this form, which is exactly equivalent to the present tense form, must have the correct endings.

There are two different ways to form the future tense of съм: one can add the future markers ще and няма да either to the verb бъда, or to съм itself. Here are both possible conjugations of "to be" in the affirmative future. To form the negative future, replace ще with няма да. The variant with бъда is somewhat more frequently used.

FUTURE TENSE: "to be"

1ˢᵗ singular	ще бъд-а	ще съм
2ⁿᵈ singular	ще бъд-еш	ще си
3ʳᵈ singular	ще бъд-е	ще е
1ˢᵗ plural	ще бъд-ем	ще сме
2ⁿᵈ plural	ще бъд-ете	ще сте
3ʳᵈ plural	ще бъд-ат	ще са

The future tense refers to an action which has not yet occurred. Because speakers often envision such an action as a totality (i.e. as bounded), perfective verbs occur very frequently in the future tense. If the sense of boundedness is absent, however, the imperfective is used. Note that in the second example the meaning of boundedness is present in the second verb only:

| Ще почáкам сáмо 5 минýти. | I'll wait five minutes only. |
| Ще чáкам да дóйдете. | I'll wait for you to come. |

7.2. Indirect object pronouns

Indirect object pronouns in Bulgarian are very similar to direct object pronouns. The following gives subject, direct object, and indirect object pronouns. The grave accent mark on the 3rd person feminine form (ѝ) is an obligatory part of Bulgarian spelling; it functions to distinguish this form from the conjunction (и).

	subject	*direct object*	*indirect object*
1st singular	áз	ме	ми
2nd singular	тѝ	те	ти
(reflexive)		се	си
3rd singular			
feminine	тя́	я	ѝ
masculine	тóй	го	му
neuter	тó	го	му
1st plural	нѝе	ни	ни
2nd plural	вѝе	ви	ви
3rd plural	тé	ги	им

The reflexive indirect object form **си** is used to indicate that the action is directed back towards the subject of the sentence. For example:

| Веселѝн забеля́зва Джу́ли и си мѝсли... | Veselin notices Julie and thinks to himself... |

Indirect object pronouns are clitics, and must obey the same word order rules as direct object pronouns: they cannot occur at the beginning of a sentence or phrase, and they must occur adjacent to the verb (or other word) on which they depend.

| Éто ти, Джу́ли. | Here you are, Julie.
[= Here are these things *for you*.] |

7.3. Usage of indirect objects

The meaning "indirect object" in Bulgarian is similar to that in English: it denotes a person or object affected by the verb in a way which is considered somehow less direct than that of a direct object. In English this meaning is conveyed either through word order or by the prepositions "to" or "for". When there is no preposition, the indirect object always comes before the direct object, as in

Give	the children	the kebabs.
verb	*indirect obj.*	*direct obj.*

The English indirect object in this sentence can also be "to the children".

In Bulgarian, by contrast, indirect objects *must* be preceded by the preposition **на**. The neutral word order is with the direct object first. The indirect object can occur first if the speaker wishes to place somewhat more emphasis on it.

Дáй	кебáпчетата	на децáта.	Give the children the kebabs.
verb	*direct obj.*	*indirect obj.*	

Дáй	на децáта	кебáпчетата.	Give the kebabs *to the children.*
verb	*indirect obj.*	*direct obj.*	

In the above examples, both the Bulgarian and the English sentences express indirect objects with a preposition. There are a number of verbs, however, which take a direct object in English but an indirect object in Bulgarian -- or, as in the example from Lesson 5 which is repeated below, which take a direct object in Bulgarian, but a prepositional phrase in English.

Помáгам	на децáта.
verb	*indirect obj.*

I'm helplng	the children
subject + verb	*direct obj.*

Áнгел	глéда	човéка.
subject	*verb*	*direct obj.*

Angel	looks	at the man.
subject	*verb*	*prep.phrase*

The lesson of these examples is that one cannot predict the status "direct object"/"indirect object" in Bulgarian directly from the structure of the corresponding English sentence. One must simply learn which verbs in Bulgarian take direct objects and which take indirect objects.

7.4. Plural of masculine monosyllabic nouns

Most masculine nouns consisting of a single syllable (and a few which have a fleeting vowel in the second syllable) add the ending **-ове** in the plural. The accent is unpredictable and must be learned. However, the addition of the definite article in the plural does not affect the place of accent.

Accent types are illustrated below. In the majority of nouns the accent stays on the stem syllable, as in type (1). In a number of nouns, however, the accent is on the final syllable of the plural ending, as in (3), and in a few nouns it is on the first syllable of the ending, as in (2). If a noun has a plural of type (2) or (3), this will be indicated in the glossary; otherwise one should assume its plural is of type (1).

(1) *stem stress*	(2) *initial end stress*	(3) *final end stress*
вку́с-ове	нож-о́ве	ветр-ове́
вла́к-ове		град-ове́
ди́м-ове		плод-ове́
по́д-ове		снег-ове́
со́к-ове		студ-ове́
сто́л-ове		час-ове́
хля́б-ове		
ци́рк-ове		
шу́м-ове		

(with article: **со́ковете, ножо́вете, плодове́те,** etc.)

7.5. Verbal prefixation and the aspect system

Prefixation is very frequent in Bulgarian. The addition of a prefix alters the meaning of a verb to a certain extent, but does not normally obscure the semantic relationship between it and other verbs with the same root. The ability to recognize the relationship between prefix and verbal root, therefore, can be a very valuable tool in vocabulary building. To aid in seeing this, the examples below are given with a hyphen separating the prefix from the rest of the verb. The first three examples, which exist only in the prefixed form, all refer to movement. In each instance, the prefix adds the meaning of the direction of the movement.

в - ли́зам / в - ля́за	enter, come in
из - ли́зам / из - ля́за	leave, go out
с - ли́зам / с - ля́за	get off, get down, descend

Most prefixes are similar in form to prepositions. They do not always have the same meaning, however. Of the three verbs above, for instance, only in one of them (влизам) does the prefix в- have the same meaning as the preposition в.

Another set of verbs which exists only in the prefixed form expresses the general meaning "carry". Although the three prefixed verbs given below are historically related to the simplex imperfective verb нóся, they are considered within the Bulgarian aspect system to be separate verbs from it.

до - нáсям / до - несá	bring
за - нáсям / за - несá	take
под - нáсям / под - несá	offer, present

Although the above six verbs are very commonly used, their form is exceptional in that the non-prefixed forms do not exist as separate verbs. It is much more usual for prefixes to be added to already existing verbs. Sometimes a prefix is even added to an existing aspectual pair. For example:

стáвам / стáна	get up, stand up
о- стáвам / о- стáна	remain

In the majority of cases, however, prefixes are added to simplex imperfectives -- those verbs which exist only in the imperfective aspect, and which designate an activity in basic and general terms. Placing a prefix before such a verb adds the idea of boundedness, and makes it perfective. Each such verb created in this way is considered to designate a new and separate verbal meaning. Sometimes this new meaning is very different from that of the simplex imperfective, and sometimes it is only slightly different from it. Here are some examples:

simplex imperfective	*meaning*	*prefixed perfective*	*meaning*
четá	read	про-четá	read to the end
		пред-по-четá	prefer
знáя	know	по-знáя	guess
белéжа	mark	за-белéжа	notice
броя́	count	пре-броя́	count up, count out
пѝя	drink	из-пѝя	drink up, drain a glass
тъ́рся	seek	по-тъ́рся	look specifically for
бъ́рзам	be in a hurry	по-бъ́рзам	hurry up
чáкам	wait	по-чáкам	wait for a bit
прáвя	do, make	на-прáвя	do, make

126

Simplex imperfectives signify basic, general actions. They do not have perfective partners. Every perfective verb formed by prefixation, however, has its own imperfective partner. The process by which these new imperfectives are derived will be studied in more detail later.

The chart below gives the above verbs as they are listed in Bulgarian dictionaries. Simplex imperfectives stand alone, while the prefixed perfectives formed from them are listed together with their aspect partners, with the imperfective form given first:

беле́жа	mark
броя́	count
забеля́звам / забеле́жа	notice
зна́я	know
изпи́вам / изпи́я	drink up
напра́вям / напра́вя	do, make *(bounded)*
пи́я	drink
позна́вам / позна́я	guess
потъ́рсвам / потъ́рся	look for, search for
поча́квам / поча́кам	wait for a bit
пра́вя	do, make
предпочи́там / предпочета́	prefer
преброя́вам / преброя́	count [out]
прочи́там / прочета́	read through to the end
тъ́рся	seek
ча́кам	wait
чета́	read

7.6. Да-phrases, continued

The most frequent meaning of a да-phrase is as an infinitive replacement. Usually the да will connect two verbs, which may or may not have the same subject.

Йскам да сля́за	I want to get off
да си ку́пя не́що.	and buy [myself] something.
Йскам да сле́зеш	I want you to get off
да ми ку́пиш не́що.	and buy me something.

The да-phrase can also be used alone. When it refers to the idea of the action in general (and does not specify an actor), it is the grammatical subject of the sentence, and the verb is in the 2nd singular. The verb in such a да-phrase can also take other personal endings if the identity of its subject is specified. In this case, да-phrases can act grammatically either as the subject or the object of the sentence.

Here are examples, followed by a schematic outline of the grammar involved:

1. Но да познаваш кухнята на един народ, не é достáтъчно.	It's not enough [just] to know the cuisine of a people.
2. Добрé е да опознáеш и странáта.	It's good to get to know the country as well.
3. Мúсля, че ще е хýбаво да прекáраме óтпуската в Бългáрия.	I think it will be nice to spend our vacation in Bulgaria.
4. Úскам да сгóтвиш кебáпчета.	I want you to make kebabs.

subject	predicate / verb	object
1. да познáваш...	не é достáтъчно	
2. да опознáеш...	е добрé	
3. да прекáраме...	ще е хýбаво	
4.	úскам	[ти] да сгóтвиш нéщо

When да-phrases are used in questions, an additional shade of meaning is often added, which is best translated by adding English "should". For instance:

А на Джýли, каквó да й кýпя?	And what about Julie? What should I buy for her?
Да слéзем ли да потъ́рсим нéщо?	Should we get off to look for something?

7.7. Pronoun reduplication

Certain definite direct objects receive special emphasis. By a process called "pronoun reduplication", an object pronoun is added to the sentence (reduplicating the noun in question). Because this pronoun also refers to the same object as the noun, it must be of the same gender as the noun in question.

Pronoun reduplication is obligatory after the introductory particle éто or after the impersonal negative ня́ма, and optional in other instances to be learned later. Here are examples:

		noun object	reduplicative pronoun
Éто я гáрата!	There's the station!	гарата	я
Éто ги кебáпчетата!	Here's the kebabs!	кебабчета	ги
Ня́ма го човéка.	No trace of him.	човека	го

128

7.8. Prepositions

(a)   The basic meaning of the preposition **при** is "by, near, at, in the vicinity of". It differs from **до**, which also means "by, near", in two ways. First, **до** can mean movement as well as location, while **при** can only mean location. Second, **до** refers to immediate proximity, while **при** refers to a more general, unspecified location.

Деца́та седя́т до Джу́ли.	The children are sitting next to Julie.
Те́ са при коли́чката с кеба́пчетата.	They are at the cart with the kebabs.

(b)   The basic meaning of the preposition **през** is "through".

То́й че́сто вли́за през прозо́реца.	He often gets in through the window.
Че́сто мина́вам през града́.	I pass through town often.

(c)   The preposition **по** can also mean "about", "approximately", "around", especially in contexts of time.

Ела́ по това́ вре́ме, тога́ва.	Come around that time, then.

Café in Shiroka Lăka, near Smolyan

129

EXERCISES

I. Rewrite the following sentences replacing the underlined phrases with the appropriate pronouns.

1. Децата декламират стихотворения на пътниците.
2. Пътниците ще покажат на момчето къде да слезе от влака.
3. Всеки ден майката чете на децата книгата.
4. Позволете на човека да вземе вестника.
5. Лелята купува ли на децата шоколад?
6. Ти казваш на Джули истината, но Джули не вярва.
7. Калина и Бойко пишат на Боб и Патриша.

II. Put everything in the following sentences into the plural.

1. Ако си гладен, вземи кебапче и плод.
2. На масата има краставица, шоколад и готварска книга.
3. Кучето обича ли детето?
4. Пада голям сняг, духа силен вятър.
5. Мястото е свободно. Седни!
6. В града живеят момче и момиче.
7. Хлябът е на масата, а шишето е в хладилника.
8. Тя носи в чантата учебник, молив, тетрадка и речник.

III. Rewrite the sentences in the future, replacing всеки ден *or* сега *with* утре.

1. Всеки ден взимам трамвая и не закъснявам за университета.
2. Сега избирам подарък за майка.
3. Ела друг път! Сега съм зает и бързам.
4. Сега купувам на децата по един сладолед.
5. Той става в 7 часа всеки ден.
6. Чакам те всеки ден след работа.
7. Сега отиваме на гарата да посрещнем Джули и Дейвид.
8. Всеки ден преброявам птиците на дървото.
9. Децата всеки ден изпиват чаша мляко, а майките - чаша кафе.
10. Сега духа силен вятър.

ADDITIONAL GRAMMAR NOTES

7.1a. Future tense

The verb бъ́да is used both as the future tense, and the imperative, of съм.

| Бъди́ добъ́р! | Be good! |
| Бъде́те то́чни! | Be on time! |

The future particle ще is unaccented. It can also occur accented; in this case it is the 3rd singular of the regular verb ща́ "want". Conjugated forms of ща́ occur most frequently after negation, and are restricted to colloquial contexts.

| ще́ не ще́ | whether one wants to or not |

7.2a. Indirect object pronouns

Indirect object pronouns follow exactly the same word order rules as those given in Lesson 5 for direct object pronouns. Recall that numbering of word order examples is cumulative across lessons. For example:

(16)
Купу́вам	ви	кеба́пчета.
verb	*IND*	*direct obj.*

I'm buying you kebabs.

(17)
А	на Джу́ли,	какво́	да	й	ку́пя?
	indirect obj.	*direct obj.*	*Cnj.*	*IND*	*verb*

And Julie, what should I buy for her?

When a verb takes two objects and both are expressed by pronouns, the indirect object pronoun precedes the direct object pronoun. Examples of this usage will be given in Lesson 9.

7.4a. Plural of masculine monosyllabic nouns

Masculine monosyllables form their plural with the ending -ове. This ending takes the form -еве in nouns ending in -й or in a soft consonant (those with the article form -ят). The stem final -й drops before this ending. A few nouns with a fleeting vowel take the -ове plural ending, losing the fleeting vowel before it. In these nouns, a final soft consonant causes the spelling -ьове. Here are examples:

singular indefinite	singular definite	plural
ча́й	ча́ят	ча́еве
це́нтър	це́нтър-ът	це́нтр-ове
о́гън	о́гън-ят	огнь-о́ве
вя́тър	вя́тър-ът	ветр-ове́

The accent in masculine nouns can shift forward to the definite form in the singular, and to both definite and indefinite forms in the plural. For some nouns this shift happens in all possible forms, for others only in the singular or the plural. Essentially, a noun's accent pattern must be learned; it is predictable, however, that accent shifts in the plural will always occur in both definite and indefinite forms. Here are some common nouns with accentual shifts (the notation (те) means that the accentuation is the same in both indefinite and definite forms).

	sing. indefinite	sing. definite	plural	(meaning)
Shift in both				
	гра́д	градъ́т	градове́ (те)	city
	пло́д	плодъ́т	плодове́ (те)	fruit
	сня́г	снегъ́т	снегове́ (те)	snow
	ча́с	часъ́т	часове́ (те)	hour
Shift in singular only				
	вку́с	вкусъ́т	вку́сове (те)	taste
	ди́м	димъ́т	ди́мове (те)	smoke
	шу́м	шумъ́т	шу́мове (те)	noise
Shift in plural only				
	вя́тър	вя́търът	ветрове́ (те)	wind

The plural of де́н (дни́) was learned in Lesson 6. The plurals of пъ́т, кра́й, and certain other masculine monosyllables, will be learned in Lesson 8.

7.5.a. Verbal prefixation and the aspect system

Almost all prefixed Bulgarian verbs are perfective, and are formed by adding a prefix to a simplex imperfective. This produces a new verb, with a new meaning. The imperfective partners of these new verbs are called "derived imperfectives", because each is derived from the corresponding perfective by one of several means, the most common of which is suffixation. All derived imperfectives belong to the a-conjugation, and most contain a characteristic suffix, such as -в- (e.g. побъ́рз-в-ам) or -ав-/-яв- (e.g. пребро-я́в-ам). The meaning of a derived imperfective is identical to that of its base perfective except for the absence of the idea of boundedness.

Bulgarian differs markedly from other Slavic languages in this respect. The fact that verbs like пра́вя, пи́ша and чета́ do not have perfective partners, and that the prefixed verbs напра́вя, напи́ша and прочета́ are considered to be separate

132

verbs, each with its own imperfective partner, may mystify the student who is familiar with the aspect system of another Slavic language. The fact that it is difficult to give an English translation for пра́вя and напра́вя which would convey the difference in meaning that goes beyond that of boundedness (aspect), or to characterize a significant difference in meaning (or any at all) between the two imperfective verbs пра́ва and напра́вям, no doubt compounds the mystification for such a student.

Yet the system makes sense to Bulgarians. Aspect, after all, is nothing more than a coherent way of defining a point of view. What matters is that the system is internally consistent, and that it makes sense to the speakers whose communication system it functions to organize.

7.8a. Prepositions

(a)   When the preposition в "in, into" occurs in front of a word beginning with в- or ф-, it is doubled. Although it is written във, it is frequently pronounced [въф]. This pronunciation of в can also occur before words beginning with a vowel, and before other consonants as well. In writing, however, only във occurs, and only when the following word begins with в- or ф-. For example:

Áз и́мам два́ хля́ба във вла́ка.
Те́ живе́ят във Флоре́нция.

Те́ хо́дят че́сто в Ирла́ндия.	[въф Ирла́ндия] *or* [ф Ирла́ндия]
Ни́е живе́ем в Со́фия.	[въф Со́фия] *or* [ф Со́фия]

(b)   The same is the case with the preposition с "with".

Със здра́ве да го но́сиш!
Áз ще до́йда със Саби́на.

А ти́ ще до́идеш с Ива́н.	[със Ива́н]
Оби́чаш ли да пи́еш кафе́ с мля́ко?	[със мля́ко] *or* [с мля́ко]

7.9.   Derivation: adjectives in -ен, nouns in -к and in -ник

The process of forming related words from the same root is called *derivation*. In verbs, the most common instance of derivation is the formation of imperfective partners for prefixed perfectives (themselves formed from simple imperfectives by the process of prefixation). The general outlines of verbal derivation will become clear to the student as s/he learns examples of aspect pairs; the details of this system will be studied in Lessons 18 and 26.

Many different words are related by derivational processes. For instance, the suffix -ен- creates adjectives from noun roots, the suffix -к- creates feminine nouns from various roots, and the suffix **-ник** creates masculine nouns from various roots. The stem to which the suffix is added is usually recognizably the same as in a word with a closely related meaning.

Learning to recognize individual suffixes, and the general patterns of word derivation, will help the student learn (and retain) new words much more quickly. Below are examples of each of these three very common suffixes.

Adjectives in -ен-

The adjectival suffix **-ен-** is usually added to a noun stem. Sometimes the stem is identical to the noun itself, and sometimes it has been slightly transformed. The suffix is freely added to foreign words as well (rendering them thereby domestic). In many such words, even the Latin suffix "-ic" has been borrowed into Bulgarian as **-ич**, as in the last three items in the chart below.

The suffix **-ен** almost always contains a fleeting vowel. The few instances where it does not (such as **чáен, чáена**, derived from **чáй**) will be noted specifically in glossary lists.

noun	*stem*	+ ен ›	*derived adjective*	*(meaning)*
свобод-á	свобод-	+ ен ›	свобóден, -дна	free
сúл-а	сил-	+ ен ›	сúлен, -лна	strong
глáд	глад-	+ ен ›	глáден, -дна	hungry
нарóд	народ-	+ ен ›	нарóден, -дна	national
трамвáй	трамвай-	+ ен ›	*трамвáен, -йна	tram
интерéс	интерес-	+ ен ›	интерéсен, -сна	interesting
дóм	дом-аш-	+ ен ›	домáшен, -шна	domestic
без мес-ó	без-мес-	+ ен ›	безмéсен, -сна	meatless
идúл-ия	идил-ич-	+ ен ›	идилúчен, -чна	idyllic
тúп	тип-ич-	+ ен ›	типúчен, -чна	typical
екзóт-ика	екзот-ич-	+ ен ›	екзотúчен, -чна	exotic

*Note the spelling rule in **трамвá-ен, трамвáй-на**: the stem-final **-й** drops out before a following front vowel, but is retained elsewhere.

Nouns in -к-

The suffix -к-, which is always followed by the feminine ending -a, is added to various stems. The use of this suffix to form nouns of profession or origin, such as **учителка** or **българка**, was studied in Lessons 1 and 3. These nouns, by definition, always refer to female human beings.

The suffix is also widely used to form nouns denoting objects or concepts. The stem to which the suffix is added can be provided by either a noun or a verb. In the examples below, imperfective verbs are given because the normal dictionary citation form is the imperfective. The stem from which the derived noun is formed carries no aspectual meaning within itself.

(1) Derivations from a noun base

noun	*stem*	+ к ›	*derived noun*	*(meaning)*
ка́рт-а	ка́рт-ич-	+ к ›	ка́ртичка	postcard
къ́щ-а	къ́щ-ич-	+ к ›	къ́щичка	little house
пло́ч-а	пло́ч-	+ к ›	пло́чка	tile

(2) Derivations from a verb base

verb	*stem*	+ к ›	*derived noun*	*meaning*
рис-у́вам	рис-ун-	+ к ›	рису́нка	drawing
глъ́т-вам	глъ́т-	+ к ›	глъ́тка	swallow
почи́в-ам	почив-	+ к ›	почи́вка	rest
греш-а́	греш-	+ к ›	гре́шка	mistake
беле́ж-а	бележ-	+ к ›	беле́жка	note

135

Nouns in -ник

This suffix creates nouns denoting either persons or objects. As in the case of the suffix -к-, the stem to which it is added can be provided by either a noun or a verb. All such nouns shift the final -к to -ц before the plural ending -и. For example:

(1) Derivations from a noun base

noun	stem	+ ник ›	derived noun	(meaning)
чáс	час-ов-	+ ник ›	часóвник, -ци	clock(s)
вой-нá	вой-	+ ник ›	войни́к, -ци	soldier(s)
чáй	чай-	+ ник ›	чáйник, -ци	teapot(s)
пъ́т	пъ̀т-	+ ник ›	пъ́тник, -ци	traveler(s)

(2) Derivations from a verb base

verb	stem	+ ник ›	derived noun	(meaning)
ýч-а *	уч-е-	+ ник ›	учени́к, -ци	pupil(s)
ýч-а *	уч-еб-	+ ник ›	учéбник, -ци	textbook(s)
реч-éш **	реч-	+ ник ›	рéчник, -ци	dictionary, -ies
белéж-а	бележ-	+ ник ›	белéжник, -ци	notebook(s)

* The derivational process is not direct; other forms have intervened. In the case of **учéбник**, the word itself is a borrowing from Russian.

** The verb **рекá** "say" has a consonant shift similar to that of **мóга**: the consonant -к appears before the endings -а, -ат; and the consonant -ч appears before the other endings.

SAMPLE SENTENCES

1. Всяка седмица ще търся в библиотеката интересни книги.

2. Ще потърся утре в библиотеката интересни книги.

3. Ще чакам да дойдете.

4. Ще почакам пет минути и тръгвам.

5. Ще купувам мляко и хляб всеки ден.

6. Утре ще купя мляко и хляб.

7. Често го виждам в Университета.

8. Ще го видя в Университета.

9. Той често влиза вкъщи през прозореца.

10. Днес той няма ключ и може да влезе вкъщи само през прозореца.

11. -- Слизате ли на другата спирка?
    -- Не. Ще ви направя място да слезете.

12. Тя чете бързо. За два дни прочита една книга.

13. -- Зная, че обичаш шоколад.
    -- Не обичам.
    -- Обичаш, обичаш, познавам по очите!
    -- Познай тогава какво ще направя сега!

14. Камен може да брои до десет. Камен преброява пътниците. Надка не може да ги преброи.

15. -- Бързам за училище.
    -- Побързай да не закъснееш за училище.

SENTENCES FOR TRANSLATION

1. "How will we get in? We don't have keys! "
   "You will help the children to get in through the window. They are small, and can get in but you can't."

2. Please tell the waiter to bring us tomatoes, cucumbers, bread and cheese. And knives and spoons, of course.

3. Come over tomorrow and bring the textbook. I want to show Julie several things.

4. How many loaves of bread [= breads] do you have? Everyone is very hungry. They will also want fruits and vegetables.

5. Here is the station, we'll get off here. Then we'll go into the station and buy two bottles of rakia and three pieces of fruit [= fruits].

6. "Do you travel a lot?"
   "Yes, I go to many villages and cities. Next year I will go to three cities and two villages. After that I will go to the seashore on vacation."

7. Please bring me notebooks, dictionaries, textbooks and pencils. I am going to study for hours and hours. I will be very busy, and won't be able to talk on the telephone.

8. Ivan is telling me that unfortunately he will not be able to come to the movies today. He will write poems for several hours. He wants to finish five new poems. Then he will recite them to the children.

9. How many children will begin school tomorrow? Seven girls and eight boys. The teacher will show them many books and pictures and will help them learn to read and write. Will they make many mistakes? Of course, everyone makes mistakes. Will they be able to read this book [through]? They will not be able to read it immediately, but they will continue to work. Then success will come.

READING SELECTION

Кореспонде́нция - (6)

---

20 окто́мври, Са́н Франци́ско

Здраве́й Бо́йко,

Патри́ша мно́го харе́сва тарато́ра, защо́то тя оби́ча вси́чки плодове́ и зеленчу́ци. Ще ку́пим бъ́лгарска готва́рска кни́га. Ту́к и́ма бога́т и́збор от готва́рски кни́ги. Патри́ша и́ма ця́ла коле́кция. А́з че́сто ѝ купу́вам готва́рски кни́ги за пода́рък. Но да позна́ваш са́мо ку́хнята на еди́н наро́д, не е́ доста́тъчно. Добре́ е да опозна́еш и страна́та. Запо́чвам да ми́сля, че ще е ху́баво догоди́на да прека́раме о́тпуската в Бълга́рия. Ни́е обикнове́но прека́рваме о́тпуската в Аме́рика. Догоди́на оба́че оча́квам да и́мам по́вече вре́ме. Патри́ша и Кали́на ве́че са прия́телки. И деца́та ще наме́рят о́бщ ези́к. Какво́ ще ка́жеш? Какъ́в пла́н ще напра́вим? И́скам пъту́ването да бъ́де интере́сно и за деца́та.

Пиши́ ми ка́к сте! Ни́е сме добре́.

Ча́кам о́тговор.

Сърде́чни по́здрави,

Ро́берт

---

3 ное́мври, Со́фия

Дра́ги Бо́б,

Чуде́сен е пла́нът да до́йдете в Бълга́рия на почи́вка. Оча́кваме да ви ви́дим ту́к в Со́фия. Опиши́ ми вку́совете на Патри́ша и деца́та. Какво́ оби́чат те́ да гле́дат? Архитекту́рата на градове́ и села́ или приро́дата? Бълга́рия е ма́лка страна́, но със ста́ра исто́рия и интере́сна приро́да. И́ма места́ по вкуса́ на все́ки чове́к. А ка́к оби́чате да пъту́вате? Оби́чате ли да пъту́вате с вла́к?

Дне́с е неде́ля. И́во е с дру́ги учени́ци от класа́ на Ви́тоша. Вре́мето не е́ мно́го ху́баво, но те́ са мла́ди и мо́гат да издъ́ржат ветрове́ и снегове́. Я́на рису́ва. Кали́на тъ́рси но́ви ду́ми в ре́чниците: и́зпитът по англи́йски е ско́ро.

По́здрави на Патри́ша и деца́та.

Вси́чко ху́баво,

Бо́йко

GLOSSARY

амѝ	but, well	ѝ	[to] her (indirect object)
архитектура	architecture	идѝлия	idyll
		ѝзбор	selection, choice
безмесен	vegetarian (adj.) : without meat)	издържам / издържа (-йш)	stand, endure
белѐжа (-иш)	mark	изпускам / изпусна	drop, let go; miss
белѐжка	note		
белѐжник	notebook, notepad	им	[to] them (indirect object)
богат	rich		
бъда	be	интерес	interest
		история	history
веднъж	once		
ветрове see вятър		какво ще кажеш?	what do you think?
ви	[to] you (pl. indirect object)	качвам / кача (-йш)	carry up, take up
вкус, -ът	taste	качвам се /	
война	war	кача се (-йш)	ascend, get on
войнѝк	soldier	клас, -ът (pl. класове)	class, grade in school
във = в	in		
вярвам	believe	ключ	key
вятър (pl. ветрове)	wind	колекция	collection
		колѝчка	pushcart
глад	hunger	край	end
глътвам / глътна	swallow	кухня	cuisine
готварски	cooking, culinary	къщичка	little house
готварска книга	cookbook		
град, -ът (pl. градове)	city	маса	table
греша (-йш)	sin, err	ми	[to] me (indirect object)
		млад	young
декламѝрам	declaim, recite	му	[to] him, it (ind. object)
догодѝна	next year		
дом, -ът (pl. домове)	home, house	на	for, to (indirect object)
домашен	home (adj.)	на другата спѝрка	at the next stop
донасям / донеса	bring	наред	in order, O.K.
достатъчен	enough	народ	people, folk
друг	next	ни	[to] us (indirect object)
дума	word	нов	new
дърво (pl. дървета)	tree	нож (pl. ножове)	knife
		няма да	won't (negative future)
екзотика	exotica, exoticism		
		обаче	however
желая	wish, desire	общ	general, common
		огън (pl. огньове)	fire
забравям / забравя	forget	опѝсвам / опѝша (-еш)	describe
зает	busy, occupied		
закъснявам / закъснея	be late	опознавам / опозная	recognize, get to know
занасям / занеса	carry, take to	от класа	from the same school class
зеленчук	vegetable		

140

о́тговор	answer	си	to oneself
отпъту́вам	set off for, depart	си́рене	white cheese
оча́квам	await, expect	сли́зам / сля́за	get off, go down, descend
па́дам / па́дна	fall	сня́г, снегъ́т	snow
па́да голя́м сня́г	it's snowing heavily	(pl. снегове́)	
перо́н	[railway] platform	со́к	juice
пла́н	plan	спи́рка	bus or tram stop
пло́д (pl. плодове́)	fruit	ста́р	old
пло́ча	tile, slab	страна́	country
по	about	сту́д, -ъ́т	cold, chill
по това́ вре́ме	about that time	(pl. студове́)	
побъ́рзвам / побъ́рзам	hurry up	със = с	with
по́вече	more	тетра́дка	notebook
пода́рък	present, gift	ти	[to] you (indirect object)
позна́вам / позна́я	know; guess	ти́п	type
позна́вам по очи́те	tell by [someone's] eyes	трамва́ен	tram (adj.)
		тъ́рся	seek, look for
пока́звам / пока́жа (-еш)	show	университе́т	university
пома́гам / помо́гна	help	учени́к	student, pupil
по́рция	portion, serving	учени́чка	student, pupil (female)
потъ́рсвам / потъ́рся	seek		
поча́квам / поча́кам	wait	харе́свам	like (see L. 12)
прека́рвам / прека́рам	spend	хлади́лник	refrigerator
при	at, by	це́нтър	center
приро́да	nature	(pl. це́нтрове)	
притесня́вам се / притесня́ се	worry	ця́л, це́ли	whole, entire
продава́ч (ка)	salesperson	ча́ен, ча́ена	tea (adj.)
пти́ца	bird	ча́й (pl. ча́еве)	tea
пъ́тник	traveler	ча́йник	teapot
пъту́ване	travels, trip	ча́с, -ъ́т	hour
		(pl. часове́)	
река́ (-че́ш)	say, utter	часо́вник	watch, clock
ре́чник	dictionary		
		ща́	want
свобода́	freedom	ще	will (future particle)
се	oneself, themselves, itself, etc.	ще́ не ще́	whether one wants or not

CULTURAL COMMENTARY

Food and drink: cheese and bread

Domestic cheese in Bulgaria is of two types. One is white and soft, and the other is yellow and hard. The white soft cheese, called "sirene" (**си́рене**) is known in the West as "feta"; and the harder yellow cheese has begun to be imported under its own name, "kashkaval" (**кашкава́л**). Both are known throughout the Balkans. "Sirene" can be made from either cow's milk or sheep's milk (or a combination of the two). The preferred kind is that made from sheep's milk. Other cheeses are imported into Bulgaria from Western Europe, and are known under their Western names. They remain a specialty item for most Bulgarians, however, and one too expensive to indulge in often.

Like many other Europeans, Bulgarians eat bread with every meal. "Fast-food" kebabs are served with a thick slice of bread.

History

Bulgaria's history is extremely old: the first state was founded in 681. Bulgarian culture flourished during the medieval period, up to the time of the Ottoman conquest in the 14th century. The modern Bulgarian state won its freedom in 1878. Bulgarian history will be outlined in greater detail in Lesson 20.

Geography: general

Bulgaria's landscape is surprisingly varied for its relatively small size. It contains several different ranges of tall mountains, most of the long basin of the Danube (**Ду́нав**) river (though not the delta area near its mouth) and a long coastal section along the Black Sea (**Че́рно мо́ре**).

School system: student life

The terminological difference between pre-university schooling and university education extends to the words for "student". To a Bulgarian, the word **студе́нт** means only university level. Any student below that level is referred to as an **учени́к / учени́чка**. There is no direct equivalent in English: the slightly archaic "pupil" and the more common "schoolchild" usually refer only to the elementary grades. Those enrolled in Bulgarian schools are called **учени́к / учени́чка** through the end of high school.

As in other countries, schoolchildren go with their classmates on recreational field trips. A favorite field trip of Sofia schools is to Vitosha, in all seasons of the year.

LESSON 8

DIALOGUE

Влакът е готов да тръгне

// Влакът ще тръгне всеки момент, а Веселин още стои на перона. Плаща на продавачката и взема кебапчетата. Ще успее ли да се качи навреме? //

Продавачката: Побързайте, господине! Ще изпуснете влака!

Веселин: Няма да го изпусна! Довиждане.

// Веселин тича и се качва в последния вагон. Помагат му двама мъже. //

Веселин: Благодаря! Къде съм? В кой вагон?

Владимир: В двайсет и четвърти. Това е последният вагон на влака. Кой вагон търсите?

Веселин: Осемнайсети.

Георги: Седнете, починете си малко! Поемете си дъх!

Веселин: Не мога. Ще изстинат кебапчетата. Децата чакат.

Георги: Млад сте за баща! Колко деца имате? Виждам, че имате много кебапчета!

Веселин: Ами... децата не са мои. Но са много сладки. И гладни! А кебапчетата са и за други пътници в купето.

Георги: Бързайте тогава. Гладни деца не могат дълго да чакат. Моите деца, например, изобщо не могат да чакат. Хайде! Владо, помогни му!

Владимир: Няма ли някой да седне на моето място?

Георги: Не се притеснявай, аз ще го пазя. Няма да го отстъпя на никого. Изпрати човека!

Владимир: Добре, ще го изпратя. Ще му помогна да занесе кебапчетата на гладните деца. Няма да изстинат кебапчетата.

BASIC GRAMMAR

8.1. Long adjective forms

The masculine form of most adjectives ends in a consonant (e.g. голя́м, ху́бав, добъ́р, мла́д). The masculine form of certain adjectives, however, ends in the vowel -и. Among these are ordinal numbers ("first", "second", etc.), all adjectives ending in -ски, and the pronominal adjective все́ки "each, every".

Cardinal numbers beyond 2 are unchanging in form. Ordinal numbers are adjectives, and must change to agree with the noun they refer to. Following are the ordinal numbers for 1 through 9:

masculine	feminine	neuter	plural	(meaning)
пъ́рв-и	пъ́рв-а	пъ́рв-о	пъ́рв-и	first
вто́р-и	вто́р-а	вто́р-о	вто́р-и	second
тре́т-и	тре́т-а	тре́т-о	тре́т-и	third
четвъ́рт-и	четвъ́рт-а	четвъ́рт-о	четвъ́рт-и	fourth
пе́т-и	пе́т-а	пе́т-о	пе́т-и	fifth
ше́ст-и	ше́ст-а	ше́ст-о	ше́ст-и	sixth
се́дм-и	се́дм-а	се́дм-о	се́дм-и	seventh
о́см-и	о́см-а	о́см-о	о́см-и	eighth
деве́т-и	деве́т-а	деве́т-о	деве́т-и	ninth

Although the masculine and the plural forms are identical, one can tell either from the noun or from the context which meaning is intended. Ordinals from 5 onwards are formed by adding the above endings to the number itself. For instance, пе́т [5] + -и gives пе́т-и [5th].

Note that the -е- in се́дем and о́сем is treated as a fleeting vowel (се́дем [7], о́сем [8], but се́дми [7th], о́сми [8th]).

The spoken form of dates always uses the ordinal form. English speakers can say either "September 15" or "September 15th", but Bulgarian speakers can only say петна́йсети септе́мври. When the date is expressed in writing by a number and not a word, the final -и is sometimes added and sometimes not. The date on which something happens is indicated by the preposition на.

В Бълга́рия учени́ците тръ́гват
    на учи́лище
        на 15-и септе́мври
        на 15 септе́мври.

In Bulgaria children start school
    on September 15th.

Ordinal numbers have both indefinite and definite forms. When these numbers name something, such as a date, an address or a reservation number, they are used in the indefinite. For example:

Днес е втори октомври.	Today is October 2nd.
Ние сме в седми вагон.	We're in car no. 7.
Живеем в Надежда, блок деветдесет и трети, вход "Б", пети етаж.	Our address is [= we live in] residential district Nadezhda, building no. 93, 2nd entrance, 5th floor.

When ordinal numbers refer to a counted place in a series, however, they are used in the definite. For example:

Ще слезете на третата спирка.	You [will] get off at the third stop.
Те живеят на петия етаж.	They live on the fifth floor.

8.2. Definite forms of adjectives

When a definite noun is modified by an adjective, the article is added to the adjective instead of the noun. If there is more than one adjective, the article is added to the first of the series. The article is placed after the adjective ending. In the case of masculine adjectives, the ending -и always appears before the article. The sequence и + ът is always written -ият. Fleeting vowels are lost before this ending. In the case of alternating root vowels, the -я- shifts to -е- before this ending.

Here are the definite and indefinite forms of the adjectives добър and голям, and of the ordinal number първи.

	masculine	*feminine*	*neuter*	*plural*
indefinite	добър	добр-а́	добр-о́	добр-и́
definite	добр-ият	добр-а́та	добр-о́то	добр-и́те
indefinite	голя́м	голя́м-а	голя́м-о	голе́м-и
definite	голе́м-ият	голя́м-ата	голя́м-ото	голе́м-ите
indefinite	пъ́рв-и	пъ́рв-а	пъ́рв-о	пъ́рв-и
definite	пъ́рв-ият	пъ́рв-ата	пъ́рв-ото	пъ́рв-ите

English and Bulgarian are alike in that when definite nouns occur preceded by adjectives, the entire phrase is considered definite. The only difference between them in this respect is that in Bulgarian the article occurs *after* the first element in this phrase instead of before it, as in English.

Here are examples of definite nouns both with and without adjectives:

feminine	Ча́нта-та	е на по́да	The bag is on the floor.
	Голя́ма-та ча́нта	е на по́да.	The big bag is on the floor.

neuter	Дете́-то	рису́ва добре́.	The child draws well.
	Ма́лко-то дете́	рису́ва добре́.	The small child draws well.

plural	Мо́ливи-те	са в ча́нтата.	The pencils are in the bag.
	Цве́тни-те мо́ливи	са в ча́нтата.	The colored pencils are in the bag.

masculine	Мо́лив-ът	е ту́ка.	The pencil is here.
subject	Черве́н-ият мо́лив	е ту́ка.	The red pencil is here.

masculine	Ви́ждаш ли	мо́лив-а?	Do you see the pencil?
object	Ви́ждаш ли	черве́н-ия мо́лив?	Do you see the red pencil?

As in definite nouns, the masculine object form drops the -т. Remember that in Bulgarian, the category "subject" includes predicate nouns, and that the category "object" includes objects of prepositions. For example:

subject

Това́ е после́дният ваго́н на вла́ка. It's the last car of the train.

object

Весели́н се ка́чва в после́дния ваго́н. Veselin gets into the last car.

8.3. Possessive pronominal adjectives

Possessive pronominal adjectives in Bulgarian are similar to other adjectives in that they change form to agree with the noun they refer to. In Bulgarian, the question word чий "whose" also belongs to this group. These adjectives, whose forms are given below, are used most frequently in the definite form, although the indefinite form can be used in certain instances.

	masculine	feminine	neuter	plural	(meaning)
1sg	мо́й	мо́-я	мо́-е	мо́-и	my/mine
2sg	тво́й	тво́-я	тво́-е	тво́-и	your(s)
3sg fem	не́ин	не́йн-а	не́йн-о	не́йн-и	her(s)
3sg masc	не́гов	не́гов-а	не́гов-о	не́гов-и	his
1pl	на́ш	на́ш-а	на́ш-е	на́ш-и	our(s)
2pl	ва́ш	ва́ш-а	ва́ш-е	ва́ш-и	your(s)
3pl	те́хен	тя́хн-а	тя́хн-о	те́хн-и	their(s)
query	чи́й	чи-я́	чи-е́	чи-и́	whose

There are fleeting vowels in both **не́ин** and **те́хен**, but their behavior is quite different. The vowel in **не́ин** is, exceptionally, -и-. As do other fleeting vowels in adjectives, it appears only in the masculine singular. However, a trace of it (in the form of the consonant -й-) is present in the remaining forms. Note that the masculine form **не́ин** has two syllables, while the stem seen in other forms (**нейн-**) has only one.

Note that the adjective meaning "their" has not only a vowel-zero alternation (**те́хен / те́хни**) but also an **е / я** alternation in the root (**те́хен / тя́хна**).

8.4. Negative and indefinite pronouns

Question words are those which request information, and with which one forms questions. Practically all such words in Bulgarian begin with к- (**ко́й, кога́, къде́, какво́**, etc.). Negative and indefinite pronouns are formed by adding the prefixes **ни-** and **ня-**, respectively, to these words. The Bulgarian system is much more symmetrical in this respect than the English one:

	identity	*time*	*place*	*character*	*manner*
question	**ко́й?** who?	**кога́?** when?	**къде́?** where?	**какъ́в?** what sort?	**ка́к?** how?
negative	**ни́-кой** no one	**ни́-кога** never	**ни́-къде** nowhere	**ни́-какъв**	**ни́-как**
indefinite	**ня́-кой** someone	**ня́-кога** sometime	**ня́-къде** somewhere	**ня́-какъв** some sort	**ня́-как** somehow

The English translation "what sort?" for **какъ́в** in the above chart does not cover all the meanings of the Bulgarian word. No translations are given for **ни́какъв** or **ни́как**, since for these words the correct translation depends on the context. The form **поня́кога** "sometimes" also exists. It differs slightly in meaning from **ня́кога** "sometime" (in the meaning "at some point in the past").

The words for "nothing" and "something" are formed by adding recognizable prefixes not to the question word **какво́** but to the more colloquial word **що́**:

negative	**ни́що**	nothing
indefinite	**не́що**	something

When the words in the "identity" column refer to human beings, they have both a subject and an object form. The subject form is the one listed above, and the object form ends in -го: **кого́, ни́кого, ня́кого**. The object form must be used whenever the pronoun is the object of the verb or of a preposition. For example:

subject

Кóй живée тýка?	Who lives here?
Нáкой чáка на вратáта.	Someone is waiting at the door.

object

С когó живéете?	Who do you live with?
На когó помáгаш?	Whom are you helping?
Вѝждаш ли нáкого?	Do you see someone?

8.5. Double negatives

In Bulgarian, as in all Slavic languages, multiple negative markers are required. If the verb is negated and the sentence includes pronouns or adverbs for which there exists a negated form, this negated form must be used. This is in contrast to English, where only one negative marker per sentence is permitted. For example:

Нѝкъде нѝкого не вѝждам.	I don't see anyone anywhere.
Тóй нѝщо не знáе.	He doesn't know anything.
Нáма да го дáм на нѝкого.	I won't give it to anyone.
Нѝкой нáма да сéдне тýка.	No one will sit down here.

8.6. Word order and the future tense

Pronoun objects of a verb in the future tense must be placed after the future markers (ще or нáма да) and before the verb.

Ще го пáзя, нáма да го отстъпя.	I'll guard it. I won't give it up.

The question marker ли occurs after the main verb when the future marker is ще. When the future marker is нáма да, the question marker occurs after the negative form нáма. For example:

Ще дóйдеш ли ýтре?	Are you coming tomorrow?
Нáма ли да дóйдеш ýтре?	Aren't you coming tomorrow?

8.7. The particles се / си with verbs

Bulgarian grammars usually refer to the particles се and си as "reflexive". Formally, these particles are object pronouns. They obey the same word order rules as object pronouns, and they are formally similar with the 1sg-2sg object pronouns:

	direct object	indirect object
1ˢᵗ singular	ме	ми
2ⁿᵈ singular	те	ти
reflexive	се	си

Functionally, however, they have a double life. They can be used either as the object of a verb, or as part of the verb itself. When used as pronoun objects, they are called "true reflexives" -- the objects of a verb whose action "reflects" back onto the subject. That is, the person who is the object of the verb is simultaneously its subject. Here are examples illustrating the difference between non-reflexive and reflexive usage. (Reflexives will be studied in more detail in Lesson 13.)

non-reflexive

Ма́йката ми́е дете́то.	The mother washes the child.
Весели́н ка́зва не́що на Джу́ли.	Veselin says something to Julie.

reflexive

Дете́то се ми́е.	The child washes [himself].
Весели́н си ка́зва не́що.	Veselin says something to himself.

More commonly, the particles **се** and **си** occur as "verbal additives", becoming part of an individual verb's meaning. In this usage, the two particles function quite differently. When the particle **се** accompanies a verb, it is usually an integral part of that verb. The complex "verb + **се**" then becomes a unique verb all its own. Here are examples of verbs with and without this particle:

+/- particle	*verb*	*(meaning)*
without	ка́звам / ка́жа	say [something]
with	ка́звам се	be called
without	приби́рам / прибера́	gather, collect
with	приби́рам се / прибера́ се	come home
without	разби́рам / разбера́	understand
with	разби́ра се *(3sg)*	of course
without	ка́чвам / кача́	lift [something]
with	ка́чвам се / кача́ се	get on [bus, train, etc.], go up
without	притесня́вам / притесня́	cause concern [to someone]
with	притесня́вам се / притесня́ се	worry

149

There is not always a predictable relationship between the meaning of a verb with **се** added, and the same verb without **се**. Sometimes the difference is one of transitivity (the ability to take a direct object), in which case there is no separate dictionary entry. But when the meaning is sufficiently different, as in the above, each of the verbs is a separate dictionary entry. (The usage of **се** to mark intransitivity will be studied in Lesson 11.)

The particles **се** and **си** function quite differently. Although **се** is obligatory, in that it is part of the verb it accompanies (and indeed, makes this verb into a new and different verb), **си** is optional. It can be added to a verb or not as the speaker chooses. When it is present, it adds the meaning of greater intimacy, of greater involvement in the action. For instance, in the expression **поемам дъх**, "catch [one's] breath", a Bulgarian could say either of the following two sentences:

Седне́те, поеме́те дъх!	Sit down and catch your breath!
Седне́те, поеме́те си дъх!	*[same]*

The second version is much more frequently heard, no doubt because it is generally perceived that someone out of breath is (or should be) highly involved in the action of catching his breath.

8.8. Prepositions

(a)   The preposition **към** means "towards". It indicates movement in the direction of a certain point, both in space and in time. It is also used in a number of idiomatic expressions to indicate relationship.

Дете́то ти́ча към гради́ната.	The child runs towards the park.
Към пе́т часа́ ще сме гото́ви.	We'll be ready towards/around 5:00.
Напосле́дък тя́ проявя́ва интере́с към средновеко́вието.	Lately she has been showing an interest in the Middle Ages.
Ще наме́риш но́вите ду́ми в допълне́нието към ре́чника.	You'll find [the] new words in the supplement to the dictionary.

(b)   The primary meaning of the preposition **от** is "from". Although many instances of it are translated with other prepositions in English, most still maintain the general idea of separation. (For more on the use of the preposition **от** in phrases of comparison, see Lesson 10.)

Ни́кой от мо́ите прия́тели не мо́же да повя́рва това́.	None of my friends can believe it.
Ни́кой не оби́ча живо́тните по́вече от Е́мили.	No one likes animals more than Emily.

(c)   The preposition **на** is used to specify intervals in space or time. The English phrases "at a distance of..." or "at intervals of..." may help the student learn this usage.

Ри́лският манасти́р е на два́ ча́са пъ́т с кола́ от Со́фия.	Rila monastery is about two hours' drive from Sofia.
Ще гъ́лташ лека́рствата на 8 ча́са.	Take the pills every 8 hours.

(d)   The preposition **през** also specifies intervals of space or time, but intervals that are skipped over.

Списа́нието изли́за през се́дмица.	The magazine comes out every other week.
Тя́ поса́жда по едно́ дърво́ през три́ къ́щи.	She plants a tree every three houses.
То́й живе́е през три́ у́лици.	He lives three streets over from here.

8.9. Demonstrative pronouns, continued

Corresponding to the pronoun **то́зи** "this" is the pronoun **о́нзи** "that". The forms are similar to those of **то́зи**. They are:

masculine	*feminine*	*neuter*	*plural*	
то́-зи	та́-зи	то-ва́	те́-зи	this
о́н-зи	она́-зи	оно-ва́	оне́-зи	that

English speakers should beware of translating "this" and "that" directly into Bulgarian. As the following example shows, the *neutral* demonstrative pronoun in English is "that", but in Bulgarian it is **то́зи** "this".

Та́зи къ́ща е мно́го ху́бава.	That house is very nice.

The difference may be schematized as follows:

	nearby	*neutral*	*distant*
English	this	that	that
Bulgarian	то́зи	то́зи	о́нзи

EXERCISES

I. Rewrite the sentences changing all underlined nouns to the appropriate pronouns:

1. Пе́тър и На́дка ня́ма да гле́дат <u>фи́лма</u> в неде́ля.
2. Ще прочете́ш ли писмо́то <u>на ба́бата</u>?
3. Ня́ма ли да пока́жеш на Ангел <u>списа́нието</u>?
4. Ще полу́чим ли <u>писма́та</u> след три́ дни́?
5. Ба́ба ня́ма ли да обере́ та́зи се́дмица <u>лу́ка</u>?
6. Ка́мен ня́ма да отстъ́пи мо́ливите <u>на На́дка</u>.
7. Ле́карят ще прегле́да <u>пацие́нтите</u> след о́бед.

II. Expand each of the following sentences by adding one or more of the following adjectives before each noun: добъ́р, интере́сен, ле́ден, ма́лък, правосла́вен, софи́йски, и́стински, америка́нски, бя́л, голя́м, цве́тен, мла́д, бъ́лгарски, пре́сен, дъ́лъг, то́пъл, на́ш, ва́ш.

1. Ще поднесе́т на го́стите плодове́ и ча́й.
2. Деца́та тъ́рсят мо́ливи.
3. Цъ́рквата и́ма исто́рия.
4. Дне́с е студе́но. Ду́ха вя́тър. Деца́та гле́дат снега́ през прозо́реца.
5. Тури́стите хо́дят на екску́рзии.
6. Адвока́тът оча́ква Де́йвид и Джу́ли с нетърпе́ние.
7. Прия́телите пи́шат писма́.

III. Rewrite the following sentences as negative.

1. То́й оти́ва ня́къде и бъ́рза.
2. Това́ ни интересу́ва, разкаже́те ни го.
3. Ня́кои да́ва на деца́та о́рехи.
4. Ма́йката ги хра́ни с лъжи́чка.
5. Те́ ня́как ще нареди́т на́шата програ́ма.
6. А́нгел ви́жда ня́кого през прозо́реца.
7. Ня́кой звъни́ на врата́та.

ADDITIONAL GRAMMAR NOTES

8.1a. Long adjective forms

All adjectives formed with the suffix -ск- add -и in the masculine form. This suffix is used to create adjectives from a number of stems. It is very frequent with proper nouns (names of places or regions). Additional suffixes are sometimes added when adjectives are formed from proper nouns. Although the proper nouns themselves are capitalized (as in English), the adjectives formed from them are not.

noun	stem	+ - ск- ›	adjective (masculine)	(meaning)
мъж	мъж-	+ - к- ›	* мъ́жк-и	masculine
и́стин-а	истин-	+ -ск- ›	и́стинск-и	true
Ри́л-а	рил-	+ -ск- ›	ри́лск-и	of Rila
Евро́п-а	европ-ей-	+ -ск- ›	европе́йск-и	European
Ку́б-а	куб-ин-	+ -ск- ›	куби́нск-и	Cuban
Визáнти-я	византий-	+ -ск- ›	византи́йск-и	Byzantine

* The adjective **мъ́жки** is formed on to this pattern, but is written without the -с-.

8.2a. Definite forms of adjectives

Adjectives can often refer to nouns which are not stated. Some such adjectives in fact now function as full-fledged nouns, three examples of which are given below. Although they look like singular neuter nouns, their plural endings show that they are essentially adjectives:

singular indefinite	singular definite	plural indefinite	plural definite	(meaning)
живо́тн-о	живо́тн-ото	живо́тн-и	живо́тн-ите	animal
контро́лн-о	контро́лн-ото	контро́лн-и	контро́лн-ите	quiz, test
дома́шн-о	дома́шн-ото	дома́шн-и	дома́шн-ите	homework

The longer forms **контро́лна ра́бота** and **дома́шна ра́бота** also exist, and also mean "quiz" and "homework", respectively. The fact that the shorter forms end in -o is proof that they now function as nouns on their own -- if the noun **ра́бота** were there but simply remained unspoken, the shorter forms would end in -a.

153

Indeed, adjectives used alone are usually understood to refer to a particular noun which does not happen to be stated. Since that noun almost always refers to something that has already been mentioned, the adjective appears in its definite form. For instance:

-- Коя́ ча́нта тъ́рсите?   "Which bag are you looking for?"
-- Голя́мата.   "The big one."

Димъ́т е опа́сен за ма́лките.   Smoke is dangerous for the small ones.
             (Here "small ones" = "children"
              in the generic usage.)

8.2b. Soft adjectives

One commonly used adjective, **син** "blue", ends in a soft consonant. To signify this, the endings of the feminine and neuter forms must be spelled with **-я** and **-ьо**, respectively. The forms of this adjective are as follows:

	masculine	*feminine*	*neuter*	*plural*
indefinite	си́н	си́н-я	си́н-ьо	си́н-и
definite	си́н-ият	си́н-ята	си́н-ьото	си́н-ите

8.3a. Possessive pronominal adjectives

Like other forms with adjectival endings, the possessive pronominal adjectives can occur in both definite and indefinite variants. The definite form is used when the topic has been mentioned before, or is known in some way. Since that which is possessed is usually a known quantity to the possessor, these adjectives tend to occur most frequently in the definite form. If the information is new, however, or if the identity of that which is possessed is unspecified, then the indefinite form will be used. Here are examples, with the presumed meaning given below in italics.

Indefinite form

Деца́та не са́ мо́и.   The children are not mine.

It is not known whether or not the speaker has children; all he says here is that the children in question are not his.

Мо́и прия́тели, напри́мер,   [Some of] my friends, for example,
 не и́скат да хо́дят на аеро́бика. don't [like to] go to aerobics classes.

The identity of the friends who don't do aerobics is not specified beyond the fact that they are among the group "friends of the speaker".

154

Definite form

Тези деца не са мойте.	These children aren't mine.
	[= aren't the ones that are mine.]

The participants in the conversation are aware that the speaker has children; what he says here is that the children in question are not the ones we know to be his.

Мойте деца, например,	My children, for example,
изобщо не могат да чакат.	can't wait at all.

For the speaker, the fact that the children are his is a given and therefore known; the new information is about their inability to wait.

8.5a. Negative expressions, continued

The negative form of the conjunction и "and" is нито, which also exists in a more colloquial variant, ни. Its most frequent use is as an intensifier. The examples below illustrate the affirmative intensifier use of и, and the parallel negative usage of нито / ни. Note that in the affirmative sentence, the English translation specifies this intensification by means of the adverb "even". The negative sentence, however, has no way to express the parallel intensification, since only one negative is allowed in English.

Тя знае много езици.	She knows many languages.
Знае и български.	She even knows Bulgarian.
Той не знае ни една дума български.	He doesn't know a word of Bulgarian.
Не разбира нито дума.	He doesn't understand a single word.

8.6a. Word order rules and the future tense

Word order rules involving the future particle ще *(Fut.)* are similar in many ways to those involving the negative particle не *(Neg.)* and the conjunction да *(Cnj.)*. These otherwise unrelated words share three important characteristics:

-- they are unaccented
-- they may begin a sentence or a clause
-- they must be followed directly by the sequence "clitic(s) plus verb" (or the verb itself if no clitics are present)

Therefore, these particles are designated by a capitalized abbreviation. This designation opposes them both to fully accented words (such as *verb*, designated all in lower case) and to true clitics (such as the short form direct object pronoun *DIR*, designated all in upper case). Examples of word order in the future tense, with numbering cumulative across lessons, are given below. Note the similarity to word order in negative constructions and да-phrases. Note also that the negative future marker ня́ма да also follows the same rules by virtue of its second member, да.

Simple future tense

Regardless of the place of ще in the sentence, a pronoun object of a verb in the future tense must be placed between the particle ще and the verb form.

(18) Áз   ще   го   пáзя.
             Fut.   *DIR*   *verb*   I will guard it.

(19) Ще   му   помóгна   да   ги   занесé.
       Fut.   *IND*   *verb*   *Cnj.*   *DIR*   *verb*   I'll help him carry them.

Similarity of future tense and negated present tense

When pronoun objects are present, the word order of future tense and negated present tense sentences is identical. The only difference is that the clitic pronoun is accented after the negative particle but not after the future particle.

(20) Ще   го   изпрáтя.
       Fut.   *DIR*   *verb*   I'll accompany him.

vs.

(21) Не   гó   изпрáщам.
       Neg.   *DIR*   *verb*   I'm not accompanying him.

(22) Ще   му   помóгна.
       Fut.   *IND*   *verb*   I'll help him.

vs.

(23) Не   мý   помáгам.
       Neg.   *IND*   *verb*   I'm not helping him.

Negated future tense

Pronoun objects after negated future verbs are treated exactly as pronoun objects after да. The notation reflects this by separating the negative future marker ня́ма да into the stressed word ня́ма *(neg.)* and the conjunction да *(Cnj.)*. Compare the similarity with the да-phrase in example (19) above.

(24) Ня́ма   да   го   отстъ́пя   на ни́кого.
       neg.   *Cnj.*   *DIR*   *verb*   *indirect obj.*   I won't give it up to anyone.

(25)

Няма	да	му	каже.
neg.	*Cnj.*	*IND*	*verb*

She won't tell him.

Simple questions in the future tense

To form a question in the future tense, add the interrogative particle **ли** immediately after the verb, as in other questions. The placement of object pronouns is not changed. These rules also apply to embedded questions.

(26)

Ще	успее	ли	да	го	купи?
Fut.	*verb*	*INT*	*Cnj.*	*DIR*	*verb*

Will he manage to buy it?

(27)

Ще	ми	помогнеш	ли?
Fut.	*IND*	*verb*	*INT*

Will you help me?

(28)

Питай	го	ще	дойде	ли.
verb	*DIR*	*Fut.*	*verb*	*INT*

Ask him if he is coming.

(29)

Не	знаем	ще	можем	ли	да	дойдем.
Neg.	*verb*	*Fut.*	*verb*	*INT*	*Cnj.*	*verb*

We don't know whether or not we'll be able to come.

Negated questions in the future tense

Questions formed from negative futures are more complex. The particle **ли** comes between the two components of the negative future marker **няма да**. In word order terms, the accented word **няма** functions as a verb; therefore it is normal that it should be followed directly by the interrogative particle.

Pronoun objects continue to follow the conjunction **да**, which is also the norm for them. Note that this rule does not allow anything to come between **да** and the verb except a pronoun object. Thus, if the subject of the verb is expressed, it is placed *after* **няма ли** but *before* **да**.

(30)

Няма	ли	да	дойдеш	утре?
neg.	*INT*	*Cnj.*	*verb*	

Aren't you going to come tomorrow?

(31)

Няма	ли	да	й	помогнеш?
neg.	*INT*	*Cnj.*	*IND*	*verb*

Won't you help her?

(32)

Няма	ли	някой	да	седне	тук?
neg.	*INT*	*subject*	*Cnj.*	*verb*	

Won't someone sit down here?

(33)

Няма	ли	да	го	питаш	ще	дойде	ли?
neg.	*INT*	*Cnj.*	*DIR*	*verb*	*Fut.*	*verb*	*INT*

Aren't you going to ask him whether or not he is coming?

157

8.7a. The particles се / си with verbs

The particles **се** and **си** can function either as reflexive objects of the verb, or as integral components of a verb's meaning. In either case, they obey the word order rules for direct and indirect object pronouns, respectively.

The addition of **се** to a verb always creates a new verb, one in which the change of meaning is not directly predictable. The addition of **си** to a verb is optional (but frequent), and the change in meaning is usually the same: the often untranslatable overtone of greater involvement and intimacy.

There are a few instances, however, where the particle **си** does change the meaning sufficiently to create a new verb. One of these is the perfective form of the verb **почѝвам** (perfective **почѝна**). This verb means "rest", and in the imperfective can be used either with or without **си**. For example:

Вѝе кáк почѝвате?	What do you do on vacation? [= How do you rest?]
Сегá си почѝвам хýбаво -- четá един ромáн.	I'm having a nice rest -- I'm reading a novel.

In the perfective, however, the verb has two different meanings. **Почѝна си** continues to mean "rest", but **почѝна** alone is a euphemism for "die", or "go to one's eternal resting place." The particle **си** in this instance functions to distinguish these two meanings.

Other verbs where the **си** can change the meaning are **лягам** (perfective **лѐгна**). Without **си**, the verb means "lie down", but with **си**, it usually means "go to bed." The verb **спѝмням си** "remember, keep a memory of" occurs only with the particle **си** attached. In this sense, exceptionally for the system, it is like a **се**-verb.

Лѐкарят кáзва на пациѐнта -- Легнѐте, ще ви преглѐдам.	The doctor says to the patient: "Lie down, and I'll examine you."
Мáйката кáзва на детѐто -- Легнѝ си, мнóго си уморѐн.	The mother says to the child: "Go to bed, you are very tired."
Нѝе си спóмняме добрóто стáро врѐме.	We remember the good old days.

8.10. Plural of masculine monosyllabic nouns, continued

Most masculine monosyllabic nouns add the ending **-ове** in the plural. A few, however, simply add **-е**. This plural ending is always accented. Except for **мъж** and **княз**, the nouns which form their plurals in this way also all take the article in **-ят**. The accent in the definite form is not predictable.

Three relatively common nouns have the irregular plural ending **-ища**. They also take the article in **-ят**.

singular indefinite	singular definite	plural	(meaning)
мъж	мъж-ъ́т	мъж-е́	man, husband
кня́з	кня́з-ът	княз-е́	prince
кра́л	кра́л-ят	крал-е́	king
ца́р	ца́р-ят	цар-е́	emperor
ко́н	ко́н-ят	кон-е́	horse
пъ́т	пъ́т-ят	пъ́т-ища	way, road
съ́н	сън-я́т	съ́н-ища	dream, sleep
кра́й	кра́-ят	кра́-ища	end

There are also several common nouns which, although they are monosyllabic, take the plural ending **-и**. Two have a fleeting vowel and the article in **-ят**, and three are unremarkable (at least in the singular).

Finally, several masculine nouns form the plural with **-а**, and one forms its plural with **-я**. The first of these endings is always accented.

singular indefinite	singular definite	plural	(meaning)
ла́кът	ла́кът-ят	ла́кт-и	elbow
но́кът	но́кът-ят	но́кт-и	nail [finger/toe]
зъ́б	зъ́б-ът	зъ́б-и	tooth
фи́лм	фи́лм-ът	фи́лм-и	film
го́ст	го́ст-ът	го́ст-и	guest
кра́к	крак-ъ́т	крак-а́	leg, foot
ли́ст	ли́ст-ът	лист-а́	leaf [on a tree]
но́мер	но́мер-ът	номер-а́	number, No.
господи́н	господи́н-ът	госпо́д-а́	Mr., gentleman
бра́т	бра́т-ът	бра́т-я	brother

Note that the noun **господи́н** loses its "singular" ending **-ин** in the plural. The noun **ли́ст** in the meaning "sheet of paper" has the plural which is more regular for a monosyllabic noun: **ли́стове**.

8.11. Conjoined phrases

Often speakers wish to emphasize the connection (or lack thereof) between words or phrases. To do this, Bulgarian simply repeats the conjunctions. Note the difference from English, where a paired set of conjunctions must be used:

и ... и	both...and
или ... или	either...or
ни ... ни	neither...nor

For example:

Тя́ зна́е и англи́йски, и бъ́лгарски.	She knows both English and Bulgarian.
То́й не зна́е ни́то англи́йски, ни́то бъ́лгарски.	He knows neither English nor Bulgarian.
Или ще до́йда, или ня́ма да до́йда.	Either I'll come or I won't.

Finally, there is a striking difference between English and Bulgarian in the construction of phrases such as "John and I" or "he and Emily". To refer to a pair of persons one of whom is being mentioned for the first time, speakers of English simply join the proper name and the singular pronoun by the conjunction "and".

Bulgarians, however, refer to the *pair* with a pronoun, and add the proper name as part of a prepositional phrase. The literal translation of such phrases, therefore, would be (in highly awkward English) "We with John", "They with Emily". This usage occurs in both subject and object positions. For example:

Ни́е с Патри́ша че́сто хо́дим на екску́рзии.	Patricia and I often go on excursions.
Те с И́во ще хо́дят на ци́рк.	S/he and Ivo are going to go to the circus.
Това́ найстина е ва́жно за на́с с Де́йвид.	It's really important for David and me.

(The object pronoun form на́с "us" will be learned in Lesson 10.)

160

8.12. Conjoined adjectives

When two nouns of different gender are modified by the same adjective, the form of the adjective depends on whether or not the nouns refer to something that can be counted. If so, then the adjective is in the plural. If not, then the adjective agrees with the first of the two nouns. For example:

Мо́ите ба́ба и дя́до живе́ят на се́ло.	My grandmother and grandfather live in the village.
Сла́га то́пъл ча́й и мля́ко на ма́сата.	She puts hot tea and milk on the table.

When the same noun is modified by two different adjectives, it retains the singular form, even though it is clearly plural in meaning. For example:

То́й зна́е и бъ́лгарски и англи́йски ези́к.	He knows both Bulgarian and English [languages].
Черве́ната и зеле́ната то́пка са по́-ху́бави от жъ́лтата.	The red and green balls are nicer than the yellow one.

(The comparison of adjectives, as in **по́-ху́бав** "nicer", will be learned in Lesson 10.)

Downtown Smolyan, central Rhodopes

161

SAMPLE SENTENCES

1. Пъ́рви януа́ри е пъ́рвият де́н на годи́ната. То́й е почи́вен де́н.

2. Йво е учени́к от о́сми кла́с. Е́мили е учени́чка от се́дми кла́с. Едина́йсети е после́дният кла́с.

3. На́шата пъ́рва кола́ е во́лга. Вто́рата ще е рено́.

4. Чове́к тру́дно науча́ва пъ́рвия чу́жд ези́к. Вто́рият и тре́тият са ле́сни.

5. Та́ня и Пе́тър живе́ят в десе́ти бло́к, на тре́тия ета́ж, в апартаме́нт петдесе́т и се́дем.

6. То́плото пря́сно мля́ко е поле́зно за здра́вето.

7. Ти́ съну́ваш ли цве́тни съ́нища?

8. Вси́чки пъ́тища во́дят към Ри́м.

9. От мла́дите листа́ на лоза́та в Бълга́рия пра́вят сарми́.

10. Учи́телката разда́ва на учени́ците ли́стове харти́я.

11. Учени́ците пра́вят номера́ на мла́дата учи́телка.

12. Ни́що не го́ интересу́ва. Ни́къде не и́ска да хо́ди.

13. Ня́мам ни́какви позна́ти в Бълга́рия.

14. Ту́к ни́кой на ни́кого не пре́чи.

SENTENCES FOR TRANSLATION

1. Will you help them? You won't help them? Why not?

2. Where do your friends live? Mine live in Nadezhda 181, entrance B, 7th floor. They don't like living on the seventh floor; they prefer the top [= last] floor.

3. Which month of the year is December? Is it the first or the last? The twenty-first day of December is the first day of winter.

4. Will you tell me where your colored pencils are? I want the blue one. Does Ivo have it? Will he put it on the table now, or will he keep it in the red bag?

5. No one knows who is coming today. No one ever knows who is coming, or when.

6. Where are the blue books and the red dictionaries? I don't see anything at all here. I know that they are somewhere but I don't know where. Who can know?

7. Will you ask them when they are leaving? I won't forget them. No one can forget them.

8. Either she knows Bulgarian or she doesn't. If she knows it now, will she forget it tomorrow?

9. Everyone remembers the good old times. Will we remember them? Won't we forget them?

10. Don't put either elbows or feet on the table! Nobody anywhere does that.

READING SELECTION

<u>А́з оби́чам да пъту́вам</u>

Том: Послѐдните почѝвни днѝ прека́рах в Со́фия. Ѝскам да вѝдя и дру́ги интере́сни места́. Не мо́жеш ли да предло́жиш не́що интере́сно за слѐдващата съ́бота?

Васил: Мо́жем да отѝдем на Вѝтоша. Това́ е люби́мото мя́сто на мно́го хо́ра в Со́фия.

Том: Вѐче бя́х та́м. Предпочѝтам да е дале́че от Со́фия. А́з оби́чам да пъту́вам. Ка́зват, че в Родо́пите е мно́го интере́сно. Мо́жем да отѝдем та́м.

Васил: Това́ е добра́ иде́я. Осве́н това́ ѝмам прия́тели в Смо́лян. Те́ ще ни пока́жат града́.

Том: Ако ѝскам да гле́дам градове́, ще оста́на в Со́фия. Интересу́ва ме приро́дата.

Васил: Не се́ бо́й, нѝкой ня́ма да те заклю́чи в апартаме́нт. Ще мо́жеш мно́го да се разхо́ждаш в приро́дата. Мо́жеш да вѝдиш и ѝстински еле́н или сърна́. Не тѝ пожела́вам да вѝдиш ѝстински гла́ден въ́лк. Въ́лците не разпозна́ват люби́телите на приро́дата и ги третѝрат като обикнове́ни хо́ра.

Том: Зна́чи в съ́бота взѝмаме вла́ка и отѝваме в Смо́лян, налѝ?

Васил: Не го́ взѝмаме, защо́то до та́м ня́ма вла́к. Мо́жем да отѝдем с дире́ктен автобу́с до Смо́лян или с вла́к до Пло́вдив, а след това́ с автобу́с. Ня́ма да е ху́баво да пристѝгнем в Смо́лян мно́го къ́сно.

Том: Ня́ма ли да пъту́ваме мно́го дъ́лго?

Васил: Ня́ма. Ня́ма да прочете́ш и еди́н ве́стник и ще бъ́дем та́м.

Том: Зна́м ка́к тѝ чете́ш ве́стници. Тѝ чете́ш до послѐдната бу́ква.

Васил: Нѝщо подо́бно. Дорѝ ня́ма да реша́ кръстосло́вицата. А от Пло́вдив до Смо́лян автобу́сите са почтѝ през еди́н ча́с.

Том: А ѝма ли интере́сни неща́ в Пло́вдив?

Васил: Разбѝра се, осо́бено в ста́рия гра́д.

Том: Вѐче запо́чвам да съжаля́вам, че ня́ма да ѝмаме вре́ме да го вѝдим.

Васил: Ще го оста́вим за дру́г пъ́т.

GLOSSARY

аеро́бика	aerobics	и ... и	both...and
америка́нски	American (adj.)	изо́бщо	in general, at all
апартаме́нт	apartment		
		изпра́щам /	send off, see off,
ба́ба	grandmother	изпра́тя	accompany
баща́	father (see L. 10)	изсти́вам /	grow/become cold
бло́к	apartment building	изсти́на	
боя́ се	fear	или ... или	either...or
бра́т (pl. бра́тя)	brother	интересу́вам	interest
бу́ква	letter (of alphabet)	и́стински	real, true
ва́жен	important	кня́з (pl. князе́)	prince
ва́ш	your, yours	кого́	whom
византи́йски	Byzantine	компле́кс	complex
во́дя	lead, take	ко́н, -ят (pl. коне́)	horse
вто́ри	second	контро́лен	control (adj.)
вхо́д	entrance	контро́лна ра́бота	exam, quiz
въ́лк (pl. въ́лци)	wolf	контро́лно	exam, quiz
		кра́й (pl. кра́ища)	district
го́ст (pl. го́сти)	guest	кра́к, -ъ́т	leg
гъ́лтам	swallow	(pl. крака́)	
гъ́лтам лека́рство	take medicine	кра́л, -ят	king
		(pl. крале́)	
деве́ти	ninth	кръстосло́вица	crossword puzzle
дире́ктен	direct	куби́нски	Cuban
дови́ждане	goodbye	към	toward
дома́шно	homework		
допълне́ние	addition, supplement	ла́кът, ла́къдят	elbow
дори́	even	(pl. ла́кти)	
дъ́лго	a long time	ле́ден, -ена	ice (adj.), frozen
дъ́х	breath, wind	лека́рство	medicine
дя́до (pl. in L. 10)	grandfather	люби́м	favorite
		люби́тел	lover, fan
европе́йски	European	ля́гам си /	go to bed
екску́рзия	excursion	ле́гна си	
еле́н	deer, stag		
ета́ж	floor [of a multi-	манасти́р	monastery
	story building]	мату́ра	matriculation [exam]
		ми́я	wash
живо́тно	animal	мо́й	my, mine
жи́лищен	residential	мора́вски	Moravian
жи́лищен компле́кс	block of apartments,	мъ́ж, -ъ́т	man, husband
	residential district	(pl. мъже́)	
жъ́лт	yellow	мъ́жки	male, masculine
заклю́чвам /	lock	наде́жда	hope
заклю́ча (-иш)		напосле́дък	lately
зеле́н	green	напри́мер	for example
зъ́б, -ъ́т (pl. зъ́би)	tooth	на́с	us (see L. 10)

наш	our, ours	познат	acquaintance
нéгов	his	полéзен	useful
нéин, нéйна	her, hers	полéзно за	good for one's health
нетърпéние	impatience	здрáвето	
ни	not, neither	получáвам /	receive, get
ни ... ни	neither... nor	получá (-иш)	
нѝкак	not at all	понякога	sometimes
нѝкакъв	none, no kind of	посáждам / посадя	seat, plant
нѝкога	never	почѝвам си /	rest
нѝкого	no one (object)	почѝна си	
нѝкой	no one (subject)	почѝвен	rest (adj.)
нѝкъде	nowhere	почѝвен дéн	day off, holiday
нѝто	not, neither	почѝна	die
нѝто (еднá) дýма	not a single word	почтѝ	almost
нѝщо	nothing	правослáвен	Orthodox [religion] (adj.)
нѝщо подóбно	nothing of the sort	прáвя номерá на	play dirty tricks on
нóкът, нóкътят	nail (on hand or foot)	преглéждам /	examine
(pl. нóкти)		преглéдам	
нóмер (pl. номерá)	number, size	предлáгам /	proffer, propose
някак	somehow	предлóжа (-иш)	
някакъв	some sort	през	(distributive) see p. 151
някога	sometime	през сéдмица	every other week
някой	someone	прéсен, прясна	fresh
някъде	somewhere	прéча (-иш)	bother
		прибѝрам /	gather, collect
óбед (or обяд)	lunch	приберá	
обикновéн	usual	прибѝрам се /	arrive home
обѝрам / оберá	plunder, pick	приберá се	
онáзи	that (feminine)	притеснявам /	worry, cause concern to,
онéзи	those	притесня	embarrass
óнзи	that (masculine)	прогрáма	program
оновá	that (neuter)	проявявам /	appear, show
осемнáйсети	eighteenth	проявя	
óсми	eighth	проявявам интерéс	take an interest in
осóбено	especially	към	
остáвям / остáвя	leave	пѫт, -ят	way, path
от	than	(pl. пѫтища)	
отстѫпвам / отстѫпя	step back, yield, give up		
		раздáвам / раздáм	give out, distribute (conj. in L.9)
пáзя	guard, protect	разкáзвам /	relate, tell
пéти	fifth	разкáжа (-еш)	
писмó	letter	разпознáвам /	distinguish, discern
по пѫтя	along the way	разпознáя	
пó-хýбав	nicer, prettier (see L. 10)	разхóждам се / разхóдя се	walk around, take a walk
повярвам	believe, give credence	решáвам /	solve
подóбен	similar	решá (-иш)	
поéмам / поéма	take, take up	решáвам	do a crossword
поéмам [си] дѫх	catch one's breath	кръстослóвица	puzzle
пожелáвам /	wish	рѝлски	Rila (adj.)
пожелáя			

сéдми	seventh	успя́вам / успéя	succeed
си́н (си́ня, си́ньо)	blue		
слéдващ	next	фи́лм (*pl.* фи́лми)	film, movie
софи́йски	of Sofia *(adj.)*		
списáние	magazine	харти́я	paper
спóмням (си) /	recall	храня́	feed, nourish
спóмня (си)			
средновекóвие	Middle Ages	цáр, -я́т (*pl.* царé)	tsar, emperor
съжаля́вам / съжаля́	regret, be sorry		
сън (*pl.* съ́нища)	dream	чáкам с нетърпéние	await eagerly
сън, -я́т	sleep	четá до послéдната	read every last word
сърнá	deer, doe	бýква	
		четвъ́рти	fourth
твóй	your, yours *(singular)*	чи́й, чия́, чиé, чии́	whose
тéхен, тя́хна	their, theirs	чýжд	foreign, alien
ти́чам	run		
тóпка	ball	шéсти	sixth
трéти	third		
трети́рам	treat	щó	what
тури́ст	tourist		
		януáри	January
уморéн	tired		

Courtyard of Rila Monastery

167

CULTURAL COMMENTARY

Housing

Most people in larger cities live not in self-standing houses, but in apartment buildings. This is especially the case in the capital city, Sofia, which is surrounded by large complexes of apartment buildings. Each of these large units is called a **жилищен комплекс**, and has an overall name, such as "Nadezhda" (**Надежда**). Although there are streets among the buildings, addresses refer not to the streets but to the numbers of the buildings (which can be in the hundreds). Each building usually has several entrances which are labeled in alphabetical order (**А, Б, В, Г**, etc.), and many floors. The numbers of the apartments do not necessarily correspond to the floors, but since there are only two to three apartments on each floor (accessible from that entrance, that is), people usually give just the floor as part of the address. It is crucial, however, especially in the case of very large apartment buildings, to know the correct entrance.

School system: exams

Written quizzes and exams taken by students in school are called **контролни работи**. The term **изпит** "examination" refers only to qualifying examinations of the sort that determine one's future. One of these is the "matura" (**матура**), taken at the end of secondary schooling. Most Bulgarians, when they hear the word **изпит**, however, think of University entrance examinations. These examinations are extremely difficult and competitive; it is often said, only partly in jest, that the hardest part of university education is being admitted.

Food and drink: milk

Yogurt (**кисело мляко**) is such a staple of the Bulgarian diet that Bulgarians often add the adjective **прясно** "fresh" to describe what in western countries is simply "milk". Bulgarians always heat fresh milk before drinking it. Sometimes they let it cool first but more often they drink it hot; the general belief is that hot milk is very healthful.

Geography: Rila

One of the many picturesque mountain areas in Bulgaria is that called Rila (**Рила**), located to the south of Sofia. It is a favorite excursion spot for both locals and foreigners, not only for the mountain sports of hiking and fishing, but because of the Rila monastery (**Рилският манастир**) nestled among the mountains. The monastery was founded in the 11th century and has been destroyed and rebuilt many times since. One tower now remains from the 12th century, but the interest is the present structure, built in the 19th century on older models. This includes a large Byzantine-style church in the center of a courtyard, with monastery cells surrounding it on all sides. The whole monastery is colorfully painted and decorated. A hotel has been built outside the monastery walls, but it is sometimes possible to sleep in the monastery itself.

Geography: the Rhodopes

The Rhodope mountains are very rugged, and wild animals roam freely; hunting is a popular sport. Settlements in the Rhodopes are small; the central city, Smolyan (**Смолян**), is a recent creation. It consists of three large villages, each of which has retained its original character to a considerable extent. Two of these, Ustovo (**Устово**) and Raykovo (**Райково**), are now equivalent to suburbs. The central village, formerly called Pashmakli (**Пашмакли**), is now "city center". There are no direct train lines to Smolyan; one can only travel there by bus.

Geography: Plovdiv

Plovdiv (**Пловдив**, ancient Philipopolli) is the second largest city in Bulgaria. A number of fine Roman ruins are to be seen there, and the old city has been restored in 19th-century style. It is situated on the main road between Sofia and Istanbul, Turkey.

Travel: trains and buses

Long-distance travel in Bulgaria is accomplished by train and bus. The train lines are run by the state, but long-distance bus travel is now carried out by a number of private companies. Most towns are serviced by one or more bus lines.

168

LESSON 9

DIALOGUE

Слава Богу, вие сте тука!

// Владимир и Веселин вървят бързо по коридора. Като минават вагоните, Веселин ги брои: двайсет и трети, двайсет и втори, двайсет и първи, двайсети, деветнайсети... //

Веселин: Най-после дойдохме! Осемнайсети! Влез, Владимире, в нашето купе, и седни малко. Поне да изядеш едно кебапче и да изпиеш една ракия.

Камен: Ура! Кебапчетата пристигат! Кой са моите?

Веселин: Ето ги твоите, ето и за другите.

Таня: Вече започвам да се притеснявам. Слязохте и никакъв ви няма.

Джули: Слава Богу, вие сте тука. Не са важни кебапчетата, важното е, че не сте останали там в Шумен.

Камен: Как да не са важни кебапчетата!?

Милена: Кебапчетата не са достатъчно солени! Някой има ли сол?

Таня: Аз имах сол тука някъде... Не я виждам.

Надка: Мамо, Камен пипа солницата сутринта.

Камен: Аз само посолих пуканките и я оставих на място.

Таня: Ето я солта. Намерих я. В чантата е. Заповядайте, госпожо.

Камен: М-м-м. Много хубави кебапчета! Наядох се. Няма да ям до утре сутринта.

Таня: Няма ли да вечеряш довечера?

Камен: Може би. Ще видим.

Таня (на Веселин): Кебапчетата са наистина много вкусни. Благодаря ви!
    (на Владимир): И на нашия гост, за неговата помощ.

Веселин: Да, много ти благодаря, Владо. Ето, вземи моите кебапчета. Давам ти ги в знак на благодарност!

Владимир: Ти не си ли гладен?

Веселин: Няма значение. Важното е, както казва Джули, че не съм останал там в Шумен.

BASIC GRAMMAR

9.1. The verbs да́м and я́м

The verbs да́м "give", я́м "eat" (and all perfective verbs formed from them), are slightly irregular in the present tense. All forms but the 1st singular follow the e-conjugation. The stem is дад- and the accent is on the theme vowel. The 1st singular, by contrast, contains only the initial consonant plus [-ам] (д + ам › да́м, й + ам › я́м). The imperative forms are also irregular. Here are the full conjugations of these verbs:

	singular	plural	singular	plural
1st person	я́м	яд-е́м	да́м	дад-е́м
2nd person	яд-е́ш	яд-е́те	дад-е́ш	дад-е́те
3rd person	яд-е́	яд-а́т	дад-е́	дад-а́т
imperative	я́ж	я́ж-те	да́й	да́й-те

9.2. Aorist tense, continued

The aorist tense is formed by adding the aorist endings (learned in Lesson 6) to the aorist theme vowel. The aorist theme vowel for most и-conjugation verbs is -и-. For comparison, here are the present and aorist tense forms of the verbs хо́дя and броя́:

	PRESENT	AORIST	PRESENT	AORIST
1st singular	хо́д-я	хо́д-их	бро-я́	бро-и́х
2nd singular	хо́д-иш	хо́д-и	бро-и́ш	бро-и́
3rd singular	хо́д-и	хо́д-и	бро-и́	бро-и́
1st plural	хо́д-им	хо́д-ихме	бро-и́м	бро-и́хме
2nd plural	хо́д-ите	хо́д-ихте	бро-и́те	бро-и́хте
3rd plural	хо́д-ят	хо́д-иха	бро-я́т	бро-и́ха

For most и-conjugation verbs, therefore, and for all а-conjugation verbs, the present and aorist theme vowels are the same. This means that the 3rd singular forms are identical. However, context is usually sufficient to indicate which meaning is intended.

170

An important group of verbs forms the aorist with two different theme vowels: these verbs have -e- in the 2nd and 3rd singular, and -o- in other persons. Most of these verbs also have a different accent in the aorist from that of the present. As examples of this type, here are the present and aorist conjugations of четá and дáм.

	PRESENT	AORIST	PRESENT	AORIST
1st singular	чет-á	чéт-ох	дáм	дáд-ох
2nd singular	чет-éш	чéт-е	дад-éш	дáд-е
3rd singular	чет-é	чéт-е	дад-é	дáд-е
1st plural	чет-éм	чéт-охме	дад-éм	дáд-охме
2nd plural	чет-éте	чéт-охте	дад-éте	дáд-охте
3rd plural	чет-áт	чéт-оха	дад-áт	дáд-оха

All prefixed forms of these verbs form the aorist tense in exactly the same manner. The aorist forms of the verb ям are parallel to those of the verb дáм.

Two very important members of this group are the motion verbs дóйда and отúда. They are noteworthy because they have different accentual patterns. The accentuation of дóйда is the reverse of other verbs in this class: it has stem stress in the present and end stress in the aorist. The accent of отúда does not change from present to aorist. Here are the present and aorist conjugations of these two verbs:

	PRESENT	AORIST	PRESENT	AORIST
1st singular	дóйд-а	дойд-óх	отúд-а	отúд-ох
2nd singular	дóйд-еш	дойд-é	отúд-еш	отúд-е
3rd singular	дóйд-е	дойд-é	отúд-е	отúд-е
1st plural	дóйд-ем	дойд-óхме	отúд-ем	отúд-охме
2nd plural	дóйд-ете	дойд-óхте	отúд-ете	отúд-охте
3rd plural	дóйд-ат	дойд-óха	отúд-ат	отúд-оха

9.3. Feminine nouns in a consonant

Most nouns ending in a consonant are masculine (влáк, трамвáй, etc.), and most nouns ending in -a are feminine (кнúга, библиотéка, etc.). However, a certain number of nouns ending in a consonant are also feminine (сóл, нóщ, помóщ, éсен, прóлет, etc.). For these nouns, the "rhyming principle" does not work. The student must learn the fact of feminine gender when learning each of these nouns, and must remember that all adjectives, demonstrative pronouns, and articles which occur with them must be marked as feminine. For example:

Дай ми солта́, мо́ля.	Give me the salt, please
Благодаря́ за ва́шата по́мощ.	Thank you for your help.
Есента́ е зла́тна.	Autumn is golden.
През пролетта́ цветя́та цъфтя́т.	Flowers bloom in the spring.
Чета́ "Хиля́да и една́ нощ".	I'm reading "1001 Nights". *

(* The noun **нощ** appears in the singular here because the title is a fixed expression; normally the plural would occur after a complex number ending in 1.)

All feminine nouns take the definite article **-та**. Note that when added to a feminine noun ending in a consonant, this article is *always* accented, and that when added to a feminine noun ending in **-a** it is *never* accented.

9.4. Past active participles as adjectives

Past active participles are adjectives formed from verbs. They describe the state that results after the verbal action they refer to has taken place. For instance, the adjective **ми́нал** "last, past" is the past active participle of the verb **ми́на** "pass".

All Bulgarian verbs can form a participle indicating that an action has been carried out. This participle is used to form several compound verb tenses, which will be learned in later lessons. The focus in this lesson is on the use of the participle as a predicate adjective.

The endings of this participle are given below. It is often called the "L-participle" because its characteristic mark is the consonant **-л-**, which occurs immediately before the gender-marking endings.

masculine	*feminine*	*neuter*	*plural*
-л	-ла	-ло	-ли

When these participles modify nouns, they function exactly as adjectives (only certain of these participles can occur in this position). In this usage, they are usually definite. For example:

Ми́налата се́дмица бе́ше мно́го тру́дна.	Last week [= the past week] was a very difficult one.
Оста́налото я́дене ще сло́жа в хлади́лника.	I'll put the leftover food in the refrigerator.

A much more frequent use of these participles is as predicate adjectives. In this usage, they retain more of their verbal meaning. Examples:

Я́дене не е́ оста́нало.	There isn't any food left.
Ва́жното е, че не сте́ оста́нали в Шу́мен.	The important thing is that you didn't remain in Shumen.
Ва́жното е, че не съ́м оста́нал в Шу́мен.	What's important is that I didn't remain in Shumen.

The last two translations of the predicative participle **оста́нал** render it as a verbal tense. This is partly because of the meaning of the verb **оста́на**, and partly because the most common usage of the L-participle is indeed within the compound tense called the "past indefinite". Even within a verbal tense, however, the participle formally continues to function as an adjective: it takes the same endings all adjectives take, and follows the same agreement rules. In meaning, it is both adjectival and verbal. It is a verb because it describes a state which is the result of a verbal action; and it is an adjective because it applies that state to the description of a person or thing.

In the case of the above example, the state is that of "remaining in Shumen". Both speakers are describing a person by noting that the present state of "remaining in Shumen" does not apply to him. The participle form must agree with the subject of the sentence. When the speaker, a male, is referring to himself, the participle must have the masculine ending. When someone else refers to him with the polite form **ви́е**, however, the participle must have the plural ending.

The complete rules for forming the L-participle will be learned in Lesson 16, and the past indefinite tense will be studied in more detail in Lessons 16 and 21.

9.5. Word order of object pronouns

When a single verb occurs with two objects, one is a direct object and one is an indirect object. If both objects are expressed by pronouns, the indirect object pronoun must precede the direct object one. These two object pronouns must occur together, in this sequence, adjacent to the verb. Here are two examples:

Сега́ ти го да́вам.	Now I'm giving it to you.
Ще им ги да́вам.	I'll give them to them.

9.6. Time expressions: time of the day

Following are the names of the portions of the day, the adverbs locating an action within that time frame, and the greeting appropriate to that time of day. Upon taking leave of someone, one says **дови́ждане** during the day but **ле́ка но́щ** at night.

time period	adverb of time	greeting	(meaning)
сýтрин	сýтрин, сутринтá	добрó ýтро!	morning
обя́д	на обя́д	дóбър дéн!	noon
следóбед	след обя́д, следóбед	дóбър дéн!	afternoon
вéчер	вéчер, вечертá	* дóбър вéчер!	evening
нóщ	през нощтá	* дóбър вéчер!	night
полунóщ	в полунóщ		midnight

* Although the word **вéчер** is usually feminine, it is masculine in the fixed expression **дóбър вéчер**. Note the accent of **дóбър** in these fixed expressions.

Usually, the definite forms of **сýтрин** and **вéчер** refer to a particular morning or evening, and the indefinite forms refer to the general idea of morning or evening. But the definite forms can also be used with the general meaning. For example:

specific

Сутринтá и́мам срéща в 9 ч.　　I have an appointment at 9 this morning.

Вечертá ще оти́да да го ви́дя.　　I'll go see him this evening.

general

Сýтрин стáвам рáно, а вéчер лягам късно.　　I get up early and go to bed late.

Сутринтá оти́вам рáно на рáбота, а вечертá се прибúрам уморéн като кýче.　　I go to work early in the morning and come home at night tired as a dog.

The chart below gives the relative terms for the time of day, looking both forward and back from the vantage point of "today":

- 2 days	- 1 day	NOW	+ 1 day	+ 2 days
óнзи дéн	вчéра	днéс	ýтре	дрýги дéн
	вчéра сутринтá	сутринтá	ýтре сутринтá	
	вчéра следóбед	(днéс) следóбед	ýтре следóбед	
	снóщи	тáзи вéчер / * довéчера	ýтре вéчер	
	мúналата нóщ	тáзи нóщ	дрýгата нóщ	

* Be careful to distinguish the adverb **довéчера** "this evening", which refers to the forthcoming evening of the same day, from the prepositional phrase **до вечéря** "until/before supper". Note also that **довéчера** can be used only in an anticipatory sense. Once one is speaking in the present, one must use **тáзи вéчер** in the meaning "this evening".

9.7. Time expressions: days and months

Names for the days of the week are formed from several roots, although the "counting" principle is evident in several of them. Names of the months of the year are, as in English, derived from Latin.

Days of the week:

понеде́лник	Monday	четвъ́ртък	Thursday
вто́рник	Tuesday	пе́тък	Friday
сря́да	Wednesday	съ́бота	Saturday
		неде́ля	Sunday

The word for "week" is се́дмица.

Months of the year:

януа́ри	January	ю́ли	July
февруа́ри	February	а́вгуст	August
ма́рт	March	септе́мври	September
апри́л	April	окто́мври	October
ма́й	May	ное́мври	November
ю́ни	June	деке́мври	December

The word for "month" is ме́сец.

Days of the week are preceded either by the preposition **в** or by a modifier; and months of the year are preceded by the preposition **през**. When the date is given, the preposition **на** is used. For example:

Ха́йде да хо́дим на Ви́тоша в неде́ля.	Let's go to Vitosha on Sunday.
Хо́дим на Ви́тоша вся́ка неде́ля.	We go to Vitosha every Sunday.
Обикнове́но хо́дим на море́то през [ме́сец] а́вгуст.	We usually go to the seashore in [the month of] August.
Ще тръ́гнем на 15-и а́вгуст.	We'll leave on August 15.

N.B.: Neither the days of the week nor the months of the year are capitalized in Bulgarian!

9.8. Time expressions: seasons of the year

The four seasons (годи́шните времена́) are as follows:

про́лет	spring	е́сен	fall
ля́то	summer	зи́ма	winter

All four names of the seasons can be preceded by the preposition през, in which case they are used with the definite article. Про́лет and е́сен are feminine nouns, with definite forms пролетта́, есента́. With these two, the preposition на can also be used, in which case they are used in the indefinite form, and are written together with the preposition as one word. All four names can also appear without the preposition. In this case, е́сен and про́лет can be used either with or without the article, but ля́то and зи́ма must always be used with the article.

In theory, the definite forms refer to the season just ahead (or just past) and the indefinite forms refer to general time. In practice, however, they are used more or less interchangeably. For example:

(През) пролетта́ цветя́та цъфтя́т.	In spring, the flowers bloom.
Напро́лет съм ня́как по́-ве́сел.	For some reason, I'm happier in the spring.
(През) ля́тото ще хо́дим на море́то.	This summer, we'll go to the seaside.
Ля́тото ще бъ́дем та́м, а не́ ту́к.	In the summer we'll be there, not here.
Гро́здето зре́е (през) есента́.	Grapes ripen in the autumn.
На́есен деца́та ще запо́чнат учи́лище.	This autumn, the children will start school.
През зи́мата вре́мето ще е студе́но.	It will be cold this winter.
Зи́мата е студе́на.	It's cold in the winter.

9.9. Time expressions: years, and numbers beyond 100

To speak of the years in Bulgarian, one needs to form numbers in the hundreds and thousands. These numerals are:

100	сто́		600	ше́стстотин
200	две́ста		700	се́демстотин
300	три́ста		800	о́семстотин
400	че́тиристотин		900	де́ветстотин
500	пе́тстотин		1000	хиля́да

176

Years are referred to by ordinal numbers. The year 1975, for example, is reckoned as the one thousand nine hundred and seventy-*fifth* year. Note that only the final number takes the ordinal form. Thus:

хиля́да де́ветстотин седемдесе́т и пе́т-а годи́н-а   1975

Years are preceded by the preposition **през**. When years are written with numerals, the abbreviation **г.** (for **годи́на**) follows. Sometimes the **-a** of the ordinal is added after the numeral, and sometimes it is omitted.

през 1975 г.	in 1975
през 1975-а г.	*(same)*

9.10.   Time expressions: "next" and "last"

To refer to time periods just past or just ahead, Bulgarians use the words **сле́дващ** "next" or **ми́нал** "last". Both are participial forms functioning as adjectives; they must therefore agree with the nouns they modify. If the time period they refer to functions as the subject of the sentence, masculine forms will have the subject ending. Usually, however, they are used in adverbial phrases, and masculine forms will therefore have the object ending. The definite form is almost always used.

subject usage, subject case

Ми́налият ме́сец бе́ше мно́го студе́н, а преди́шният не то́лкова.	Last month was very cold, but the month before not so much.

adverbial usage, object case

Сле́дващата се́дмица ще хо́дим та́м.	We'll go there next week.
То́й бе́ше във Ва́рна ми́налия ме́сец.	He was in Varna last month.

If the preceding or coming time periods are not the ones that are immediately past or ahead, respectively, the modifiers **преди́шен** "previous" or **предстоя́щ** "forthcoming" are used.

9.11.   Conjunctions: като vs. както

The conjunctions **като** and **ка́кто** are both translated roughly "as". The difference in meaning is that **като** refers to simultaneous actions, while **ка́кто** expresses a relationship of similarity. The conjunction **като** also means "when".

177

Като минáва вагóните, Веселúн ги брой.	As he passes through the cars, Veselin counts them.
Вáжното е, кáкто Джýли кáзва, че не съм остáнал в Шýмен.	The important thing is that, as Julie says, I didn't remain in Shumen.
Тóй закъснява кáкто вúнаги. Пáк ще изпýсне влáка!	He's late, as always. He's going to miss the train again!

Another difference between them is that като can also function as a preposition with a noun object following, whereas кáкто can only be followed by a full phrase containing a verb.

9.12. Prepositions

A number of prepositions have idiomatic meanings when they function as a part of time expressions. Here is a review of the commonest of these:

в	недéля	on Sunday
на	15(-и) áвгуст	on August 15th
през	áвгуст	in August
през	ля́тото	during the summer
през	1975 г.	in 1975
през	деня́	during the day
през	нощтá	at night
по	обя́д	around noon

178

EXERCISES

I. Rewrite the following sentences in the past tense, changing any adverbs of time to вче́ра, *and changing the aspect as necessary.*

1. Следо́бед науча́ваме но́вите ду́ми.
2. На́дка разда́ва на пъ́тниците по една́ рису́нка.
3. Ку́чето ска́ча на легло́то.
4. Ви́е дне́с получа́вате о́тговор на писмо́то.
5. Деца́та са гла́дни и затова́ проявя́ват нетърпе́ние.
6. Пъ́тниците сли́зат еди́н след дру́г от вла́ка.
7. Сутринта́ съм свобо́дна и оти́вам на ки́но.

II. Rewrite the following sentences, changing plural to singular.

1. Прека́рахме прия́тни ве́чери с мо́ите прия́тели.
2. В хоте́лите и́ма свобо́дни ста́и.
3. То́пло е. Отвори́ врати́те и прозо́рците!
4. Прия́телките на Та́ня зна́ят и дру́ги ху́бави пе́сни.
5. Дне́с учени́чките и учени́ците ще полу́чат коле́ти.
6. Те́нджерите, ча́йниците и лъжи́ците са на ма́сите.
7. В те́зи кварта́ли и́ма бо́лници.
8. През ю́ни нощи́те са кра́тки, а дни́те са дъ́лги.

III. Rewrite the following sentences, changing all underlined nouns to the appropriate pronouns.

1. Нали́ си добро́ момче́, Ка́мене, отстъпи́ <u>папага́ла</u> <u>на На́дка</u>.
2. На Но́ва годи́на роди́телите разда́ват <u>на деца́та</u> <u>пода́ръци</u>.
3. Дими́тър и Миле́на но́сят <u>на свекъ́рвата</u> <u>сни́мки</u>.
4. Де́йвид предла́га <u>ве́стника</u> <u>на Джу́ли</u>.
5. Бо́йко подна́ся <u>кафе́то</u> <u>на го́стите</u>.
6. Ня́ма ли да пока́жете <u>на Бо́б</u> <u>къ́щата</u>?
7. А́нгел съобща́ва <u>на Де́йвид</u> <u>новини́те</u>.

ADDITIONAL GRAMMAR NOTES

9.2a. Aorist tense, continued

Optional stress shifts in the aorist

All verbs whose aorist theme vowel is the same as the present theme vowel have identical forms in the 3rd singular present and 3rd singular aorist. Some speakers of Bulgarian will shift the stress to the theme vowel in the aorist form to emphasize the fact that the form means "past" and not "present". This stress shift is acceptable only in non-prefixed forms. The possible forms, therefore, are:

	present	simple aorist		prefixed aorist
1st singular	хо́д-я	хо́д-их	or ход-и́х	разхо́д-их се
3rd singular	хо́д-и	хо́д-и	or ход-и́	разхо́д-и се

Many speakers do not shift stress at all, and those who do will usually vacillate between stem stress and end stress in the aorist forms.

This stress shift is possible with all non-prefixed verbs which have the aorist theme vowel -и- or -а- (thus it applies also to certain of the aorist forms to be learned in subsequent lessons). However, none of the sentences, dialogues and reading selections in this textbook will exemplify this optional accentuation.

Aorist in -ox, continued

Verbs which form the aorist in -ox all belong to the e-conjugation. Their 1st singular present forms (the dictionary form) end in a consonant preceded by -a. With a very few exceptions (which will be noted below), they all have end stress in the present. This fact can obscure the presence of an alternating stem vowel. since the -я- alternant appears only when the vowel is accented. Certain verbs of this group, therefore, have the stem vowel -e- throughout the present tense, but an alternating vowel in the aorist. The verbs сека́ and облека́ are given as examples; the verb съблека́ is conjugated according to the same format.

	PRESENT	AORIST	PRESENT	AORIST
1st singular	сек-а́	ся́к-ох	облек-а́	обля́к-ох
2nd singular	сеч-е́ш	се́ч-е	облеч-е́ш	обле́ч-е
3rd singular	сеч-е́	се́ч-е	облеч-е́	обле́ч-е
1st plural	сеч-е́м	ся́к-охме	облеч-е́м	обля́к-охме
2nd plural	сеч-е́те	ся́к-охте	облеч-е́те	обля́к-охте
3rd plural	сек-а́т	ся́к-оха	облек-а́т	обля́к-оха

Note the shift of the stem-final -к in these verbs to -ч whenever the theme vowel (either present or aorist) is -е. Note also that not every verb of this class with stem-final -к has an alternating vowel. The aorist tense of тека́, for instance, is те́кох.

The motion verb оти́да is one of the few verbs within this class with no shifting stress. The other three are also motion verbs: вля́за, сля́за, and изля́за. Thus, the aorist of вля́за is вля́зох. The 3rd singular forms of these verbs are alike in present and aorist: both are вле́зе. There is no optional stress shift to the end in the aorist forms of this group.

9.3a. Feminine nouns in a consonant

Because these nouns end in a consonant, there is always a sequence of [consonant + т] in the definite form. If this sequence contains [т + т], *both* consonants are pronounced. This is done by lengthening the "t" sound.

It is not always possible to know which nouns ending in a consonant will be feminine; most must be learned. Because all nouns ending in the suffix -ост are feminine, their gender is predictable and they have no need of special marking. Other feminine nouns ending in a consonant will be marked as feminine in glossary listings, in the following manner:

> ве́чер, -та́

9.5a. Word order of object pronouns

If a verb takes two objects and both are pronouns, the indirect object must precede the direct one. This sequence *(IND-DIR)* obeys all the word order rules learned earlier:

-- it *cannot* begin a sentence
-- it *must* occur directly adjacent to the verb
-- if ли is present, it must *follow* this particle
-- if ще, да or не is present, it must be placed *between* this particle and the verb

Examples are given on the next page, with the numbering cumulative across lessons. The rules are straightforward, but it will take a great deal of practice before their implementation feels natural. Because unaccented words are pronounced together with the following (or preceding) word, they are harder to decipher when heard, and harder to produce quickly if one must plan one's sentence consciously. The more unaccented words there are strung together, the more concerted attention it is necessary to pay.

(34)

Да́вам	ти	ги.
verb	*IND*	*DIR*

I give them to you.

(35)

Сега́

ти	ги	да́вам.
IND	*DIR*	*verb*

Now I'm giving them to you.

(36)

Да́ваш	ли	ми	ги?
verb	*INT*	*IND*	*DIR*

Are you giving them to me?

(37)

Не	ти	ги	да́вам.
Neg.	*IND*	*DIR*	*verb*

I'm not giving them to you.

(38)

Ще	ти	ги	даде́	ли?
Fut.	*IND*	*DIR*	*verb*	*INT*

Will he give them to you?

(39)

Ня́ма	да	ти	ги	даде́.
neg	*Cnj.*	*IND*	*DIR*	*verb*

He won't give them to you.

9.6a. Time expressions: periods of the day

There is a relatively close fit between English and Bulgarian as concerns words for the periods of the day. Several non-correspondences should be noted, however. First, Bulgarians use **су́трин** to refer to the earlier part of the morning, usually until about 9:00 or (at the latest) 10:00. The period between that and 12:00 noon is usually called **преди́ обя́д**.

The corresponding expression, **след обя́д**, can mean either the early afternoon, or the entire afternoon. For the idea "noon", Bulgarians invariably say **обя́д**, but for the idea "midnight" they can say either **полуно́щ** or **12 часа́ през нощта́**. Finally, the early hours of the morning when one is still usually asleep can also be referred to as part of the night.

в че́тири часа́ през нощта́   at 4 in the morning
в че́тири часа́ сутринта́   *[same]*

Second, the words for "noon" and "evening" are similar to the words for the meals eaten at those times:

time of day	**обя́д**	noon	**ве́чер**	evening
meal	**о́бед**	lunch	**вече́ря**	supper

The word **обя́д** is used with both meanings, but the word **о́бед** means only "lunch".

Adjectives referring to times of the day are in general derived directly from the word for that time by addition of the suffix -ен. In a few cases, the stem contains the suffix -ш-, and, in one instance, the stem is different.

time of day	stem	+ ен ›	adjective
с-у́трин	утрин-	+ ен- ›	у́тринен, у́тринна
обя́д	обед-	+ ен- ›	о́беден, о́бедна
следо́бед	следобед-	+ ен- ›	следо́беден, следо́бедна
ве́чер	вечер-	+ ен- ›	вече́рен, вече́рна
но́щ	нощ-	+ ен- ›	но́щен, но́щна
дне́с	днеш-	+ ен- ›	дне́шен, дне́шна
вче́ра	вчера-ш	+ ен- ›	вче́рашен, вче́рашна
у́тре	утре-ш-	+ ен- ›	у́трешен, у́трешна
сно́щи	снощ-	+ ен- ›	сно́щен, сно́щна

These adjectives are used frequently in phrases such as **дне́шен де́н** "today", **о́бедно вре́ме** "noontime", **но́щно вре́ме** "nighttime", and the like.

Similar adjectives are formed from the adverb **сега́** and the future form **бъ́де**: these mean "present" and "future", respectively. They are used to refer to time periods in general and to two of the verbal tenses already learned (the names of other verbal tenses will be learned later):

сега́шно вре́ме	present tense
бъ́деще вре́ме	future tense

9.7a. Time expressions: days of the week

Calendars in Bulgaria begin the week with Monday (as opposed to most countries in the West, where they begin with Sunday). The fact that Monday is the first day of the week can be seen from the names for Tuesday (**вто́рник**), Thursday (**четвъ́ртък**) and Friday (**пе́тък**), which contain the stems of the words 2nd, 4th and 5th, respectively. The fact that Wednesday (**сря́да**) is considered the middle day of the week can seen from its name, which is a variant form the word **среда́** "middle".

The names for the other three days have a different origin. The word for Saturday (**съ́бота**) comes from the word "sabbath"; and the word for Sunday (**неде́ля**) comes from an old Slavic word meaning "no-work". The name for Monday (**понеде́лник**) means simply "that which comes after Sunday". Finally, the word for "week" (**се́дмица**) contains the number 7, corresponding to the seven days of the week.

9.10a. Adverbs with time expressions

The conventions "B.C." and "A.D." are expressed in two different ways. The cutoff point (the birth of Christ) is expressed either as **но́вата е́ра** "the new era" or **Рождество́ Христо́во** "the birth of Christ". The phrases are:

преди́ н.е.	*or*	преди́ Р.Хр.	B.C.
от н.е.	*or*	след Р.Хр.	A.D.

Although the phrase **сле́дващата годи́на** "next year" exists, the adverb **догоди́на** is used much more frequently in this meaning.

To focus on the length and duration of a period of time, the modifier **цял/це́ли** "entire, all" is used. It is sometimes used with the preposition **през,** but more frequently it occurs without a preposition. Like all adjectives, this modifier has both definite and indefinite forms. In theory, definite forms refer to a particular time period and indefinite ones to generalized situations.

In the case of **цял,** however (as in the case of the seasons), this distinction is being lost. Today Bulgarians use both forms in both meanings (to refer to a particular time period, or to state a general observation). Context is usually sufficient to tell which is meant.

Дне́с цял / це́лия де́н ще чета́, а вечерта́ ще изведа́ ку́чето на разхо́дка.	I'll read all day long, and in the evening walk the dog.
Ця́ла / ця́лата су́трин го ня́ма.	He hasn't showed up the entire morning.
Ця́ла / ця́лата ве́чер ще слу́шаме му́зика.	We'll listen to music the whole evening.

If the preposition **по** is present, only the indefinite form of **цял** can be used. Conversely, if duration is expressed with the preposition **през,** only the definite form (either of **цял** or of a noun) can be used. For example:

По цял де́н прика́зва по телефо́на.	She talks on the phone all day. [= a whole day at a time]
Ня́кои ча́кат по це́ли се́дмици.	Some people [have to] wait for weeks [at a time].
През це́лия де́н ще съм зае́т.	I'll be busy the whole day.
Следи́ го през ця́лото вре́ме какво́ пра́ви.	She watches what he's doing the whole time.
Ще бъ́дем та́м през це́лия ме́сец.	We'll be there the whole month.
Рабо́тя през деня́, а спя́ през нощта́.	I work in the daytime and sleep at night.

9.13. Subject inversion

The normal word order in Bulgarian, as in English, is "subject - predicate":

The kebabs	aren't important.
Кеба́пчетата	**не са́ ва́жни.**
subject	*(negated) predicate*

English, in fact, must obey this word order rule. Only with certain sentences can one reverse the order of subject and predicate. Furthermore, in order to do so, one must usually reformulate the sentence considerably, often changing its meaning somewhat. Consider the sentences above, in which "the kebabs" is the subject, and "aren't important" is the predicate. Here are two ways one can invert the order of subject and predicate in this sentence in English. Note that each makes fairly complex changes in word order, and that the second sentence even splits the old predicate into two different clauses:

What's	important is	not	the kebabs.	
	(old predicate,	*negated)*	*old subject*	

It's	not	the kebabs	that	are important.
	(negation)	*old subject*	*subordinating conjunction*	*old predicate*

Bulgarian, however, can reverse the order of subject and predicate of any sentence, and can do so without making any other changes in the sentence. This process is called "subject inversion" because the placement of the subject is inverted with respect to the normal word order. The effect of this shift is to focus more attention on the subject. The first of the sentences given below is neutral. The second suggests that while the kebabs themselves aren't important, perhaps something else is.

Кеба́пчетата	**не са́ ва́жни.**	The kebabs aren't important.
subject	*predicate*	

Не са́ ва́жни	**кеба́пчетата.**	The kebabs aren't important...
predicate	*subject*	

SAMPLE SENTENCES

1. -- Мо́ля, да́й ми ръкави́ците.
   -- Ня́ма да ти ги да́м. Те́ са мръ́сни.

2. -- Вода́та в ча́йника ври́. И́скаш ли ча́й?
   -- Да́, донеси́ ми го в ста́ята.

3. Търго́вецът купу́ва сто́ката на е́дро. Прода́вам му я е́втино.

4. Къ́сно е. Фи́лмът по телеви́зията ве́че е ми́нал.

5. А́нгел не е́ ту́к. Зами́нал е за Ва́рна.

6. Ле́гнал е да спи́. И́зпитът е свъ́ршил.

7. Слъ́нцето гре́е през деня́, а луна́та през нощта́.

8. Ще те ви́дя през дру́гата се́дмица.

9. През сле́дващата годи́на то́й ще у́чи бъ́лгарски.

10. Ця́л де́н спя́, защо́то рабо́тя ця́ла но́щ.

11. Ве́чер не е́ мно́го работоспосо́бен. Ве́чер гле́даме телеви́зия.

12. По о́бед магази́ните са затво́рени. Ще позвъни́м по телефо́на на о́бед.
    Ба́бата спи́ следо́бед.

13. През зи́мата слъ́нцето заля́зва ра́но следо́бед, а през ля́тото -- къ́сно ве́чер.

14. Дове́чера ще слу́шаме му́зика. У́тре сутринта́ замина́ваме.

15. Ве́че е о́бедно вре́ме, а мо́ят о́бед о́ще не е́ гото́в.

16. Мно́го тру́дно наме́рихме добра́ учи́телка по английски за дете́то.

17. Ко́й ви да́де адре́са на то́зи ле́кар?

18. Ка́мен сутринта́ изя́де две́ я́бълки, три́ са́ндвича с кашкава́л и еди́н
    сладоле́д. И сега́ па́к е гла́ден. Стра́шен апети́т и́ма това́ дете́.

SENTENCES FOR TRANSLATION

1. All the knives, forks and spoons are in the cupboard. Will you give them to me? And where is the salt? Please give it to me also.

2. Marina has classes in the morning from 9 to 12. At noon she goes home for lunch. In the afternoon she works in the library from 2 to 4, and then she listens to music until dinnertime. In the evening after dinner she studies several more hours. Then she says "Good night" to everyone and goes to bed.

3. Has Ivo left? There's no sign of him anywhere. Last Friday he was here, but apparently this week he is traveling.

4. My birthday is next Tuesday. When is your birthday? I prefer to have a birthday in the fall. And you?

5. We came at 2:00 and went into the library. The girl there gave us each a book, and we read the books for two hours. We waited one more hour, and finally we left the library and went to the movies.

6. Julie got off the train, walked around the station a bit, and then got on again. She counted all the cars of the train, and then she counted them again.

7. She received his letter on July 5th, 1983, and read it during the night. The next day everyone asked her what was in the letter. "Nothing," she answered. His second letter came on August 31st of the following year. She also read it during the night, but on the next day, September 1st, 1984, no one asked her what was in the letter. Apparently everyone had forgotten. "I can give it to them," she thought. "Then they will remember." But she didn't give it to anyone.

8. 1968 was a very important year. Many people remember it very well.

9. Yesterday Marin bought 235 pencils and 547 notebooks. Apparently he wants to become a wholesale merchant. Will he sell them to us cheap?

10. "Don't eat all the fruits at once, please. Oh, did you eat them already?" "Yes, we certainly ate our fill."

READING SELECTION

Кореспонде́нция - (7)

---

14 ное́мври, Сан Франци́ско

Здраве́й Бо́йко,

Пи́таш какво́ ни интересу́ва. С една́ ду́ма о́тговорът е ле́сен: вси́чко. Това́ ще е пъ́рвото пъту́ване на деца́та в Евро́па. Го́твим се за не́го с вси́чки си́ли. Патри́ша прочете́ ве́че мно́го кни́ги за Евро́па. И́скаме деца́та да запо́мнят това́ пъту́ване.

Патри́ша мно́го оби́ча и ста́ра, и но́ва архитекту́ра. Мо́же да стой с часове́ в ня́коя баро́кова цъ́рква. В после́дно вре́ме архитекту́рата интересу́ва и Е́мили, но засега́ я привли́ча преди́мно европе́йското средновеко́вие. Подари́хме ѝ ня́колко албу́ма, но тя́ предпочи́та да пъту́ва, а не́ да чете́. Гла́вно я интересу́ват оба́че живо́тните. Ни́кой не ги оби́ча по́вече от Е́мили. Тя́ и́ма костену́рка и ха́мстер. Не зна́я кой ще ги гле́да, дока́то сме в Бълга́рия.

На́шите синове́ и́мат о́бщи спо́ртни интере́си. Ма́йкъл, ка́кто и И́во, плу́ва, лови́ ри́ба. Ми́налата неде́ля хо́дихме два́мата за ри́ба. А́з оби́чам да хо́дя пеша́, за да си почи́вам от ра́ботата в бо́лницата. Че́сто изли́заме на разхо́дка.

Ча́кам с нетърпе́ние тво́ите предложе́ния. По́здрави вкъ́щи,

Ро́берт

---

25 ное́мври, Со́фия

Дра́ги Бо́б,

Ра́двам се да полу́ча то́лкова бъ́рзо о́тговор. Това́ е тво́ето четвъ́рто писмо́. Ви́ждам голя́м напре́дък в тво́я бъ́лгарски ези́к. Да́дох писмо́то на мо́ите прия́тели да го ви́дят. Ни́кой не мо́же да повя́рва, че у́чиш бъ́лгарски без учи́тел.

В Бълга́рия иде́те да ви́дите Ри́лския манасти́р, сре́дище на бъ́лгарската средновеко́вна култу́ра. То́й е висо́ко в Ри́ла, на два́ ча́са пъ́т с кола́ от Со́фия. Това́ е мъ́жки манасти́р. А́з и́мам прия́тели та́м и мо́га да уредя́ да спи́м в манасти́ра, а не́ в хоте́ла. Си́гурно ще е интере́сно да ви́дите отвъ́тре живо́та на и́стински правосла́вен манасти́р. От манасти́ра мо́жете да пра́вите и́злети нао́коло. Вода́та в ри́лските реки́ е чи́ста и мно́го студе́на. Пъстъ́рвата така́ва вода́ оби́ча. На Ри́ла Ма́йк ще мо́же да хва́не и́стинска пъстъ́рва. Ри́лският манасти́р и́ма интере́сна византи́йска архитекту́ра.

И́во пра́ща специа́лни по́здрави на Е́мили. То́й се ра́два, че тя́ оби́ча живо́тните, и мно́го и́ска да ѝ пока́же на́шия тарале́ж. Тарале́жът живе́е под легло́то на И́во и пла́ши Я́на.

Вси́чко ху́баво,

Бо́йко

GLOSSARY

адре́с	address	дру́ги де́н	the day after tomorrow
албу́м	album, picture-book		
апети́т	appetite	е́втин	cheap, inexpensive
апри́л	April	е́дър	large
		е́ра	era
баро́ков	baroque (adj.)	е́сен, -та́	fall, autumn
благода́рност	thanks, thankfulness		
бо́г	god, God	живо́т	life
Бо́же	Oh God, Oh my God		
бъ́дещ	future (adj.)	заля́звам / заля́за	set [of the sun]
бъ́деще вре́ме	future tense	замина́вам /	leave, depart
		зами́на	
ве́сел	happy, gay, lively	запо́мням /	remember
ве́чер, -та́	evening	запо́мня	
ве́чер, вечерта́	in the evening	засега́	at present, for now
вече́рен	evening (adj.)	зи́ма	winter
вече́рям	eat dinner	зла́тен	golden
вре́ме (pl. времена́)	verbal tense	зна́к	sign
вря́	boil (intransitive)	значе́ние	meaning
вто́рник	Tuesday	зре́я	ripen
вче́ра	yesterday		
вче́ра следо́бед	yesterday afternoon	изве́ждам / изведа́	take out, lead away
вче́ра сутринта́	yesterday morning	изве́ждам ку́чето	walk the dog
вче́рашен	yesterday's	на разхо́дка	
		изя́ждам /	eat up
гла́вен	main, chief	изя́м (-яде́ш)	
гла́вно	mainly		
гле́дам	look after	ка́кто	as
годи́шен	yearly, annual	кварта́л	district, living area
годи́шните времена́	seasons [of the year]	костену́рка	turtle
го́твя се	prepare, get ready	кра́тък	short
гре́я	warm, heat [up]	култу́ра	culture
гро́зде	grapes (collective)		
		ле́к	light, easy
да́вам / да́м (даде́ш)	give	ле́ка но́щ	good night
две́ста	two hundred	ловя́	catch
де́ветстотин	nine hundred	ловя́ ри́ба	fish, catch fish
деке́мври	December	луна́	moon
Де́н на	Thanksgiving Day	ля́то (pl. лета́)	summer
благодарността́			
дне́шен	today's	ма́й	May
дне́шен де́н	this very day	ме́сец	month
добро́ у́тро	good morning	ми́нал	past
до́бър ве́чер	good evening	мо́же би	maybe
	(fixed accent)	мръ́сен	dirty
дове́чера	this evening		
дока́то	while, until	н.е. = но́вата е́ра	(see p. 184)

189

на е́дро	wholesale	през нощта́	at night
нае́сен	in the fall	през 1975 г.	during 1975
нао́коло	around, round about	привли́чам /	attract, draw
напре́дък	progress, gain	привлека́ (-че́ш)	
напро́лет	in the spring	прика́звам	talk, converse
науча́вам /	learn	прия́тен	pleasant
науча́ (-иш)		про́лет, -та́	spring
на́яждам се /	eat one's fill,	пу́канка (sg. rare)	[piece of] popcorn
ная́м се (-яде́ш се)	gorge on	пъстъ́рва	trout
ное́мври	November		
но́щ, -та́	night	работоспосо́бен	efficient, productive
но́щен	night (adj.)	Р.Хр. = Рождество́ Христо́во	
но́щно вре́ме	nighttime	разхо́дка	walk, stroll
ня́ма значе́ние	it doesn't matter	ра́но	early
		река́	river
о́беден	lunch, noon (adj.)	ри́ба	fish
о́бедно вре́ме	lunchtime	роди́тел	parent
обя́д	lunch, noon	рождество́	Christmas
о́нзи де́н	day before yesterday	ръкави́ца	glove
о́семстотин	eight hundred		
оста́нало	remaining, left, left-over	с вси́чки си́ли	with all one's strength, full tilt
от н.е.	A.D.	с една́ ду́ма	in a word
от Р.Хр.	A.D.	с часове́	for hours [on end]
отвъ́тре	from within	са́ндвич	sandwich
		свекъ́рва	mother-in-law (of wife)
па́к	again	сега́шен	present-day, current
папага́л	parrot	сега́шно вре́ме	present tense
пе́сен, -та́	song	се́демстотин	seven hundred
(pl. пе́сни)		сека́ (-че́ш)	cut
пе́тстотин	five hundred	си́гурно	surely, certainly
пе́тък	Friday	си́н, -ъ́т	son
пеша́	on foot	(pl. синове́)	
пи́пам	touch, handle	ска́чам /	jump
пла́ша (-иш)	frighten	ско́ча (-иш)	
плу́вам	swim	сла́ва	glory
подаря́вам / подаря́	give (away), give a present	сла́ва Бо́гу	thank God
		след обя́д	afternoon, after lunch
позвъня́вам /	call	след Р.Хр.	A.D.
позвъня́		следо́беден	afternoon (adj.)
полуно́щ	midnight	слъ́нце	sun
по́мощ, -та́	help	слъ́нцето гре́е	the sun is shining
поне́	at least	сно́щен	last night's
понеде́лник	Monday	сно́щи	yesterday evening, last night
посоля́вам / посоля́	salt		
преди́ н.е.	B.C.	со́л, -та́	salt
преди́ Р.Хр.	B.C.	соле́н	salted
преди́мно	primarily	солни́ца	salt shaker
преди́шен	previous	специа́лен	special
предложе́ние	proposition, suggestion	спо́ртен	sports (adj.)
		сре́дище	center
предсто́ящ	forthcoming, impending	средновеко́вен	medieval
		сре́ща	meeting, appointment
през деня́	in the daytime	сря́да	Wednesday

ста́я	room	ха́мстер	hamster
сто́ка	goods, commodity	хва́щам / хва́на	grasp, seize, catch
стра́шен	terrible, fearful	хиля́да (*pl.* хи́ляди)	thousand
су́трин, -та́	morning	хо́дя за ри́ба	go fishing
су́трин, сутринта́	in the morning	хо́дя пеша́	go for a walk, walk [not ride]
та́зи ве́чер	this evening	хоте́л	hotel
та́зи но́щ	tonight	Христо́в	Christ's
тарале́ж	hedgehog		
тека́ (-че́ш)	flow	цъфтя́	bloom
три́ста	three hundred		
търго́вец	merchant	четвъ́ртък	Thursday
		че́тиристотин	four hundred
уре́ждам / уредя́	arrange, settle		
у́тре ве́чер	tomorrow evening	ше́стстотин	six hundred
у́тре сутринта́	tomorrow morning		
у́трешен	tomorrow's	ю́ни	June
у́тринен	morning *(adj.)*		
у́тро	morning	я́дене	food, meal
		я́м, яде́ш	eat
февруа́ри	February		

CULTURAL COMMENTARY

School systems: first day of school

School in Bulgaria always begins on September 15th. Children who begin first grade on that date are honored with small gifts.

Religion

Bulgarians belong to the Eastern Orthodox church, called in Bulgarian правосла́вна цъ́рква. During the Ottoman occupation, the church was administered from Constantinople by the Greek bishopric. The independent Bulgarian exarchate was established in 1870-71. Many Bulgarians today are practicing Orthodox Christians, and the cultural heritage of Orthodoxy has been very important in Bulgarian history.

Although it was technically possible to practice religion openly during the socialist regime, it was extremely difficult to do so without surrendering the possibility of social or professional advancement. Christmas was not celebrated, and the main winter holiday was New Year's. Christmas is now celebrated once more, but it has become a habit for many to think of the general holiday period as "New Year's."

LESSON 10

DIALOGUE

<u>А ви́е же́нен ли сте?</u>

Ангел: А́з съвсе́м забра́вих, че и́мам дома́ти в ча́нтата. От на́шата гради́на. Мно́го вървя́т с кеба́пчетата. Заповя́дайте!

// Вси́чки взи́мат по еди́н дома́т и благодаря́т. //

Ангел: Вземе́те о́ще. Страхо́тни дома́ти, а Де́йвид?

Дейвид: Да́, арома́тни са.

Ангел: Вземе́те, де! Вземе́те о́ще по еди́н. А́з и́мам мно́го.

Джули: Взе́х еди́н, сти́га то́лкова. Благодаря́!

Надка: Ма́мо, Ка́мен взе́ вто́ри дома́т!

Ангел: Бра́во, мо́ето момче́, ра́двам се, че ти е по вкуса́.

Владимир: Мно́го вку́сно. Благодаря́ ви мно́го за вси́чко! А сега́ да си вървя́. Бра́т ми си́гурно се чу́ди къде́ изче́знах.

Веселин: А, зна́чи, Гео́рги ти е бра́т. Ви́ждам, че прили́ча на те́бе. То́й по́-голя́м ли е от те́бе, или по́-ма́лък?

Владимир: По́-голя́м е. С пе́т годи́ни. То́й е же́нен, и́ма ве́че две́ деца́.

Камен: Като ме́не и На́дка, нали́? Едно́ момче́ и едно́ моми́че?

Владимир: Да́, то́чно. Са́мо че те́хните са по́-ма́лки от ва́с.

Камен: Кое́ е по́-голя́мо? Момче́то ли?

Владимир: Да́. Синъ́т им ста́на на че́тири годи́ни, а дъщеря́ им е на две́.

Камен: Чи́чо, ти́ че́сто ли хо́диш у тя́х? Кажи́ ни за тя́х! Момче́то и́ма ли си ста́я?

Таня: Ка́мене, мълчи́. Пусни́ чове́ка да си тръ́гне. Ня́ма ну́жда вси́чко да зна́еш.

Владимир (на Таня): Оставе́те го да пи́та, не се́ притесня́вайте. А́з не бъ́рзам.

(на Камен): Пле́менниците ми живе́ят в една́ ста́я с роди́телите си. Но тя́хната ста́я е голя́ма и све́тла. Деца́та ня́мат своя́ ста́я.

Камен: Та́тко не ни́ да́ва да и́маме отде́лни ста́и. То́й и́ма кабине́т, но ни́кога не си́ е вкъ́щи. Не разби́рам защо́ не мо́га да спя́ в не́говия кабине́т. Кабине́тът му е голя́м и све́тъл.

Таня(на Камен): Ка́мене, нали́ чу́ какво́ ти ка́зах? Сти́га то́лкова!

(на Владимир): Мъжъ́т ми рабо́ти извъ́н Со́фия, и че́сто пъту́ва. Вя́рно е, че ря́дко го ви́ждаме.

Веселин: И а́з постоя́нно пъту́вам. Ми́налия ме́сец пропу́снах свето́вното пъ́рвенство по фу́тбол покрай те́зи пу́сти командиро́вки. Все́ ме ня́ма вкъ́щи.

Дейвид: А ви́е же́нен ли сте?

Theater, downtown Varna

BASIC GRAMMAR

10.1. Aorist tense, continued

Verbs of the **e**-conjugation form the aorist tense according to several different types. Those verbs whose stem ends in the consonant -**н**-, such as **стáн-а**, **срéщн-а** or **вързн-а**, all take the aorist theme vowel -**а**-. Verbs whose stems end in -**ш** or -**ж** also take the aorist theme vowel -**а**-. Before this theme vowel, these stem-final consonants appear as -**с** and -**з**, respectively. Here are the present and aorist conjugations of these two types. Representing the first is the aorist of **стáна**, and representing the second is the aorist of **пúша**.

	PRESENT	AORIST	PRESENT	AORIST
1st singular	стáн-а	стáн-ах	пúш-а	пúс-ах
2nd singular	стáн-еш	стáн-а	пúш-еш	пúс-а
3rd singular	стáн-е	стáн-а	пúш-е	пúс-а
1st plural	стáн-ем	стáн-ахме	пúш-ем	пúс-ахме
2nd plural	стáн-ете	стáн-ахте	пúш-ете	пúс-ахте
3rd plural	стáн-ат	стáн-аха	пúш-ат	пúс-аха

The second type (**пúша**, aorist **пúсах**) also includes **кáжа** (aorist **кáзах**). These are the verbs which have been identified in glossary lists according to the format

пúша (-еш)

in order to differentiate them from verbs whose stems also end in -**ш** or -**ж** but which belong to the **и**-conjugation, and are identified in glossary lists according to the format

пýша (-иш).

Note that *only* in the former group, the **e**-conjugation verbs, is the -**ш** (or -**ж**) shifted to -**с** (or -**з**) in the aorist. Since this group of verbs is much smaller than the other, the student should learn the few verbs which belong to it. S/he can then predict that all other verbs whose stems end in -**ш** or -**ж** will belong to the **и**-conjugation.

A third type includes verbs whose 1st singular ends in -**я** preceded by -**и** or -**у**. These verbs have *no* theme vowel: the aorist endings are added directly to the verb root. In the verbs **взéма**, **поéма** and **приéма**, which also belong to this group, the stem-final consonant -**м**- is dropped in the aorist. Representing this type are the aorist conjugations of **пúя** and **взéма**, with the present given alongside for comparison:

	PRESENT	**AORIST**	*PRESENT*	**AORIST**
1ˢᵗ singular	пи́-я	пи́-х	взе́м-а	взе́-х
2ⁿᵈ singular	пи́-еш	пи	взе́м-еш	взе́
3ʳᵈ singular	пи́-е	пи	взе́м-е	взе́
1ˢᵗ plural	пи́-ем	пи́-хме	взе́м-ем	взе́-хме
2ⁿᵈ plural	пи́-ете	пи́-хте	взе́м-ете	взе́-хте
3ʳᵈ plural	пи́-ят	пи́-ха	взе́м-ат	взе́-ха

10.2. Long form pronoun objects

Bulgarian has two types of pronoun objects, "long" and "short". The short forms were learned in Lessons 5 and 7. The long forms are given below, together with the short forms for comparison. The primary usage of the long form pronoun objects is after prepositions.

	Direct object		**Indirect object**	
	short	*long*	*short*	*long*
1ˢᵗ singular	ме	ме́не	ми	на ме́не
2ⁿᵈ singular	те	те́бе	ти	на те́бе
3ʳᵈ sing. feminine	я	не́я	ѝ	на не́я
3ʳᵈ sing. masculine	го	не́го	му	на не́го
3ʳᵈ sing. neuter	(= masc. form)		(= masc. form)	
1ˢᵗ plural	ни	на́с	ни	на на́с
2ⁿᵈ plural	ви	ва́с	ви	на ва́с
3ʳᵈ plural	ги	тя́х	им	на тя́х

Here are examples of the use of these forms after prepositions. For the use of the comparative degree of adjectives, see below.

Той по́-голя́м ли е от те́бе?	Is he older than you?
Като ме́не и На́дка, нали́?	Like me and Nadka, right?
Техните са по́-ма́лки от ва́с.	Theirs are younger than you.
Кажи́ ни за тя́х!	Tell us about them!

10.3. Short form possessive constructions

Bulgarian also has long and short ways of expressing possession. The long forms are мо́й, тво́й, etc. (similar in usage to English "my", "your", etc.). The short form possessives are identical to the short form indirect object pronouns.

The short form possessives are more frequently used, especially if the relationship between possessor and possessed is a close one. In this usage, the noun which is possessed *must* be in the definite form, and the short form possessive pronoun follows *immediately* after the definite article. The possessive forms express the identity of the possessor (in 3rd singular, this also includes the gender).

The rule requiring short form possessives to follow immediately after the definite article also applies when the possessed noun is modified by an adjective.

Синъ́т им е на четири годи́ни.	Their son is four years old.
Позна́ваш ли сина́ им?	Do you know their son?
Кабине́тът му е голя́м и све́тъл.	His office is big and light.
Мъжъ́т ми рабо́ти мно́го.	My husband works a lot.
Пле́менниците ми живе́ят в една́ ста́я.	My nieces/nephews live in the same room.
Голя́мата ми ча́нта е та́м.	My big bag is over there.

Only nouns of family relationship are exempt from this rule. When these nouns occur in the singular before a short form possessive, they must be in the indefinite form, except for **мъж** "husband" and **син** "son", which *do* take the definite article before the possessive short form. For example:

Дъщеря́ им е на две́ годи́ни.	Their daughter is two years old.
Бра́т ми и́два сега́.	My brother is coming along now.
Жена́ ви къде́ рабо́ти?	Where does your wife work?
Сестра́ ѝ рису́ва мно́го добре́.	Her sister draws very well.

but:

На ко́лко годи́ни е синъ́т им?	How old is their son?
Мъжъ́т ви къде́ рабо́ти?	Where does your husband work?

All plural forms with short-form possessives are definite, however. Compare the difference between singular and plural in the following:

Сестра́ ми замина́ва за Ва́рна.	My sister is leaving for Varna.
Сестри́те ми са мно́го зае́ти.	My sisters are very busy.

10.4. The usage of свой and си

Bulgarian, like all Slavic languages, has a separate category of reflexive possessive forms whose function is to indicate that the possessor of the object noun and the subject of the sentence are the same. These forms are translated variously -- "his", "his own", "my", "my own", etc.

If the subject and the possessor are the same, then these possessive forms -- **свой** (long) or **си** (short) -- *must* be used. Although it may seem evident from the context who the possessor is (as is the case in most English sentences), if a form other than **свой/си** is used, a Bulgarian will necessarily conclude that the possessor is someone other than the subject. For example:

Possessor of the diary:

Тя́ пи́ше в дне́вника си.	She is writing in her diary.	*the writer*
Тя́ пи́ше в дне́вника ѝ.	*(same)*	*another female*

If the possessed noun is the subject of the sentence, the modifier **свой/си** cannot be used. Here are examples in which the English "their"/"their own" is rendered by different Bulgarian possessive forms. In the first and third sentences, the reflexive forms **свой** and **си** mark the noun possessed by the subject of the sentence. In the second sentence, however, the possessed noun is the subject; therefore the modifier **те́хен** must be used in place of **свой**.

Пле́менниците ми живе́ят в една́ ста́я с роди́телите си.	My niece and nephew live in the same room as their parents.
Но тя́хната ста́я е голя́ма и ху́бава.	But their room is nice and big.
Деца́та ня́мат своя́ ста́я.	The children do not have their own room.

Note also that the English translation uses "their" in the first two instances above, and "their own" in the third. This is because in the first two cases the identity of the possessor is obvious and the idea of possession is not central to the meaning of the sentence. In the third, however, the identity of the possessor is what the sentence is about. Therefore, the emphatic "own" is added.

The contrast between Bulgarian and English lies in the fact that English speakers may choose whether or not (through the addition of the word "own") to introduce the extra idea of reflexivity. But Bulgarian speakers do not have a choice -- they are obliged to mark every possessed object for the identity of the possessor. When translating into Bulgarian, therefore, always verify whether the possessor and the subject are identical or different, and choose the appropriate possessive form accordingly.

10.5. The particle **си** with verbs, continued

Speakers of Bulgarian frequently add the particle **си** to a verb, thereby giving the verb a meaning of greater involvement and intimacy. It is difficult to translate this added meaning precisely, since in most cases it depends on the verb itself; sometimes it is not even possible to express this added distinction in English.

When added to motion verbs, for instance, the particle **си** suggests that the speaker is moving towards "his/her own space". This can mean "go home", "return to where one came from" or simply to "move off in one's own undefined direction". The destination is not necessarily "home", but is rather the very loosely defined idea of "space one is attached to at the moment". Here are several examples (note that none of the several possible translations states explicitly that "home" or "back" is the intended destination):

А сегá да си вървя́.	And now I'll be off.
	And now I'll get moving.
	And now I need to move on.
Пусни́ човéка да си трьгне!	Let the man get going!
	Let the man leave!
	Let the man get on his way!

When added to verbs of state or possession, the particle **си** increases the sense of connectedness between possessor and possessed:

Момчéто и́ма ли си стáя?	Does the boy have his own room?
	Does the boy have a room to himself?
Тóй и́ма кабинéт, но ни́кога не си́ е вкъ́щи.	He has a study, but he's never home.
	He has a study, but he never spends any time in it.

10.6. Comparative and superlative degree of adjectives

Comparison of adjectives in Bulgarian is straightforward. The comparative degree (equivalent to "more + *adjective*" in English) is formed by prefixing **пó-** to the adjective, and the superlative degree (equivalent to "most + *adjective*" in English) is formed by prefixing **нáй-** to the adjective. The comparative and superlative degree of adverbs is formed in the same manner.

Each of these particles is accented. Comparative and superlative forms, therefore, each have *two* accents. The hyphen joining the particle and the adjective is a required part of Bulgarian spelling.

Тóй пó-голя́м ли е, или пó-мáлък?	Is he older or younger?
Сестрá ми е нáй-мáлката.	My sister is the youngest.
Пишéте пó-чéсто!	Write more often!

198

The English "than" and "of" in comparative sentences are both expressed in Bulgarian by the preposition **от**. When the comparison is with a verb, the conjunction **отколкото** is used.

То́й е по́-голя́м от ме́не.	He is older than me.
Тя́ е на́й-ма́лката от вси́чки.	She is the youngest of all.

То́й е по́-у́мен, отко́лкото **изгле́жда.**	He's smarter than he looks.
Пише́те ни по́-че́сто, отко́лкото **пи́шете сега́.**	Write us oftener than you do now.

Superlatives can also be used simply to magnify the meaning of an adjective.

В това́ учи́лище учени́ците **у́чат на́й-разли́чни неща́.**	Pupils in that school learn all sorts of things.

10.7. Masculine nouns ending in a vowel

Certain masculine nouns denoting human beings end in either **-a** or **-o**. The plural of these nouns is always **-и**. It is added directly to the stem of nouns whose singular is **-a**, but is preceded by the suffix **-овц-** in nouns whose singular ends in **-o**.

All these nouns carry a certain emotional overtone; the most common ones denote family relationships. For instance:

singular	*plural*	*(meaning)*
бащ-а́	**бащ-и́**	father
дя́д-о	**дя́д-овци**	grandfather
чи́ч-о	**чи́ч-овци**	uncle (father's side)
ву́йч-о	**ву́йч-овци**	uncle (mother's side)
та́тк-о	**та́тк-овци**	Dad

The noun **коле́г-а** "colleague" also belongs in this group. It refers either to a male colleague or to the general category; a female colleague is **коле́жка**.

Like all nouns ending in **-a** or **-o**, these nouns take a rhyming article. Adjectives, articles or pronouns which agree with (or refer to) them, however, must be in the masculine form. For example:

Дя́дото седи́ с деца́та. То́й им **разка́зва за ста́рото вре́ме.**	Grandpa is sitting with the children. He's telling them about the old days.

| Бащата на Лиляна не é стар. | Lilyana's father is not old. |
| Моят баща говори с твоя дядо. | My father is talking with your grandfather. |

Nicknames for male persons also frequently end in -o. Plurals of these names are formed with -овци, but they are rarely encountered.

proper name	*nickname*	*proper name*	*nickname*
Владимир	Влад-о	Александър	Саш-о
Димитър	Митк-о	Петър	Петь-о

10.8. Prepositions

(a)   The preposition **у** means "at the home of" or "among". Be careful to differentiate this from **при**, which means "at, with, in the presence of" (wherever that person may be at the moment). For example:

Ела у дома!	Come over to the/our house!
Стой при мене!	Stay by me!
Отиват у вас на гости.	They're going over to visit you.
Отивам при него за съвет.	I'm going to him for advice.
Завеждам децата у учителката (на гости).	I'm taking the children over to their teacher's house.
Завеждам децата при учителката.	I'm taking the children to see the teacher.
Певецът предизвиква възторг у публиката.	The singer enraptured [= evoked rapture in] the audience.

(b)   The prepositions **от** and **с** are used in phrases of comparison as follows:

Камен е по-голям от Надка.	Kamen is older than Nadka.
Той е по-голям с две години.	He is older by two years.
Тя е най-малка от всичките.	She is the youngest of all.

(c)   When used after verbs of communication, the preposition **за** means "about".

| Кажи ни за тях! | Tell us about them! |
| Носи съобщение за колет. | She has got a notice about a package. |

EXERCISES

I. Replace the underlined nouns or phrases by the appropriate pronouns.

1. Слу́шай <u>баща́ си</u>, то́й на ло́шо ня́ма да те нау́чи.
2. Ка́мене, слу́шай <u>роди́телите си</u> като На́дка.
3. У <u>Миле́на и Дими́тър</u> все́ки де́н и́ма го́сти.
4. Кажи́ <u>на Áнгел</u> да пи́ше по́-че́сто <u>на ма́йка си</u> за <u>Де́йвид.</u>
5. А <u>на ма́ма и та́тко</u> ня́ма ли да даде́ш бонбо́н?
6. Съсе́дът благодари́ <u>на бояджи́ята</u> за ху́бавата му ра́бота.
7. Учи́телката пи́та <u>деца́та</u> за <u>писа́телите.</u>

II. Fill in the blank with an appropriate possessive pronoun.

1. Зна́еш ли, къде́ е жена́ _____?
2. Су́трин то́й разгова́ря с ку́чето _____.
3. Едно́то писмо́ е за ме́не, а дру́гото за сестра́ _____. Áз прочи́там пъ́рво
    _____, а по́сле _____.
4. Пе́тър ка́зва: "Запозна́йте се, това́ е жена́ _____." Ива́н ка́зва: "Жена́
    _____ си́гурно зна́е за ме́не. Ни́е сме ста́ри прия́тели." Пе́тър ка́зва:
    "Áз че́сто разка́звам на жена́ _____ за те́бе."
5. В неде́ля Та́ня и сестра́ _____ во́дят _____ деца́ на ци́рк. Та́ня
    ка́зва на сестра́ _____ : "_____ деца́ мно́го се разби́рат с
    _____."
6. Бо́б получа́ва чести́тки от _____ прия́тели и от прия́телите на
    Патри́ша. _____ прия́тели живе́ят в Бо́стън, а _____ в
    Чика́го.
7. Две́ съсе́дки разгова́рят. Една́та ка́зва: "Мо́ля те, пусни́ _____ ко́тка
    да поигра́е с _____ деца́ в гради́ната."

III. Rewrite each sentence in the past tense, replacing все́ки де́н *or* сега́ *with* вче́ра.

1. Боря́на все́ки де́н пи́ше писма́ на прия́телките си.
2. Деца́та пи́ят все́ки де́н то́пло мля́ко на заку́ска.
3. Все́ки де́н след вече́ря ти́ взи́маш ку́чето да го разхо́диш.
4. Писмо́то е гото́во. Сега́ го пу́скам в по́щенската кути́я.
5. Ка́мен и На́дка вся́ка су́трин ка́зват на ма́йка си "добро́ у́тро".
6. Сега́ чу́ваме учи́лищния звъне́ц.
7. Сега́ вла́кът присти́га на га́ра Со́фия.

ADDITIONAL GRAMMAR NOTES

10.1a. Aorist tense, continued

Verbs like **пиша** and **кажа** shift the stem-final consonant in the aorist form. This consonant shift is the same one that was seen between certain perfective and derived imperfective aspect forms. (Derived imperfectives will be discussed in more detail in Lesson 18.)

consonant: ш *or* ж	*consonant:* с *or* з	
perfective	*imperfective*	*aorist*
опиш-а разкаж-а	опис-вам разказ-вам	опис-ах разказ-ах

The verbs **къпя** "bathe" and **капя** "drip, leak" belong to the e-conjugation, and form their aorists with the theme vowel -a- (**къпах**, etc. and **капах** etc.). Their 1st singular present forms, in -я, are irregular.

Verbs whose 1st singular ends in -я preceded by -у or -и (e.g. **пия, чуя**) lack a theme vowel in the aorist. This group also includes verbs in -ая if they have at least two syllables preceding the ending. Thus, **копая** and **позная** belong to this group, as seen below (only 1st singular and 1st plural forms are given). The verb **зная**, whose aorist will be learned in the next lesson, does *not* belong to this group.

	PRESENT	**AORIST**	*PRESENT*	**AORIST**
1st singular	копая	копах	позная	познах
1st plural	копаем	копахме	познаем	познахме

10.2a. Long form pronoun objects

Short form pronouns have different shapes for indirect and direct objects. Long form pronouns, however, function like nouns. The object form alone has the meaning "direct", and the object form preceded by **на** has the meaning "indirect".

	direct	*indirect*
Noun object	Камен	на Камен
Pronoun object	мене	на мене

Third-person long form pronoun objects are similar to the possessive adjectives; this similarity can help the student remember them.

pronouns	*3sg* her не́-я	*3sg* him/it не́го	*3pl* them тя́х
	3sg her(s)	*3sg* his/its	*3pl* their(s)
possessive adjective (f.) *possessive adjective (m.)*	не́-йна не́-ин	не́го-ва не́го-в	тя́х-на те́х-ен

The long form reflexive pronoun, **се́бе си**, always appears with long and short forms together. This usage will be studied in more detail in Lesson 11. The pronouns **ме́не** and **те́бе** are sometimes written and spoken without the final syllable. There is no difference in meaning. For example:

Ще до́йдеш ли с ме́н?   Will you come with me?

10.3a. Word order in short form possessive constructions

Short form indirect object pronouns express relationship in two ways. They can be added to a noun, (e.g. **бра́т му** "his brother"), or they can depend on a form of the copula **съм** in predicative sentences. In the latter instance, indirect object pronouns follow the copula directly. This sequence *(COP-IND)* then follows the word order rules learned in Lesson 5: it must occur adjacent to the predicate (immediately before it if possible), and it must occur immediately after the negative or interrogative particles. Note that *IND* also applies to **си** in its meaning "verbal additive signifying greater intimacy", and that the same word order rules apply.

As in the case of all word order examples, numbering of the following examples is cumulative across lessons.

(40) **Ти́**   **си**   **ми**   **ста́р позна́т.**
 subject *COP* *IND* *pred. noun*
          You are an old acquaintance of mine.

(41) **Те́**   **са**   **му**   **ве́рни прия́тели.**
 subject *COP* *IND* *pred. noun*
          They are my faithful friends.

(42) **Ви́е**   **не**   **сте́**   **му**   **прия́тел.**
 subject *Neg.* *COP* *IND* *pred. noun*
          You're not his friend.

(43) **Ни́е**   **ни́кога**   **не**   **сме́**   **си**   **вкъ́щи.**
 subject   *Neg.* *COP* *IND* *pred. adverb*
          We're never at home.

Word order with 3rd singular copula

If the copula form is 3rd singular, however, the word order is reversed. The sequence, to which the above rules also apply, is *IND-3rdCOP*. Special care must be taken to learn this difference! Examples are given below.

(44)   А, зна́чи   Гео́рги

ти	е	брат.
IND	*3rdCOP*	*pred. noun*

       subject

Oh, that means Georgi is your brother.

(45)   Позна́вам я,   тя́

ми	е	коле́жка.
IND	*3rdCOP*	*pred. noun*

       subject

I know her -- she is my colleague.

(46)   То́й   ни́кога

не	си	е	вкъщи.
Neg.	*IND*	*3rdCOP*	*pred. adverb*

       subject

He's never at home.

The above rule will take on great importance when the student learns the past indefinite tense in Lesson 16, for it will also govern the ordering of pronoun objects with respect to the verbal auxiliary.

Word order in negative interrogative sentences

When both negative and interrogative particles are present, either the copula OR the indirect object short form pronoun, whichever is first in sequence, is placed between them. It is important to remember that only *one* clitic can occur in this position. Examples are give below; this word order rule will be drilled in greater detail in Lesson 13.

(47)   Ти́

не	си	ли	му	прия́тел?
Neg.	*COP*	*INT*	*IND*	*pred. noun*

       subject

Aren't you his friend?

(48)   То́й

не	ти	ли	е	прия́тел?
Neg.	*IND*	*INT*	*3rdCOP*	*pred. noun*

       subject

Isn't he your friend?

10.4a. The usage of сво́й and си

When the possessor is other than 1st or 2nd person, Bulgarians must specify whether it is equivalent to the subject of the sentence or not: in the first case they must use сво́й / си, and in the second case they must use a non-reflexive possessor. When the possessor is 1st or 2nd person, Bulgarians theoretically have the option to use either reflexive or non-reflexive possessors.

In practice, however, they almost always use сво́й / си. If they are using a short form possessive, си is chosen almost exclusively. If a speaker uses a long form possessive, s/he will tend to use сво́й unless s/he wishes to place special emphasis on the possessive relationship, in which case s/he will use мо́й, тво́й, etc.

10.9. Kinship terms

All societies have terms for family relationships. Much of the Bulgarian terminology is organized in a manner similar to that of English. The following chart gives some of the major kinship terms:

	male	*female*	*generic*
parent	баща́	ма́йка	роди́тел
parent (affectionate)	та́тко	ма́ма	
child	син	дъщеря́	дете́
sibling	брат	сестра́	
grandparent	ба́ба	дя́до	
grandchild	вну́к	вну́чка	*
spouse	мъж	жена́	
spouse (generic)	съпру́г	съпру́га	*
niece/nephew	пле́менник	пле́менница	*
cousin	братовче́д	братовче́дка	*
fiancé	годени́к	годени́ца	*
newlywed, groom/bride	младоже́нец	младоже́нка бу́лка	*
parent-in-law of wife	све́къръ	свекъ́рва	
parent-in-law of husband	тъст	тъ́ща	
parents of couple	сват	сва́тя	
step-parent	вто́ри баща́	вто́ра ма́йка маще́ха	

* The feminine term is used exclusively for females, but the masculine term can refer either to a male person or to the general concept. For instance, the form вну́ци (plural of the masculine form вну́к) can refer either to grandchildren in general, or to a specific group of grandchildren at least one of whom is male. The plural form вну́чки refers to a group of grandchildren who are all female.

In the case of nieces, nephews and fiancés, the plural forms are ambiguous. Пле́менници, for instance, is the plural of both пле́менник (meaning either "nephew" or the general category "sibling's child") and пле́менница ("niece"). Note, by the way, that the plural form съпру́ги refers exclusively to females; the corresponding masculine plural is съпру́зи.

The terms сва́т and сва́тя refer to the relationship which obtains between the parents of a young married couple. They continue to bear this relationship to each other (and to use these terms for each other) throughout their lives. Wives and husbands use separate terms to refer to the parents of one's spouse.

The names for "uncle" and "aunt" are complex. Many Bulgarians use only ле́ля for "aunt" and чи́чо "father's brother" or ву́йчо "mother's brother" for "uncle". The full set of terms will be presented in Lesson 22.

10.10. Derivation: nouns in -ица, -джия, -джийка; possessive adjectives in -ов, -ев

Nouns in -ица

The suffix **-иц-**, followed by the ending **-а**, forms feminine nouns of various sorts. There is often the overtone of something "smaller" or more delicate in some way. These nouns are usually formed from other nouns, but they can be formed from words of any class. For example:

noun	stem	+ иц- ›	derived noun	(meaning)
пле́мен-ник	племен-н-	+ иц- ›	пле́менниц-а	niece
госпо́д-ин	госпож-	+ иц- ›	госпо́жиц-а	Miss
стран-а́	стран-	+ иц- ›	стра́ниц-а	page
ви́л-а	вил-	+ иц- ›	ви́лиц-а	fork

adjective	stem	+ иц- ›	derived noun	(meaning)
ху́бав	хубав-	+ иц- ›	хубави́ц-а	beauty

numeral	stem	+ иц- ›	derived noun	(meaning)
се́дем	седм-	+ иц- ›	се́дмиц-а	week

The suffix **-иц-** is normally used to form neutral words such as the above. In certain cases, however, it is used to form emotionally loaded words, which are of masculine gender. Here is an example of one such noun, which is formed from the stem of the verb **пи́я** plus the suffix **-ан-**:

> То́й е голя́м пия́ница.   He's quite the drinker.

Nouns in -джия, -джийка

The suffix **-джий-** is borrowed into Bulgarian from Turkish, where it has numerous meanings. One of these, that denoting profession, has been borrowed into Bulgarian as well. Some of the Bulgarian nouns formed with this suffix have neutral meaning, but others are felt as ironic in varying degrees.

In masculine nouns, the suffix is followed by the ending **-а** (resulting in the spelling **-джия**). Feminine nouns can also be formed by adding the suffix **-к-**, again followed by the ending **-а** (resulting in the spelling **-джийка**). These nouns designate a female practitioner of the profession in question.

In the chart below, the first three nouns have neutral meaning, and the second three have what is often called "expressive" (emotionally charged) meaning.

noun	meaning	stem	+ джий(ка) ›	derived nouns	meaning
по́ща	mail	пощ-а-	+ джий(ка) ›	по́щаджи-я по́щаджий-ка	letter-carrier
боя́	paint	бой-а-	+ джий(ка) ›	бояджи́-я бояджи́й-ка	painter
сто́п	stop	стоп-а-	+ джий(ка) ›	сто́паджи-я сто́паджий-ка	hitchhiker
дво́йка	failing grade	двойк-а-	+ джий(ка) ›	дво́йкаджи-я дво́йкаджий-ка	high school dropout
кавга́	quarrel	кавг-а-	+ джий(ка) ›	кавгаджи́-я кавгаджи́й-ка	brawler
че́йндж	currency exchange office	чейндж-а-	+ джий(ка) ›	че́йнджаджи-я че́йнджаджий-ка	unofficial money-changer

Possessive adjectives in -ов, -ев

The suffix -ов- appears in numerous family names. It is by origin a possessive suffix. The surname Сто́йков, for instance, refers to those who are part of the family of someone named Сто́йко. Similarly, the surname Бояджи́ев refers to those who are part of the family of someone known as a бояджи́я (a painter). This same suffix is also used to derive adjectives from nouns. This suffix is usually -ов-, but after certain consonants it is -ев-.

noun	stem	+ ов- / ев- ›	derived adj.	(meaning)
слъ́нц-е	слъ́нч-	+ ев- ›	слъ́нчев	sunny
гро́зд-е	грозд-	+ ов- ›	гро́здов	grape
портока́л	портокал-	+ ов- ›	портока́лов	orange
баро́к	барок-	+ ов- ›	баро́ков	Baroque
Хри́ст	Христ-	+ ов- ›	Христо́в	Christ's
не́г-о	нег-	+ ов- ›	не́гов	his

207

10.11. Consonant shifts in derivation

Certain stem-final consonants are frequently replaced by other consonants before certain derivational suffixes. These replacement patterns are not random, but occur according to predictable patterns. Here are some examples:

consonant	*replacement*
- г -	- ж -

коле́г - а	коле́ж - ка
кни́г - а	кни́ж - ка
сня́г	снеж - и́нка

consonant	*replacement*
- ц -	- ч -

лъжи́ц - а	лъжи́ч - ка

consonant	*replacement*
- к -	- ч -

учени́к	учени́ч - ка
вну́к	вну́ч - ка
екзо́тик - а	екзоти́ч - ен
мля́к - о	мле́ч - ност
зна́к	знач - е́ние

Gorge in the Rhodope Mountains
(southern Bulgaria)

208

SAMPLE SENTENCES

1. Майка му много го обича. И той много обича майка си. Неговата майка е добре.

2. Таня казва, че мъжът ѝ често пътува. Таня моли мъжа си да не пътува често. Нейният мъж често не си е вкъщи.

3. Кажи на твоята жена, че чакам утре сутринта да ми се обади.

4. Той казва на жена си на другия ден да му позвъни по телефона.

5. Тя жена ли му е на него? Не, те не са женени.

6. Това жена му ли е? Не, това е негова братовчедка.

7. Запознайте се, жена ми. Моята жена е адвокат.

8. Лиляна си има три деца. Лиляна и Младен си имат три деца.

9. Иди си, късно е вече.

10. Моят сват често боледува. Синът ми е женен за най-голямата му дъщеря. Той има три дъщери от първия си брак.

11. Камен и Надка са брат и сестра.

12. Свекърва ми и майка ми са добри приятелки. Те заедно водят внуците си на разходка. Моите деца обичат своите баби.

13. Те са близки приятелки. Купуват си дрехи от един и същ магазин.

14. Тя приказва все едно и също, откакто я познавам.

15. Виждам, че те имат едни и същи грешки в контролното.

16. Децата станаха на десет години.

17. Вече знам. Казаха ми за това още в България.

18. Димитър чу от приятелите си последните новини.

19. Багажът не беше много и затова Таня взе малката чанта.

20. -- Какво прави баща ти в момента?
    -- Боядисва предната врата.

21. Един и същ бояджия им боядисва къщите.

SENTENCES FOR TRANSLATION

1. Mother called the painter on the phone but he wasn't at home. Tomorrow she will ask him, "When will you come to paint our house?" Our neighbors are painting their own house, but we don't want to paint ours.

2. Come with us to the movies! Or maybe you prefer to go with them? Probably, because they'll go in their car, but we will walk. Ivo and I always walk to the movies. We talk about the film, and we also talk about you and Marina!

3. Last night Lilyana told me about her mother. Her mother went to America last year, and met her American aunts and uncles. She took her youngest daughter with her, but her older children didn't go. They stayed home with their father.

4. Where's Marin? He left [to go home]. His father is ill, and he wants to stay with him.

5. My brother wrote me from Plovdiv -- he's coming tomorrow. But I have no room in my apartment, because all my cousins are staying with me. Can he sleep at your place? You are my closest friend, and you are also a good friend of his.

6. Nadka put her red pencils into her bag but left her blue pencils on the floor. Her mother asked, "Nadka, why did you put only some pencils in your bag?" Nadka said, "My blue pencils are bigger than my red pencils". Her older brother Kamen then said, "No, they are smaller. And I of course know because I am two years older than you."

7. Her uncle drinks a lot. If she goes to see him, he will want her to sit and drink with him. For that reason, she goes to her grandmother's more often than she goes to her uncle's. With her grandmother, she drinks only tea.

8. "Do you know Sabina?"
   "Yes, of course. She is my colleague. I have been working with her for more than three years. Her younger sister Boryana is also our colleague, but she works in a different office and I see her rarely. Yesterday I invited her to come have dinner with us."

READING SELECTION

Кореспонде́нция - (8)

29 деке́мври, Со́фия

Дра́ги Патри́ша и Бо́б,

Тъ́кмо сега́ полу́чихме писмо́то на Бо́б и бъ́рзам да отгово́ря. Деца́та го доне́соха ведна́га след заку́ска. Покрай пра́зниците по́щата оба́че рабо́ти осо́бено ба́вно. Дано́ та́зи чести́тка за Но́вата годи́на присти́гне навре́ме поне́ за сле́дващата Но́ва годи́на.

Пожела́ваме ви от сърце́ мно́го здра́ве, ра́дости и успе́х във вси́чко!

Ни́е ня́маме пра́зник като ва́шия Де́н на благодарността́, но Бъ́дни ве́чер, навече́рието на Ко́леда, е мно́го ва́жен пра́зник за на́с.

Тога́ва е после́дният де́н от ко́ледните по́сти и затова́ приго́твихме са́мо по́стни го́зби: бо́б, зе́ле, турши́я, о́рехи, суше́ни плодове́. На ма́сата сло́жихме от вси́чко по ма́лко, за да родя́т и догоди́на ни́вите, лозя́та и гради́ните. Ни́е с Бо́йко изпи́хме по една́ ча́ша ви́но и за ва́ше здра́ве. За Бъ́дни ве́чер го́сти не ка́нихме, празну́вахме, ка́кто обикнове́но, в те́сен семе́ен кръ́г.

Та́зи Но́ва годи́на съвпа́дна с кръ́гла годи́шнина от на́шата сва́тба с Бо́йко. Затова́ пока́нихме мно́го бли́зки родни́ни на го́сти. Бо́йко посре́щна роди́телите си на га́рата и ги дока́ра ту́к с кола́та. Ста́нахме мно́го (са́мо братовче́дите ни са се́дем ду́ши) и затова́ ни́е със свекъ́рва ми ве́че почна́хме да ше́таме. Тя́ ще напра́ви ба́ницата с късме́тите. Баща́ ми ще до́йде след ра́бота за́едно с Бо́йко: те́ рабо́тят в една́ и съ́ща бо́лница и на Но́ва годи́на и́мат дежу́рство. Дя́до Мра́з ще донесе́ на вси́чки деца́ пода́ръци. Ба́бите и дя́довците, ле́лите и чи́човците се го́твят за сурвака́рите и съби́рат но́ви лъ́скави моне́ти. Накра́тко Но́ва годи́на обеща́ва да бъ́де ве́села и шу́мна, ни́що че па́к ня́ма сня́г.

Мно́го се ра́дваме на ва́шите писма́. Пише́те ни по́-че́сто.

Ва́ша

Кали́на

GLOSSARY

арома́тен	aromatic	дано́ присти́гне навре́ме	let's hope it gets there on time
ба́ница	banitsa (baked pastry)		
ба́ница с късме́ти	banitsa with small fortunes in it	дво́йка	"2", failing mark in school
баро́к	Baroque	дво́йкаджия, -ийка	high school dropout
благодаря́	thank, pay gratitude	де	*(intensifying particle)*
бли́зък	close *(adj.)*	дежу́рен	on duty
бли́зки са	they are close friends	дежу́рство	duty
бо́б	beans	дне́вник	diary
боледу́вам	be ill	дока́рвам / дока́рам	drive to, bring to
бонбо́н	candy		
боя́	paint	дре́ха	article of clothing
бояджи́я, -и́йка	house painter; paint or dye merchant	дре́хи	clothes, clothing
		дъщеря́	daughter
боя́ди́свам	paint, dye, color	дя́до *(pl.* дя́довци)	grandfather
бра́во	bravo	Дя́до Мра́з	Jack Frost
бра́к	marriage	Дя́до Ко́леда	Santa Claus
бу́лка	bride		
Бъ́дни ве́чер	Christmas Eve	еди́н и съ́щ	[one and] the same
в една́ ста́я с	in the same room as	же́нен, -ена	married
ва́с	you *(direct object)*		
ве́рен, вя́рна	true, faithful	за	about
вя́рно е, че...	it's true that...	заве́ждам / заведа́	take somewhere, lead
ви́ла	pitchfork	заку́ска	breakfast
ви́лица	fork	запозна́вам се / запозна́я се	meet, get acquainted
вну́к	grandson		
вну́чка	granddaughter	звъня́ по телефо́на	telephone
все́	always, constantly		
все́ ме ня́ма	I'm never there	извъ́н	out of, outside
все́ о́ще изби́рам	I'm still looking	изче́звам / изче́зна	disappear
все́ едно́ и съ́що	[it's] always the same thing		
		кавга́	quarrel, dispute
		кавгаджи́я, -и́йка	quarrelsome person, brawler
вто́ра ма́йка	stepmother		
вто́ри баща́	stepfather	ка́ня	invite
ву́йчо *(pl.* ву́йчовци)	uncle (mother's brother)	ка́пя (-еш)	drip, leak
		кни́жка	booklet; driver's license
възто́рг	delight, rapture	коле́га	colleague
вървя́ с	go well with	Ко́леда	Christmas
вървя́ си	get going	ко́леден	Christmas *(adj.)*
вя́рно *see* ве́рен		коле́жка	female colleague
		командиро́вка	business trip
годени́к	fiancé	копа́я	dig
годени́ца	fiancée	ко́тка	cat
годи́шнина	anniversary	кръ́г, -ъ́т	circle
		кръ́гъл	round, circular
дано́	let's wish, if only	кръ́гла годи́шнина	decade anniversary

кути́я	box	пока́нвам / пока́ня	invite
късме́т	fortune, luck	покрай	because of
		портока́л	orange
ло́зе (*pl.* лозя́)	vineyard	портока́лов	orange (*adj.*)
лъ́скав	shining, bright	по́ст	Lent; fast
		по́стен	Lenten, pertaining to fasting
ма́щеха	stepmother		
ме́не	me (*direct object*)	постоя́нен	constant
младоже́нец	bridegroom, newlywed	постоя́нно	constantly
		по́чвам / по́чна	begin, start
младоже́нка	bride, newlywed	по́щаджия, -и́йка	letter carrier, postman
мле́чност	milkiness	по́щенска кути́я	mailbox
моне́та	coin	по́щенски	postal
мра́з	frost, chill	пра́зник	holiday
мълча́ (-и́ш)	be silent, fall silent	празну́вам	celebrate
		пре́ден	front, anterior
навече́рие	the eve of; vigil	предизви́квам / предизви́кам	provoke, defy
най-	most... (*superlative degree particle*)	предизви́квам възто́рг у	enrapture
най-мно́го	the most	приго́твям / приго́твя	prepare
най-разли́чни неща́	all sorts of things		
накра́тко	in short, briefly	приемам / прие́ма	accept
на́с	us (*direct object*)	прили́чам	look like, resemble
не́го	him (*direct object*)	пропу́скам / пропу́сна	skip, let pass
не́я	her (*direct object*)		
ни́ва	[corn]field	пу́блика	public
ни́що, че ня́ма	it doesn't matter if there isn't any	пу́скам / пу́сна	let, allow; drop
		пу́скам писмо́	mail a letter
Но́ва годи́на	New Years	пу́ст	empty
		пу́сти командиро́вки	[these] blasted business trips
оба́ждам се / оба́дя се	call on the phone, get in touch with	пъ́рвенство́	championship
обеща́вам / обеща́я	promise	ра́дост	joy
осо́бен	special, particular	ра́ждам / родя́	bear, give birth to, be fruitful
отгова́рям / отгово́ря	answer		
отка́кто	[ever] since	разгова́рям	converse
отко́лкото	than	разли́чен	different, various
		разхо́ждам / разхо́дя	take for a walk
певе́ц	singer		
пети́ца	"5" (second-best mark in school)	ре́дки *see* ря́дък	
		родни́на	relative
писа́тел (ка)	writer	родя́ *see* ра́ждам	
пия́ница	drunkard, tippler	ря́дък, ре́дки	rare
пле́менник	nephew	ря́дко	rarely
пле́менница	niece		
по́-	more...(*comparative degree particle*)	сва́т (*or* сва́тя)	in-law
		сва́тба	wedding
по́-голя́м	older	све́кър	father-in-law (to wife)
по́-ма́лък	younger	свето́вен	world (*adj.*)
пожела́вам от сърце́	send heartfelt wishes	све́тъл	light (*adj.*)
поигра́вам / поигра́я	play for a while	сво́й	own (*adj.*)

213

семе́ен	family, domestic	тъ́ща	mother-in-law (to husband)
сестра́	sister		
слъ́нчев	sunny	тя́х	them *(direct object)*
снежи́нка	snowflake		
сре́щам / сре́щна	meet	у	at the home of
ста́вам / ста́на	become, get to be	у дома́	at home, at one's house
ста́ваме мно́го	there gets to be a lot of us		
		у́мен	smart, intelligent
(синъ́т им)	(their son)	учи́лищен	school *(adj.)*
ста́на на че́тири	has turned four	учи́лищен звъне́ц	school bell
сти́га то́лкова	that's enough		
сто́п	stop-sign; hitchhiking	фу́тбол	soccer
сто́паджия, -ийка	hitchhiker		
сурвака́р	survakar (New Year's wassailer)	че́йндж	currency exchange office
		че́йнджаджия, -ийка	unofficial money changer
суше́н	dried		
съве́т	advice	чести́т	happy *(in greeting)*
съвпа́дам / съвпа́дна	coincide, concur	чести́та Но́ва Годи́на	Happy New Year
съпру́г, съпру́га	spouse		
сърце́	heart	чести́тка	greeting card
		чи́чо *(pl.* чи́човци)	uncle (father's brother)
та́тко *(pl.* та́тковци)	dad	чу́вам / чу́я	hear
те́бе	you *(direct object)*		
те́сен семе́ен кръ́г	immediate family	шести́ца	"6" (best mark in school)
турши́я	pickles; pickled vegetables		
		ше́там	do housework; be active
тъ́кмо	just, exactly	шу́мен	noisy
тъ́кмо сега́	just this minute		
тъ́ст	father-in-law (to husband)		

New Year's in downtown Veliko Tărnovo

214

CULTURAL COMMENTARY

Families: kinship terms; living quarters

Bulgarians maintain contact with extended families, as seen by the complex system of family-relationship names. Young urban Bulgarians no longer distinguish all the different terms for "brother-in-law" or "sister-in-law", and some have also begun to confuse certain of the terms for "uncle" and "aunt". If the particular relationship exists in one's own family, however, it is likely that the correct word will be used (and that the younger generation will learn it). When one marries, the appropriate terms for parents-in-law are always used.

Living quarters in Bulgaria (and especially in Sofia) are crowded. If a family has more than one child, it is almost unheard of that each child would have his or her own room. Often, in fact, the children of a family will share the only bedroom while the parents sleep in the living room.

Sports

As in other European countries, soccer is called "football" (футбол), and is by far the most popular spectator sport.

Forms of address: surnames

Many Bulgarian surnames contain the suffix -джий-, which is of Turkish origin and indicates professional affiliation. Today, of course, this means only that someone among one's ancestors once practiced that profession. The parallel with English "Smith" or "Miller" is an obvious one.

School system: grading

Grades in school range from 6 (the equivalent of an A) down to 2, which is a failing grade. A grade of 6 (шестица) or 5 (петица) is regarded with pride; other grades are not mentioned unless necessary.

Traveling: currency

Formerly, it was possible to change currency only in banks and officially-sponsored tourists offices. Now, private offices for currency changing abound. The exchange rate varies among them, but usually only slightly. One is advised to change money in one of these offices (and to obtain a receipt). It is not advisable to change money on the street.

Food and drink: fasting; banitsa; holiday customs connected with food

Fasting is part of the Eastern Orthodox religion. Most religious adherents abstain from eating meat every Friday (and some do so on Wednesday as well). The most important fasting periods of the Orthodox calendar, however, are the periods preceding Christmas and Easter. There are three general forms of fasting. According to the mildest type, one abstains from eating the flesh of creatures (meat or fish), but is allowed to eat that which they produce (that is, eggs and milk). According to the intermediate type of fast, one can eat only things that grow from the ground, on trees or on vines. The most rigid type is a total fast.

Постни гозби are dishes that are allowed during the fasting period. Examples (according to the intermediate type) are vegetables, fruits, nuts, beans and wine; or (according to the mild type) the above plus dishes such as yogurt soup, fried eggs or banitsa. On the final evening of the Christmas fast, Бъдни вечер, it is believed that to focus one's attention on these foods is to encourage the earth to be fertile during the coming year. According to one folk custom, the male and female heads of the household go out to visit each fruit tree at Christmastime. The male carries an ax and threatens to cut each tree down, but the female stops him and encourages the tree to grow and be fruitful.

Banitsa (баница) is a baked pastry filled with white cheese and eggs. On New Year's, a special banitsa is baked with fortunes (късмети) in it, and sliced so that a fortune, foretelling his or her luck for the coming year, is within each family member's portion. Traditionally, the fortunes are small pieces of cornel branch, each with a bud, cut in different shapes. The cook who bakes the banitsa keeps a list of which shape corresponds to which fortune, and reads it out as the fortunes are discovered. Alternatively, one can write fortunes on small slips of paper and bake them in the banitsa.

Holiday customs: Christmas and New Year's

It is the accepted norm to send greetings on New Year's. The phrase **честита Нова година** ("Happy New Year") is often abbreviated to **ЧНГ**. New Year's day itself is the day dedicated to Saint Vasil; it is customary to pay visits to friends and relatives on the afternoon of New Year's day.

The popular name for Christmas is **Коледа**; the word is a survival from pre-Christian times. The religious name is **Рождество**, which is a word from the church ritual meaning "birth". It refers not to any birth, but only to the birth of Christ. The term for Christmas Eve, **Бъдни вечер**, is related to that of the **бъдник** or Yule log.

Dyado Mraz (**Дядо Мраз**), literally "Grandfather Frost", is the Bulgarian functional equivalent of Santa Claus. He brings children presents which they have requested in advance.

Another New Year's custom connected with cornel wood is that of "surva" (**сурва**) or "survakane" (**сурвакане**); it is practiced with great enjoyment on the morning of New Year's day. Using decorated branches of cornelwood called "survachki" (**сурвачки**) that have been purchased in advance, young children strike their elder relatives lightly on the back. As they do so, the "survakari" (**сурвакари**) -- i.e., the children -- chant the following tune:

Сурва сурва година, весела година
Живо здраво догодина, догодина, до амина.

These relatives in turn give the children shiny new coins, which they have been collecting in advance. Since Bulgarian children usually do not receive allowances or spending money, this New Year's money is a special treat.

New Year's in Sofia, near the University

216

LESSON 11

DIALOGUE

<u>Хáйде да се чýкнем за младожéнците!</u>

Влади́мир: Áз да вървя́, че ме чáкат. Пáк заповя́дайте на гóсти в нáшето купé.

Дими́тър (на Веселин): Е, кажéте де! Жéнен ли сте?

Веселин: Óще не съм.

Áнгел: А-а! Ергéн си, знáчи. Ня́ма ли да се жéниш?

Веселин: Еди́н дéн мóже и да се ожéня. Всé óще изби́рам.

Áнгел: Каквó тóлкова изби́раш?

Дими́тър: Ожени́ се! Ня́ма да съжаля́ваш. Ви́ж ме мéне! Ни́е сме младожéнци. Жéнени сме съвсéм отскóро.

Джули: Чести́то! Да сте жи́ви и здрáви!

Áнгел: Хáйде да се чýкнем за младожéнците. За мнóго годи́ни! Жáлко, че ня́маме шампáнско, но и раки́ята ще свъ́рши рáбота.

Джули: Когá бéше свáтбата?

Милена: Преди двé сéдмици. След товá хóдихме на свáтбено пътешéствие на морéто. Бéше мнóго хýбаво -- тóпло, слъ́нчево, вéсело. Видя́хме и прия́тели. Еднá вéчер хóдихме на ки́но. Глéдахме ня́каква комéдия. Умря́хме от смя́х. Мнóго добрé си почи́нахме.

Дими́тър: А сегá оти́ваме при мáйка ми в Сóфия. На Милéна свекъ́рвата. Не сé познáват óще. Ще се срéщнат за пъ́рви пъ́т.

Милена: Вчéра се обáдихме по телефóна да ѝ кáжем когá присти́гаме. Си́гурно ще ни чáка на гáрата.

Таня: Амá кáк такá мáйка ви не дойдé на свáтбата? Бóлна ли бéше?

Ангел: Къдé ще живéете? В Со́фия или във Вáрна?

Димитър: Във Вáрна. Ня́ма да стои́м дъ́лго в Со́фия. Ще поразхо́дя женá си из Со́фия. По́сле се връ́щаме.

Камен: Мáмо, Нáдка не и́ска да ми въ́рне мо́лива. Кажи́ ѝ, че е мо́й. Не é нéин!

Надка: Тво́ите мо́ливи ти ги дáдох вси́чките. Ти́я са си мо́и.

Таня: Не сé кáрайте, децá. Мо́ливи и́ма за вси́чки. Ня́ма да се занимáвам сáмо с вáс.

Джули: Хáйде, децá, елáте да ви почетá, а пъ́к вие по́сле ще ми попéете.

Камен: Áз вчéра пя́х, днéс Нáдка да пéе.

Джули: Кои́ са нáй-люби́мите ви кни́ги?

Надка: Мéчо Пýх!

Камен: Я́н Бибия́н на лунáта!

Джули: Тогáва ще ви почетá и от двéте. Седнéте до мéне.

Seaside café "At the Old Lighthouse", Nesebăr

BASIC GRAMMAR

11.1. Aorist tense, continued

A number of different verb types form the aorist with the theme vowel -а- (sometimes spelled -я-). Among these are all и-conjugation verbs which do not form the aorist with the theme vowel -и-. If the final stem consonant is -ч, -ж, or -ш, the theme vowel is spelled -а- : мълча́ (1sg. present) мълча́х (1sg. aorist). Otherwise it is spelled -я-.

In this verb group, the aorist theme vowel is always accented. Note that although the vowel in stressed -а-/-я- in the present is pronounced as [ъ/йъ], stressed -а-/-я- in the aorist is pronounced as [а́] or [я́]. Thus 1sg. present мълча́ is pronounced [мълчъ́] but 3sg. aorist мълча́ is pronounced [мълча́].

Nearly all и-conjugation verbs which form the aorist in -ах or -ях have end stress in both present and aorist. The one exception in this group is ви́дя, which has stem stress in the present and end stress in the aorist.

Below are the present and aorist tense forms of вървя́ and ви́дя.

		PRESENT	**AORIST**	*PRESENT*	**AORIST**
1ˢᵗ	*singular*	върв-я́ [йъ]	върв-я́х [я́х]	ви́д-я	вид-я́х [я́х]
2ⁿᵈ	*singular*	върв-и́ш	върв-я́ [я́]	ви́д-иш	вид-я́ [я́]
3ʳᵈ	*singular*	върв-и́	върв-я́ [я́]	ви́д-и	вид-я́ [я́]
1ˢᵗ	*plural*	върв-и́м	върв-я́хме	ви́д-им	вид-я́хме
2ⁿᵈ	*plural*	върв-и́те	върв-я́хте	ви́д-ите	вид-я́хте
3ʳᵈ	*plural*	върв-я́т [йъ́т]	върв-я́ха	ви́д-ят	вид-я́ха

The verb мо́га also forms its aorist according to this pattern (even though it is an e-conjugation verb). Its stem is that of the 3sg. present, мож-. Thus: 1sg. present мо́га, 1sg. aorist можа́х; 2sg. present мо́жеш, 2sg. aorist можа́, etc.

Two other types form the aorist with the theme vowel -я-. One includes verbs which end in -ея in the present: the aorist stem of these verbs is formed by dropping the stem-final -е. The other includes certain common verbs whose stem-final consonant is -р, e.g. умра́ and спра́. The present and aorist conjugations of живе́я and умра́ are given below.

		PRESENT	AORIST	PRESENT	AORIST
1st	singular	живе́-я	жив-я́х	умр-а́ [ъ]	умр-я́х
2nd	singular	живе́-еш	жив-я́	умр-е́ш	умр-я́ [я]
3rd	singular	живе́-е	жив-я́	умр-е́	умр-я́ [я]
1st	plural	живе́-ем	жив-я́хме	умр-е́м	умр-я́хме
2nd	plural	живе́-ете	жив-я́хте	умр-е́те	умр-я́хте
3rd	plural	живе́-ят	жив-я́ха	умр-а́т [ът]	умр-я́ха

11.2. Emphatic and doubled pronouns

To place emphasis on a pronoun object, Bulgarians have two options. One is to use the long-form pronoun in either sentence initial or sentence final position. This places extremely high emphasis on the pronoun. For example:

Кого́ тъ́рсиш? Ме́не ли тъ́рсиш?	Who are you looking for? *Me?*
Чове́кът не тъ́рси ме́не, а те́бе.	It's not *me* the man's looking for, but *you*.
Да́йте ми, мо́ля, еди́н килогра́м кафе́. А на не́я полови́н ки́ло.	Please give me a kilo of coffee. And give *her* a half kilo.
-- На те́бе ли да го да́м?	"Is it *you* I should give it to?"
-- Не́, не́, да́йте го на не́го.	"No, no, give it to *him*."

The other option is to use both long form and short form objects together, e.g. ме́не (long) + ме (short), or на ме́не (long) + ми (short).   Here are examples:

На ме́не ми да́йте че́твърт сала́м.	Give me a quarter-kilo of salami.
Не́го го ви́ждаме че́сто.	We see him often.

As the translations indicate, the doubled usage of pronoun objects carries considerably less emphasis. The meaning is somewhere in between that of the short form used alone (neutral) and the long form used alone (emphatic).

There are two possible types of word order in such sentences. In one (illustrated above), the doubled pronoun object begins the sentence and is followed immediately by the verb, with nothing intervening. When the verb occurs elsewhere in the sentence, however, the pronoun objects are separated. This is because each of

220

the two objects has its own word rules to obey. Long form objects usually stand at the beginning of the sentence, while short form objects must be directly adjacent to the verb. The following examples illustrate the joint action of these two rules:

На ме́не ни́що не ми́ ка́зва.	S/he doesn't [ever] tell me anything.
На не́го ще му ка́жеш ли?	Will you tell him?

11.3. "Experiencer" constructions

In Bulgarian, indirect pronoun objects appear in a number of very frequently used expressions. One is the "experiencer" construction, which conveys the idea that someone feels a particular way or is in a particular state. For instance:

Студе́но ми е.	I'm cold.	Ще ти ста́не то́пло.	You'll be [too] hot.
Бе́ше ѝ добре́.	She felt fine.	Мно́го ми е ло́шо.	I feel terrible!
Не му́ е добре́.	He's not well.		

The general meaning of all the above sentences is that the subject experiences a certain state. In English, the experiencer is the actual subject of the verb "be", "feel", etc. In Bulgarian, however, these sentences have no subject. The state is expressed by an adverb, and the identity of the experiencer is expressed by an indirect object pronoun. The basic verb is съм, although the verb ста́вам / ста́на can occur in the past and future tenses when the idea of "become" is present. The verb form is *always* 3rd singular.

When a present-tense state is expressed, the order of words is very rigid. This is because short form pronoun objects must stand directly before the 3rd singular copula e, and because they cannot begin a sentence. The only possible choice, therefore, is for either the adverb or the negative particle to begin the sentence.

affirmative	Добре́ ми е.	I'm fine.
interrogative	Добре́ ли ти е?	Are you OK?
negative	Не ми́ е добре́.	I don't feel [so] good.

In the future or past tenses, when it is possible for the verb form to begin the sentence, two different word orders are possible:

past	Добре́ ми бе́ше.	*or*	Бе́ше ми добре́.	I was fine.
	Добре́ ми ста́на.	*or*	Ста́на ми добре́	I'm OK now. *
future	Добре́ ще ми бъ́де.	*or*	Ще ми бъ́де добре́.	I'll be fine.
	Добре́ ще ми ста́не.	*or*	Ще ми ста́не добре́.	I'll get better.

* = I got better.

When these sentences are negated, however, only one word order is possible:

present	Не ми́ е добре́.	I'm not well.
past	Не ми́ бе́ше добре́.	I didn't feel [so] good.
future	Ня́ма да ми е добре́.	I won't be OK.

The doubled indirect object can also be used. When the identity of the experiencer is expressed as a noun, the doubled form *must* be used. For example:

present	На Кали́на не ѝ е добре́.	Kalina's not feeling so well.
future	На студе́нтите добре́ ли ще им ста́не?	Will the students be OK?
past	На Стоя́н не му́ бе́ше добре́.	Stoyan didn't feel good.

11.4. Transitivity, reciprocity, and the particle ce

When the particle ce is added to a verb, it changes the meaning of that verb. Sometimes the change of meaning can only be rendered idiomatically, as in ка́звам (perfective ка́жа) "say, tell" vs. ка́звам се (imperfective only) "be named". Usually, however, one of several definable meanings is added. One of the most frequent of these added meanings is *intransitivity*.

A transitive verb is one that takes a direct object: it expresses the idea of an action which has a direct result on someone or something. An intransitive verb, by contrast, does not (and cannot) take a direct object. It simply expresses the fact that an action "happens". Here are examples of the same verbs used both transitively and intransitively. In each case, the particle ce makes the verb intransitive.

transitive
    Връ́щам кни́гите в библиоте́ката.   I'm returning the books to the library.
intransitive
    Връ́щам се ведна́га след това́.   I'm returning immediately after that.

transitive
    Ма́йката събу́жда деца́та в 7 ч.   Mother wakes the children at 7 a.m.
intransitive
    Деца́та се събу́ждат в 7 ч.   The children wake up at 7 a.m.

transitive
    Ня́ма да ви занима́вам с това́.   I won't bother you with this.
intransitive
    Ня́ма да се занима́вам са́мо с ва́с.   I can't be concerned only with you.

Another meaning the particle ce can add is that of reciprocity. Sometimes this is translated as an object of the sort "each other", and sometimes it is just understood from the context. The verbs in such sentences, of course, must be in the plural. Here are examples of the same verbs used transitively and with reciprocal meaning:

transitive
>Ще го ви́дим ли дове́чера? — Will we see him this evening?

reciprocal
>Ще се ви́дим ли дове́чера? — Will we see each other this evening?

transitive
>Ни́е го сре́щаме че́сто на у́лицата. — We meet him on the street often.

reciprocal
>Ще се сре́щнат за пръ́в пъ́т. — They will meet for the first time.

If the verb is one which takes an indirect object, the reciprocal meaning is expressed with the particle **си**. For instance:

>Ха́йде да си гово́рим на "ти́". — Let's speak to each other as "ти".

11.5. Adverbs of direction and location

The adverb **къде́** means "where" both as location and direction. For example:

| *location* | **Къде́ живе́еш?** | Where do you live? |
| *direction* | **Къде́ оти́ваш?** | Where are you going? |

If a more vivid sense of direction is desired, the directional adverb **накъде́** is used.

| *vivid direction* | **Ти́ накъде́?** | Where are you off to? |
| | **Накъде́ оти́ваш?** | *(same)* |

Certain common adverbial compounds used in answer to this question also are formed with **на-**. Here are the base forms, followed by examples of usage.

| го́ре | up | въ́н | in | ля́во | left |
| до́лу | down | въ́тре | out | дя́сно | right |

>**Оти́вам наго́ре.** — I'm going up.
> [... надо́лу / наля́во / надя́сно] — [...down/left/right]

>**Изли́заме навъ́н.** — We're going outside.
>**Ха́йде да вле́зем навъ́тре в гора́та.** — Let's go deeper into the woods.

The adverb **откъде́** means "from where?". This question is often answered by adverbs formed from **от-** plus the base forms given above. For example:

>**Откъде́ и́два?** — Where is he coming from?
>**Сли́за отго́ре.** — He's coming down [from above].

Йдва отдо́лу.	She's coming up [from below].
Йдва отля́во / отдя́сно.	It's coming from the left/from the right.
Миризма́та йдва отвъ́н.	The smell is coming from outside.
Ня́кой излиза отвъ́тре.	Someone's coming out [from inside].

Frequently, the на- and the от- adverbs are combined. For example:

Вода́та тече́ отго́ре надо́лу.	Water runs downhill [from up to down].
Ни́е пи́шем отля́во надя́сно, а в ара́бските страни́ пи́шат отдя́сно наля́во.	We write from left to right, but in Arabic countries they write from right to left.

The prefix в-, in the meaning of location, can also be added to certain of the above base forms. For example:

-- Къде́ е магази́нът?	"Where's the store?"
-- Ту́ка вля́во.	"Here, on the left."
Вдя́сно от те́бе са очила́та ми. Пода́й ми ги, мо́ля.	My eyeglasses are on your right -- give them to me, please.

11.6. Demonstrative pronouns: тоя

The pronoun то́я "this" is a variant form of то́зи. Bulgarians use it frequently, especially in speech. The demonstrative о́нзи "that" has similar variant forms. Here are both sets:

masculine	*feminine*	*neuter*	*plural*	*(meaning)*
то́-зи	та́-зи	то-ва́	те́-зи	this
то́-я	та́-я	т-у́й	ти́-я	*(same)*
о́н-зи	она́-зи	оно-ва́	оне́-зи	that
о́н-я	она́-я	он-у́й	они́-я	*(same)*

The masculine form то́зи is sometimes shortened to то́з (in writing as well as in speech). The adverb така́ "thus" also has the variant form тъ́й.

11.7. Social interactional formulas

The form of да which sometimes called "modal" appears in a number of formulaic expressions, especially those connected with congratulations or good wishes.

One of the most frequent of these is (in literal translation) "May you be alive and healthy!". It is often said to someone upon departure, roughly equivalent to the archaic English "Fare thee well", and is frequently used as an expression of congratulations, in the sense of "best wishes". The same phrase is used, although somewhat less commonly, with the imperative бъди́ (plural бъде́те). For example:

Да сте жи́ви и здра́ви!	May you be well and healthy!
Бъде́те жи́ви и здра́ви!	Be well and healthy!

The verb meaning "toast" (in the literal sense of touching glasses and drinking) is чу́кам се (perfective чу́кна се). It is introduced by either да or ха́йде да. Toasts themselves are usually expressed with the preposition за. For example:

Ха́йде да се чу́кнем за младоже́нците!	Let's toast the newlyweds!
За мно́го годи́ни!	Here's to many [happy] years!
Наздра́ве!	Cheers! To your health!

11.8. Prepositions

(a)   The preposition из refers to non-directional movement within a closed area. Students of other Slavic languages should pay particular attention to this meaning.

Ще разхо́дя жена́ си из Со́фия.	I'll show my wife around Sofia.
Ще пъту́ваме из Бълга́рия.	We're going to tour Bulgaria.

(b)   The preposition за is used in toasts, either literal (when raising a glass) or metaphorical (general expression of good wishes).

За успе́х на и́зпита!	Here's to success on the exam!

EXERCISES

I. Rewrite the following sentences, doubling the pronouns.

1. Ти́ ли ѝ ка́за за това́?
2. -- Дру́гата годи́на библиоте́ката ще и́ма ли те́зи списа́ния?
   -- Не́, ня́ма да ги получа́ваме.
3. На́шите прия́тели благодари́ха ли им за помощта́?
4. -- Заду́шно е. Ня́ма ли да отво́рите те́зи прозо́рци?
   -- Не ги́ отва́ряме, за да не ста́ва тече́ние.
5. Ско́ро ли го оча́квате да до́йде?
6. -- Нахра́ни ли деца́та?
   -- Нали́ зна́еш, че а́з ни́кога ня́ма да ги оста́вя гла́дни.
7. Ще го напи́ша кога́то и́мам вре́ме.

II. Compose negative and interrogative "experiencer" sentences as follows:

Model: Дими́тър (present tense) ле́сно

Answer: На Дими́тър не му́ е ле́сно.   На Дими́тър ле́сно ли му е?

1.	Кали́на	(past tense)	добре́
2.	Студе́нтите	(future tense)	тру́дно
3.	Деца́та	(present tense)	заба́вно
4.	Ма́йка ми	(past tense)	ло́шо
5.	Ка́мен и На́дка	(future tense)	студе́но
6.	Ле́карят	(past tense)	добре́
7.	Баща́ му	(present tense)	ве́село

III. Fill in the blank with се *ONLY if the meaning requires it.*

1. Те́ _____ опла́каха от не́го на учи́телката.
2. Дру́гия ме́сец ще _____ же́ним на́шата ма́лка дъщеря́.
3. Каче́те _____ по стъ́лбите, асансьо́рът не рабо́ти.
4. Ви́е Ива́н ли _____ ка́звате?
5. Младоже́нците ще ви _____ въ́рнат пари́те, кога́то мо́гат.
6. Те́ _____ оже́ниха преди пе́т годи́ни и и́мат две́ деца́.
7. Джу́ли и Де́йвид ще _____ въ́рнат в Аме́рика в кра́я на ля́тото.

ADDITIONAL GRAMMAR NOTES

11.1a. Aorist tense, continued

The verb спя́ (2sg. спи́ш) is irregular in that it spells the aorist theme vowel as -a- and not -я-. Its aorist is thus 1sg. спáх, 2sg. спá, etc. As in other verbs, the vowel in the -я́ ending of the present tense is pronounced [-йъ́], while the -á ending of the aorist is pronounced [-á].

Verbs with monosyllabic stems in -ая (such as ля́я, зня́я) form the aorist with the theme vowel -я-. All prefixed forms of these verbs (except those of зня́я) also form the aorist with -я-. Verbs in -ая with disyllabic stems (such as копáя), and prefixed forms of зня́я (e.g. познáя), however, have no theme vowel in the aorist. Here are the present and aorist forms of ля́я and познáя:

	PRESENT	**AORIST**	*PRESENT*	**AORIST**
1ˢᵗ singular	ля́-я	ля́-ях	познá-я	познá-х
2ⁿᵈ singular	ля́-еш	ля́-я	познá-еш	познá
3ʳᵈ singular	ля́-е	ля́-я	познá-е	познá
1ˢᵗ plural	ля́-ем	ля́-яхме	познá-ем	познá-хме
2ⁿᵈ plural	ля́-ете	ля́-яхте	познá-ете	познá-хте
3ʳᵈ plural	ля́-ят	ля́-яха	познá-ят	познá-ха

11.2a. Emphatic and doubled pronouns

The pronoun себе

The reflexive pronoun себе occurs only in the doubled form, and only in the form себе си. This phrase expresses both direct and indirect object meanings.

-- Когó ви́ждаш в огледáлото?	"Whom are you looking at in the mirror?"
-- Ви́ждам себе си в нéго.	"I see myself in it."
-- На мéне ли говóриш?	"Are you talking to me?"
-- Нé, на себе си.	"No, to myself."
За себе си ако не сé погри́жиш, за когó ще се погри́жиш?	If you don't look after yourself, then who are you going to look after?

Word order with doubled pronouns

Doubled pronoun phrases -- comprising a long form and a short form pronoun object -- are encountered very frequently in Bulgarian. The two pronouns mean exactly the same thing, but since one of them is a clitic and the other a fully accented word, they are subject to very different word order rules.

Accented words can, in principle, occur anywhere in the sentence. The long form of a doubled object, however, almost always stands at the beginning of the sentence, although in certain instances it can also stand at the end of the sentence. Short form objects obey the rules already learned for clitics: they cannot begin a sentence, they stand immediately adjacent to the verb, and they follow directly the particles да, ще or не.

Combining these two sets of rules, one sees that the short object can directly follow the long one, if the sequence of objects is followed directly by the verb. More frequently, however, the verb occurs near or at the end of the sentence. Care must then be taken that both sets of word order rules are applied correctly. The following examples (with numbering cumulative across lessons) illustrate these rules. As clitics, the short form objects are identified in capital letters (*IND, DIR*). As fully accented words, the long form objects are identified in lower case letters (*indirect obj., direct obj.*)

(49) | На ме́не | ни́що | ни́кога | не | ми́ | да́ва. |
| *indirect obj.* | *direct obj.* | | *Neg.* | *IND* | *verb* |

She doesn't ever give me anything.

(50) | Не́я | ще | я | ви́диш | ли? |
| *direct obj.* | *Fut.* | *DIR* | *verb* | *INT* |

Will you see her?

(51) | Ха́йде и | на тя́х | да | им | го | пока́жем. |
| | *indirect obj.* | *Cnj.* | *IND* | *DIR* | *verb* |

Let's show it to them too.

(52) | Тя́ | жена́ | ли | му | е | на не́го? |
| *subject* | *predicate* | *INT* | *IND* | *3ʳᵈCOP* | *indirect obj.* |

Is she his wife?

11.3a. "Experiencer" constructions

Experiencer constructions also occur frequently with doubled pronoun objects. The rules outlined above apply to them as well, of course.

(53) | На не́я | не | й | е | добре́. |
| *indirect obj.* | *Neg.* | *IND* | *3ʳᵈCOP* | |

She doesn't feel good.

(54) | На тя́х | не | им | бе́ше | добре́. |
| *indirect obj.* | *Neg.* | *IND* | *verb* | |

They didn't feel well.

(55)   На тях | няма   да   им   бъде | добре.
indirect obj. | neg.   Cnj.   IND   verb |

They won't feel well.

(56)   На него   добре | ли   ще   му   стане? |
indirect obj. | INT   Fut.   IND   verb |

Will he get better?

(57)   Добре | ли   му   беше | на Иван?
| INT   IND   verb | indirect obj.

Were things OK [in the end] for Ivan?

11.4a.   Transitivity, reciprocity, and the particle ce

A large number of verbs can occur both in the transitive form (accompanied by a direct object) and the intransitive form (accompanied by the particle **ce**). For some verbs, the intransitive is the more neutral of the two, and in this case the transitive variant takes on a more causative meaning. The same is true of certain reciprocal verbs. Here are examples of usage, with the more neutral intransitive variant given first.

intransitive
   Синът ми се жени скоро.   My son is getting married soon.
transitive
   Скоро ще женя сина си.   Soon I'll be marrying off my son.

intransitive
   Ще се разходим из София.   We'll stroll around Sofia [and see the
                                             sights].
transitive
   Ще разходя жена си из София.   I'm going to take my wife around Sofia
                                             [and show her the sights].

reciprocal
   Не се карайте, деца.   Don't fight, children.
transitive
   Не ме карай да те чакам.   Don't make me wait for you.

Certain reciprocal verbs can retain the **ce** and still occur with a seemingly transitive meaning. In these cases, the object is a prepositional phrase. For example:

   Утре ще се срещнем с него.   We'll meet him tomorrow.
   Той се кара често с нас.   He argues with us often.

Several verbs are particularly interesting in this regard. One is **интересувам**, whose transitive usage is as in English. When used intransitively, it adds **ce** and takes the preposition **от**. The verb **опла́квам** "mourn" is similar: in the intransitive version (with the meaning "complain") it adds **се** and takes the preposition **от**.

The verb **се́щам се** "remember, call to mind" also belongs to this category. Although this verb is transitive in English, in Bulgarian it is an intransitive verb marked by **се**. Like other verbs of mentioning, thinking etc., it takes an object with the preposition **за**. For the transitive meaning, the related verb **подсе́щам** "remind" is used. For all these verbs, examples of which are given below, the intransitive version is the one more commonly encountered.

intransitive

    Интересу́вам се от средновеко́вието. | I'm interested in the Middle Ages.

transitive

    Интересу́ва ме средновеко́вието. | The Middle Ages interest me.

intransitive

    От какво́ се опла́квате? | What are you complaining about?

transitive

    Жи́в да го опла́чеш. | It makes your heart bleed to see him. (literally: it's as if you mourn him alive.)

intransitive

    По це́ли ме́сеци не се́ се́ща за ма́йка си. | For months at a time he won't remember [to think of] his mother.

transitive

    Ако не го́ подсе́тя, ня́ма и по телефо́на да ѝ се оба́ди. | If I don't remind him, he won't get in touch with her even by phone.

11.5a. Adverbs of direction and location

There are numerous adverbs of location which are formed either with the prefix **от-** (and to a lesser extent, **на-**), or without a prefix altogether. These usages are idiomatic. For example:

Че́тните номера́ на къщите са отля́во, а нече́тните -- отдя́сно. | The even-numbered houses are on the left, and the odd-numbered ones on the right.

То́й седи́ отля́во (от ля́вата ми страна́). | He's sitting on my left (on my left side).

Въ́тре гори́ о́гън -- ела́ въ́тре. | There's a fire inside -- come on in.

Навъ́тре в гора́та и́ма мно́го я́годи. | There are a lot of strawberries in the woods.

Боли́ ме отвъ́тре, като чу́вам таки́ва неща́.	It pains me [inside] to hear such things.

Деца́та си игра́ят въ́н.	The children are playing outside.
Деца́та си игра́ят отвъ́н.	*(same)*
Деца́та си игра́ят навъ́н.	*(same)*

Perhaps the most frequently used of these is the idiomatic formula го́ре-до́лу, which corresponds to English "more or less":

Така́ го́ре-до́лу ми́сля и а́з.	That's more or less what I think, too.

11.5b. The noun пъ́т

The noun пъ́т "time" occurs in expressions like "the first time", "the second time", "every time", "some time" and the like. The plural is **-и**. There is no quantified form: the plural is used after numbers and other quantifiers.

This noun usually occurs in the indefinite form, although the definite form is possible if the speaker has a specific "time" in mind. As in other adverbials of time formed from masculine nouns (e.g. ми́налия ме́сец), the definite *object* form is used.

Все́ки пъ́т, кога́то я ви́ждам, забра́вям да ѝ ка́жа за те́бе.	Every time I see her I forget to tell her about you.
За пъ́рви пъ́т ще во́дим деца́та в Евро́па.	We're taking the children to Europe for the first time.
После́дния пъ́т, кога́то се видя́хме, бе́ше през деке́мври.	The last time we got together was in December.
Ще ми́на ня́кой пъ́т да си поприка́зваме.	I'll drop by some time so we can have a chat.
Ни́е се видя́хме са́мо еди́н пъ́т, и то закра́тко.	We met only once, and for a very short time at that.
Два́ пъ́ти, три́ пъ́ти, ня́ма значе́ние ко́лко пъ́ти звъ́ня по телефо́на и все́ не мо́га да го наме́ря.	Twice, three times, it doesn't matter how many times I call, he's never there.

11.7a. Social interactional formulas

Another way to express congratulations is with phrases containing the adjective **честит**. If the occasion is not specified, one uses the adverbial form. If the occasion is specified, the adjective **честит** modifies the noun signifying it. For example:

Честита Нова година!	Happy New Year!
Честит рожден ден!	Happy birthday!
Честита Баба Марта!	Happy first day of spring!
Честит празник!	Happy holiday!
Честито!	Congratulations!

The greeting for one who has just arrived is composed of the adverb **добре** and the L-participle of the verb **дойда**. This phrase, which means literally "well come", must carry the adjectival ending appropriate to the person(s) being welcomed.

greeting	*(meaning)*	*addressee*
Добре дошл-и!	Welcome!	*a group or a single person spoken to as* **вие**
Добре дошл-а!	Welcome!	*a female spoken to as* **ти**
Добре дош-ъл!	Welcome!	*a male spoken to as* **ти**
Добре дошл-о!	Welcome!	*a child, animal or neuter object*

The imperative form **заповядай** (plural **заповядайте**) is used on a number of occasions. It is said on moving aside to let someone pass, on handing someone something (either as a gift or as a purchase), on extending an invitation, or on asking someone in. Examples below are given in the plural form; of course, the singular is used in speaking to someone addressed as **ти**.

Заповядайте, минете.	After you.
Ето, заповядайте.	Here [you are].
Заповядайте на гости у нас.	Come by and see us [sometime].
Заповядайте!	Come in!

11.9. Definiteness and numbers

Numbers can be used in the definite form when the group they refer to is spoken of as a specified, known unit. If the unit is 1, the definite form usually signals a contrast between "the one" and "the other". In the plural, **едни(те)** is used in the sense "some, certain ones".

Of course, numbers higher than 1 cannot distinguish singular and plural. Definite articles for these numbers are either **-та** (any number form ending in **-a)** or **-те**. For numbers 4 and higher the accent shifts to the definite article.

Here is a synopsis of the forms and their accentuation, followed by examples.

number	masculine		neuter	feminine	(plural)
1	еди́н-ият		едно́-то	една́-та	едни́-те
	personal	*non-personal*			
2	два́ма-та	два́-та		две́-те	
3	три́ма-ата		три́-те		
4	четири́ма-та		четири-те́		
	etc.		etc.		

Една́та врата́ е отво́рена, а дру́гата не е́.	One of the doors is open, and the other one isn't.
Едни́те вли́зат, а дру́гите излѝзат.	Some come in, and others go out.
Разхо́жда ме по едни́ кри́ви у́лици.	He's taking me down some crooked streets.
А ви́е два́мата, ела́те след 1 ча́с.	As for you two, come back in an hour.
Три́те жени́ ча́кат на опа́шка.	The three women are waiting in line.
Това́ бе́ше през петдесетте́ годи́ни.	That was during the 50s.

When definite numbers are preceded by the conjunction и, the meaning is "all of..." (or, in the case of the number 2, "both"). For example:

И два́мата мъже́ и́дват да ни помо́гнат.	Both men are coming to help us.
Ще почета́ и от две́те кни́ги.	I'll read a bit from both of the books.
Ще до́йдат и три́мата.	All three of them will come.
И три́те яйца́ са развале́ни.	All three eggs went bad.

The ordinal number пъ́рви can also appear without the final -и in certain idiomatic expressions. The form without the -и is spelled differently: the sequence -ър- is replaced by the sequence -ръ-. For example:

Ще се сре́щнат за пръ́в пъ́т.	They will meet for the first time.

11.10.   The conjunction че, continued

The conjunction **че** often suggests a mild degree of causality. In such instances, it is best left untranslated into English, since the English conjunction "because" would convey too much of a causal relationship. For example:

Ха́йде, че съм гла́ден!	Let's go! I'm hungry!
А́з да вървя́, че ме ча́кат.	I'm on my way; they're waiting for me.

NOTE: A comma is **nearly always** written before **че,** regardless of either the meaning, or the spoken form, of the sentence.

11.11.   The particle де

The particle **де** suggests increased interaction in conversation, often verging on impatience.

Кажи́ де! Же́нен ли си?	So tell me! Are you married [or not]?
Ха́йде де! Да тръ́гваме!	Come on! Let's get going!

SAMPLE SENTENCES

1. Лиля́на се пла́ши от ми́шки. Младе́н ѝ ка́зва: Не сé плаши́, ня́ма ни́що стра́шно.

2. Ма́лките деца́ вя́рват в Торбала́н и се пла́шат от не́го.

3. -- Óх, ка́к ме стре́сна!
   -- Не сé стря́скай, а́з съм.

4. Ка́мен и На́дка не сé разби́рат мно́го добре́: те́ се разби́рат като ку́че и ко́тка.

5. Два́мата бра́тя ка́рат коли́те си по еди́н и съ́щ на́чин.

6. Не сé се́щам каква́ пе́сен мо́жем да изпе́ем. Подсети́ ме за ня́коя ху́бава пе́сен.

7. Спо́мням си добро́то ста́ро вре́ме.

8. Спо́мняш ли си ко́лко стру́ва еди́н трамва́ен биле́т в Со́фия?

9. Ако не заку́си, след о́бед ще му ста́не ло́шо.

10. На Лиля́на ѝ ста́ва ло́шо в самоле́т.

11. Ка́мене, ло́шо ли ти е? Защо́ си то́лкова бле́д?

12. И два́мата бя́хме бо́лни. Сега́ на ме́не ми е по́-добре́, а то́й о́ще не мо́же да ста́ва от легло́то.

13. На ме́не ми е я́сно за какво́ ста́ва ду́ма, на те́бе я́сно ли ти е?

14. На не́я все́ ѝ е студе́но, а на не́го му е горе́що. То́й отва́ря прозо́реца, тя́ го затва́ря.

15. Наку́де́ ме во́диш? Та́м ня́ма пъ́т.

16. Върви́ш наля́во до пресе́чката, по́сле зави́ваш.

17. Пъте́ката е тя́сна: отля́во и́ма планина́, а отдя́сно -- про́паст.

SENTENCES FOR TRANSLATION

1. How is your father? I saw him yesterday and he wasn't so well then. What is the matter with him?

2. Boris and Marina don't speak to each other any more. They are always fighting. Things aren't going very well for them. I wanted to help them but I couldn't. Could you?

3. Will you wake up on time, or do you want me to wake you up? Don't complain if I wake you earlier than you want. It's better than waking up too late.

4. Congratulations on your new house! May you live there many long and happy years!

5. Ivan is cold, can you give him his jacket please? The children were cold before, but then their mother brought them their jackets and now they are no longer cold.

6. The students are all upset [feeling bad], because they have an exam tomorrow. Last night they were so cold they couldn't study. Today they will help each other study, though.

7. Are you all right? You say you're OK, but I'm worried about you. You say you are going to the left and then you go to the right, and you say you are going up and then you go down.

8. I don't understand. He sold you the kebabs for ten leva, but he sold me kebabs for fifteen leva. I don't want to complain to everyone, but to you I'll complain!

9. Your friends had a lot of fun last night -- they watched a film, saw many of their favorite actors, and died laughing. Why couldn't you watch the film with them? Were you really ill? Are you better now?

10. There are so many new places to visit -- I'm interested in all of them. But I am most interested in the mountains. I always feel great in the mountains. My sister does too -- we both are happy when we are in the mountains.

READING SELECTION

Кореспонде́нция - (9)

7 януа́ри

Дра́ги Бо́б,

Ни́е сме, ка́кто ви́наги през зи́мната вака́нция, на го́сти за ня́колко дни́ у мо́ите роди́тели. Дойдо́хме ведна́га след Но́ва годи́на. Роди́телите ми са ве́че ста́ри и еди́нствената им ра́дост в живо́та са люби́мите вну́ци. Като по́вечето ста́ри хо́ра не и́скат да променя́т на́вafter на́виците си и да до́йдат да живе́ят при нас. Мно́го им се мо́лихме, но не можа́хме да ги убеди́м. Къ́щата им ту́ка е, разби́ра се, несравни́мо по́-голя́ма и удо́бна от на́шия апартаме́нт в Со́фия. Но на нас ще ни е прия́тно те́ да са по́-бли́зо до нас. И ни́е на тя́х ще мо́жем по́вече да пома́гаме, и те́ на нас. Я́на и осо́бено И́во са мно́го привъ́рзани към сво́ите ба́ба и дя́до: като ма́лък И́во прека́ра три́ годи́ни в Смо́лян при тя́х. Я́вно, докато са здра́ви (да чу́кна на дърво́), ще са ту́к, пък по́сле ще ви́дим.

Ма́йка ми е мно́го дово́лна, че сме на го́сти в Смо́лян. Ше́та от су́трин до ве́чер из къ́щи. Вче́ра ни пра́ви ба́ница, о́ня де́н -- коко́шка с ки́село зе́ле. Да́же не се́ се́ща да се опла́ква от здра́вето си.

Ни́е с баща́ ми ти́я дни́ постегнахме къ́щата -- зна́еш ка́к са ста́рите къ́щи, в тя́х все́ и́ма по не́що счу́пено.

Ту́к кли́матът е суро́в, а къ́щата на роди́телите ми ня́ма, разби́ра се, па́рно отопле́ние. Кали́на е зимо́рничава и все́ ѝ е студе́но. Вче́ра да́же ѝ ста́на ло́шо, но дне́с ѝ е по́-добре́. Докато бе́ше студе́но, държа́хме деца́та по́вече въ́тре. Дне́с оба́че вре́мето оме́кна и те́ изля́зоха навъ́н. Я́на напра́ви голя́м сне́жен чове́к с но́с от мо́рков, а И́во си игра́е с ку́чето на двора. О́ще три́ дни́ и ще се връ́щаме в Со́фия. Мо́же би та́м ще ни ча́ка писмо́ от ва́с.

На те́бе и на семе́йството ти пожела́вам да сте жи́ви и здра́ви.

Сърде́чни по́здрави,

Бо́йко

P.S. Пра́щам та́зи ка́ртичка да ви́дите ко́лко са ху́бави ро́дните ми Родо́пи.

23 януа́ри

Дра́ги Бо́йко,

Ня́ма да повя́рваш, но дне́с полу́чихме едновре́менно ва́шите писма́ от
29 деке́мври и 7 януа́ри. Мно́го благодари́м за ху́бавите ка́ртички. Патри́ша
се ка́ни да пи́ше отде́лно на Кали́на в о́тговор на новогоди́шната чести́тка.
Родо́пите изгле́жда найстина заслужа́ват да ги посети́м за ня́колко дни́.
Какви́ интере́сни места́ и́ма та́м? В Бълга́рия а́з чу́х от коле́гите са́мо за
зи́мния куро́рт Бо́ровец, но дали́ и́ма сми́съл да оти́дем до та́м, щом ще бъ́дем
в Бълга́рия през ля́тото?
Въобще́, защо́ не ми́ разка́жеш по́вече за планини́те в Бълга́рия? А́з
видя́х са́мо Ви́тоша. Мно́го е ху́бава. Хо́дих до та́м це́ли два́ пъ́ти. Еди́ния
пъ́т, ка́кто си́гурно си спо́мняш, се качи́хме с те́бе и с И́во на Че́рни връ́х. А
ня́колко дни́ по-къ́сно ме во́диха да вече́ряме на Копи́тото. Изгле́дът къ́м
но́щна Со́фия от рестора́нта бе́ше чуде́сен.
В едно́ от преди́шните си писма́ ти́ ми пи́са за Ри́ла. Ни́е с Патри́ша
ве́че твъ́рдо реши́хме да посети́м Ри́лския манасти́р.
Че́тохме за нестина́рите в Стра́нджа. Ка́к ми́слиш, по кое́ вре́ме да
оти́дем, за да ги ви́дим?
Е́то че па́к те затру́пах с въпро́си. Ча́каме с нетърпе́ние о́тговора ти.

По́здрави от вси́чки ни

Бо́б

GLOSSARY

абони́рам	subscribe	едновре́менен	simultaneous
ара́бски	Arab *(adj.)*	ерге́н	bachelor
асансьо́р	elevator		
		жа́лко	too bad, pity
Ба́ба Ма́рта	Granny March (har-	же́ня	marry off
	binger of spring)	же́ня се	get married
биле́т	ticket	жи́в	live, living, alive
блед	pale	жи́в да го	it makes your heart bleed
		опла́чеш	to see him
вдя́сно	on the right		
вля́во	on the left	за	to *(in a toast)*
врѣх, върхъ́т	summit; tip	за какво́ ста́ва	what's the matter, what's
(pl. върхове́*)*		ду́ма	it about
връ́щам се /	return, go back	за мно́го годи́ни	many happy returns
въ́рна се		за да	in order to *(conjunction*
вълше́бник	magician, wizard		*of purpose)*
вън	out	за да не ста́ва	so there won't be a draft
въобще́	in general	тече́ние	
въпро́с	question	заба́вен	amusing, fun
въ́тре	in, inside	закра́тко	for a short while
		заку́свам / заку́ся	eat breakfast
го́ре	up	занима́вам	interest, occupy
го́ре-до́лу	more or less	занимавам се с	be occupied with
горе́щ	hot	заслужа́вам /	deserve, be worth
горя́	burn	заслу́жа (-иш)	
		затру́пвам /	cover up, bury under;
да сте жи́ви и	here's to your life	затру́пам	pile up
здра́ви	and health	затру́пвам с	burden with questions
да́же	even	въпро́си	
дали́	whether, if; *(question*	зи́мен	winter *(adj.)*
	particle)	зи́мен куро́рт	ski resort
дали́ и́ма сми́съл?	does it make any	зимо́рничав	sensitive to the cold
	sense?		
двор	yard	и то	at that
де́сен, дя́сна	right	игра́я на дво́ра	play in the yard
до́лу	down	игра́я си	play around
добре́ дошла́	welcome *(to female)*	из	around, throughout
добре́ дошли́!	welcome *(to a group*	из къ́щи	around the house
	or a formal		*(fixed phrase)*
	acquaintance)	изпя́вам / изпе́я	sing [to the end]
добре́ дошъл	welcome *(to male)*	и́ма сми́съл	it makes sense
добро́то ста́ро вре́ме	the good old days	интересу́вам се от	be interested in
дошъл	come		
дърво́ *(pl.* дърва́*)*	wood	как така́	how is it that, how can
държа́ (-и́ш)	hold, keep		that be
дя́сна *see* де́сен		ка́ня се	plan, intend
		ка́рам се	scold, quarrel
еди́нствен, -ена	single, only	като ма́лък	when he was little

ка́чвам се по стъ́лбите	climb the stairs	о́ня	that (variant of о́нзи)
кли́мат	climate	опа́шка	tail; line, queue
кога́то	when (conjunction)	опла́квам / опла́ча (-еш)	mourn, lament
коко́шка	hen, fowl	опла́квам се / опла́ча се (-еш)	complain, grumble
коме́дия	comedy		
куро́рт	resort	отвъ́н	from outside
		отго́ре	from above
ла́я	bark	отдо́лу	from below
ля́в (pl. ле́ви)	left, Left	отдя́сно	from the right
		отля́во	from the left
мече́	bear cub	отопле́ние	heating
Ме́чо Пух	Winnie the Pooh	отско́ро	(since) quite recently
миризма́	smell, scent	очила́ (pl. only)	eyeglasses
ми́шка	mouse		
мо́же	it's possible	пара́	coin
		па́рен	steam (adj.)
на́вик	habit	пари́	money
навъ́н	outside (directional)	па́рно отопле́ние	central heating
навъ́тре	inside (directional)	пе́я	sing
наго́ре	up (directional)	пла́ша се (-иш)	be frightened, fear
надо́лу	down (directional)	по́вечето	the majority
надя́сно	to the right	погри́жвам се / погри́жа се (-иш)	take care of, look after
наздра́ве	cheers, to your health!		
накъде́	to where	пода́вам / пода́м (-даде́ш)	hand, pass, reach
наля́во	to the left		
нахра́нвам / нахра́ня	feed	поприка́звам	have a chat
не рабо́ти	it's out of order	попя́вам / попе́я	sing a little
несравни́м	incomparable	поразхо́ждам	take for a brief stroll
нестина́р	fire-dancer	посеща́вам / посетя́	visit
нестина́рство	fire-dancing, fire-walking		
		постя́гам /постѐгна	tighten, fasten; prepare, fix up
нече́тен	odd-numbered		
новогоди́шен	New Year's	почи́там, почета́	read for a bit
новогоди́шна чести́тка	New Year's greeting	пресе́чка	intersection
		привъ́рзан	tied, bound, attached
нос, -ъ́т (pl. носове́)	nose	проме́ням / променя́	change
ня́ма ни́що стра́шно	there's nothing to be afraid of		
		про́паст, -та́	abyss, cavern
		пък	but, yet, and, while
оба́ждам се по телефо́на	call on the phone	пъте́ка	(foot)path
		пътеше́ствие	trip
огледа́ло	mirror		
оже́нвам / оже́ня	marry	ра́бота	job; matter
оже́нвам се / оже́ня се	get married	рабо́тя	work, be in operation
		разва́лен	spoiled, rotten
оме́квам / оме́кна	soften, grow milder	разхо́дка из града́	city tour
она́я	that (variant of она́зи)	реша́вам / реша́ (-и́ш)	decide
они́я	those (variant of оне́зи)	ро́ден	one's own, native
		ро́дно мя́сто	birthplace
ону́й	that (variant of онова́)		
		сала́м	sausage

самолéт	airplane	тóя	this (*variant of* тóзи)
свáтбен, -ена	wedding (*adj.*)	туй	this (*variant of* товá)
свáтбено пътешéствие	honeymoon	тъй	thus (*variant of* такá)
сéбе си	oneself (*reflexive object form*)	убеждáвам / убедя́	persuade (*see L. 14*)
		удóбен	convenient/comfortable
семéйство	family	умúрам / умрá	die
сéщам се / сéтя се	recall, come to mind, think of, remember	умúрам от смя́х	die laughing
смúсъл	sense, meaning	хáйде да се чýкнем	let's have a toast
смя́х, смехъ́т (*pl.* смеховé)	laughter	чáкам на опáшка	wait in/on line
снéжен	snow (*adj.*)	чéрен	black
снéжен човéк	snowman	честúт прáзник	happy holiday
спúрам / спрá	stop	честúт рождéн дéн	happy birthday
стоя́	stay in one place	честúто	congratulations!
стря́скам / стрéсна	startle, scare	чéтвърт, -тá	quarter
стря́скам се / стрéсна се	be startled, take fright	чéтен	even-numbered
		чýкам / чýкна	knock, clink
стъ́лба	step, ladder	чýкам на дървó	knock on wood
сурóв	severe	чýкам се / чýкна се	clink glasses, toast
счýпен, -ена	broken		
събýждам / събýдя	wake		
събýждам се / събýдя се	wake up, awaken	шампáнско	champagne
такъ́в (такáва, такóва, такúва)	such	ще свъ́рши рáбота	that'll do the job
такúва нещá	such things	щом	as soon as, since, as, if, once
тáя	this (*variant of* тáзи)		
твъ́рд	hard, firm, steadfast	я́вен	open, obvious
твъ́рдо решáвам	firmly resolve	я́вно	clearly
тúя	these (*variant of* тéзи)	я́года	strawberry
		яйцé (*pl.* яйцá)	egg
то	then (*particle*)	я́сен	clear
торбá	bag, sack	я́сно ми е	I get it, it's clear

241

CULTURAL COMMENTARY

Families: relationship patterns; residences

The parent-child relationship in Bulgaria is a very close one. It is nearly unthinkable, for instance, that a mother will not be present at her son's wedding: only the most drastic of unforeseeable circumstances would prevent her attendance.

The grandparent-grandchild relationship is also very close. It is not uncommon for children to spend very long periods of time at the home of the grandparents. Sometimes this is from necessity, as the parents both must work and cannot look after their children properly. It is also, however, traditional to keep the tie between the generations alive in this way.

As a rule, there is a large difference between city residences and country ones. Those in the city are small, cramped, and often in large apartment buildings with no open space for children to play. Those in the country are frequently large and roomy, but they lack central heating (and sometimes even indoor plumbing).

Literature: children's books

Many favorite children's books from other languages have been translated into Bulgarian, among them A. A. Milne's *Winnie the Pooh* (Мечо Пух) and L. F. Baum's *The Wizard of Oz* (Вълшебникът от Оз). There are also many fine children's books written in Bulgarian, one of which is *Jan Bibian on the Moon* (Ян Бибиян на луната), by the well-known author Elin Pelin (Елин Пелин, 1878-1949).

Geography: seaside and mountain resorts

The Black Sea coast is a favorite vacation spot. There are many fine beaches, resorts and small tourist spots. Bulgarians speak of it simply as морето ("the sea"). The other favorite vacation spot is the mountains; there are numerous resorts. One of the best known (for both summer and winter sports) is Borovets (Боровец), in the northern Rila mountains. Another is Pamporovo (Пампорово) in the Rhodopes. Being within the city limits of Sofia, Vitosha mountain is not considered a resort. Nevertheless it has ski lifts and tourist hotels, which are frequently visited. The hotel at Kopitoto (Копитото) has a good restaurant and a fine view of the city. Hiking to the top of Vitosha, at Cherni vrǎkh (Черни връх) is a favorite activity.

Geography: Strandzha

The far southeastern corner of Bulgaria is called Strandzha (Странджа). One of the archaic folk customs formerly practiced there is that of "nestinarstvo" (нестинарство) or fire-walking. The fire-walkers (нестинари) would be moved to state of ecstasy which would allow them to dance barefoot on live coals without getting burned. The custom is now recreated for tourists with a simulation of live coals.

Customs and beliefs: Baba Marta; Torbalan

"Granny March" (Баба Марта) is the personification of the month of March; spring is said to begin on the first day of March. (For the custom of "martenitsi", see Lesson 13.)

Torbalan (Торбалан) is a mythical character in Bulgarian children's folklore. He carries a large sack (торба), and is said to scoop up naughty children into his sack and carry them off.

LESSON 12

DIALOGUE

Защо́ га́бровците ре́жат опа́шките на ко́тките?

Веселин: Ко́лко е часъ́т? Ко́лко о́ще и́ма до Го́рна Оря́ховица?

Дейвид: Та́м ли ще сли́зате?

Веселин: Да́. Та́м тря́бва да се прехвъ́рля на дру́г вла́к, на вла́ка за Га́брово.

Дейвид: Каже́те ни не́що за фестива́ла. Какво́ ста́ва та́м?

Веселин: Мно́го е интере́сно и заба́вно. Га́бровци разпра́вят мно́го ви́цове. Ще ви разка́жа еди́н. Защо́ га́бровците ре́жат опа́шките на ко́тките?

Джули: Защо́?

Веселин: За да не изсти́ва ста́ята, като вли́зат и излли́зат през зи́мата.

Дейвид: Но това́ е ужа́сно!

Веселин: Защо́?

Дейвид: Нали́ живо́тните и́мат права́! Ня́ма ли при ва́с общество́ за защи́та на права́та на живо́тните? Тря́бва да и́ма, на вся́ка цена́!

Веселин: Това́ е ви́ц. Зна́ете ли какво́ е ви́ц?

Дейвид: Не ми́ харе́сват таки́ва ви́цове.

Надка: Ма́мо, заболя́ ме гъ́рлото!

Милена: Катоседи́ш на тече́ние, така́ е!

Таня: Ка́мене, те́бе боли́ ли те гъ́рлото?

Камен: Не́, са́мо моми́четата ги боли́.

Таня: Кажи́ ми, найстина ли ти е добре́?

Камен: Добре́ ми е ма́мо, че́стна ду́ма.

Дейвид: Кажéте ми óще нéщо за фестивáла. Каквó прáвите? Сáмо вѝцове ли си разпрáвяте?

Веселин: Не знáм тóчно, тé всяка годѝна измѝслят нéщо нóво. Мѝналата годѝна организѝраха карнавáлно шéствие. Вчéра във Вáрна случáйно срéщнах едѝн приятел от Гáброво. Мнóго се зарáдвах да го вѝдя. Сáмо че тóй бéше мнóго заéт. Поговóрихме си с нéго за фестивáла на крáк, като вървяхме по улицата. Чух от нéго, че сегá подгóтвят голéми изненáди. Затовá отѝвам да вѝдя със сóбствените си очѝ. Защó не дóйдете с мéн? Самѝ ще вѝдите. Сѝгурен съм, че мнóго ще харéсате фестивáла.

Дейвид: Каквó мѝслиш, Джули? Да отѝдем ли?

Джули: Мóже.

Monument to the April Uprising, Dryanovo Monastery
near Veliko Tarnovo

244

BASIC GRAMMAR

12.1. Aorist tense, conclusion

There is a small group of verbs whose aorist is irregular. The aorist theme vowel -a- is added to a stem which has lost its internal vowel. This group includes **берá** and all its prefixed forms, as well as **перá, дерá** and their prefixed forms. Below are the present and aorist tense forms of **перá** and **разберá**.

	PRESENT	**AORIST**	*PRESENT*	**AORIST**
1st singular	пер-á	пр-áх	разбер-á	разбр-áх
2nd singular	пер-éш	пр-á	разбер-éш	разбр-á
3rd singular	пер-é	пр-á	разбер-é	разбр-á
1st plural	пер-éм	пр-áхме	разбер-éм	разбр-áхме
2nd plural	пер-éте	пр-áхте	разбер-éте	разбр-áхте
3rd plural	пер-áт	пр-áха	разбер-áт	разбр-áха

12.2. Usage of the aorist tense

The Bulgarian aorist tense is used to convey the simplest, most straightforward of past tense meanings: the fact that an action happened. It is formed freely from verbs of both aspects. The crucial factor in determining which aspect to use is the meaning desired, and the degree of boundedness associated with that meaning. Consider the following narration, in which the aorist verb forms are underlined:

-- Тú каквó <u>прáви</u> вчéра?　　“What did you do yesterday?”

-- <u>Ýчих</u> чéтири чáса,　　“I studied for four hours,
　　а пóсле <u>пúх</u> кафé.　　　and then had [some] coffee.
　　<u>Изпúх</u> трú кафéта.　　　I drank three cups of coffee.”

-- <u>Наýчи</u> ли нéщо　　“Did you learn something/anything
　　за тéзи чéтири чáса?　　in those four hours?”

-- <u>Наýчих</u> правилáта　　“I learned the rules of the road.”
　　на пътното движéние.

Each of these above verbs relates what the speaker “did”. Some of what she did was more bounded in meaning, and for these actions perfective verbs (“learn”, “drink [up a certain amount]”) were used. When no boundedness was implied, imperfective verbs (“do”, “study”, “drink ”) were used.

　　English can only sometimes render this distinction formally, such as through the opposition between “study” and “learn”. More frequently, the English distinction must be understood from the context. Bulgarians, however (as well as students learning to speak and write Bulgarian) must always make a conscious choice between a bounded (perfective) or an unbounded (imperfective) verb form.

12.3. Impersonal verbs

Bulgarian has four verb forms called "impersonal", which express the meanings of existence, non-existence, possibility and necessity. Two have been learned already and two will be learned in this lesson. Each impersonal verb is formally equivalent to the 3sg. form of a fully conjugated verb. The two sets are:

conjugated verb	meaning	impersonal verb	meaning
и́мам	have	и́ма	there is/are
ня́мам	not have	ня́ма	there isn't/aren't
мо́га	can, be able	мо́же	maybe, OK
тря́бвам	be necessary to	тря́бва	must, have to

Of the conjugated verbs, only **тря́бвам** is new to the student. The subject of this verb (and of the sentence) is the person or thing needed, and the one who needs it is expressed as the indirect object. Here are examples:

О, Миле́на! То́чно ти́ ми тря́бваш!	Oh, Milena! You're just whom I need! [= Exactly you are necessary to me.]
Тря́бват им цве́тни мо́ливи.	They need colored pencils. [= Colored pencils are necessary to them.]
Тря́бва им един добъ́р ре́чник.	They need a good dictionary. [= A good dictionary is necessary to them.]

The unchanging form **тря́бва** (equivalent to the 3sg. form of **тря́бвам**) is much more commonly encountered. In its meaning as an impersonal form. it either stands alone or is followed by a да-phrase. Although impersonal **тря́бва** does not have a grammatical subject, the да-phrase does, and this subject may or may not be expressed. A literal translation of **тря́бва** would be "it is necessary that...", but the more normal translation is "have to", "must", "need to". Here are examples:

То́й тря́бва да у́чи. Тря́бва да у́чи.	He's got to study.
А́з тря́бва да рабо́тя дове́чера. Тря́бва да рабо́тя дове́чера.	I have to work tonight.
Ни́е тря́бва да сле́зем ту́ка. Тря́бва да сле́зем ту́ка.	We need to get off here.

Ти́ тря́бва да до́йдеш навре́ме!	You must arrive on time!
Тря́бва да до́йдеш навре́ме!	

Compare the above examples with the usage of conjugated **тря́бва** (from **тря́бвам**):

Тря́бва му добъ́р адвока́т.	He needs a good lawyer.
Тря́бват му добри́ адвока́ти.	He needs good lawyers.

Although the impersonal form **мо́же** can be literally translated "it is possible that...", the more normal translation is "may" or "might". In fact, the difference between the Bulgarian impersonal form **мо́же** and the conjugated verb **мо́га** is roughly parallel to that between English "might" and "can". For example:

impersonal **мо́же**

Мо́же да рабо́тя дове́чера.	I might work tonight.
	[= it's a possibility]
Мо́же ли да вля́за?	May I come in?

conjugated **мо́же**, from **мо́га**

Мо́га да рабо́тя дове́чера.	I can work tonight.
	[= I'm able and willing]
Не мо́га да вля́за, че ня́мам клю́ч.	I can't get in, I don't have a key.

12.4. "Third-person" verbs

Bulgarian has several verbs which occur only in the third person. These verbs are *not* impersonal -- they have singular and plural forms, and they take a subject. They are listed in the dictionary in their 3rd singular forms.

The most common of these verbs is **боли́** "hurt". The subject of this verb is always the body part which hurts, and the object of the verb is the person who experiences pain. Sentences with **боли́** are similar in many ways to the "experiencer" constructions learned in Lesson 11. The primary differences are that the pronoun object is a *direct* object, and that the verb has a subject, with which it must agree.

Боли́ ме глава́та.	I have a headache.
Боли́ го стома́хът.	He has a stomachache.
Боли́ я зъбъ́т.	She has a toothache.
Боля́т я зъ́бите.	Her teeth hurt.

247

As in experiencer constructions, the doubled object can also be used, and *must* be used, when the experiencer of the body-part pain is expressed as a noun. Since the experiencer of the pain is grammatically a direct object, masculine nouns must have the definite object ending.

Мéне ме болú главáта.	I have a headache.
Нéя я боля́т зъ́бите.	Her teeth hurt.
Калúна я болú ухóто.	Kalina has an earache.
Úво го болú гъ́рлото.	Ivo has a sore throat.
Студéнта го болú кракъ́т.	The student's leg hurts.

When the ailment is of a single type but concerns a number of experiencers, the verb can be either singular or plural. The plural form of the noun/pronoun object is sufficient to indicate the multiplicity of sufferers.

-- Кáмене, тéбе болú ли те гъ́рлото?	"Kamen, do you have a sore throat?"
-- Не, сáмо момúчетата ги болú.	"No, only girls have sore throats."

The aorist of болú is боля́ (on the model of the verb вървя́, aorist вървя́х). The meaning is that something hurt at some point in the past but no longer does now. With the prefix за-, the meaning is "begin to hurt." For example:

Вчéра ме боля́ главáта.	I had a headache yesterday.
Мúналата сéдмица Лиля́на я боля́ха очúте.	Lilyana's eyes hurt last week.
Заболя́ха ги главúте от миризмáта.	They got headaches from the smell.

12.5. Verbs of "liking"

To express the idea of "like" or "love" in general, Bulgarians use the verb обúчам. It is used with infinitive replacements (да-phrases) and with certain nouns.

Нáдка обúча да рисýва.	Nadka likes to draw.
Децáта мнóго обúчат да хóдят на цúрк.	The children love going to the circus.
Обúчаш ли класúческа мýзика?	Do you like classical music?
Обúчам те.	I love you.
Обúчам те мнóго.	I like you a lot.

By contrast, positive reactions to a particular thing or event, or particular single instances of "liking", are expressed with the verb **харесвам** (perfective **харесам**).

Ти кой песни най-много харесваш?	Which songs do you like the best?
Хареса ли филма?	Did you like the film?
Много си хубава -- сигурно ще те хареса.	You're lovely -- of course she'll like you.

Peculiar to this verb is the ability to alternate transitive with intransitive usage. The above examples illustrate the transitive use: direct objects are clearly present. In the intransitive usage of this verb, the subject (the one who does the liking) is transformed into an indirect object experiencer (the one to whom something is pleasing).

Тази песен ми харесва.	That's a nice song -- I like it.
Харесва ли ти моята рокля?	Do you like this dress on me?
-- Много ни хареса филмът.	"We liked the film a lot."
-- А на мене не ми хареса.	"Not me -- I didn't like it."

In most cases, it is difficult to render into English the difference between transitive and intransitive **харесвам** without a larger context. In general, however, the focus of the intransitive usage is less upon the "action" of liking (or not liking) and more upon the object which produces this reaction. Both uses of the verb mean "like [something]"; indeed Bulgarians use the two forms of this verb largely interchangeably.

12.6. Embedded questions, continued; the use of дали

Embedded questions, studied in Lesson 4, are questions which are integrated into another sentence, usually as the object of a verb. In terms of word order, it is important to remember that they reproduce the order of the original question exactly.

original question	Ще бъдеш ли там?	Will you be there?
embedded question	Питай го ще бъде ли там.	Ask him if he will be there.

Speakers of English must take care not to translate "if" in sentences such as the above by Bulgarian **ако**. A rule of thumb is: if one can substitute "whether" for "if" in the English, then one must use **ли** (and not **ако**) in the Bulgarian.

Embedded questions of this sort may also be formulated with the conjunction дали. In this case, the interrogative particle ли is dropped, and the conjunction stands at the beginning of the embedded sentence. Note the similarity between the word order of English "if/whether" sentences and Bulgarian дали sentences:

Пи́тай го	дали́	ще бъ́де та́м.
Ask him	if/whether	he will be there.

12.7. The pronoun сам

The emphatic pronoun са́м has two different meanings. One is equivalent to English "by/for oneself" and the other is equivalent to English "alone". There is a certain overlap between the two meanings, as in English, where the phrase "by oneself", can refer either to the state of being unaccompanied, or to self-initiated action.

Here are the forms, followed by examples of usage:

masculine	*feminine*	*neuter*	*plural*
са́м	сама́	само́	сами́

Ела́те с ме́н! Сами́ ще ви́дите.	Come with me! You'll see for yourselves.
Ти́ сама́ ли пъту́ваш? Ха́йде да се́днем за́едно.	Are you traveling alone? Let's sit together.

One must be careful to distinguish the adverb са́мо "only" from the neuter pronominal adjective само́ (in either of the above two meanings). For example:

са́мо "only"

Са́мо едно́то дете́ рису́ва; дру́гите гле́дат телеви́зия.	Only the one child is drawing; the others are watching TV.

само́ "alone, by oneself"

Дете́то седи́ само́ в ста́ята и рису́ва.	The child is sitting alone in his room and drawing.
Дете́то напра́ви та́зи рису́нка само́, без мо́я по́мощ.	The child did the drawing all by himself, without [any] help from me.

12.8. Names of body parts

Names of many body parts which come in pairs, including those for hands, feet, eyes, and ears, have irregular plurals. The singular and plural forms in Bulgarian are:

sg. indef.	sg. def.	pl. indef.	pl. def.	(meaning)
ръка́	ръка́та	ръце́	ръце́те	hand, arm
кра́к	кракъ́т	крака́	крака́та	foot, leg
око́	око́то	очи́	очи́те	eye
ухо́	ухо́то	уши́	уши́те	ear

The nouns око́ and ухо́ are neuter, but they have the plural ending -и.

Church in Nesebăr, detail

EXERCISES

I. Fill in the blanks with the proper form of харе́свам *or* оби́чам.

1. Джу́ли _____ ма́лките деца́ и живо́тните.
2. _____ ли ви та́зи ста́я?
3. На́дка _____ да ѝ чета́т при́казки.
4. Какво́ _____ по́вече: шокола́д или сладоле́д?
5. Ни́е не _____ таки́ва къ́си приче́ски.
6. То́й _____ приро́дата и затова́ хо́ди че́сто на екску́рзии.
7. Все́ки живе́е, ка́кто му _____.

II. Fill in the blanks with one of the following: мо́же, и́ма, ня́ма, тря́бва; *or with a conjugated form of* мо́га, и́мам, ня́мам, *or* тря́бвам.

1. _____ да е голя́ма хубави́ца, но не е́ мно́го любе́зна.
2. Извине́те, сега́ не _____ да ви пока́ня, мно́го бъ́рзам.
3. Не говори́, кога́то _____ какво́ да ка́жеш.
4. Деца́та _____ да слу́шат ма́йка си и баща́ си.
5. Ако _____ пари́, _____ да ви даде́м наза́ем.
6. В университе́тската библиоте́ка _____ мно́го кни́ги за Бълга́рия.
7. Те́ не _____ да рабо́тят, кога́то _____ го́сти.

III. Fill in the blanks with an appropriate form of the verb боли́ (*choose between* боли́, боля́т, боля́, боля́ха, заболя́, заболя́ха).

1. Ако те _____ зъ́бите, иди́ на зъболе́кар.
2. Ка́мен е добре́, ве́че ни́що не го́ _____.
3. След вече́ря Миле́на я _____ глава́та.
4. Ако ви _____ крака́та, седне́те да си почи́нете.
5. То́лкова се умори́ха, че вси́чки ги _____ очи́те.
6. _____ ни усти́те да повта́ряме, че това́ е гре́шка.
7. Ми́налия ме́сец тя́х пак ги _____ стома́х.

ADDITIONAL GRAMMAR NOTES

12.1a. Relationship between aorist and present tense forms

Mastery of the Bulgarian verb system comes from an understanding not only of its different forms, but also of their interrelationships. In every dictionary (and in the glossary lists in this book) verbs appear in their present tense forms. One is therefore inclined to think that the present tense *is* the verb, and that everything else is derived from it.

In actuality, the verb is a complex of many forms, and is based upon the relationship between the present and the aorist tenses. Some verb forms are derived from the present tense, and others are derived from the aorist tense. Neither the present nor the aorist is primary, and both are essential.

To truly know a verb, therefore, one must know
>   (a) its present tense form;
>   (b) its aorist tense form;
>   (c) the relationship that obtains between them.

The chart which follows is intended to guide the student internalize this knowledge in the most economic fashion.

Nearly every verb in Bulgarian belong to one of nine basic types. Conjugating a newly learned verb, therefore, is simply a matter of learning which type it belongs to. In the chart, these types are exemplified wherever possible by non-prefixed verbs. This is to underscore the fact that although adding a prefix changes the *meaning* of a verb, it does not alter its *form*. For instance, once the student learns all the forms for бера́, s/he then knows all the forms for разбера́, прибера́, and any other verb composed of "prefix + бера́".

The organizing principle of the chart is the theme vowel, and the characteristic sign of a type is the combination of present and aorist theme vowels. The verb forms given as examples are 1st plural. For clarity, forms are divided as follows:

	root	*theme vowel*	*ending*
	ход	и	хме

The following conventions are used:

The theme vowel **[-a-]** denotes a general category which includes both **-а-** and **-я-**.
The notation **[-C-]** denotes a category which includes the consonants **-с-** and **-з-**.
The notation **[-C'-]** denotes a category which includes the consonants **-ш-** and **-ж-**.

RELATIONSHIP BETWEEN PRESENT AND AORIST TENSE FORMS

	tense	theme vowel	examples		
1.	Present	-a-	глéд-а-ме	и́ск-а-ме	вечéр-я-ме
	Aorist	-a-	глéд-а-хме	и́ск-а-хме	вечéр-я-хме
2.	Present	-и-	хóд-и-м	бро-и́-м	у́ч-и-м
	Aorist	-и-	хóд-и-хме	бро-и́-хме	у́ч-и-хме
3.	Present	-и-	върв-и́-м	мълч-и́-м	сто-и́-м
	Aorist	-a-	върв-я́-хме	мълч-á-хме	сто-я́-хме
4.	Present	-e-	пи́-е-м	взéм-е-м	копá-е-м
	Aorist	---	пи́ -- хме	взé -- хме	копá -- хме
5.	Present	-e-	чет-é-м	сеч-é-м	влéз-е-м
	Aorist	-o-	чéт-о-хме	ся́к-о-хме	вля́з-о-хме
6.	Present	-e-	срéщн-е-м	въ́рн-е-м	стáн-е-м
	Aorist	-a-	срéщн-а-хме	въ́рн-а-хме	стáн-а-хме
7.	Present	-e -e	живé-е-м	изпé-е-м	закъснé-е-м
	Aorist	-- -a	жив--я́-хме	изп--я́-хме	закъсн--я́-хме
8.	Present	-C' -e-	пи́ш-е-м	кáж-е-м	
	Aorist	-C -a-	пи́с -а-хме	кáз -а-хме	
9.	Present	-ep -e-	пер-é-м	бер-é-м	
	Aorist	- p -a-	пр -á-хме	бр -á-хме	

There are six different combinations of present and aorist theme vowels: these are represented by types 1 through 6 in the above chart. Types 7 through 9 have the same present/aorist theme vowel relationship as type 6. Each of these latter three types also has a change in the shape of the stem.

Type 8 is characterized by consonant shifts [с › ш] and [з › ж]. The observant student will note that this is the same consonant shift seen in imperfective derivation. Compare the forms below, all 1st singular.

Consonant			Verb form
с *or* з	(пре)пи́сах	(раз)ка́зах	Aorist
	препи́свам	разка́звам	Derived imperfective
ш *or* ж	препи́ша	разка́жа	Prefixed perfective
	пи́ша	ка́жа	Simplex imperfective

Within type 4, the verb взе́ма also has a stem change which, once learned, is predictable: the stem-final consonant -м disappears in the aorist. **Прие́ма, пое́ма** and **зае́ма** are all conjugated in the same manner.

The accent is usually the same in both present and aorist of any one verb. There is an optional accent shift in the unprefixed aorist of types 1, 2, 6 and 8. Only in verbs of type 5, however, is there an obligatory accent shift. Practically all these verbs have end stress in the present and stem stress in the aorist. Only one verb exhibits the reverse shift, and several verbs do not shift stress at all. The student should learn the latter verbs as exceptions. Examples below are 1st plural forms.

Tense	*Present*	*Aorist*
Accent		
Regular shift	чете́м	че́тохме
Exceptional shift	до́йдем	дойдо́хме
Lack of shift	оти́дем	оти́дохме
	вле́зем	вля́зохме
	etc.	

All verbs in type 3 are end stressed in both present and aorist; the only exception is ви́дя (with stem stress in the present). Verbs of the и-conjugation which are end-stressed are thus more likely to belong to type 3 than to type 2.

As seen in the chart on the preceding page, the primary basis for the nine-type classification is conjugation form. However, there are certain correlations between stem type and meaning. Type 7 verbs, for instance, are all derived from adjectives and signify that one is in (or coming into) the state described by that adjective. Furthermore, type 2 verbs are practically all transitive (with a few exceptions like хо́дя), and type 3 verbs are practically all intransitive (again, with a few exceptions like ви́дя). This latter difference can aid the student in remembering which of the verbs with present tense in -и- forms its aorist in -и- (type 2), and which forms its aorist in -а- (type 3).

12.2a. Aspect in the aorist tense

The Bulgarian aorist tense is formed freely from both aspects of the verbs. The name of this tense in Bulgarian can be misleading, therefore, for it suggests that the aorist tense and the perfective aspect are related. Here are the terms:

Aspect		свършен *Perfective*	несвършен *Imperfective*
Tense	мина́ло	свъ́ршено	
		Aorist	

The crux of the terminological confusion rests in the word **свършен**, which literally means "completed". There is indeed a certain overlap between the aorist tense (whose literal name is "past completed tense") and the perfective aspect (whose literal name is "completed aspect"), in that the meaning of each does indicate a certain degree of completedness.

This overlap will be discussed in more detail in Lesson 14. Here it is important to note that the choice of aorist tense does *not* predetermine the choice of perfective aspect. The meaning of the aorist is concerned with the *fact* of past action, and not its potential boundedness. The boundedness is signalled by the choice of perfective aspect, and rests within the verb itself.

12.3a. Impersonal verbs

Although impersonal verbs are often used with да-clauses (especially **тря́бва**), they also occur frequently alone. Used in this way, **и́ма** and **ня́ма** express the idea of existence/availability or its absence; and **мо́же** and **тря́бва** express the idea of possibility or necessity. Numerous different translations are possible. For example:

-- И́ма ли за́хар?	"Is there [any] sugar?"
-- И́ма, заповя́дайте.	"Yes, here [it is]."
И́ма вре́ме.	There's [plenty of] time.
Съжаля́вам, ама́ ту́ка ня́ма ни́що.	I'm sorry, but there's nothing here.
Ня́ма тако́ва не́що.	There's no such thing.
И́скам да те пи́там не́що, мо́же ли?	I want to ask you something, is that OK?
-- Да оти́дем ли?	"Should we go?"
-- Мо́же.	"We could."
Зна́м, че не и́скаш, ама́ тря́бва.	I know you don't want [to], but you have to.

12.4a. "Third-person" verbs and word order

Definiteness in body-ache constructions

In body-ache sentences (with the verb **боли**), the affected body-part acts as the subject. When the ailment is a common one and the experiencer is singular, the noun naming the body-part is either definite or indefinite, with little or no difference in meaning. For instance:

Боли́ ме глава́.	I have a headache.
Боли́ ме глава́та.	*(same)*

In the case of multiple experiencers, however, the presence or absence of the article is determined by the number of the verb. A singular verb indicates a generalized view (hence indefinite), while a plural verb demands more specificity (hence definite).

Заболя́ ги глава́ от миризма́та.	They got headaches from the smell.
Заболя́ха ги глави́те от миризма́та.	*(same)*

Word order in body-ache constructions

The verb **боли** occurs either with a single short-form pronoun object or with a doubled object; there is little difference in meaning. When the sufferer is named by a noun, the doubled object is obligatory. When doubled objects are used, the noun (or long form pronoun object) must begin the sentence. The short form object obeys its normal word order rules. Here are examples (numbered cumulatively across lessons):

(58) Надка ви́наги я боли́ гъ́рлото.
direct obj. *DIR verb* *subject*

Nadka's always got a sore throat.

(59) Ме́не не ме́ боли́ глава́та.
direct obj. *Neg. DIR verb* *subject*

I don't have a headache.

(60) Ива́н боли́ ли го стома́хът?
direct obj. *verb INT DIR* *subject*

Does Ivan have a stomachache?

Other similar constructions

Another common 3rd person verb is **вали́**, which refers to precipitation. Its subject is rain, snow, hail or the like. When no subject is used, rain is assumed as the default case. In the singular, the verb is normally used alone, although it can have a subject. In the plural, however, it must have an explicitly stated subject.

present tense

-- Вали́ ли?	"Is it raining?"
-- Ве́че не вали́.	"Not any more."
Вали́ като из ведро́.	It's pouring buckets.
Валя́т си́лни дъждове́.	We're having a lot of rain.

aorist tense

Вче́ра валя́ ця́л де́н.	It rained all day yesterday.
Преди 5 мину́ти заваля́.	It started to rain five minutes ago.
Вче́ра валя́ мно́го сня́г -- деца́та мно́го се ра́дваха.	It snowed a lot yesterday -- the children were delighted.
През зи́мата валя́ха мно́го снегове́.	There were many snowstorms last winter.

There are also a few verbs which occur almost exclusively in the 3rd person form. But as they are listed in dictionaries in the 1st person form, they do not technically belong to this group. These include треса́ "shake, shiver" and сърбя́ "itch". The person who feels the shivers or the itches is expressed, as in the case of боли́, in the direct object form. For example:

Сърби́ го ля́вата ръка́.	His left hand itches.
Тресе́ ме.	I've got the shivers.
Хе́м боли́, хе́м сърби́.	You can't have it both ways.
	[*literally*: First it hurts, then it itches.]

In the same way as body afflictions are expressed by 3rd person verbs, certain emotional states are expressed by nouns. The similarity between the two constructions is that in each case the person affected is expressed by a direct object pronoun. Emotional states commonly described in this way are сра́м "shame", я́д "anger", стра́х "fear", гну́с "loathing". For example:

Ужа́сно я е стра́х от ми́шки.	She's terrified of mice.
Я́д ме е на не́я.	I'm angry at her.
Ме́н ме е гну́с от те́бе.	You nauseate me.
Сра́м ме е.	I'm ashamed. [*also*: I'm shy.]
Не те́ е сра́м!	Shame on you! [*also*: For shame!]
Ка́к не те́ е сра́м!	You ought to be ashamed of yourself.

12.8a. Names of body parts

Here is a list of body-part names, given for ease of reference in alphabetical order according to the English term. Correspondences in meaning are relatively close, although there is some potential confusion in the terms for limbs. The words ръка́ and кра́к apply both to the entire upper and lower limbs, respectively, and to their extremities (hand or foot, respectively). Context will usually determine which is meant; if necessary, terms such as "palm [of the hand]" or "sole [of the foot]" are used. Similarly, пръст and но́кът refer to the digits and their nails on both hands and feet, and па́лец can mean either "thumb" or "big toe", depending on the context.

NAMES OF BODY PARTS (alphabetical by English term)

коре́м	abdomen		пета́	heel
гле́зен	ankle		черво́	intestine
гръб	back		коля́но	knee
брада́	beard, chin		кра́к	leg, foot *
за́дник	behind, rear end		у́стна	lip
кръв	blood		че́рен дроб	liver
ко́ст	bone		(бя́л) дро́б	lung
ко́кал	bone		уста́	mouth
мо́зък	brain		му́скул	muscle
гърда́	breast		но́кът	nail
бу́за	cheek		ши́я	neck
гръд or гърди́	chest		вра́т	neck
бради́чка	chin		но́с	nose
у́хо	ear		небце́	palate
ла́кът	elbow		дла́н	palm
око́	eye		ра́мо	shoulder
ве́жда	eyebrow		ко́жа	skin
ми́гла	eyelash		стъпа́ло	sole
лице́	face		сто́мах	stomach
пръст	finger		бедро́	thigh
юмру́к	fist		гърло	throat
че́ло or чело́	forehead		гу́ша	throat
коса́	hair		па́лец	thumb, big toe
ръка́	hand, arm		ези́к	tongue
глава́	head		сли́вица	tonsil
сърце́	heart		зъб	tooth
			ки́тка	wrist

* нога́   leg *(poetic, dialectal)*

SAMPLE SENTENCES

1. Мо́же да мо́же, а мо́же и да не мо́же.
2. Ти́ мо́же да и́скаш, но каква́ е по́лзата, що́м не мо́жеш.
3. Мо́же ли да вля́за в цъ́рквата с ша́пка на глава́та?

4. Вла́къ́т тря́бва да присти́гне все́ки моме́нт.
5. Тря́бва да гово́ря с не́го, но не мо́га да го наме́ря.

6. Все́ки моме́нт мо́же да завали́.
7. Деца́та ги боли́ глава́ от мно́го уро́ци.

8. И́ма ли ня́кой да ча́ка за до́ктор Петро́в?
9. Какво́ и́ма?
10. Ня́ма дру́г като не́го.

11. Ту́к боли́ ли?
12. Па́к заваля́, а а́з не си́ но́ся чадъ́ра.
13. Заваля́ дъ́жд и ни измо́кри до ко́сти.
14. Вали́ гра́д.

15. От бо́лката му поте́коха съ́лзи.
16. Тя́ че́те докла́д на конфере́нцията.

17. То́й си оти́де и ни́кога ве́че не го́ видя́хме.
18. Пи́са, пи́са и ни́що не напи́са.
19. Те́ живя́ха щастли́во за́едно.

20. Деца́та харе́сват та́зи при́казка.
21. Си́нята ша́пка му харе́са по́вече.
22. Вче́ра обра́хме чере́шата и свари́хме сла́дко.
23. Та́ня изпра́ вси́чки дре́хи на деца́та и ги простря́.

24. Ха́йде да не го́ ча́каме, то́й и са́м ще ни наме́ри.
25. Ти́ сама́ ли изпле́те то́зи пуло́вер?

26. Пи́тах го дали́ е гла́ден, но забра́вих да го попи́там жа́ден ли е.
27. Не зна́м със за́хар ли пи́ете кафе́то.
28. Чу́дя се дали́ да си взе́ма жиле́тката или да я оста́вя.

SENTENCES FOR TRANSLATION

1. "Why does my head hurt so much? I wonder what I did?"
   "When did it start hurting? Is it the rain? I always get a headache if it starts raining. If it rains my head hurts, but not if it snows. Isn't that strange?"

2. We have to leave for the station immediately if we want to get there on time. Ask Marina if she wants to come with us. Does she still have a backache or is she better now?

3. All mothers love their children, even when they are ill. My sister, for instance, had an earache, a toothache and a stomachache all at the same time, and it was terrible for both her and my mother. But my mother never complained at all.

4. That was a great movie, I really liked it. Marin didn't like it, though. After the film he said, "That was a terrible film. I'm never going to the movies again." I couldn't understand him. But of course he'll go again. Movies are a necessity for him.

5. We might be able to come over tonight, if Nadka and Kamen are better. Both of them have toothaches. It's hard for them.

6. Do you like to watch soccer on TV? Or do you prefer to go to the stadium? Do you like to watch TV in general? Some people don't like TV at all. I don't like most of the programs, and I don't know if they will ever show better programs.

7. How many fingers do you see? Two or three? Now show me all your fingers.

8. How is your elbow? Is it still hurting? Both of my elbows hurt. But my hands are OK. That's good, because I need my hands.

9. Marina called me on the phone last night, she was in a terrible state. Her mother all of a sudden got a sharp pain in her stomach, and they were very frightened. Where was the doctor? They phoned, but they couldn't find him. Then, thank goodness, her brother came, and he took all of them to the hospital. Her mother is better now, although it still hurts.

10. "Do you need this book?"
    "Yes, I have to study this evening. Don't you have to study? How will you learn your lessons if you don't study? My father always calls to ask me if I am studying, and of course I always say yes."

READING SELECTION

<u>Ýтре е съ́бота</u>

Марин: Ало́. Пла́мен мо́же ли да се оба́ди, мо́ля.

Пламен: На телефо́на.

Марин: Не можа́х да ти позна́я гласа́. Ви́ж какво́, и́скам да ти напра́вя едно́ предложе́ние. Ýтре е съ́бота. Това́ е де́н за култу́рни развлече́ния. Като́ култу́рни хо́ра, и ни́е тря́бва да оти́дем ня́къде.

Пламен: Добре́. Ве́че ми омръ́зна да гле́дам телеви́зия ве́чер. Какво́ предла́гаш?

Марин: И́маме голя́м и́збор: теа́тър, ки́но, о́пера, какво́ ли не́. Не зна́м какви́ са вку́совете ти.

Пламен: Сами́ят а́з оби́чам да хо́дя на о́пера. Осве́н това́ звучи́ на́й-култу́рно.

Марин: О́пера ли? Опомни́ се. Живе́ем във века́ на те́хниката. Пу́скаш си компа́кт ди́ск и все́ едно́ си в за́лата. Пъ́к и на́й-добри́те певци́ са по чужби́на.

Пламен: В такъ́в слу́чай да оти́дем на ки́но. Зна́еш ли програ́мата на кина́та?

Марин: Защо́ да я зна́м. Срещу на́с да́ват ви́деокасети под на́ем. Мо́же да гле́даш какво́то пои́скаш, дори́ на́й-но́вите фи́лми. Ни́е и́маме широ́ко разби́ране за а́вторското пра́во.

Пламен: Ма́й оста́ва да оти́дем на теа́тър.

Марин: Помисли́ логи́чно. Ако пие́сата е интере́сна, ня́ма да и́ма биле́ти. Ако и́ма биле́ти, пие́сата не е́ интере́сна. По́-добре́ е са́м да си чете́ш пие́сите, ня́ма защо́ да ти ги чете́ режисьо́р.

Пламен: Зна́чи избира́ме между ви́деокасета, компа́кт ди́ск и сбо́рник с пие́си. А съ́що и телеви́зия.

Марин: Не съвсе́м. Почти́ забра́вих. Ýтре и́ма ма́ч. Игра́ят "Ле́вски" и "ЦСКА". Това́ са на́й-популя́рните отбо́ри.

Пламен: Не мо́же ли да го гле́даме по телеви́зията? Ще мо́жем да гле́даме повторе́ния.

Марин: Защо́ ти е повторе́ние? Ако ня́кой изпу́сне го́л, то́й ня́ма да го вка́ра на повторе́нието. На стадио́на е по́-интере́сно и мо́жеш да ви́каш на во́ля.

Пламен: Вя́рно. Нали́ гово́рим за культу́рно развлече́ние? Съгла́сен съм, но ти́ ще се реди́ш на опа́шката за биле́ти.

Марин: Ку́пих биле́тите о́ще вче́ра. Хо́дя на то́зи ма́ч от дете́. И не забра́вяй да си взе́меш чадъ́р. Мо́же да вали́.

Пламен: Ще взе́ма чадъ́р, а съ́що и аспири́н. И благодаря́ за бога́тия и́збор.

Марин: Ви́наги мо́жеш да разчи́таш на ме́не. Зна́чи, у́тре ще се оба́дя па́к да се разбере́м къде́ ще се сре́щнем. Дочу́ване.

Пламен: Добре́. Дочу́ване.

Theater of the Bulgarian Army, Sofia

GLOSSARY

áвторски	author's	голя́мо движе́ние	lots of traffic
áвторско пра́во	copyright	гра́д	hail
ало́	hello (on the phone)	гръ́б, гърбъ́т	back
ама	but	(pl. гърбове́)	
áрмия	army	гръ́д, -та́ (or гърди́)	chest
аспири́н	aspirin	гу́ша	neck, throat
		гърда́	breast, bosom
бедро́	thigh	гъ́рло	throat
бера́	pick, gather		
боли́ (3rd person only)	hurt	да́вам на за́ем	loan
боли́ ме глава́та	I have a headache	да́вам под на́ем	rent out
боля́т ме очи́те	my eyes hurt	движе́ние	movement; traffic
бо́лка	pain	дера́	skin, fleece, tear, scratch
брада́	beard; chin	дла́н	palm of the hand
бради́чка	chin	докла́д	report
бу́за	cheek	дочу́ване	goodbye (on the phone)
бя́л дро́б	lung	дро́б, -ъ́т (pl. дро́-	lung
		бове or дробове́)	
в такъ́в слу́чай	in that case	дъ́жд, -ъ́т	rain
вали́ (3rd person only)	rain, etc.	(pl. дъждове́)	
	(precipitation)		
вали́ (дъ́жд)	it's raining	жиле́тка	waistcoat, cardigan
вали́ сня́г	it's snowing		sweater
вали́ гра́д	it's hailing	заболя́ва ме /	start to hurt
вали́ като из ведро́	it's raining buckets	заболи́ ме	
валя́т си́лни	it's raining heavily	(3rd person only)	
дъждове́		заболя́вам /	get sick
ведро́	bucket	заболе́я	
ве́жда	eyebrow	заваля́ва / завали́	begin to precipitate
ве́к, -ъ́т	century	(3rd person only)	
ви́д, -ъ́т	aspect, view,	за́дник	behind, rear end
	appearance	зае́мам / зае́ма	take up, occupy
ви́деокасета	video cassette	за́ла	hall
ви́ж какво́	(topic focuser)	зара́двам се	cheer up
ви́кам	shout, yell	за́хар, -та́	sugar
ви́кам на во́ля	shout to one's heart's	защи́та	defense
	content	звуча́ (-и́ш)	sound
ви́ц	joke	звучи́ добре́	that sounds good
вка́рвам / вка́рам	push in, drive in	зъболе́кар	dentist
вка́рам го́л	score [a goal]		
во́ля	will, desire	изми́слям /	think up, invent
вра́т	back of the neck	изми́сля	
		измо́крям /	drench, soak
глава́	head	измо́кря	
гла́с, -ъ́т (pl. гласове́)	voice	измо́крям се	get soaked to the skin
гле́зен	ankle	до ко́сти	
гну́с ме е	[I] feel nauseated	изнена́да	surprise
го́л	goal (in sports)	изпи́рам / изпера́	do laundry, wash

изпли́там / изплета́	knit, twist	обаждам се / обадя се	come to the phone
изпу́скам го́л	miss [a goal]		
и́мам пра́во	have the right	общество́	society
		око́ (*pl.* очи́)	eye
ка́к не те́ е сра́м!	you should be ashamed!	омръ́звам / омръ́зна	tire, bore
каква́ е по́лзата	what's the use	омръ́зва ми	I'm bored
какво́ ли не́	whatever, whatnot (*see L. 17*)	о́пера	opera
		опо́мням се / опо́мна се	come to (one's) senses
какво́то	whatever (*see L. 17*)	опомни́ се!	snap out of it!
карнава́лен	carnival (*adj.*)	организи́рам	organize
ки́тка	wrist	от дете́	since childhood
ко́жа	skin	отбо́р	team
коля́но (*pls.* колена́ *or* колене́)	knee		
		па́лец	thumb, big toe
компа́кт ди́ск	compact disk	пера́	wash
конфере́нция	conference	пета́	heel
коре́м	abdomen, belly	пие́са	play
коса́	hair	повта́рям / повто́ря	repeat
ко́ст, -та́	bone		
кръ́в, -та́ (*pl.* къ́рви)	blood	повторе́ние	repeat, replay
културе́н	cultural	поговорвам / поговоря	talk for a bit
къ́с	short	подго́твям / подго́твя	prepare
лице́	face		
логи́чен	logical	пои́сквам / пои́скам	want, wish, ask for
ма́й	it seems, in all probability	по́лза	use, advantage
		поми́слям / поми́сля	think about
ма́й оста́ва да оти́дем та́м	I guess we have to go there	популя́рен	popular
		поти́чам / потека́ (-че́ш)	start flowing
ма́ч	[sports] match, game		
между	between, among	правила́ на пъ́тното движе́ние	traffic laws, rules of the road
ме́н = ме́не		пра́вило	rule
ми́гла	eyelash	права́та на живо́тните	animal rights
ми́нало свъ́ршено вре́ме	aorist tense		
		пра́во	[legal] right
мо́зък	brain	прехвъ́рлям се / прехвъ́рля се	transfer; shift
му́скул	muscle		
		при́казка	tale, story
на вся́ка цена́	at any price, at all costs, absolutely	приче́ска	haircut, hair style
		прости́рам / простра́	stretch out
на кра́к	hastily		
на телефо́на	speaking! (on the phone)	прости́рам дре́хи	hang clothes out to dry
на́ем	rent	пръ́ст (*pl.* пръ́сти)	finger, toe
наза́ем	loan	пуло́вер	sweater
не те́ е сра́м!	shame on you!	пъ́тен	road, traveling
небце́	palate [roof of mouth]		
несвъ́ршен	incomplete, imperfect	разби́рам се / разбера́ се	come to an understanding, agree
несвъ́ршен ви́д	imperfective aspect		
нога́	leg (*dialectal, poetic*)	разби́ране	understanding

265

развлечéние	amusement	трябва (*3rd person only*)	must, should
разпрáвям / разпрáвя	tell, relate	(тóй) трябва да дóйде	he needs to come
разчи́там	rely on, count [on]	трябва му адвокáт	he needs a lawyer
рáмо (*pl.* раменá *or* раменé)	shoulder	трябвам	be necessary to
редя́	arrange, put in order		
редя́ се на опáшка	get/wait in line	ужáсен	terrible
рéжа (-еш)	cut, slice	уморя́вам се / уморя́ се	get tired, become exhausted
режисьóр	director	университéтски	university (*adj.*)
рóкля	dress	устá	mouth
ръкá (*pl.* ръцé)	hand, arm	ýстна	lip
		ухó (*pl.* уши́)	ear
сáм, самá, самó, сами́	alone, [the] very, by oneself		
сами́ят áз	I myself	харéсвам / харéсам	like
сбóрник	collection	хéм (хем ... хем)	both...and...; not only..., but...
свъ́ршен, -ена	complete, perfect		
свъ́ршен ви́д	perfective aspect		
сли́вица	tonsil	ценá	price
случáен	chance, accidental	централен	central
случай	instance		
случáйно	by chance	чадъ́р (*pl.* чадъ́ри)	umbrella
сóбствен, -ена	one's own	чéло (*or* челó)	forehead
срáм, -ъ́т (*pl.* срáмове *or* срамовé)	shame, modesty	червó	intestine
		чéрен дрóб	liver
срáм ме е	I'm ashamed/shy	черéша	cherry
срещу	against, opposite, across from	чéстен	honorable, honest
		чéстна дýма	word of honor
стадиóн	stadium	чужби́на	abroad
стомáх	stomach		
страх, -ъ́т (*pl.* страховé)	fear, dread	шéствие	procession, train
		широ́к	wide, broad
страх ме е (от)	I'm afraid [of]	широ́ко разби́ране	liberal interpretation
стъпáло	sole (of the foot)	ши́я	neck
съглáсен	in agreement		
сълзá (*pl.* съ́лзи *or* сълзи́)	tear (from the eye)	щастли́в	happy
съ́рби́ (*3rd person only*)	itch	юмрýк	fist
тéхника	technology	я́д	anger
тóчно	just	я́д ме е (на)	I'm angry (at)
тресá	shake		
тресé ме	I've got the shakes; I've got a fever		

266

CULTURAL COMMENTARY

Traveling: train lines

Two main train lines connect the capital city of Sofia with the Black Sea port of Varna: one runs through the center of the country and one further to the north. Transfers can be made to smaller towns in the interior from major points along this line. The north central town of Gorna Oryakhovitsa (Го́рна Оря́ховица) is the transfer point for Gabrovo, which is situated between the two main arteries.

Politics: animal rights

The cause of animal rights has not yet penetrated to Bulgaria. Certain "protective" societies are known, however; among them is a society dedicated to the conservation of nature (общество́ за защи́та на приро́дата).

Entertainment: music; sports

Like other world capitals, Sofia has numerous theater companies and its own symphony, opera and ballet companies. Bulgarians love music, especially singing; and Bulgaria is known for its fine opera singers. Many of these have emigrated to the West.

Recorded music, both on cassettes and compact disks, is easily available in Bulgaria, as are videocassettes of recent films. Although copyright laws are somewhat more lax than in the West, there is probably the same amount of illegal copying in Bulgaria as in other countries (and the same difficulties of enforcement).

The main sports stadium in Sofia is named after the revolutionary hero Vasil Levski (Васи́л Ле́вски, 1837-1873). It seats 55,000 spectators. Soccer is the game played there most often, but it is also used for track and field events. The traditional rival soccer teams are the ЦСКА (Центра́лен спо́ртен клу́б на а́рмията, the "Central Army Sport Club") and the Ле́вски ("Levski") team.

National theater "Ivan Vazov", Sofia

LESSON 13

DIALOGUE

<u>Щом те боли́ гъ́рлото, облечи́ се!</u>

Таня: На́дке, щом те боли́ гъ́рлото, облечи́ се. И о́ня де́н, дока́то се разхо́ждахме из ботани́ческата гради́на, те́бе те боле́ше гъ́рлото.

Надка: Не и́скам да се обли́чам. Добре́ ми е така́.

Таня: Не ме́ ли разбра́? Ведна́га си облечи́ жиле́тката!

Надка: Ще си я облека́ след ма́лко. Ако ме заболи́ по́вече.

Таня: Не спори́. Като те заболи́ по́вече, ще е къ́сно да се обли́чаш.

Надка: Добре́. След ма́лко. Но и Ка́мен да се облече́!

Таня: Не́ след ма́лко, а сега́.

Камен (на Надка): Защо́? Те́бе те заболя́ гъ́рлото, ти́ се облечи́. Ме́не не ме́ боли́.

Таня: Покажи́ ми ръце́те си. Аха́, мръ́сни са. Тря́бва да се изми́еш. Ту́ка и́ма ма́лко вода́. Ела́ да ти поле́я да си изми́еш ръце́те.

Камен: Ми́х се преди ма́лко, дока́то На́дка гово́реше с те́бе. Не и́скам па́к да се ми́я.

Таня: Кога́? Не те́ видя́х. Слу́шай, Ка́мене. На́дка ве́че се обле́че и ти́ тря́бва да се изми́еш. Това́ е.

Веселин: Ско́ро ще сли́зам, да си взе́ма дови́ждане. Какво́ реши́хте, Джу́ли? Ще до́йдете ли с ме́н?

Джули: Ни́е с Де́йвид тря́бва да продължи́м за Со́фия, и́маме ра́бота та́м. Ако я свъ́ршим бъ́рзо, мо́же да до́йдем в Га́брово.

Веселин: Мо́га ли с не́що да ви бъ́да поле́зен? И́мам мно́го позна́ти в Со́фия.

Джули: Ни́е тря́бва да се сре́щнем с профе́сор Алекса́ндър Попо́в, археоло́г. Не го́ ли позна́вате случа́йно?

Веселин: Какъ́в късме́т! Позна́вам го добре́. То́й ми е родни́на.

Джули: Наѝстина ли!

Веселин: А бе, защо́ да не до́йда и а́з с ва́с до Со́фия да ви предста́вя?

Дейвид: Да не изпу́снете заради на́с фестива́ла?

Веселин: Ѝма о́ще ма́лко вре́ме, докато фестива́лът запо́чне. Ако́ свъ́ршим бъ́рзо всѝчко в Со́фия, ще отѝдем за́едно. Налѝ и́скате да посетѝте фестива́ла?

Downtown Sofia

BASIC GRAMMAR

13.1.   The imperfect tense, introduction

     Bulgarian has two simple past tenses, the aorist and the imperfect. The 3rd singular form of the imperfect will be learned in this lesson. The theme vowel of the imperfect is -е- or -а-/-я-, and the 3rd singular ending is -ше. The full conjugation of the imperfect will be learned in Lesson 14.

     Both the aorist and the imperfect refer to actions which took place in the past. Of the two tenses, the aorist is the more neutral: it simply states the *fact* of past action. The imperfect tense has a more specific meaning, in that it concentrates on the *duration* of a past action over a certain period of time. For example:

aorist

        Вчéра ме боля́ главáта.   Yesterday my head hurt.

imperfect

        Осóбено мнóго болéше зад   It hurt particularly in the area behind
          очйте.   my eyes.

aorist

        Вчéра Лиля́на говóри с   Lilyana spoke with the director
          дирéктора.   yesterday.

imperfect

        Мйх се преди мáлко, докато   I washed a while ago, while Nadka
          Нáдка говóреше с тéбе.   was talking with you.

     Both instances of the aorist above refer to simple facts of past action: someone had a headache, or someone carried out a particular conversation. Both instances of the imperfect, however, focus on the duration of the action. That is, while the headache was going on (duration), it was centered in a particular spot; and while a certain conversation was going on (duration), the fact of washing got accomplished.

     The use of the imperfect will be discussed in more detail in Lesson 14.

13.2.   The past tense of impersonal verbs

     The past tense of impersonal verbs is identical with the 3rd singular imperfect ending. For these verbs, however, this ending simply means "past": there is no separate aorist form. Thus:

present	*past*		*present*	*past*
и́ма	и́маше		тря́бва	тря́бваше
ня́ма	ня́маше		мо́же	мо́жеше

Translations vary, especially in the case of **тря́бва**, which means "supposed to", "must", "ought to", or "should have", depending on the context. It is crucial to remember that although the meaning of the sentence is "past tense", the verb after **да** remains in the *present tense* form.

И́маше мно́го интере́сен фи́лм по телеви́зията.	There was a really interesting film on TV.
Ня́маше ни́каква ну́жда да и́дваш сно́щи.	There really was no need for you to [have] come last night.
По ця́л де́н го ня́маше вкъ́щи.	He often was gone for the whole day.
Тря́бваше да помо́ля за извине́ние.	I ought to have asked [your] pardon.
То́лкова ми бе́ше зле́, че тря́бваше да пови́кам ле́каря през нощта́.	I was in such a bad state that I had to call the doctor during the night.
Мо́жеше и ме́не да пови́кате!	You could have called *me*, you know!
Мо́жеше по́-кро́тко да гово́риш.	You might have spoken more gently.

13.3. Reflexive verbs

The particles **се** and **си** are frequently combined with verbs, to which they add various shades of meaning. The particle **се** can add the meanings of intransitivity or reciprocity, or can simply create a verb of a different meaning. The particle **си** adds the meaning of "greater involvement in the action"; it can also function as a short form possessive when the possessor is identical with the subject of the sentence.

Both these particles are called "reflexive", because they serve in various ways to reflect the verbal action away from a potential direct object and back towards the subject of the sentence. When attached to verbs of the general category "caring for the body", these particles convey the reflexive meaning in its purest form. For this reason, such verbs are called "true reflexives."

When used without the reflexive additive, these verbs are transitive. They take a direct object, and signify that the relevant action is performed upon someone or something else. When the reflexive particle **се** is added, the meaning is that the subject performs the action on or for himself. The object of the verb is now the particle **се**, and the verb is said to be reflexive. A literal English translation would add the object "himself", "yourself"; correct English simply names the action.

Below are eight of the most common of these verbs, followed by examples of transitive and reflexive usage.

verb	(meaning)	verb	(meaning)
бърша	wipe, dry	обличам / облека́	put on clothes, dress
къ́пя	bathe	обу́вам / обу́я	put on shoes, stockings, etc.
ми́я	wash	събли́чам / съблека́	take off clothes, undress
ре́ша	comb	събу́вам / събу́я	take off shoes, stockings, etc.

transitive

Надка облича и съблича ку́клите си.	Nadka dresses and undresses her dolls.
Седни́ да те събу́я.	Sit down and I'll take your shoes off.

reflexive

-- Къде́ е Ка́мен?	"Where's Kamen?"
-- В ба́нята. Ми́е се.	"In the bathroom. He's washing."
Студе́но е навъ́н. Облечи́ се!	It's cold outside. Put [something] on!

Reflexive verbs can also take the particle **си**. The meaning continues to be that the subject performs the action on or for himself. But when **си** is present, there is always another object in the sentence, either a noun or pronoun. If this direct object refers to a body part, it is always in the definite form; if it refers to a piece of clothing it can be either definite or indefinite. In English, the indefinite objects are treated as any indefinite object, but the definite objects are translated with possessive adjectives such as "my", "your", etc. Here are examples:

Ка́мен се ми́е - ми́е си лице́то.	Kamen is washing -- washing his face.
Ведна́га си облечи́ жиле́тката!	Put your sweater on right away!
Да си облека́ бя́ла ри́за дове́чера?	Should I wear a white shirt this evening?

13.4. Word order in negative-interrogative sentences

A negative-interrogative sentence contains both the negative and the interrogative particles. It follows basic word order rules: the negative particle **не** always precedes the verb and the interrogative particle **ли** usually follows it.

When clitics are present, the word order changes dramatically. Clitics continue to occur in sequence, preceded directly by the negative particle. The interrogative particle, however, must follow the first clitic in sequence, no matter what its meaning. The word order (and specifically the position of the object in the sentence) is thus quite different from that of those with short form pronoun objects. Compare the following examples:

| Не позна́ваш ли Ива́н? | Don't you know Ivan? |
| Не го́ ли позна́ваш? | Don't you know him? |

| Не да́дох ли кни́гата на Ива́н? | Didn't I give the book to Ivan? |
| Не му́ ли я да́дох? | Didn't I give it to him? |

| На те́бе не е́ ли прия́тел? | Isn't he a friend of yours? |
| Не ти́ ли е прия́тел? | Isn't he your friend? |

13.5. Modal да, continued

The modal meaning of да is most strongly present when there is no verb preceding it. In these instances, да-phrases communicate (to a greater or lesser extent) wishes or desires of the speaker. When the verb following да is 3rd person, the wish is especially strongly felt. It can be expressed as a fervent desire, or even as a veiled order (depending, of course, on the context). For example:

| Ела́те в 3 ч. И И́во да до́йде. | Come at 3:00. Have Ivo come too. |
| Да сле́зем ли? | Let's get off, shall we? |

| Да живе́е демокра́цията! | Long live democracy! |
| И Ка́мен да се облече́! | Kamen has to get dressed too! |

13.6. Iterative imperatives

Affirmative imperatives are normally in the perfective aspect and negative imperatives normally in the imperfective aspect. Perfective aspect is chosen in the affirmative imperative because the speaker is usually referring to a specific, completed act. If the speaker wishes a repeated action, however, then an imperfective verb is used. For example:

| Затвори́ врата́та! | Close the door! |
| Не затва́ряй врата́та! | Don't close the door! |

Пише́те ни по́-че́сто!	Write more often!
Оба́ждайте се!	Keep in touch!
Сла́гайте дре́хите си на мя́сто!	Put your clothes where they belong!

13.7. The verb бъда

The verb бъда "be" can be seen as the bounded form of съм. It is used in forming both the future tense and the imperative mood of съм. It can also appear after да if the meaning is one of boundedness.

То́й ще бъ́де в кабине́та от 9 ч.	He will be in his office from 9:00 on.
Бъде́те така́ добъ́р да ми напра́вите ко́пие от това́ писмо́.	Be so good as to make me a copy of that letter.
Мо́га ли с не́що да ви бъ́да поле́зен?	Can I be of help to you in some way?

13.8. The conjunction докато

The conjunction **докато** has different meanings depending on the aspect of the verb which follows. If the verb is imperfective, **докато** has the unbounded meaning "while", but if the verb is perfective, **докато** has the bounded meaning "until". Perfective **докато** can, but need not be, followed by the particle **не,** with no essential change in meaning.

Examples are given below. Bounded and unbounded conjunctions will be discussed in more detail in Lesson 17.

unbounded

Ми́х се преди ма́лко, докато На́дка гово́реше с те́бе.	I washed a while ago, while Nadka was talking with you.
Докато е студе́но, ще държи́м деца́та въ́тре.	So long as it's cold we'll keep the children inside.

bounded

И́ма о́ще ма́лко вре́ме, докато фестива́лът запо́чне.	There's still a little time left before the festival begins.
Мя́сто не мо́жеше да си наме́ри, докато не ги́ чу́ една́ су́трин.	She couldn't settle down until she finally heard them one morning.

13.9. Prepositions

The preposition **по** has a wide range of idiomatic meanings. It indicates different sorts of connection, depending on the particular expression. For example:

Мно́го прика́зва по телефо́на.	She talks on the phone a lot.
И́маше ху́бав фи́лм по телеви́зията сно́щи.	There was a good film on TV last night.
Тря́бва да гово́рим по по́вод на това́.	We have to talk in connection with that.
Оти́ваме та́м по ба́нски.	We go there in our bathing suits.
Тря́бва да яде́ш по три́ пъ́ти на де́н.	One should eat three times a day.

EXERCISES

I. Fill in the blanks with **се** *or* **си** *as appropriate.*

1. Véче е късно. Вре́ме е да _____ оти́ваме.
2. Тя́ е мно́го елега́нтна. Ви́наги _____ обли́ча ху́баво.
3. Кога́то оти́ва в университе́та, то́й _____ обли́ча я́кето и джи́нсите.
4. Су́трин вси́чки _____ ми́ят или _____ къпят, ако и́ма то́пла вода́.
5. На́дка е о́ще ма́лка и не мо́же да _____ ми́е сама́ лице́то и ръце́те.
6. Ту́к е горе́що. Съблечи́ _____ палто́то.
7. Та́зи къ́рпа е чи́ста. Мо́жете да _____ избъ́ршете в не́я.
8. Деца́, затва́ряйте _____ уста́та, кога́то голе́мите разгова́рят.
9. Ка́мен от ма́лък мо́же са́м да _____ обу́ва обу́щата.
10. Вси́чки _____ ми́ят ръце́те преди́ я́дене, а Ка́мен не _____ ги ми́е.
11. Кога́то _____ изми́еш, ела́ при ме́не на то́пло.

II. Rewrite the following as negative questions.

1. Ка́за ли му го?
2. То́й пои́ска ли ти автогра́ф?
3. На не́го ли му да́доха кни́га за награ́да?
4. Пи́са ли ни подро́бно за те́зи неща́?
5. На ва́с съобщи́ха ли ви за промя́ната в програ́мата?
6. Ни́е че́сто игра́ем те́нис за́едно.
7. Дими́тър все́ки де́н се оба́жда на ма́йка си по телефо́на.

*III. Fill in the blanks with the appropriate verb form (*боли́, тря́бва, и́ма, ня́ма, мо́же*) in present, aorist or imperfect tense.*

1. Ка́мен дне́с е по́-добре́. Пъ́рви де́н не го́ _____ ни́що.
2. Вче́ра то́й бе́ше по́-зле́. Ця́л де́н го _____ глава́та.
3. Кога́то то́й бе́ше бо́лен от гри́п, мно́го го _____ глава́та.
4. Ако _____, ще препи́шем това́ писмо́ о́ще веднъ́ж.
5. Вче́ра то́й _____ ра́бота и зато́ва не _____ да до́йде.
6. Ела́ непреме́нно. Ако ме _____ вкъ́щи, _____ да ми оста́виш беле́жка в по́щенската кути́я.
7. То́й _____ и по́-добре́ да напи́ше докла́да, но _____ вре́ме.

ADDITIONAL GRAMMAR NOTES

13.3a. Reflexive verbs: word order

When used with reflexive verbs, the particle **ce** functions exactly as a direct object, with the special meaning "object which is identical with the subject of the sentence". The particle **си** functions as a combination of "indirect object" and "possessive". This similarity of function is seen also in their form, as the first three lines of the pronoun object chart from Lesson 7 demonstrate:

	subject	*direct object*	*indirect object*
1ˢᵗ singular	áз	ме	ми
2ⁿᵈ singular	тú	те	ти
(reflexive)		се	си

These similarities extend to word order as well. The reflexive particles **ce** and **си** obey exactly the same word order rules as the appropriate object pronouns. Examples are given below, with numbering cumulative across lessons.

(61) Лéкарят кáзва на пациéнта да се съблечé.
        Cnj. DIR verb

> The doctor tells the patient to get undressed.

(62) Чú ли ме? Веднáга си облечú жилéтката.
        IND verb | *direct obj.*

> Did you hear me? Put your sweater on *now*!

(63) Ще си я облекá след мáлко.
        Fut. IND DIR verb

> I'll put it on in a bit.

(64) Ще си облечé ли бя́ла рúза?
        Fut. IND verb INT | *direct obj.*

> Will he wear a white shirt?

13.4a. Word order and intonation in negative-interrogative sentences

Negative-interrogative sentences in Bulgarian are particularly tricky, for two different reasons: they follow a word order rule which has little similarity to any other rules learned, and they have a characteristic intonation which sounds unnatural to speakers of English.

When no pronoun objects are present, the negative particle precedes the verb and the interrogative particle follows it, as in (65) below. When clitic pronoun objects are present, they follow the negative particle directly. The interrogative particle ли must then be placed after the first clitic in the string, *no matter what it means*.

This rule differs from all others learned previously, which required a specific grammatically marked form to follow the negative particle or to precede the interrogative one. On the basis of only examples (66) or (67), for instance, one might be tempted to say simply that the correct sequence in negative interrogative sentences would be:

"negative particle + pronoun object(s) + interrogative particle"

However, examples (68) through (70) show that the rule makes reference only to the sequence of clitic forms. The student should study these examples carefully, and be aware that special effort will be required to internalize this word order pattern.

(65)

Не	и́скаш	ли	сладоле́д?
Neg.	*verb*	*INT*	*direct obj.*

Don't you want [any] ice cream?

(66)

Не	го́	ли	позна́ваш?
Neg.	*DIR*	*INT*	*verb*

Don't you know him?

(67)

Не	и́м	ли	пома́га?
Neg.	*IND*	*INT*	*verb*

Isn't he helping them?

(68)

Не	ти́	ли	го	да́дох?
Neg.	*IND*	*INT*	*DIR*	*verb*

Didn't I give it to you?

(69)

Не	ти́	ли	е	прия́тел?
Neg.	*IND*	*INT*	*3ʳᵈCOP*	*predicate noun*

Isn't he your friend?

(70)

Не	си́	ли	му	прия́тел?
Neg.	*COP*	*INT*	*IND*	*predicate noun*

Aren't you his friend?

The characteristic rhythm of negative-interrogative sentences is due to two separate facts about Bulgarian intonation. The first is that the negative particle always focuses attention on the following accented word, and second is that the interrogative particle causes high tone on the preceding word. Any word surrounded by these two particles, therefore, carries a particularly strong accent. This intonation pattern is especially striking when a clitic is the word that is surrounded, because clitics do not otherwise carry any accent at all.

In English, high intonation in the middle of a sentence marks special emphasis. The same is true in Bulgarian when the question particle ли is placed after any word *other* than the verb. For instance:

В събота на <u>кино</u> ли ще хо́диш?   Are you going to the *movies* on Saturday? [and not somewhere else?]

<u>В събота</u> ли ще хо́диш на кино́?   Are you going to the movies on *Saturday?* [and not some other day?]

The high intonation of negative-interrogative sentences, however -- even higher than that of simple questions because of the negation -- is normal and neutral in Bulgarian. In each of the questions below, for instance, the capitalized form is pronounced much louder and with much higher tone than anything else in the sentence. An English ear will hear surprise (and almost shock) in this intonational pattern. In Bulgarian, however, it carries neutral meaning, and is the only way such sentences can be pronounced.

Те́бе не ТЕ́ ли боли́ гъ́рлото?   Doesn't your throat hurt?
На Ива́н не МУ́ ли е добре́?   Isn't Ivan well?

13.9a. Prepositions

Prepositions are not accented, but are rather pronounced together with the following noun or pronoun object as a single word. Prepositions of two or more syllables, such as между, срещу, or заради, are sometimes given in dictionaries (although not in the glossaries to this book) with accent on the final syllable. In very slow speech, or in instances when it is necessary to pronounce these words alone, they do bear a light accent on the final syllable.

The same is true of conjunctions such as ако, като or докато. Only when a conjunction is formed from an adverb, such as ка́кто or кога́то, does it bear an accent of its own in the speech stream.

13.10. Pronoun reduplication and inverted word order

A definite noun object is obligatorily "reduplicated" by the corresponding short form pronoun object in a number of sentence patterns. One of these is after е́то or ня́ма, and another is in experiencer and body-ache constructions. For review, consider the following:

Ето го трамвая!	There's the tram!
Калина я няма.	Kalina's not around.

Иван го боли зъб.	Ivan has a toothache.
На Надка ѝ е студено.	Nadka is cold.

Bulgarians also have the option to reduplicate a noun object if they wish to place a certain emphasis on it. The most common way to express emphasis is to reverse the order of verb and object; frequently a reduplicated pronoun object is added as well.

As an example, compare the neutral form of a sentence with a definite direct object, followed by its emphatic form with inversion and doubling. The emphasis is not strong, and the difference is difficult to render adequately in English translation.

Не помня телефонния номер.	I don't remember the phone number.
Телефонния номер не го помня.	*(same)*

13.11. Derivation: diminutive suffixes

Bulgarian, like other Slavic languages, has several suffixes which are termed "diminutive". They form nouns from other nouns, and add the meaning of smallness. One of the commonest of these is the suffix -ч-, which is frequently followed by the neuter ending -e.

In some nouns this -ч- is derived from a final -к or -ц in the base noun, and in others it is a separate suffix added to the noun stem. Below are examples of both types of neuter derived diminutives.

base noun	*stem*	+ -ч- ›	*derived noun*	*(meaning)*
човек	чове[к]-	+ -ч- ›	чове́че	dwarf
прозор-ец	прозор-[ц]-	+ -ч- ›	прозо́рче	small window
мом-ък	мом-[к]-	+ -ч- ›	мом-че́	boy
	мом-и-	+ -ч- ›	моми́че	girl
кеба́п	кебап-	+ -ч- ›	кеба́пче	grilled or stewed meat
нож	нож-	+ -ч- ›	нож-че́	[razor] blade
живот-но	живот-ин-	+ -ч- ›	животи́нче	little animal
българ-ин	българ-	+ -ч- ›	бъ́лгарче	young Bulgarian
друга́р	другар-	+ -ч- ›	друга́рче	young friend

Certain nouns in -a form diminutives according to a similar pattern. If the noun stem ends in -к or -ц, this consonant shifts to -ч-. The suffix -к- is then usually added before the feminine ending -a. Most of these nouns signify something of a smaller size; sometimes they simply mean "feminine", however.

base noun	stem	+ -ч- к- ›	derived noun	(meaning)
ма́ртеница	мартени[ц]	+ -ч-к- ›	ма́ртени-чка	small martenitsa
учени́к	учени[к]-	+ -ч-к- ›	учени́-чка	female pupil
ма́са	маси-	+ -ч-к- ›	ма́си-чка	small table

13.12. "Third-person" verbs, continued

Certain verbs, such as боли́ and вали́, are used only in the third person. A few other verbs of this sort express the idea of a feeling or a state which happens to one. Among these are досмеша́ва "feel like laughing" and досрамя́ва "feel ashamed". These are used most frequently in the past tense. Досрамя́ва expresses the experiencer as the direct object, while досмеша́ва expresses it as the indirect object.

Досрамя́ ме да си по́искам по́вече.	I felt [too] ashamed to ask for more.
Ма́лко ми досмеша́ като го полу́чих.	I chuckled to myself when I got it.

Museum-house "Todor Kableshkov", Koprivshtitsa

SAMPLE SENTENCES

1. Ако ти е студéно, не сé мúй.
2. Измúй се, облечú се и да трúгваме, че закъснávаме.
3. Кáмене, тú си голámо момчé, мóжеш сáм да се измúеш.

4. Тá се облúча мнóго хýбаво.
5. Тóй се облúча спóртно. Нúкога не сú слáга вратоврúзка.

6. Тресé ме. Тý се облúчам, тý се съблúчам.
7. През лáтото тá се съблúча по бáнски и се печé на слúнце на балкóна.
8. Не ходú бóс! Тýк не é тóлкова чúсто. Обýй се!

9. Нáдка е мáлка, не мóже да се обýе самá и да си завúрже врúзките на обýвките. Мáйка ù я обýва.

10. Кúпе се по трú пúти на дéн и всé мрúсен се чýвства.

11. Не тú ли стáна неудóбно да го пúташ за товá?
12. Не вú ли стúга, че съм тýка?
13. Не гó ли знáеш какúв е?
14. Не мé ли чý като те извúках?

15. Йдвайте ни пó-чéсто на гóсти!
16. Проверávай редóвно далú пóщата е дошлá.
17. Полúвай цветáта, докато ме нáма.

18. Мóжеше да не мú затвáряш вратáта под носá.
19. Тé трábваше вéче да са тýк.

20. Кáк мóже да взéмеш ключа без разрешéние -- трábваше да пúташ.
21. На твóите годúни трábваше да си пó-разýмен.
22. Вчéра úмаше сáмо двé яйцá в хладúлника, а днéс нáма нито еднó.
23. Не сú спóмням заглáвието на кнúгата.
24. Заглáвието на кнúгата не сú го спóмням.

25. Не ù кáзаха нéговото úме. Нéговото úме не ù го кáзаха.
26. Изáдох послéдното яйцé. Послéдното яйцé го изáдох.

SENTENCES FOR TRANSLATION

1. You ought to have come earlier. Then we could have studied together all evening. Now we only have one hour to prepare for the test!

2. There used to be a shoe store here. Where is it? Do you know where they sell shoes now?

3. Kamen is a big boy now. Every day he puts on his own shirt, pants, shoes and socks. Nadka still needs her mother's help. Her mother puts on her shoes and socks for her.

4. Wait until I dry my hands, please. Then I can write down the telephone number for you. You'll call them tonight, won't you?

5. Mother dresses the children in the morning, and Father bathes them in the evening. They both put them to bed: Mother sings them a song and Father reads them a story. When the children are bigger, they will do all these things themselves.

6. That shirt is dirty, you'd better put on a clean one.

7. "Where is my tie? You were supposed to wash it for me!"
   "Didn't I give it to you? Yes, there it is, on the bed."

8. "We like martenitsi. Usually our Bulgarian friends send them to us, but when I opened their letter yesterday, there was nothing in it."
   "They didn't put it in the letter for you? Here, take this one. Everyone should have a martenitsa in the spring. You should have had one last week."

9. Where's Ivan? He isn't here. He wasn't here yesterday either. He could have written us a note so that we'd know where he is. Yes, he ought to have written us a note.

10. "I'm cold. I want to put on my sweater, but I don't know where it is."
    "Well, if you're cold then I'm hot. I'll take off my sweater and you can put it on. Then we'll both be fine."

11. Boris came in, took off his jacket and shoes, and sat down. Then he got up again, went into the bathroom, and washed his hands and face. He couldn't dry himself, though, because there was no towel.

12. Where's your coat? Didn't you take it off just a bit ago?

READING SELECTION

<u>Кореспонде́нция - (10)</u>

15 февруа́ри, Со́фия

Дра́ги Патри́ша, Бо́б, Е́мили и Ма́йкъл,

Чести́та Ба́ба Ма́рта! Пожела́ваме ви и през та́зи про́лет да бъ́дете здра́ви и бо́дри, бе́ли и черве́ни като те́зи ма́ртеници!

У на́с в Бълга́рия хо́рата смя́тат, че пролетта́ настъ́пва на пъ́рви ма́рт. Предста́вяме си то́зи ме́сец като ста́ра жена́, намръ́щена и капри́зна, но с добро́ сърце́. И́мето ѝ е Ба́ба Ма́рта. По това́ вре́ме доли́тат от ю́г и пъ́рвите щъ́ркели. Те́ ви́наги се връ́щат у дома́ си, в своето гнездо́. Една́ дво́йка ста́ри позна́йници си сви́ха гнездо́ преди три́ годи́ни на коми́на на на́шата къ́ща в Смо́лян. И нали́ щъ́ркелите но́сят късме́т, на́шите ги ча́кат с нетърпе́ние вся́ка годи́на да се въ́рнат. Ми́налата годи́на бе́ше студе́но и те́ ма́лко закъсня́ха. Да зна́ете ка́к се притесни́ мо́ята свекъ́рва... мя́сто не мо́жеше да си наме́ри, дока́то не ги чу́ една́ су́трин да тра́кат с клю́н.

На пъ́рви ма́рт деца́та и мно́го въ́зрастни си зака́чват ма́ртеници за здра́ве. Преди мно́го годи́ни а́з за пъ́рви пъ́т подари́х ма́ртеница на Бо́йко и ми ста́на мъ́чно, че то́й я забо́де под реве́ра на сако́то си. Попи́тах се не ме́ ли оби́ча, от кого́ ли и́ска да скри́е мо́ята ма́ртеница? Тря́бваше да ми́нат мно́го годи́ни, за да разбера́, че то́й (ка́кто и дру́ги мъже́) се смуща́ва да но́си откри́то ма́ртеница. Към кра́я на ме́сеца мно́го хо́ра зака́чват ма́ртениците си на ня́кое дърво́, та те́ и на не́го да донеса́т здра́ве. Но, разби́ра се, деца́та се ра́дват на ма́ртениците на́й-мно́го. Ми́налата годи́на мно́го бли́зки да́доха ма́ртенички на Я́на и тя́ се оки́чи с тя́х като новогоди́шна елха́. Закачи́ две́ и на люби́мата си ку́кла. Я́на и не́йните прия́телки устро́иха не́що като мо́дно реви́ю с ма́ртеници.

И́во оба́че от ня́колко годи́ни се смя́та за прекале́но голя́м за таки́ва "дети́нски ра́боти".

Сърде́чни по́здрави от вси́чки ни. Оба́ждайте се.

Кали́на

2 март, Сан Франциско

Драга Калина,

Малко ми досмеша, като получих онзи ден писмото ти и го отворих, а от него паднаха двуцветните вълнени пискюли. Ние смятахме, че пролетта настъпва на 21 март, в деня на пролетното равноденствие. Тази година обаче тя настъпи за нас рано -- като в България. Вчера Емили предизвика фурор на училище с мартеницата си. Майкъл обаче отказа да си я сложи. Бои се, че приятелите му ще се смеят. Не си сложи той мартеницата, но и на Емили не пожела да я подари. Скри я при другите си съкровища в дървената кутия под леглото.

Старите обичаи са смешни понякога, но животът без тях е скучен, нали?

Апропо, едни мои приятели много се интересуват от народна музика. Те ми подсказаха да си купя една българска плоча с изумителна автентична народна музика. Записът е от някакъв фестивал в Копривщица. Ти можеш ли да ми разкажеш повече за този фестивал?

Ваша

Патриша

Storks on a chimney (central Bulgaria)

GLOSSARY

автенти́чен	authentic	животи́нче	little animal
автогра́ф	autograph	забо́ждам / забода́	stick, pin
апропо́	apropos, by the way	завъ́рзвам / завъ́ржа (-еш)	tie
балко́н	balcony	завъ́рзвам връ́з-ките на обу́вки	tie shoelaces
ба́нски	bathing; swimsuit		
бо́дър	lively, cheerful	загла́вие	title
бо́лен от гри́п	down with the flu	зад	behind
боле́ше	was hurting (2-3sg. imperfect)	зака́чвам / закача́ (-и́ш)	hang, suspend
бо́с	barefoot	за́пис	recording
ботани́ческа гради́на	botanical garden	зара́ди	for the sake of
ботани́чески	botanical	затва́рям врата́та под носа́ [на]	shut the door in [someone's] face
бъ́лгарче	young Bulgarian		
бъ́рша (-еш)	wipe, rub	зле́	bad, badly
взе́мам си дови́ждане	make one's farewells	избъ́рсвам / избъ́рша (-еш)	wipe, dry
вратовръ́зка	necktie	изви́квам / изви́кам	cry, call out
връ́зка	tie, string, shoelace		
въ́лнен, -ена	wool, woolen	извине́ние	excuse, pardon
гнездо́	nest	изми́вам / изми́я	wash up
гово́реше	was talking (2-3sg. imperfect)	изуми́телен	amazing, astounding
гри́п	influenza, flu	капри́зен	capricious
		кеба́п	grilled or stewed meat
дво́йка	pair	клю́н	beak
двуцве́тен	two-colored	коми́н	chimney
демокра́ция	democracy	ко́пие	copy
дети́нски	children's	кро́тък	gentle
дети́нски ра́боти	kid stuff	ку́кла	doll, puppet
джи́нси	jeans	къ́рпа	cloth, towel
дире́ктор	director		
дока́то не	until	любя́	love, be in love with
доли́там / долетя́	come flying, fly up to		
досмеша́ва ме / досмеше́е ме (3rd person only)	feel like laughing	ма́ртеница	see p. 287
		ма́ртеничка	small martenitsa
		ма́сичка	little table
досрамя́ва ме / досраме́е ме (3rd person only)	feel ashamed	миле́я	hold dear, care for
		мо́ден	fashionable
		мо́дно ревю́	fashion show
друга́рче	playfellow, playmate	мо́мък (pl. момци́)	young man
дъ́рвен (-ена)	wood, wooden		
		мъ́чен	hard, difficult
ела́ да ти поле́я	let me pour water [over your hands]	награ́да	reward, prize
елха́	fir tree	намръ́щен (-ена)	sullen, gloomy

285

нари́чам / нарека́ (-че́ш)	call, name	предста́вям си / предста́вя си	imagine
настъ́пвам / настъ́пя	come on, set in, occur	прекале́н	too great, unconscionable
не спори́	don't argue	прекале́но голя́м	way too big
непреме́нен	indispensable, necessary	препи́свам / препи́ша (-еш)	rewrite, copy
непреме́нно	by all means	проверя́вам / проверя́	check, verify, test
неудо́бен	inconvenient		
новогоди́шна елха́	New Year's tree	прозо́рче	small window
но́жче	[razor] blade	проле́тен	spring (adj.)
		проле́тно равноде́нствие	vernal equinox
обича́й	custom, convention		
обли́чам / облека́ (-че́ш)	dress [someone]	промя́на (pl. проме́ни)	change
обли́чам се / облека́ се (-че́ш)	put on, don	профе́сор	professor
обли́чам се спо́ртно	wear/put on casual clothing	равноде́нствие	equinox
		разреше́ние	permission
обу́вам / обу́я	put something on someone's foot	разу́мен	sensible, rational
		ра́нен	early
обу́вам се / обу́я се	put something on over the foot	реве́р	lapel
		ревю́ (neuter)	revue, show
обу́ща	footwear	редо́вен	regular; in order
оки́чвам / оки́ча (-иш)	adorn, decorate	ре́ша (-еш)	comb
		ри́за	shirt
отка́звам / отка́жа (-еш)	cancel, refuse		
		сако́	jacket
откри́то	openly, aboveboard	сви́вам / сви́я	bend, fold, roll
		сви́вам гнездо́	build a nest
палто́	coat	скри́вам / скри́я	hide
пека́ (-че́ш)	bake	ску́чен	boring
пека́ се на слъ́нце	sunbathe	сме́шен	funny, humorous
пискю́л	tassel, pendant	сме́я се	laugh
пло́ча	phonograph record	смуща́вам се / смутя́ се	get confused, be embarrassed
по ба́нски	wearing swimsuits		
по по́вод	regarding, in connection with	смя́там / сме́тна	reckon, count
		смя́там (за)	consider [to be]
пови́квам / пови́кам	call, call out	споря́	dispute, contend
по́вод	occasion, cause	ста́на ми мъ́чно	I had a hard time
подро́бен	detailed	сти́гам / сти́гна	reach, arrive at
подро́бно	in detail	събли́чам / съблека́ (-че́ш)	undress [someone]
подска́звам / подска́жа (-еш)	hint, prompt		
		събли́чам се / съблека́ се (-че́ш)	undress, get undressed
позна́йник	acquaintance		
позна́йница	acquaintance (f.)	събу́вам / събу́я	take [something] off [someone's] foot
поли́вам / поле́я	pour		
поли́вам цветя́та	water the flowers	събу́вам се / събу́я се	take something off one's foot
помо́лвам / помо́ля	beg, ask		
по́мня	remember	съкро́вище	treasure
попи́твам се / попи́там се	ask oneself, wonder	та	and; so that
		та́ча (-иш)	respect
предста́вям / предста́вя	present, offer	телефо́нен	telephone (adj.)

те́нис	tennis	чове́че	dwarf
това́ е!	that's that!	чу́вствувам се	feel
тра́кам	rattle	(*or* чу́вствам се)	
устро́йвам / устроя́	arrange, organize	щъ́ркел	stork
фуро́р	furor	юг	south
хо́дя бо́с	go barefoot	я́ке	jacket

CULTURAL COMMENTARY

Customs and beliefs: martenitsi; storks

A "martenitsa" (ма́ртеница) is a small decoration made of red and white yarn wound into tassels. It is worn pinned or tied to one's lapel throughout the month of March. Friends give martenitsi to each other to mark the coming of spring. It is especially customary to give children martenitsi, and to mail them to friends in other countries. The colors are thought to symbolize the health of springtime: cheeks that are red and skin that is white (that is, not jaundiced). The custom is one in which Bulgarians take great delight.

Storks (щъ́ркели) are very common birds in the Balkans. They often build their nests on rooftops near chimneys; to have a stork's nest on one's house is considered a sign of good luck. In addition, their return from winter migrations is considered to be a clear sign of spring.

Forms of address, and a poem

Forming diminutives with the suffix -ч- is quite common "at home" (within Bulgaria), but less so when referring to persons or things outside Bulgaria. Although Bulgarians could in principle refer to an English child as англича́нче, they would not do so automatically. The word бъ́лгарче, on the other hand, is extremely common. Part of this may be due to the following poem that every Bulgarian schoolchild knows:

А́з съм бъ́лгарче. Свобо́дно
в кра́й свобо́ден а́з живе́я.
Вси́чко бъ́лгарско и ро́дно
лю́бя, та́ча и миле́я.

I am a Bulgarian child. Freely
I live, in a free land.
Everything Bulgarian and native
is what I love, esteem and hold dear.

А́з съм бъ́лгарче. Оби́чам
на́ш'те планини́ зеле́ни.
Бъ́лгарин да се нари́чам
пъ́рва ра́дост е за ме́не.

I am a Bulgarian child. I love
our mountains green.
To be able to say I am Bulgarian
is the most joyful of things for me.

Folklore: Koprivshtitsa festival

It has been customary to hold a large folk festival every five years in the mountain town of Koprivshtitsa. Lovers of Bulgarian folk music come from all over the world for this festival. It will be described in Lesson 16.

LESSON 14

DIALOGUE

На гáрата в Сóфия

// Влáкът приближáва гáра Сóфия с мáлко закъснéние. На перóна чáкат мнóго хóра, между тя́х един слáб човéк с мустáци и, мáлко пó-далéче, една мнóго елегáнтно облéчена дáма. Веднáга щом влáкът спи́ра, от нéго сли́зат пъ́рво Тáня с децáта, пóсле Милéна и Дими́тър, а след товá дру́гите. //

Камен: Тáтко! Ти́ дойдé!

Петър: Разби́ра се! Току́-що получи́х вáшето писмó от Вáрна. Намéрих го в пóщенската кути́я, когáто се въ́рнах от рáбота. В нéго пи́шеше, че ще присти́гате с тóзи влáк. Тря́бваше да побъ́рзам, за да дóйда наврéме да ви посрéщна.

Таня: И́маме късмéт, че си в Сóфия. Каквá изненáда!

Петър: Нали́ знáеш, че áз съм по изненáдите. Вкъ́щи ви чáка óще еднá изненáда! É, децá, кáк прекáрахте на морéто? Каквó прáвихте? Хýбаво ли бéше?

Камен: О, мнóго хýбаво, тáтко. Сáмо и́сках ти́ да си с нáс!

Надка: Тáтко, тáтко! Áз се научи́х да плýвам.

Петър: Брáво, мóето моми́че!

Таня: Не мóжех да я извáдя от морéто. Стоéше по ця́л дéн във водáта.

Надка: Ви́ж, тáтко, каквó гердáнче и́мам. Нали́ е мнóго слáдко?

Петър: Дá, мнóго е хýбаво. Кóй ти го подари́?

Таня: Ни́е с Нáдка вся́ка су́трин съби́рахме óхлювчета на плáжа. И Кáмен ни помáгаше. Пóсле изби́рахме нáй-хýбавите и ги ни́жехме на гердáни. Áз нани́зах нáй-хýбавия гердáн.

Петър: А за тéбе, Кáмене, гердáн ня́ма ли?

Камен: Áз съм мъ́ж. Защó ми е на мéне гердáнче? На мéне мáма ми ку́пи шнóрхел!

288

* * * * * * * * * * * *

Димитър: Погледни, мило! Виж, майка ми ни маха оттам. Ела да ви запозная.

Милена: Боже, колко добре е облечена! Всички ли софиянки се обличат така? А виж ме мен на какво приличам след тоя дълъг път. Какво ли ще помисли за мен?

Димитър: Не се притеснявай, мило. Много си хубава. Сигурно ще те хареса. Мамо, ето ни най-после.

Павлина: Митенце! Ти пристигна!

Димитър: Ние пристигнахме, мамо. Запознай се, това е Милена. Милена, майка ми.

Павлина: Вие сигурно сте уморени от пътя. Хайде, таксито ни чака. Как пътувахте?

Милена: Без приключения.

* * * * * * * * * * *

Таня: Хайде, деца, да тръгваме.

Надка: Нали и лелята ще дойде с нас?

Таня: Тя си има работа. Пусни я. Кажи ѝ довиждане.

Надка: Не, аз искам тя да дойде с нас. Искам да ѝ покажа куклите си.

Таня: Пусни сега лелята. Пусни я, че бърза. Но може в неделя да отидем заедно на Витоша. Джули, обади ни се. Ето нашия телефон.

Джули: Не знам дали в неделя все още ще съм в София. Зависи какво ще каже професорът. Но ще ви се обадя на всяка цена, след като нещата се изяснят.

BASIC GRAMMAR

| 14.1. The imperfect tense: form |

The endings of the imperfect tense are like those of the aorist; only the second and third singular are different. The imperfect endings are:

	singular	plural
1st	-х-	-хме
2nd	-ше	-хте
3rd	-ше	-ха

These endings are preceded by one of two theme vowels: -a- (or -я-), used in a-conjugation verbs, and the alternating -я-/-e- vowel, used in all other verbs. Examples of the imperfect conjugation are given below, in each case together with the present and the aorist for comparison.

For a-conjugation (type 1) verbs, the aorist and the imperfect are identical except for second and third singular. Context is usually sufficient to know which is meant.

(type 1)	PRESENT	IMPERFECT	AORIST
1st singular	глéд-ам	глéд-ах	глéд-ах
2nd singular	глéд-аш	глéд-аше	глéд-а
3rd singular	глéд-а	глéд-аше	глéд-а
1st plural	глéд-аме	глéд-ахме	глéд-ахме
2nd plural	глéд-ате	глéд-ахте	глéд-ахте
3rd plural	глéд-ат	глéд-аха	глéд-аха

For all other verbs, the shape of the theme vowel depends upon the accent and upon the shape of the ending which follows. According to the general rule, the alternating vowel -я-/-e- always appears as -e- when unstressed. In the majority of verb types, therefore, the theme vowel will be -e-.

(type 2)	PRESENT	IMPERFECT	AORIST
1st singular	хóд-я	хóд-ех	хóд-их
2nd singular	хóд-иш	хóд-еше	хóд-и
3rd singular	хóд-и	хóд-еше	хóд-и
1st plural	хóд-им	хóд-ехме	хóд-ихме
2nd plural	хóд-ите	хóд-ехте	хóд-ихте
3rd plural	хóд-ят	хóд-еха	хóд-иха

When the theme vowel is accented, it appears as -e- in the second and third singular and -я- or -a- elsewhere. For example:

(type 3)

	PRESENT	**IMPERFECT**	*AORIST*
1st singular	върв-я́х	върв-я́х	върв-я́х
2nd singular	върв-и́ш	върв-е́ше	върв-я́
3rd singular	върв-и́	върв-е́ше	върв-я́
1st plural	върв-и́м	върв-я́хме	върв-я́хме
2nd plural	върв-и́те	върв-я́хте	върв-я́хте
3rd plural	върв-я́т	върв-я́ха	върв-я́ха

The *endings* of the imperfect tense are straightforward: there are only the above types. *Stems*, though, can be different. This is because the imperfect tense is formed from the present tense stem. When the present (= imperfect) and aorist stems are identical, as in the above examples, the aorist and imperfect paradigms differ only in their endings. Indeed, when the stems are the same and the theme vowel is -a- or -я-, the aorist and imperfect paradigms are identical except for the second and third singular forms.

The following are examples of verbs whose imperfect stem differs from the aorist stem. Because the endings are predictable, only the first person plural forms are given. Note in each case the similarity with the present tense stem, *including accent*.

(type 5)

	PRESENT	**IMPERFECT**	*AORIST*
1st plural	чет-е́м	чет-я́хме	че́т-охме

(type 8)

	PRESENT	**IMPERFECT**	*AORIST*
1st plural	пи́ш-ем	пи́ш-ехме	пи́с-ахме

(type 9)

	PRESENT	**IMPERFECT**	*AORIST*
1st plural	бер-е́м	бер-я́хме	бр-а́хме

If there is a consonantal alternation within the present tense (as in мо́га and сека́), the stem is taken from the third singular (and not the first singular). For example:

	PRESENT	IMPERFECT	AORIST
1ˢᵗ singular	мо́г-а	мо́ж-ех	мож-а́х

	PRESENT	IMPERFECT	*AORIST*
1ˢᵗ singular	сек-а́	сеч-а́х	ся́к-ох

14.2. Usage of the imperfect tense

The imperfect is formally unique in that it is marked both for past tense (by the presence of the consonant -x- in the endings) and for present tense (by the use of the present tense stem of the verb).

Its meaning is a similar mixture. In terms of time frame, it clearly locates an action in the past. In all other ways, the meaning is that of the present tense: it describes an action or state that is either in progress at the moment in question, is habitually repeated, or is a general fact. As examples, consider the following pairs, in which the verb forms are underlined to focus upon this contrast:

present

Все́ки де́н <u>чете́</u> ве́стник.　　He reads the newspaper every day.

imperfect

Мака́р и на море́то,　　　　　Even though [he was] at the seashore,
　　то́й <u>чете́ше</u> ве́стник все́ки де́н.　　he read the newspaper every day.

present

Тя́ <u>хо́ди</u> мно́го на ки́но.　　She goes to the movies a lot.

imperfect

По́-ра́но мно́го <u>хо́деше</u> на ки́но.　　She used to go to the movies a lot.

present

Ти́ какво́ <u>пра́виш</u> в моме́нта?　　What are you doing right now?

imperfect

Ти́ какво́ <u>пра́веше</u> в то́зи моме́нт?　　What were you doing right then?

present

Ни́е сега́ ве́че не <u>пи́ем</u> мно́го.　　We don't drink much any more.

imperfect

А тога́ва -- а́х, ка́к <u>пи́ехме</u>!　　But back then -- boy, how we used to drink!

present

      Той <u>и́два</u> редо́вно   He comes over regularly
         да игра́е бридж с та́тко ти.   to play bridge with your father.

imperfect

      Той <u>и́дваше</u> редо́вно   He used to come over regularly
         да игра́е бридж с та́тко ти.   to play bridge with your father.

In fact, the only essential thing that separates each of the two pairs is the time frame: the sentences with a present tense verb describe an action occurring "now", and the sentences with an imperfect tense verb describe an action which was occurring "then".

The most appropriate English translations of the imperfect are "used to do" or "would do" (in the case of a repeated or habitual action) and "was doing", "were doing" (in the case of a single durative action).

14.3. Contrast of aorist and imperfect tenses

Both the aorist and imperfect tenses are concerned with past action. The aorist is the more neutral of the two: it focuses upon the fact of an action that happened in the past, but does not add any further information. The imperfect, however, concentrates on the duration of the action over a certain period of time. The English past progressive ("was doing", "were going") often renders this meaning exactly. In other instances, the English simple past is necessary. In these cases, context provides the necessary information of repetition or duration.

In the following examples, the main verb forms are underlined to focus on this contrast:

aorist

      <u>Ми́слих</u>, ми́слих,   I thought and thought,
         но ни́що не <u>изми́слих</u>.   but didn't think up anything.

imperfect

      То е, защо́то   That's because
         <u>ми́слех</u> под напреже́ние.   I was thinking under pressure.

aorist

      Вче́ра той <u>оти́де</u> на конферéн-   Yesterday he went to the conference
         цията и <u>слу́ша</u> два́ докла́да.   and listened to two papers.

imperfect

      Пъ́рвият бе́ше мно́го ску́чен.   The first was very boring. In the
         Отнача́ло той внима́телно   beginning he listened
         <u>слу́шаше</u>, но по́сле   attentively, but after that his
         внима́нието му се притъпи́.   attention wavered.

The usage of the imperfect is seen especially well in the narration of past events. The imperfect is used to set the frame for a story, and to involve the listener in the events of that time frame. For instance:

<u>Вървях</u> по у́лицата, ра́но-ра́но. Пти́ците <u>пе́еха</u>. [...]	I was walking down the street, early in the morning. The birds were singing. [...]
<u>Връ́щах се</u> с такси́ от бо́лницата. <u>И́маше</u> голя́мо движе́ние. [...]	I was coming from the hospital by taxi. There was a lot of traffic. [...]

If the speaker uses only imperfective verbs, the focus remains on the scene, and on the mood of the particular durative time frame. But if (as is often the case) the speaker goes on to narrate specific events that then happened within that time frame, s/he switches to the aorist. Thus, the imperfect is used to relate things that were going on in the background, while the aorist is used to relate things that happened, events in the foreground.

The following narrative illustrates this contrast between aorist and imperfect.

Imperfect

Го́твех си вече́ря. По́мня, че се чу́дех къде́ е солта́.	I was making dinner. I remember wondering where the salt was.

(actions going on in the background)

Aorist

Изведнъ́ж си́лно ме заболя́ коре́мът.	Suddenly I got a sharp pain in my abdomen.

(foregrounded story-line event)

Imperfect

Ми́слех отнача́ло, че ще ми ми́не...	I thought in the beginning that it would go away...

(state, background information)

Aorist

...и продължи́х да го́твя.	...and I resumed cooking.

(foregrounded single event, i.e. the "decision" to continue)

Но не отми́на...	But it didn't go away...

(foregrounded story-line event, leading to conclusion of story)

Simple past

...и тря́бваше да изви́кам бъ́рза по́мощ.	...and I had to call the ambulance.

(conclusion of story)

14.4. Indirect discourse

Speech which is quoted directly is called "direct discourse", and that which is rephrased in the speaker's own words is called "indirect discourse". The relationship between the two is particularly important when one rephrases something that was said, thought or felt at some time in the past. Consider the contrast between direct discourse and indirect discourse in the following English sentences:

Type of discourse		verb
direct	She said, "I am going to the movies."	am going
indirect	She said that she was going to the movies.	was going
direct	You wrote, "We will arrive today by train."	will arrive
indirect	You wrote that you would arrive today by train.	would arrive
direct	I thought: "It will be nice to visit Bulgaria."	will be
indirect	I thought it would be nice to visit Bulgaria.	would be
direct	My only desire was: "I wish you were with us."	were
indirect	I wished only that you had been with us.	had been

The speaker is talking of something in the past, and therefore the verb of the main sentence is in the past tense ("said", "wrote", "was"). The verb of a direct quote remains exactly as it was at the moment it was spoken, written, thought or felt. When an English speaker reformulates this quote as indirect discourse, however, s/he must indicate the time distance by shifting the quoted verb into the past.

Bulgarian does *not* make this shift. All verbs in indirect discourse remain in the same tense as when originally spoken, written or thought. Compare the Bulgarian translations of the above sentences:

Type of discourse		verb
direct	Ка́за: "Оти́вам на ки́но."	оти́вам
indirect	Ка́за, че оти́ва на ки́но.	оти́ва
direct	Ви́е напи́сахте: "Ще присти́гнем днес с влак."	ще присти́гнем
indirect	Ви́е напи́сахте, че ще присти́гнете днес с влак.	ще присти́гнете
direct	Поми́слих си: "Ху́баво ще е да посети́м Бълга́рия."	ще е
indirect	Поми́слих си, че ще е ху́баво да посети́м Бълга́рия.	ще е
direct	Еди́нственото ми жела́ние беше: "И́скам ти да си с нас!"	си
indirect	Еди́нственото ми жела́ние беше ти да си с нас.	си

Note that this requirement applies not only to neutral speech or thought, but also to wishes and desires. Thus, while most instances of indirect discourse occur after the conjunction **че**, some also occur after **да**.

It is necessary for speakers of English to pay particular attention to this rule. The shift of tenses is made so naturally (and unconsciously) in English that it will seem second nature to reproduce it in Bulgarian. It will take practice to catch all the instances where this English-based tendency must be overcome.

14.5. Subordinate clauses

A complex sentence is one in which two simple sentences (each with its own verb) are joined. When they are part of a single sentence, each of the simpler sentences is called a "clause". One, the main clause, stands alone, while the other, the subordinate clause, is joined to it by a conjunction.

Many such conjunctions are already familiar to the student. They are summarized here to illustrate their use in complex sentences.

че   that

Зна́я, че в та́зи сладка́рница и́ма ху́бав сладоле́д.	I know that there is nice ice cream in that sweet-shop.

ако   if

Ако вали́, ня́ма да мо́жем да оти́дем на Ви́тоша у́тре.	If it rains, we won't be able to go to Vitosha tomorrow.

докато   while

Докато ви́е два́мата прика́звахте, а́з приго́твих вси́чко.	While you two were chatting, I got everything ready.

като   as, when

Като вървя́хме по у́лицата, то́й ми разка́зваше за фестива́ла.	As we walked down the street, he told me about the festival.
Като живе́ех у тя́х на кварти́ра, пла́щах висо́к на́ем.	I paid a high rent when I lived in their apartment.

ка́кто   as, like

Ще напра́вим то́чно ка́кто ни съве́твате.	We will do exactly as you advise us.

щом since, as, if, as soon as

Щом вла́кът спи́ра, сли́зат пъ́тниците от не́го.	As soon as the train stops, the passengers get off.
Щом те боли́ гъ́рлото, облечи́ се!	If your throat hurts, put something on!

кога́то when

Наме́рих го, кога́то се въ́рнах от ра́бота.	I found it when I came home from work.

There are also a number of conjunctions which are formed of two components. The most common of these are the following:

преди́ да before

Преди́ да тръ́гнем, ще ти се оба́дим.	I'll give you a call before we set out.
Преди́ да ми ка́же, че е от Аме́рика, ми́слех, че е бъ́лгарка.	Before she told me she was from America, I thought she was Bulgarian.

сле́д като after, once, on

Сле́д като взе́х лека́рството, се почу́вствувах по́-добре́.	After I took the medicine, I felt better.
Ще ви се оба́дя, сле́д като неща́та се изясня́т.	I'll give you a call once things get clarified.

бе́з да without

Тъ́рсихме, тъ́рсихме, бе́з да наме́рим ни́що.	We looked and looked without finding anything.

Note that the English translation of "бе́з да + verb" must use a gerundial form (e.g. "finding") as its object.

EXERCISES

I. Put each sentence into the frame "По-ра́но..., ама ве́че не́." *("Earlier..., but not any more").*

1. Ка́мен и На́дка ста́ват все́ки де́н в се́дем часа́.
2. През ля́тото че́сто вали́.
3. Те́ хо́дят вся́ка се́дмица на Ви́тоша.
4. Те́ и́скат да се запозна́ем.
5. А́нгел ви́наги закъсня́ва за ра́бота.
6. Ни́е че́сто игра́ем те́нис за́едно.
7. Дими́тър все́ки де́н се оба́жда на ма́йка си по телефо́на.

II. Rewrite in indirect discourse.

1. Ста́рата жена́ пи́та: "Ко́й звъни́?"
2. Пе́тър се интересу́ва: "Ко́й бе́ше то́зи чове́к с очила́та? Видя́х го, като говоре́ше с Та́ня."
3. Та́ня пожела́ на младоже́нците: "Бъде́те щастли́ви!"
4. Го́стите помоли́ха: "Мо́же ли да се оба́дим по телефо́на?"
5. На́дка ка́зва: "Боли́ ме гъ́рлото."
6. Дими́тър предла́га на прия́телите си: "Остане́те о́ще ма́лко с на́с!"
7. Джу́ли мо́ли деца́та: "Не ви́кайте то́лкова, ще събу́дите ма́йка си!"

III. Fill in the blanks with one of the following conjunctions: ако, бе́з да, докато, ка́кто, като, кога́то, преди́ да, че, щом.

1. _____ не ми ка́жеш вси́чко, ня́ма да си тръ́гна.
2. То́й си тръ́гна, _____ фи́лмът свъ́рши.
3. Те́ ви́наги се оба́ждат, _____ ще закъсне́ят.
4. _____ не и́скаш, не и́двай с на́с.
5. Ве́чер _____ заспи́, тя́ чете́ рома́н.
6. То́й, _____ подози́ра, бе́ше пъ́лно ко́пие на знамени́тия актьо́р.
7. _____ я видя́, ще и́ ка́жа.

ADDITIONAL GRAMMAR NOTES

14.1a. The imperfect tense: form

Formally, the imperfect tense is a mixture of the present and the aorist: it has the stem of the present and the endings of the aorist. Indeed, those features which are *different from* the aorist are precisely those which are *identical to* the present. This is seen especially clearly in verbs of type 4 and 7. Note also that while the aorist sometimes lacks a theme vowel, the imperfect always has one.

(type 4)

	PRESENT	**IMPERFECT**	*AORIST*
1ˢᵗ plural	взём-ем	взём-ех-ме	взé- -хме

(type 4)

	PRESENT	**IMPERFECT**	*AORIST*
1ˢᵗ plural	чу́-ем	чу́-ех-ме	чу́- -хме

(type 7)

	PRESENT	**IMPERFECT**	*AORIST*
1ˢᵗ plural	живé-ем	живé-ех-ме	жив- -я́хме

For all but type 1 verbs, the imperfect theme vowel is the alternating vowel **-я-/-е-**. According to the basic rule, **-е-** appears when unstressed or when the following syllable contains a front vowel, and **-а-** appears elsewhere. In the case of the imperfect tense, two exceptions must be made to this rule.

The first concerns the 1ˢᵗ and 2ⁿᵈ plural endings **-хме, -хте**. Despite the fact that these endings contain a front vowel, the theme vowel preceding them continues to be **-а-** if it is stressed (**четя́хме, чстя́хтс**). Apparently the consonant **-х-** blocks the application of this rule.

The second concerns verbs whose imperfect stem ends in **-ч, -ж, -ш** or **-й**. According to the rule, **-е-** should appear in 2-3sg., and **-а-** should appear elsewhere. This rule is indeed observed in the forming the imperfect of these verbs. Many Bulgarians, however, use the theme vowel **-е-** in all imperfect forms of these verbs. Below are given both the variant forms and the regular forms:

(type 3)

	PRESENT	IMPERFECT	IMPERFECT variant	AORIST
1st singular	мълч-á	мълч-áх	мълч-éх	мълч-áх
2nd singular	мълч-и́ш	мълч-éше	мълч-éше	мълч-á
3rd singular	мълч-и́	мълч-éше	мълч-éше	мълч-á
1st plural	мълч-и́м	мълч-áхме	мълч-éхме	мълч-áхме
2nd plural	мълч-и́те	мълч-áхте	мълч-éхте	мълч-áхте
3rd plural	мълч-áт	мълч-áха	мълч-éха	мълч-áха

Verbs in which this variant is commonly heard are държá, стоя́, секá and the like. The apparent tendency is to increase the formal differentiation between aorist and imperfect.

14.2a. Additional uses of the imperfect tense

The imperfective aspect is used to express simultaneity with another ongoing action. In contrast to the aorist, which signifies the sequential occurrence of past actions, the imperfect emphasizes the fact that both actions are past, and that neither is any more specified in time than the other. For example:

Тóй говóреше по телефóна, а ти́ каквó прáвеше?	What were you doing while he was talking on the phone?
Тóй и́дваше у нáс, докато тáтко ти рабóтеше в министéрството.	He used to come by to see us when * your father was working at the Ministry. *during the time period when*
С нáс пътýваха двáма америкáнци -- ня́ма да повя́рваш кóлко хýбаво говóреха бъ́лгарски!	There were two Americans traveling with us -- you wouldn't believe how well they spoke * Bulgarian! *during the time of the traveling*

The imperfect can also be used to ask someone to repeat something which was said in the present tense. Here, the meaning remains "present", but the added information is that of politeness. The distancing effect of the past tense verb form acts to smooth over somehow the fact that communication was not achieved properly the first time around. This usage is also found in English.

Кáк бéше нéговото и́ме?	What was his name? [= What did you say his name was?]
Когá присти́гаше самолéтът?	When was the plane due? [= When did you say the plane was due?]

14.3a. Contrast of aorist and imperfect tenses

In the case of the verb **мо́га** "can, be able", the difference between aorist and imperfect usages is particularly tricky. This is partly because English translations are almost completely unable to convey this difference, and partly because of the ambiguous meaning of the verb in its past tense form, "could".

When the past tense of "can" refers to the fact of (in)ability, the contrast between aorist **можа́х** and imperfect **мо́жех** is similar to the contrast in other verbs. For example:

aorist: fact of action

Тя́ не можа́ да понесе́ оби́дата и се разпла́ка.	She couldn't deal with the insult and burst into tears.

imperfect: emphasis on duration of action

Тя́ си оти́де, защо́то не мо́жеше по́вече да пона́ся оби́дите му.	She left, because she could no longer bear his insults.

aorist: fact of action

-- Ти́ можа́ ли да ви́диш фи́лма сно́щи?	"Did you manage to watch that film last night?"
-- Не можа́х. Мно́го бя́х умо́рен и си ле́гнах ра́но.	"I didn't. I was very tired and went to bed early."

imperfect: emphasis on duration of action

-- А а́з случа́йно го видя́х. Не мо́жех да заспя́ и затова́ включих телеви́зора.	"I just happened to watch it. I couldn't fall asleep and so turned on the TV."

When the past tense of "can" refers to the possibility of an action, however, then the imperfect form **мо́жех** means "could have (but didn't)". This conditional usage of the imperfect will be treated in greater detail in Lessons 22 and 23.
    Here is one example of this contrast:

aorist: fact of action

Не можа́х да ти се оба́дя, защо́то ня́мах вре́ме.	I wasn't able to call because I didn't have time.

imperfect: possibility of action

Мо́жех да ти се оба́дя, но не и́сках да те притесня́вам.	I could have called but I didn't want to disturb you.

14.3b. Imperfect tense and imperfective aspect

The names of the two simple past tenses (imperfect and aorist) and of the two aspects (imperfective and perfective) are even more similar in Bulgarian than they are in English. The chart below, given already in shortened form in Lesson 12, shows the Bulgarian names and their English equivalents. Recall that the literal meaning of the Bulgarian adjective **свършен** is "completed."

Aspect (вид)				
		свършен *Perfective*		несвършен *Imperfective*
Tense (вре́ме)	ми́нало	свършено *Aorist*	ми́нало	несвършено *Imperfect*

Such a striking similarity in names seems to suggest a corresponding similarity in fact. It is important to be aware of this similarity, but also of the differences. The imperfect and aorist tenses, and imperfective and perfective aspects, are *not* interchangeable.

The aorist tense can be formed from both perfective and imperfective verbs. The meaning of the aorist is the fact of action in the past, and the meaning of aspect is the presence or absence of the idea of boundedness. One can think of the fact of past action in either bounded or unbounded terms: if it is past bounded action, the verb is perfective aorist (**то́й го напра́ви**), and if it is past unbounded action, the verb is imperfective aorist (**тя́ пра́ви не́що**). There is some overlap between the idea "specific point in past time" (aorist tense) and "bounded action" (perfective aspect), but the two categories are far from synonymous.

Similarly, the imperfect tense can be formed from both imperfective and perfective verbs. The meaning of the imperfect is "durative or habitual past action, the frame of a narrative" -- action not bound to any particular point in time. Here there is more overlap of meaning. Verbs which lack the general idea of boundedness (imperfective verbs) tend to occur more often in contexts which express the absence of temporal boundedness. Nevertheless, there are situations in which a bounded (perfective) verb can be used with the meaning "repeated or habitual past action". These specific situations, which are conditioned by the presence of certain conjunctions, will be studied in Lesson 17.

Yet the terminological parallel noted above is neither coincidental nor illusory: there is a similarity between the two sorts of boundedness. That expressed by the opposition aorist vs. imperfect is concerned with a perception of past time, and that expressed by the opposition perfective vs. imperfective is concerned with a perception of the nature of verbal activity. The general idea of aspect is present in both, and it is not altogether wrong to say that both these oppositions are aspectual in nature. Indeed, some grammarians speak of "subordinate aspect" (that which is limited to the frame of past time) and "superordinate aspect" (that which is concerned with all verbal activity). While the student must learn both the forms and the meanings as they are associated with these separate categories, s/he should also be aware of the underlying importance of aspect as an organizing principle of the Bulgarian verb system.

14.5a. Subordinate clauses

The compound conjunctions **преди́ да** and **сле́д като** mean "before" and "after", respectively. *Both* components of the conjunction must be present. This is particularly important to remember in the case of **преди́ да**, because it is possible for these two components to be separated from one another in the sentence. That is, the word order rule which requires the verb of a **да**-phrase to follow immediately after it supersedes the word order rule which keeps the two components of the conjunction together. Thus when the subject of the verb following **да** must be included, it comes *between* the conjunction and the **да**. For instance:

Ти́ тря́бва да присти́гнеш, преди́ то́й да си ле́гне.	You must get here before he goes to bed.

Special care must be taken not to confuse the conjunctions **преди́ да** "before" and **сле́д като** "after" with the prepositions **преди́** (**пред**) and **след**, which also mean "before" ("in front of") and "after", respectively. Each of the conjunctions contains two words, and must be followed by an entire verbal phrase, whereas each of the prepositions is a single word, which must be followed by a noun or pronoun.

conjunction **преди́ да**
    Тя́ навя́рно ще присти́гне   She'll probably arrive before he does.
    преди́ то́й да до́йде.
  vs.

preposition **пред**
    Четири́мата стоя́т пред бло́ка.   The four of them are standing in front of the apartment building.

preposition **преди́**
    Тря́бва да до́йдеш преди́ еди́н.   You have to come before 1:00.

conjunction **сле́д като**
    Сле́д като присти́гнеш, ще ни   After you get here, you'll tell us
    разка́жеш си́чко.   everything.
  vs.

preposition **след**
    След я́денето поднесо́ха кафе́.   After dinner, they served coffee.

    След пе́т годи́ни ни́кой ня́ма да   At the end of five years, no one will
    си спо́мня за това́.   remember that.

14.6. Neuter nouns, continued

Foreign words ending in -и and -у are treated as neuter nouns in Bulgarian. For example:

singular indefinite	singular definite	plural indefinite	plural definite	(meaning)
такси́	такси́то	такси́та	такси́тата	taxi
меню́	меню́то	меню́та	меню́тата	menu

A number of other "words" are considered to be neuter in gender. Among these are the spoken form of certain very common abbreviations. Note that in these instances the letters are spoken followed by the vowel -е- (and not the vowel -ъ-, as in the normal "naming" of a letter of the alphabet).

ГДР   (Герма́нска демократи́ческа репу́блика)   ›   ге́дере́ (то)
DDR [the former East German republic]

СДС   (Съю́з на демократи́ческите си́ли):   ›   се́десе́ (то)
UDF [Union of Democratic Forces] *

БСП   (Бъ́лгарска социалисти́ческа па́ртия):   ›   бе́сепе́ (то)
BSP [Bulgarian Socialist Party] *

* political parties within Bulgaria

Former Communist Party headquarters, downtown Sofia

SAMPLE SENTENCES

1. Един баща́ се ка́раше на синове́те си. Объ́рна се към по́-голе́мия.
   -- Защо́ ту́к е то́лкова мръ́сно? Какво́ пра́ви вче́ра ця́л де́н?
   -- Мота́х се.
   -- А бра́т ти какво́ пра́веше?
   -- Пома́гаше ми.

2. То́й гле́даше телеви́зия по ця́л де́н, но то́зи фи́лм ня́как му се изплъ́зна.

3. Изкъ́па се, обле́че се, изчи́сти си обу́вките и, тъ́кмо като си връ́зваше вратовръ́зката, телефо́нът иззвъня́. Дока́то гово́реше по телефо́на, кафе́то му изкипя́. Ста́на му я́сно, че и дне́с ня́ма да му върви́.

4. Вче́ра видя́х Гео́рги на у́лицата. То́й върве́ше под ръка́ с едно́ мно́го ху́баво моми́че и му разка́зваше не́що сме́шно. Моми́чето го гле́даше влюбено. Като свъ́рши ра́зказът, моми́чето се разсмя́, а Гео́рги го целу́на.

5. Тога́ва те́ тру́дно живе́еха, а сега́ им е по́-добре́.
6. То́й бе́ше то́лкова уморе́н, че не мо́жеше да държи́ очи́те си отво́рени.

7. Те́ можа́ха да напра́вят пре́вода без гре́шка.
8. Те́ мо́жеха да напра́вят пре́вода и без гре́шка, ако внима́ваха.

9. В Бълга́рия като ки́хнеш, ти ка́зват "Наздра́ве!", а като се оку́пеш -- "Чести́та ба́ня!"

10. Дире́кторът дикту́ваше бъ́рзо на секрета́рката си, като погле́ждаше от вре́ме на вре́ме през прозо́реца.

11. Като пора́снеш, ще ста́неш инжене́р.

12. Профе́сорът съобщи́, че и́зпитът по бъ́лгарски ези́к ще се проведе́ след три́ дни́.

13. Попи́тах го от кого́ се страху́ва, но то́й не ми́ отгово́ри.
14. А́з мно́го се зара́двах, кога́то то́й ми ка́за, че у́тре присти́га в Со́фия.

15. Ще ти се разсъ́рдя, ако не и́ ка́жеш, че то́й се оба́жда все́ки де́н да пи́та за не́я.

16. Бе́з да я пи́тат, ка́за, че отда́вна зна́е за това́, но пе́т пари́ не да́ва.

SENTENCES FOR TRANSLATION

1. He told us he would arrive today, but he's not here yet. Are you sure you heard him correctly?

2. "Tell me again what happened last night. You were washing the dishes..."
   "I was washing the dishes, and thinking about my exam the next day, when I heard a loud sound. Did something fall, I wondered. I went into the next room to look. Nothing. Nadka was sitting there, playing with her dolls, dressing them and undressing them. I asked her whether she had heard anything. And then I saw the mirror on the floor, all in pieces."

3. While I was talking on the phone, someone came into the house and took our television set! What a terrible world this is.

4. "What did Milena write in her letter?"
   "She said she was sorry there had been no letter from her for so long, but that she was very busy at her new job, and that she would write again as soon as she could."

5. Don't forget to put the money into the envelope before you mail the letter. After the postman takes the letter, it will be too late.

6. She wanted to call you earlier, but didn't have your phone number. I'll give it to her as soon as I see her. I know that you'll understand without asking.

7. I think Peter is in love. Did you see him this morning? He was standing in front of Katia's house and gazing at her window. He stood there for more than an hour without moving! And I myself stood there for a full fifteen minutes before he noticed me.

8. We used to study much more than we do now. Last year, for instance, we studied three hours every night. We used to drink a lot more coffee then too.

9. My mother told me that when she was young she used to write poems. She would lie in bed and look at the moon, and then she would get up, take her pencil and notebook, and write down her thoughts.

READING SELECTION

<u>Новини</u>

2 април

Здравей Пламене,

Имам за тебе една добра и една лоша новина. Ще започна с лошата: Помниш ли новия ми костюм? Сигурно го помниш, защото май беше единствен. Купих си го за вашата сватба. Нали кумът трябва да е представителен. Избирахме го заедно с Лиляна повече от два часа. Въртях се пред огледалото и се оглеждах. Мислех, че ще го нося дълго, защото изглеждаше много здрав, но сега от него става само парцал. Ето как стана това.

Отивах на работа както обикновено, с велосипеда. Лиляна ме убеждаваше да не карам велосипеда с костюма. Убеждаваше ме, но не ме убеди. Имахме банкет в службата и исках да се издокарам. Движех се по обичайния си път. Знам го наизуст и мога да го мина със затворени очи. Всичко беше добре, но се появи онзи хлапак. Изглеждаше съвсем обикновено момче -- седеше на една пейка на тротоара и ядеше сандвич. Носеше фланелка с надпис "University of California - Berkeley" и шапка от вестник. Със свободната ръка си подпираше брадичката. Тъкмо минавах покрай него, когато хлапакът извика: "Чичко, задното ти колело се върти напред!" Изтръпнах от ужас. Погледнах надолу и назад. Наистина се въртеше напред. Докато мислех дали това е наред, велосипедът продължаваше напред -- и с двете колела -- право към кофата за боклук. Сега сакото е скъсано, а панталоните са целите в петна. Обърнах се, но хлапакът изчезваше зад ъгъла. Като че ли се смееше.

Добрата новина е, че спечелих от тотото. Знаеш какво е тото -- в тази игра може да спечелиш, но обикновено губиш (или почти винаги губиш) пари, като познаваш числа. Казват, че най-сигурният начин е да сънуваш числата. Приготвях закуска за децата, когато съобщаваха числата по радиото. Не вярвах на ушите си -- четири от шест. Тази игра я играех от четири-пет години, но досега все нямах късмет. Така се зарадвах, че пържените филийки на децата почти изгоряха. Може би ще има за нов костюм!

Какви новини при тебе? Добри или лоши?

Марин

GLOSSARY

актьо́р	actor
банке́т	banquet
бе́з да	without (relative conjunction)
боклу́к	rubbish, garbage
бри́дж	bridge (card game)
БСП [pron. бесепе́]	BSP (Bulgarian Socialist Party)
в слу́жбата	at work
велосипе́д	bicycle
включвам / включа (-иш)	include
влю́бен	in love
внима́ние	attention
внима́нието му се притъпи́	his attention wandered
внима́телен	attentive
вървя́ под ръка́	walk arm in arm
въртя́ се	turn around, rotate
ГДР [pron. геде́ре́]	GDR (DDR, former East Germany)
герда́н	necklace, collar
герма́нски	German
гу́бя	lose
дви́жа се (-иш)	move, go
демократи́чески	democratic
дикту́вам	dictate
дне́с ня́ма да ми върви́	today's not going to be my day
жела́ние	wish, desire
зави́си от ва́с	it depends on you
зави́си то́й какво́ ще ка́же	it depends what he will say
зави́ся	depend
зад ъ́гъла	around the corner
за́ден	back, rear (adj.)
закъсне́ние	delay; tardiness
запозна́вам / запозна́я	acquaint [someone] with
игра́	play, game; playing
изва́ждам / изва́дя	take/bring out, produce, extract
изга́рям / изгоря́	get burned, burn up
издока́рвам се / издока́рам се	dress up

иззвъня́вам / иззвъня́	ring [out]
изкипя́вам / изкипя́	boil over
изкъ́пвам се / изкъ́пя се	bathe, take a bath
изплъ́звам се / изплъ́зна се	slip out, slip through
изтръ́пвам / изтръ́пна	fall asleep (of a body part)
изтръ́пвам от у́жас	freeze with terror
изчи́ствам / изчи́стя	clean up, clean out
изясня́вам / изясня́	clear up
и́мам си ра́бота	have things to do
инжене́р	engineer
като че ли́	as if, apparently
като че ли́ се сме́еше	he appeared to be laughing
кварти́ра	apartment, quarters
ки́хам (or ки́хвам) / ки́хна	sneeze
колело́	wheel; bicycle
костю́м	suit
ко́фа	pail, bucket
ко́фа за боклу́к	garbage can
ку́м, -ъ́т	godfather
кума́	godmother
мака́р	at least
мака́р че	although, even though
ма́хам	wave
ми́нало несвъ́р-шено вре́ме	imperfect tense
министе́рство	ministry
мо́там се (or мота́я се)	fool around
муста́ци (pl.)	mustache
навя́рно	probably
на́дпис	inscription
нани́звам / нани́жа (-еш)	string together
напре́д	ahead, forwards
напреже́ние	pressure, tension
науча́вам се / науча́ се (-иш)	learn
ни́жа (-еш)	thread, string together
оби́да	insult
обича́ен	customary

308

облечен, -ена	dressed	работа	work, business
обръщам се / обърна се	turn	радио	radio
		разказ	story
оглеждам / огледам	survey, examine	разплаквам се / разплача се (-еш)	burst into tears
оглеждам се / огледам се	look at one's reflection		
окъпвам се / окъпя се (-еш)	bathe	разсмивам се / разсмея се	burst out laughing
		разсърдвам се / разсърдя се	get angry
от време на време	from time to time		
отминавам / отмина	pass by, leave behind	рано-рано	very early
отначало	at the beginning	република	republic
охлюв	snail shell		
		с малко закъснение	a little late
панталон (or панталони)	pants	СДС [pron. седесе]	SDS (UDF, Union of Democratic Forces)
партия	party		
парцал	rag	скала	rock, cliff
пет пари не давам	I don't give a damn	скъсан	torn
петно	spot	слаб	weak, thin
плаж	beach	сладкарница	sweet shop
по изненадите съм	[I] like surprises	след като	after (relative conjunction)
по-рано	earlier, before; "used to"		
		служба	service, position
поглеждам / погледна	have/take a look	софиянец	Sofia resident
		софиянка	Sofia resident (f.)
погледни	look! look over there!	социалистически	socialist
		спечелвам / спечеля	win, gain, earn
подозирам / подозра	suspect, be suspicious		
подпирам / подпра	prop up, support	страхувам се	fear, be afraid of
подпирам си брадичката	[sit] with chin in hand	състоя се	consist of; take place
		съюз	union
познавам число	pick/guess a number		
понасям / понеса	carry off; sustain, endure	такси (neuter)	taxi
		току-що	just, now, barely
понасям обида	bear/sustain an insult	тото	lottery, pool
		тротоар	sidewalk
попитвам / попитам	ask, inquire		
пораствам / порасна	grow up	убеждавам	try to convince
почувствувам	have the feeling, become aware	убедя	convince
		ужас	horror
появявам се / появя се	appear		
		фланелка (or фанелка)	T-shirt
превод	translation		
преди да	before (relative conjunction)	филийка	little slice
		филия	slice
представителен	personable, distinguished		
		хлапак	kid
приключение	adventure		
притъпявам / притъпя	blunt, dull	число	number
провеждам се / проведа се	be conducted, be implemented	шнорхел	snorkel
пълно копие	exact replica	ъгъл (pl. ъгли)	corner
пържени филийки	French toast		

309

CULTURAL COMMENTARY

Geography: Black Sea and its coastal cities

The majority of Bulgarians try to go to the Black Sea for a summer holiday. There are many fine beaches: swimming, sunbathing, snorkeling, gathering of shells, and other normal beach sports are part of the holiday. There are also interesting historical sites nearby, particularly the scattered remains of the Byzantine town of Nesebăr (Несébър). These ruins, of especial interest to medievalists, are located on a peninsula only accessible over a long causeway. Nesebăr is located on the Black Sea coast to the north of the port of Burgas (Бургáс).

Customs and beliefs: kum; April Fool's Day

Important family ceremonies such as weddings and christenings are marked not only by the appropriate ritual events but also by the adoption into the family of someone as "sponsor" of this event. The name given to this sponsor is "kum" (кỳм, feminine form кумá). The custom corresponds to that of the "godfather" and "godmother" for a newly-born child. In Bulgaria, this custom is extended to weddings as well. The person chosen as one's "kum" bears that relationship throughout life.

The custom of playing practical jokes on "April Fool's Day" (April 1st) is widespread in Bulgaria, as in the West.

City life: lottery; T-shirts

The state lottery in Bulgaria is called "toto" (тóто). One buys a lottery ticket with 49 numbers printed on it, and guesses which will be the chosen numbers. Up to six numbers are chosen: he who guesses all six correctly wins the largest prize; one also wins with five or four correct guesses. The correct numbers are announced on the radio and printed in the newspaper.

T-shirts and sweatshirts with the names of Western universities on them are very popular in Bulgaria. Those who wear them may possibly have had some connection with the university named; normally, however, there is no such connection.

Food and drink: "fried slices"

"Fried slices" (пържени филийки) of bread are a popular breakfast, especially for children. The Western equivalent is French toast.

LESSON 15

DIALOGUE

<u>Да оти́дем да ха́пнем ня́къде?</u>

Джули: В Со́фия е по́-прохла́дно, отко́лкото на море́то. Поча́кайте ме ма́лко. Йскам да си изва́дя жиле́тката от ча́нтата.

Веселин: Со́фия е по́-висо́ко.

Дейвид: Така́ ли? А мя́стото изгле́жда съвсе́м ра́вно.

Веселин: Софи́йското поле́ е на пе́тстотин и петдесе́т ме́тра над мо́рското равни́ще.

Ангел: По́-ху́баво от море́то ня́ма, нали́ Дейвид? При на́с в Балчи́к и кли́матът е ме́к, и ри́ба мо́же да си хва́не чове́к. През ля́тото от софия́нци не мо́жем да се разми́нем. И чужде́нци и́дват на почи́вка.

Веселин: Де́йвид, Джу́ли, да оти́дем да ха́пнем ня́къде, а? А́з стра́шно съм огладня́л.

Ангел: Ха́йде да оти́дем. А́з зна́м едно́ мно́го ху́баво мя́сто. Ми́налата годи́на, като бя́х в командиро́вка в Со́фия, вся́ка ве́чер хо́дехме та́м с прия́тели.

Дейвид: Ами́ добре́, а́з съм ве́че мно́го гла́ден. И жа́ден! Йма ли та́м на това́ мя́сто ху́бави напи́тки?

Джули: А́з ще ви помо́ля да ме извини́те, мно́го съм уморе́на. Две́ но́щи не съм спа́ла и дне́с и́скам да си ле́гна по́-ра́но.

Веселин: Чове́к тря́бва да яде́ три́ пъ́ти на де́н! Дне́с сте на еди́н са́ндвич с кашкава́л ця́л де́н. Не е́ доста́тъчно!

Джули: Ймам едно́ ки́село мля́ко в ста́ята и това́ ми сти́га. А́з не съм сви́кнала да я́м по мно́го.

Веселин: Ка́кто и́скате. А́з ще ви изпра́тя до вкъ́щи. Ви́ждам, че ча́нтата ви е те́жка. А́нгеле, ви́е с Де́йвид мо́же да и́дете тога́ва да вече́ряте без на́с.

Ангел: Да тръ́гнем за́едно, мо́жем да наме́рим ня́кое мя́сто по пъ́тя.

311

// Джули, Дейвид, Ангел и Веселин си взимат багажа и излизат от чакалнята на гарата. Тръгват към спирката на трамвая. //

Веселин: Довечера ще се обадя на Сашо да уредя среща за утре.

Дейвид: Кой е този Сашо?

Веселин: Професорът, бе! Александър Попов! Нали искахте да се срещнете с него?

Джули: Да, разбира се. Много мило от ваша страна, че ни помагате.

Веселин: Къде да ви се обадя да ви кажа кога ще е срещата?

Джули: Не помня телефонния номер наизуст, трябва да попитам хазайката.

Веселин: Ето го нашия трамвай! Хайде да се качваме.

GLOSSARY

мек	soft, mild	размина́вам се /	pass each other,
ме́тър	meter	размина́ се	blow over
мо́рски	sea *(adj.)*		
мо́рското равни́ще	sea level	сви́квам / сви́кна	get used to, grow accustomed to
над	above	софи́йското поле́	the plain around Sofia
		страна́	part, side
от ва́ша страна́	on your part		
		хаза́йка	landlady
поле́	field, plain	ха́пвам / ха́пна	eat, have a bite
прохла́ден	cool		
		чака́лня	waiting room
ра́вен	even, flat		
равни́ще	level, standard, plain		

GRAMMAR

The style of this grammar lesson is telegraphic. Its aim is to summarize the essence of Bulgarian grammar, both those elements which have been learned and those which are to come. Brief examples are given after general statements; for fuller descriptions, usage and further examples, the student should consult the relevant grammar sections in preceding lessons.

The grammar summary is followed by a section summarizing word order rules, and by sample paradigms of all verbal tenses and moods.

15.1. Review of noun forms

Gender

Nouns in Bulgarian are masculine, feminine, or neuter. To a large extent, one can tell the gender from the form of the noun. Most masculine nouns end in a consonant (мъж, ден, студент), but some end in -а or -о; these all refer to human beings (баща, колега, дядо). Most feminine nouns end in -а (жена, книга, порция) but a number end in a consonant (нощ, сутрин, младост). Most neuter nouns end in -о or -е (мляко, море) but a few loan words end in -и or -у/-ю (такси, кенгуру, меню). The category "plural" is often listed together with gender in charts of grammatical endings ("masculine/feminine/neuter/plural").

Plural

The plural ending for practically all feminine nouns and most masculine nouns is -и. The plural ending for all neuters is [-a]. It is written -я in some instances (общежития, цветя, лозя) and is preceded by the sequences -ен- or -ет- in others (времена, момчета). Most masculine monosyllabic nouns have the plural ending -ове (влакове, плодове). A few have -е (мъже), -а (листа, братя), -ища (пътища, краища) or -и (дни, зъби).

Definiteness

Nouns are made definite by affixing the definite article. If the noun form ends in -о or -а, the article rhymes with it (селото, дядото; селата, бащата, листата, жената). Otherwise the form of the article is determined by gender.

Feminine nouns take -та. This article is never stressed when it follows a vowel, and always stressed when it follows a consonant (порцията, жената, but сутринта). Neuter nouns take -то (селото, детето). Plural nouns take -те (жените, мъжете, влаковете, нощите).

Masculine nouns take -ът (влакът, студентът) unless the final consonant is soft, in which case the article is -ят (лекарят, денят). Consonant softness is apparent only before endings beginning in the back vowels -а (definite -- конят, or quantified -- 2 коня) or -о (plural -- огньове). Masculine definite nouns distinguish two cases in the singular, subject (студентът, лекарят, часът) and object (студента, лекаря, часа). The latter definite article, when stressed, is always pronounced [ъ].

Quantification

Feminine and neuter nouns are in the plural after numbers or other quantifiers (двé кни́ги, двé селá, ня́колко нещá). Masculine nouns add the "quantified" ending, which is identical to the definite object form except for a possible difference in accent placement (двá часá vs. двá чáса). Masculine nouns signifying human beings are in the plural after numbers; special numbers are used for 2-6 (двáма студéнти, три́ма мъжé, but дéвет лéкари).

Accent

Feminine nouns almost always keep their accent on the same syllable. Neuter plurals ending in -a are always end stressed; if the singular is stem stressed, the accent will shift (сéло / селá, мля́ко / млекá but месó / месá). Neuter plurals in -ета or -я do not shift stress. Some masculine nouns shift stress to the article but others do not (чáс, часъ́т but влáк, влáкът); similarly, some masculine plurals in -ове stress the ending but others do not (градовé, дъждовé, but блóкове, вкýсове). The quantified ending is never accented.

15.2. Review of pronoun forms

Personal pronouns

Subject personal pronouns are stressed (áз, ти́, тóй). Object personal pronouns are of two types, stressed (also called "long form", мéне, тéбе, нéго) and unstressed (also called "short form"). Short form object pronouns distinguish two cases, direct object (ме, те, го) and indirect object (ми, ти, му). Short form pronouns are clitics and follow strict word order rules. Long forms distinguish "direct object" from "indirect object" by the addition of a preposition (мéне vs. на мéне). In certain instances long form and short form pronouns are used together.

The category "short form pronoun" also includes the so-called reflexive particles се and си, which are frequently added to verbs. In possessive constructions, short form indirect object pronouns are either attached to nouns or used adjacent to the copula in predicate constructions. All these short forms are clitics, and obey strict word order rules. A synopsis of these rules is given in section 15.6.

Demonstrative, interrogative, indefinite, negative and intensive pronouns

Demonstrative (тóзи, óнзи), interrogative (кóй), and descriptive interrogative (какъ́в) pronouns change form to agree with the noun which is referred to. If no noun is present the default form for demonstratives and descriptive interrogatives is neuter but for the simple interrogative it is masculine (товá, каквó; but кóй). Interrogative pronouns of both sorts (as well as various adverbs) can be made indefinite or negative by prefixing ня- or ни- (ня́кой, ня́какъв; ни́кой, ни́какъв). They can be made relative by the addition of the particle -то, which will be learned in Lesson 17.

The intensifier pronoun сáм changes form to agree with the noun which is referred to (самá, самó, сами́). There is no default form.

314

Possessive pronouns

Possessive pronouns change form to agree with the noun modified (мо́й, мо́я; тво́й, тво́я; не́гов, не́гова). They are sometimes called "long form possessives" to differentiate them from the short form indirect object pronouns used to indicate possession. They function as adjectives in that they can affix a definite article if the noun modified is definite (мо́ят баща́, тво́ята сестра́). The possessive interrogative чи́й is declined in the same way; the use of its definite form in relative constructions will be learned in Lesson 17.

Both the long form and short form possessives use the so-called "reflexive" form (сво́й, сво́я; си) if the identity of "possessor" is equivalent to that of "subject of the sentence".

15.3. Review of adjectives

Adjectives agree with the noun modified: the possible endings are masculine (но́в), feminine (но́ва), neuter (но́во) or plural (но́ви). Adjectives take definite or indefinite form depending on the definiteness of the noun they modify. When they modify a definite noun, they (and not the noun) carry the definite article marker (но́вият блок, но́вата къ́ща, но́вото мя́сто, но́вите градове́). In the case of a definite masculine noun, adjectives also carry the mark which differentiates subject from object (мла́дият студе́нт [subject] vs. мла́дия студе́нт [object]). They can also appear in the definite form without a noun, in which case a noun is understood (ма́лките [деца́]).

Most masculine adjectives end in a consonant in the indefinite form (но́в, ху́бав). Some adjectives have -и in the masculine indefinite form (бъ́лгарски, деве́ти, etc.). All masculine adjectives have -и- before the definite article (но́вият, ху́бавият [= но́в-и-ъ̀т, ху́бав-и-ъ̀т]).

15.4. Review of numbers

Cardinal numbers

The number for 1 doubles as the indefinite article; it has forms for all three genders and the plural (еди́н, една́, едно́, едни́). The number 2 has one form for masculine (два́) and another for neuter and feminine (две́). Other numbers have only a single form (три́, че́тири, пе́т, etc.). The teens are formed by affixing -на́йсет (двана́йсет, трина́йсет, etc.) and the decades by adding -йсет or -десе́т (три́йсет, четири́йсет, петдесе́т, etc.). Compound numbers are formed by addition, with the conjunction и (два́йсет и три́).

Variant "personal" numbers exist from 2 to 6 (два́ма, три́ма, etc.). They are used when the quantified group includes at least one male person.

All cardinal numbers can take the definite article. The number 1 takes adjectival definite forms (еди́ният, една́та, etc.). Numbers ending in -а take a rhyming article (два́та, два́мата), and all others take -те. For numbers 4 and above, this article is accented (четири́те, деветте́, осемдесетте́). Adding the conjunction и focuses on the group as an entirety (и два́мата, и две́те).

Ordinal numbers

The ordinals for 1 and 2 are unrelated to the cardinals (пъ́рви, вто́ри), those for 3 and 4 are similar (тре́ти, четвъ́рти), and those from 5 on are formed by adding -и to the cardinal (пе́ти, ше́сти, се́дми, etc.). In rare instances the ordinal for 1 can appear without the final -и (as in за пръ́в пъ́т). Ordinals take the regular endings for adjectives, including the definite article (пъ́рвият, пъ́рвата, etc.)

15.5. Review of verbal forms

Note: summary paradigms of all verbal forms are given in section 15.7.

Unity of individual verbs

Every verb is a unit, and can appear in all conjugational forms. The verb is composed of a prefix (such as в-, от-, раз-), a stem (such as -каз-, пис-), one or more suffixes (such as -в-, -ав-, -н-) and an ending. Endings are composed of a theme vowel (such as -е-, -и-) and one of the personal endings (such as -я, -м, -ме). Not every verb form has all these components.

Prefixes can change the meaning of the verb, but they do not change its conjugational forms. Once a verb form is known, all verbs formed from it by prefixation are conjugated in the same manner. A "simplex" verb is a verb without a prefix.

Aspect

Most verbs exist in two separate forms, one of which carries the added meaning of "boundedness". The verb with the bounded meaning is called perfective, and the one without it is called imperfective. A number of verbs exist only in the imperfective form (съм, и́мам). Most simplex imperfective verbs can be prefixed and thereby made perfective; when this happens an imperfective verb is created to make an aspect pair (пи́ша › о-пи́ша › о-пи́с-вам); this process is reviewed in Lesson 18. Some verbs are paired from the outset (връ́щам / въ́рна or ста́вам / ста́на); a very few of these pairs can, via prefixation, yield a new aspect pair (о-ста́вам / о-ста́на).

Some prefixes carry a predictable meaning, and the system whereby these prefixes create verb "clusters" is known to linguists as *Aktionsarten*. This system is the topic of Lesson 26. The manner in which aspect pervades the Bulgarian verbal system, and its expression in a generalized past form, is the topic of Lesson 29.

Tense

Verb tenses are simplex or compound. Simplex tenses are expressed in a single word (present, пи́ша; aorist, пи́сах; imperfect пи́шех), and compound tenses are composed of auxiliary plus verb form (future, ще оста́на, ня́ма да оста́на; past indefinite, оста́нал съм). Compound tenses yet to be learned, and the lesson in which they are to be presented, comprise the past indefinite with transitive verbs (Lesson 16), the past anterior (Lesson 18), and several tenses connected with future forms (future in the past, Lesson 22; future anterior, future anterior in the past -- Lesson 23).

There are three conjugations in the present tense, identified by the three theme vowels (-a-, -и-, -e-). The 1st singular present is the dictionary form, and the conjugation type to which each verb belongs is largely predictable from this form.

The form of the aorist tense is only partially predictable from that of the present tense, and it is best to learn the two tenses together. There are nine types which govern the organization of simplex tenses (and, as it happens, of passive participles).

The future tense is formed by prefixing an unchanging particle to the present tense forms. Word order rules concerning clitic pronoun objects are slightly more complex with compound tenses.

Mood

Verbal mood expresses the attitude of a speaker. Moods are also either simplex or compound. Simplex moods are the indicative and the imperative. The imperative (ела́!, пиши́!, ви́ж!) is formed from both perfective and imperfective verbs and has two forms, a singular and a plural (ви́ж/ви́жте, кажи́/каже́те). The indicative covers all the nine tenses summarized above (some of which are simplex in form and others of which are complex).

Complex moods are yet to be learned; these are the renarrated (Lessons 24-25) and the conditional (Lesson 27-28).

Participles

Participles are both verbal and nominal. They are formed from verbs and carry the idea of the verbal action, but they function like adjectives and change to agree with a particular noun or nominal idea.

Past active participles, also called "L-participles" (ми́нал, дошъ́л, оста́нал), are used attributively, predicatively, and in the formation of verbal tenses and moods (the past indefinite tense, the past and future anterior tenses, and the renarrated mood). These participles constitute the backbone of the Bulgarian tense-mood system. The aorist L-participle, formed from the aorist stem, is used in the majority of these tenses and moods. The imperfect L-participle, formed from the imperfect stem (Lesson 24), is used in the remainder.

Past passive participles (же́нен, позна́т) will be learned in Lesson 17; summary paradigms are given below in 15.7. They are used as adjectives and in the passive verbal constructions which will be learned in Lesson 18.

Present active participles (сле́дващ) are used primarily as adjectives; their formation will be learned in Lesson 23. The verbal noun (гу́бене) and the verbal adverb (гле́дайки) also express the idea of verbal activity. These unchanging forms will be learned in Lessons 19 and 23, respectively.

15.6. Word order rules

Examples of word order rules were given in Lessons 5 though 13. Below is a synopsis of these rules, followed by a list of the abbreviations used in them. The lesson number where the rule was introduced appears in the left margin.

Rules

[5]   *(x) + DIR + verb*
      verb + DIR
      Cnj. + DIR + verb
      Neg. + DIR + verb
      verb + INT + DIR
      Neg. + DIR + INT + verb
      Neg. + verb + INT

      predicate + COP
      Neg. + COP + predicate
      predicate + INT + COP
      Neg. + COP + INT + predicate

[6]   *Part. + verb*
      Part. + DIR + verb

[7]   any *DIR* can be replaced by *IND*

[8]   *Fut. + DIR + verb*
      neg. + Cnj. + DIR + verb
      Fut. + verb + INT
      Fut. + DIR + verb + INT
      neg. + INT + Cnj. + verb
      neg. + INT + Cnj. + DIR + verb
      neg. + INT + subject + Cnj. + verb

      Fut. + DIR + verb + Cnj. + DIR + verb
      Fut. + verb + INT + Cnj. + DIR + verb

[9]   *verb + IND + DIR*
      any *IND* or *DIR* can be replaced by *IND + DIR* sequence

[10] *subject + COP + IND + predicate*
      subject + Neg. + COP + IND + predicate
      subject + IND + 3^{rd}COP + predicate
      subject + Neg. + IND + 3^{rd}COP + predicate
      subject + Neg. + COP + INT + IND + predicate
      subject + Neg. + INT + IND + 3^{rd}COP + predicate

[11] *direct obj. + (x) + Neg. + DIR + verb*
      indirect obj. + (x) + Neg. + IND + verb
      Neg. + DIR + verb + direct obj.
      Neg. + IND + verb + indirect obj.

      Neg. can be replaced by *Fut.* or *Cnj.* in the above

[12]   *direct obj. + (x) + DIR + verb + subject*
       direct obj. + Neg.+ DIR + verb + subject
       direct obj. + verb + INT + DIR + subject

[13]   *Neg. + IND + INT + DIR + verb*
       Neg. + IND + INT + 3ᵈCOP + predicate
       Neg. + CÒP + INT + IND + predicate

Abbreviations

CLITICS
    always unstressed
    cannot stand in initial position
    must obey strict word order rules

DIR	direct object pronoun	ме те се го я ни ви ги
IND	indirect object pronoun	ми ти си му ѝ ни ви им
INT	interrogative particle	ли
COP	copula/auxiliary except 3ʳᵈ sg.	съм си сме сте са
3ᵈCOP	copula/auxiliary 3ʳᵈ sg.	е

PARTICLES
    unstressed
    unchanging in form
    must stand at head of clitic string
    can be in initial position

Cnj.	subordinating/modal conjunction	да
Neg.	negative particle	не
Fut.	future particle	ще
Part.	hortative particle	я

WORDS
    fully stressed
    changing in form
    no normal word order restrictions

(x)	optional stressed word(s)	varied
subject	noun, pronoun	varied
verb	simplex or participle	varied
predicate	noun, adjective, phrase	varied
direct obj.	full form pronoun	мéне тéбе нéго нéя нáс вáс тя́х
indirect obj.	preposition + pronoun	на + above
neg.	negative [+ *Cnj.*]	ня́ма

15.7. Sample verbal paradigms

SIMPLEX TENSES

Present

	a-*conjugation*		**и**-*conjugation*		**е**-*conjugation*	
1ˢᵗ singular	гле́дам	отва́рям	ви́дя	държа́	пи́я	чета́
2ⁿᵈ singular	гле́даш	отва́ряш	ви́диш	държи́ш	пи́еш	чете́ш
3ʳᵈ singular	гле́да	отва́ря	ви́ди	държи́	пи́е	чете́
1ˢᵗ plural	гле́даме	отва́ряме	ви́дим	държи́м	пи́ем	чете́м
2ⁿᵈ plural	гле́дате	отва́ряте	ви́дите	държи́те	пи́ете	чете́те
3ʳᵈ plural	гле́дат	отва́рят	ви́дят	държа́т	пи́ят	чета́т

Aorist

	a-*conjugation*		**и**-*conjugation*		
1ˢᵗ singular	гле́дах	отва́рях	но́сих	видя́х	държа́х
2ⁿᵈ singular	гле́да	отва́ря	но́си	видя́	държа́
3ʳᵈ singular	гле́да	отва́ря	но́си	видя́	държа́
1ˢᵗ plural	гле́дахме	отва́ряхме	но́сихме	видя́хме	държа́хме
2ⁿᵈ plural	гле́дахте	отва́ряхте	но́сихте	видя́хте	държа́хте
3ʳᵈ plural	гле́даха	отва́ряха	но́сиха	видя́ха	държа́ха

	е-*conjugation*					
1ˢᵗ singular	пи́х	че́тох	въ́рнах	живя́х	пи́сах	пра́х
2ⁿᵈ singular	пи́	че́те	въ́рна	живя́	пи́са	пра́
3ʳᵈ singular	пи́	че́те	въ́рна	живя́	пи́са	пра́
1ˢᵗ plural	пи́хме	че́тохме	въ́рнахме	живя́хме	пи́сахме	пра́хме
2ⁿᵈ plural	пи́хте	че́тохте	въ́рнахте	живя́хте	пи́сахте	пра́хте
3ʳᵈ plural	пи́ха	че́тоха	въ́рнаха	живя́ха	пи́саха	пра́ха

Imperfect

	a-*conjugation*		**и**-*conjugation*		**е**-*conjugation*	
1ˢᵗ singular	гле́дах	отва́рях	но́сех	държа́х	пи́шех	четя́х
2ⁿᵈ singular	гле́даше	отва́ряше	но́сеше	държе́ше	пи́шеше	чете́ше
3ʳᵈ singular	гле́даше	отва́ряше	но́сеше	държе́ше	пи́шеше	чете́ше
1ˢᵗ plural	гле́дахме	отва́ряхме	но́сехме	държа́хме	пи́шехме	четя́хме
2ⁿᵈ plural	гле́дахте	отва́рятхе	но́сехте	държа́хте	пи́шехте	четя́хте
3ʳᵈ plural	гле́даха	отва́ряха	но́сеха	държа́ха	пи́шеха	четя́ха

All these tenses are negated by placing **не** before the verb form.

COMPOUND TENSES

Future affirmative

	а-*conjugation*	и-*conjugation*	е-*conjugation*
1ˢᵗ singular	ще гле́дам	ще ви́дя	ще чета́
2ⁿᵈ singular	ще гле́даш	ще ви́диш	ще чете́ш
3ʳᵈ singular	ще гле́да	ще ви́ди	ще чете́
1ˢᵗ plural	ще гле́даме	ще ви́дим	ще чете́м
2ⁿᵈ plural	ще гле́дате	ще ви́дите	ще чете́те
3ʳᵈ plural	ще гле́дат	ще ви́дят	ще чета́т

Future negative

	а-*conjugation*	и-*conjugation*	е-*conjugation*
1ˢᵗ singular	ня́ма да гле́дам	ня́ма да ви́дя	ня́ма да чета́
2ⁿᵈ singular	ня́ма да гле́даш	ня́ма да ви́диш	ня́ма да чете́ш
3ʳᵈ singular	ня́ма да гле́да	ня́ма да ви́ди	ня́ма да чете́
1ˢᵗ plural	ня́ма да гле́даме	ня́ма да ви́дим	ня́ма да чете́м
2ⁿᵈ plural	ня́ма да гле́дате	ня́ма да ви́дите	ня́ма да чете́те
3ʳᵈ plural	ня́ма да гле́дат	ня́ма да ви́дят	ня́ма да чета́т

Past indefinite affirmative

	а-*conjugation*	и-*conjugation*		е-*conjugation*	
1ˢᵗ singular	гле́дал съм	но́сил съм	видя́л съм	пра́л съм	че́л съм
2ⁿᵈ singular	гле́дал си	но́сил си	видя́л си	пра́л си	че́л си
3ʳᵈ singular	гле́дал е	но́сил е	видя́л е	пра́л е	че́л е
1ˢᵗ plural	гле́дали сме	но́сили сме	виде́ли сме	пра́ли сме	че́ли сме
2ⁿᵈ plural	гле́дали сте	но́сили сте	виде́ли сте	пра́ли сте	че́ли сте
3ʳᵈ plural	гле́дали са	но́сили са	виде́ли са	пра́ли са	че́ли са

Past indefinite negative

	а-*conjugation*	и-*conjugation*	е-*conjugation*
1ˢᵗ singular	не съ́м гле́дал	не съ́м но́сил	не съ́м че́л
2ⁿᵈ singular	не си́ гле́дал	не си́ но́сил	не си́ че́л
3ʳᵈ singular	не е́ гле́дал	не е́ но́сил	не е́ че́л
1ˢᵗ plural	не сме́ гле́дали	не сме́ но́сили	не сме́ че́ли
2ⁿᵈ plural	не сте́ гле́дали	не сте́ но́сили	не сте́ че́ли
3ʳᵈ plural	не са́ гле́дали	не са́ но́сили	не са́ че́ли

Singular forms of the participle change according to the gender of the subject; гле́дала съм (не съ́м гле́дала), но́сила съм (не съ́м но́сила), видя́ла съм (не съ́м видя́ла), пра́ла съм (не съ́м пра́ла), че́ла съм (не съ́м че́ла), etc. are used if the subject is feminine.

Past anterior

	а-*conjugation*	и-*conjugation*		е-*conjugation*
1ˢᵗ singular	бях гле́дал	бях но́сил	бях видя́л	бях чел
2ⁿᵈ singular	бе́ше гле́дал	бе́ше но́сил	бе́ше видя́л	бе́ше чел
3ʳᵈ singular	бе́ше гле́дал	бе́ше но́сил	бе́ше видя́л	бе́ше чел
1ˢᵗ plural	бя́хме гле́дали	бя́хме но́сили	бя́хме виде́ли	бя́хме че́ли
2ⁿᵈ plural	бя́хте гле́дали	бя́хте но́сили	бя́хте виде́ли	бя́хте че́ли
3ʳᵈ plural	бя́ха гле́дали	бя́ха но́сили	бя́ха виде́ли	бя́ха че́ли

Singular forms of the participle change according to the gender of the subject; бях гле́дала, бях но́сила, бях видя́ла, бях че́ла, etc. are used if the subject is feminine. The negative is formed by placing не before the entire form.

Future anterior affirmative

	а-*conjugation*	и-*conjugation*	е-*conjugation*
1ˢᵗ singular	ще съм гле́дал	ще съм но́сил	ще съм чел
2ⁿᵈ singular	ще си гле́дал	ще си но́сил	ще си чел
3ʳᵈ singular	ще е гле́дал	ще е но́сил	ще е чел
1ˢᵗ plural	ще сме гле́дали	ще сме но́сили	ще сме че́ли
2ⁿᵈ plural	ще сте гле́дали	ще сте но́сили	ще сте че́ли
3ʳᵈ plural	ще са гле́дали	ще са но́сили	ще са че́ли

Future anterior negative

	а-*conjugation*	и-*conjugation*	е-*conjugation*
1ˢᵗ singular	ня́ма да съм гле́дал	ня́ма да съм но́сил	ня́ма да съм чел
2ⁿᵈ singular	ня́ма да си гле́дал	ня́ма да си но́сил	ня́ма да си чел
3ʳᵈ singular	ня́ма да е гле́дал	ня́ма да е но́сил	ня́ма да е чел
1ˢᵗ plural	ня́ма да сме гле́дали	ня́ма да сме но́сили	ня́ма да сме че́ли
2ⁿᵈ plural	ня́ма да сте гле́дали	ня́ма да сте но́сили	ня́ма да сте че́ли
3ʳᵈ plural	ня́ма да са гле́дали	ня́ма да са но́сили	ня́ма да са че́ли

Singular forms of the participle change according to the gender of the subject; ще (ня́ма да) съм гле́дала, ще (ня́ма да) съм но́сила, ще (ня́ма да) съм че́ла, etc. are used if the subject is feminine.

Future in the past affirmative

	а-*conjugation*	и-*conjugation*	е-*conjugation*
1ˢᵗ singular	щях да гле́дам	щях да но́ся	щях да чета́
2ⁿᵈ singular	ще́ше да гле́даш	ще́ше да но́сиш	ще́ше да чете́ш
3ʳᵈ singular	ще́ше да гле́да	ще́ше да но́си	ще́ше да чете́
1ˢᵗ plural	щя́хме да гле́даме	щя́хме да но́сим	щя́хме да чете́м
2ⁿᵈ plural	щя́хте да гле́дате	щя́хте да но́сите	щя́хте да чете́те
3ʳᵈ plural	щя́ха да гле́дат	щя́ха да но́сят	щя́ха да чета́т

Future in the past negative

	a-*conjugation*	и-*conjugation*	e-*conjugation*
1ˢᵗ singular	нямаше да гле́дам	нямаше да но́ся	нямаше да чета́
2ⁿᵈ singular	нямаше да гле́даш	нямаше да но́сиш	нямаше да чете́ш
3ʳᵈ singular	нямаше да гле́да	нямаше да но́си	нямаше да чете́
1ˢᵗ plural	нямаше да гле́даме	нямаше да но́сим	нямаше да чете́м
2ⁿᵈ plural	нямаше да гле́дате	нямаше да но́сите	нямаше да чете́те
3ʳᵈ plural	нямаше да гле́дат	нямаше да но́сят	нямаше да чета́т

Future anterior in the past affirmative

	a-*conjugation*	и-*conjugation*	e-*conjugation*
1ˢᵗ singular	щя́х да съм гле́дал	щя́х да съм но́сил	щя́х да съм че́л
2ⁿᵈ singular	ще́ше да си гле́дал	ще́ше да си но́сил	ще́ше да си че́л
3ʳᵈ singular	ще́ше да е гле́дал	ще́ше да е но́сил	ще́ше да е че́л
1ˢᵗ plural	щя́хме да сме гле́дали	щя́хме да сме но́сили	щя́хме да сме че́ли
2ⁿᵈ plural	щя́хте да сте гле́дали	щя́хте да сте но́сили	щя́хте да сте че́ли
3ʳᵈ plural	щя́ха да са гле́дали	щя́ха да са но́сили	щя́ха да са че́ли

Future anterior in the past negative

	и-*conjugation*	e-*conjugation*
1ˢᵗ singular	нямаше да съм но́сил	нямаше да съм че́л
2ⁿᵈ singular	нямаше да си но́сил	нямаше да си че́л
3ʳᵈ singular	нямаше да е но́сил	нямаше да е че́л
1ˢᵗ plural	нямаше да сме но́сили	нямаше да сме че́ли
2ⁿᵈ plural	нямаше да сте но́сили	нямаше да сте че́ли
3ʳᵈ plural	нямаше да са но́сили	нямаше да са че́ли

Singular forms of the participle change according to the gender of the subject; щя́х/нямаше да съм но́сила, щя́х/нямаше да съм че́ла, etc. are used if the subject is feminine.

MOODS

Indicative: all the paradigms given above.

Imperative

	type 1		*type 2*		*irregular*	
singular	чети́	носи́	гле́дай	бро́й	ви́ж	вле́з
plural	чете́те	носе́те	гле́дайте	бро́йте	ви́жте	вле́зте

Conditional

	a-*conjugation*	и-*conjugation*		e-*conjugation*
1st singular	бих гле́дал	бих но́сил	бих видя́л	бих че́л
2nd singular	би гле́дал	би но́сил	би видя́л	би че́л
3rd singular	би гле́дал	би но́сил	би видя́л	би че́л
1st plural	би́хме гле́дали	би́хме но́сили	би́хме виде́ли	би́хме че́ли
2nd plural	би́хте гле́дали	би́хте но́сили	би́хте виде́ли	би́хте че́ли
3rd plural	би́ха гле́дали	би́ха но́сили	би́ха виде́ли	би́ха че́ли

Singular forms of the participle change according to the gender of the subject; бих гле́дала, бих но́сила, бих видя́ла, бих че́ла, etc. are used if the subject is feminine. The negative is formed by placing **не** before the entire form.

Renarrated

The form of the renarrated mood depends on the tense which is being renarrated.

Present/imperfect affirmative renarrated

	a-*conjugation*	и-*conjugation*	e-*conjugation*
1st singular	гле́дал съм	но́сел съм	четя́л съм
2nd singular	гле́дал си	но́сел си	четя́л си
3rd singular	гле́дал	но́сел	четя́л
1st plural	гле́дали сме	но́сели сме	чете́ли сме
2nd plural	гле́дали сте	но́сели сте	чете́ли сте
3rd plural	гле́дали	но́сели	чете́ли

Present/imperfect negative renarrated

	a-*conjugation*	и-*conjugation*	e-*conjugation*
1st singular	не съм гле́дал	не съм но́сел	не съм четя́л
2nd singular	не си гле́дал	не си но́сел	не си четя́л
3rd singular	не гле́дал	не но́сел	не четя́л
1st plural	не сме́ гле́дали	не сме́ но́сели	не сме́ чете́ли
2nd plural	не сте́ гле́дали	не сте́ но́сели	не сте́ чете́ли
3rd plural	не гле́дали	не но́сели	не чете́ли

Singular forms of the participle change according to the gender of the subject; гле́дала съм (не съм гле́дала), но́села съм (не съм но́села), четя́ла съм (не съм четя́ла), etc. are used if the subject is feminine.

Future/future in the past affirmative renarrated

	a-*conjugation*	и-*conjugation*	e-*conjugation*
1st singular	щял съм да глéдам	щял съм да нóся	щял съм да четá
2nd singular	щял си да глéдаш	щял си да нóсиш	щял си да четéш
3rd singular	щял да глéда	щял да нóси	щял да четé
1st plural	щéли сме да глéдаме	щéли сме да нóсим	щéли сме да четéм
2nd plural	щéли сте да глéдате	щéли сте да нóсите	щéли сте да четéте
3rd plural	щéли да глéдат	щéли да нóсят	щéли да четáт

Singular forms of the participle change according to the gender of the subject; щяла съм да глéдам, щяла съм да нóся, щяла съм да четá, etc. are used if the subject is feminine.

Future/future in the past negative renarrated

	a-*conjugation*	и-*conjugation*	e-*conjugation*
1st singular	нямало да глéдам	нямало да нóся	нямало да четá
2nd singular	нямало да глéдаш	нямало да нóсиш	нямало да четéш
3rd singular	нямало да глéда	нямало да нóси	нямало да четé
1st plural	нямало да глéдаме	нямало да нóсим	нямало да четéм
2nd plural	нямало да глéдате	нямало да нóсите	нямало да четéте
3rd plural	нямало да глéдат	нямало да нóсят	нямало да четáт

Future anterior/future anterior in the past affirmative renarrated

	и-*conjugation*	e-*conjugation*
1st singular	щял съм да съм нóсил	щял съм да съм чéл
2nd singular	щял си да си нóсил	щял си да си чéл
3rd singular	щял да е нóсил	щял да е чéл
1st plural	щéли сме да сме нóсили	щéли сме да сме чéли
2nd plural	щéли сте да сте нóсили	щéли сте да сте чéли
3rd plural	щéли да са нóсили	щéли да са чéли

Future anterior/future anterior in the past negative renarrated

	и-*conjugation*	e-*conjugation*
1st singular	нямало да съм нóсил	нямало да съм чéл
2nd singular	нямало да си нóсил	нямало да си чéл
3rd singular	нямало да е нóсил	нямало да е чéл
1st plural	нямало да сме нóсили	нямало да сме чéли
2nd plural	нямало да сте нóсили	нямало да сте чéли
3rd plural	нямало да са нóсили	нямало да са чéли

Singular forms of the participle change according to the gender of the subject; щяла съм да съм глéдала (нямало да съм глéдала), щяла съм да съм нóсила (нямало да съм нóсила), щяла съм да съм чéла (нямало да съм чéла), etc. are used if the subject is feminine.

325

Past indefinite/past anterior affirmative renarrated

	a-*conjugation*	и-*conjugation*	e-*conjugation*
1st singular	бил съм гле́дал	бил съм но́сил	бил съм че́л
2nd singular	бил си гле́дал	бил си но́сил	бил си че́л
3rd singular	бил гле́дал	бил но́сил	бил че́л
1st plural	били́ сме гле́дали	били́ сме но́сили	били́ сме че́ли
2nd plural	били́ сте гле́дали	били́ сте но́сили	били́ сте че́ли
3rd plural	били́ гле́дали	били́ но́сили	били́ че́ли

Past indefinite/past anterior negative renarrated

	a-*conjugation*	и-*conjugation*	e-*conjugation*
1st singular	не съм бил гле́дал	не съм бил но́сил	не съм бил че́л
2nd singular	не си бил гле́дал	не си бил но́сил	не си бил че́л
3rd singular	не бил гле́дал	не бил но́сил	не бил че́л
1st plural	не сме́ били́ гле́дали	не сме́ били́ но́сили	не сме́ били́ че́ли
2nd plural	не сте́ били́ гле́дали	не сте́ били́ но́сили	не сте́ били́ че́ли
3rd plural	не били́ гле́дали	не били́ но́сили	не били́ че́ли

Singular forms of the participle change according to the gender of the subject; била́ съм гле́дала (не съм била́ гле́дала), била́ съм но́сила (не съм била́ но́сила), била́ съм че́ла (не съм била́ че́ла), etc. are used if the subject is feminine.

Aorist affirmative renarrated

	a-*conjugation*	и-*conjugation*		e-*conjugation*	
1st singular	гле́дал съм	но́сил съм	видя́л съм	пра́л съм	че́л съм
2nd singular	гле́дал си	но́сил си	видя́л си	пра́л си	че́л си
3rd singular	гле́дал	но́сил	видя́л	пра́л	че́л
1st plural	гле́дали сме	но́сили сме	виде́ли сме	пра́ли сме	че́ли сме
2nd plural	гле́дали сте	но́сили сте	виде́ли сте	пра́ли сте	че́ли сте
3rd plural	гле́дали	но́сили	виде́ли	пра́ли	че́ли

Aorist negative renarrated

	a-*conjugation*	и-*conjugation*	e-*conjugation*
1st singular	не съм гле́дал	не съм но́сил	не съм че́л
2nd singular	не си гле́дал	не си но́сил	не си че́л
3rd singular	не гле́дал	не но́сил	не че́л
1st plural	не сме́ гле́дали	не сме́ но́сили	не сме́ че́ли
2nd plural	не сте́ гле́дали	не сте́ но́сили	не сте́ че́ли
3rd plural	не гле́дали	не но́сили	не че́ли

Singular forms of the participle change according to the gender of the subject; гле́дала съм (не съм гле́дала), но́сила съм (не съм но́сила), видя́ла съм (не съм видя́ла), пра́ла съм (не съм пра́ла), че́ла съм (не съм че́ла), etc. are used if the subject is feminine.

TENSE / MOOD neutralization

Generalized past (perfective)

	а-*conjugation*	и-*conjugation*	е-*conjugation*
1ˢᵗ singular	гле́дал съм	но́сил съм	че́л съм
2ⁿᵈ singular	гле́дал си	но́сил си	че́л си
3ʳᵈ singular	гле́дал е	но́сил е	че́л е
1ˢᵗ plural	гле́дали сме	но́сили сме	че́ли сме
2ⁿᵈ plural	гле́дали сте	но́сили сте	че́ли сте
3ʳᵈ plural	гле́дали са	но́сили са	че́ли са

Generalized past (imperfective)

	а-*conjugation*	и-*conjugation*	е-*conjugation*
1ˢᵗ singular	гле́дал съм	но́сел съм	четя́л съм
2ⁿᵈ singular	гле́дал си	но́сел си	четя́л си
3ʳᵈ singular	гле́дал е	но́сел е	четя́л е
1ˢᵗ plural	гле́дали сме	но́сели сме	чете́ли сме
2ⁿᵈ plural	гле́дали сте	но́сели сте	чете́ли сте
3ʳᵈ plural	гле́дали са	но́сели са	чете́ли са

Singular forms of the participle change according to the gender of the subject;
гле́дала съм (не съ́м гле́дала), но́сила/но́села съм (не съ́м но́сила/но́села),
че́ла/четя́ла съм (не съ́м че́ла/четя́ла), etc. are used if the subject is feminine.

PARTICIPLES AND OTHER FORMS

Past active participle - aorist stem

	а-*conjugation*		и-*conjugation*		
masc. singular	гле́дал	отва́рял	но́сил	видя́л	държа́л
fem. singular	гле́дала	отва́ряла	но́сила	видя́ла	държа́ла
neut. singular	гле́дало	отва́ряло	но́сило	видя́ло	държа́ло
plural	гле́дали	отва́ряли	но́сили	виде́ли	държа́ли

	е-*conjugation*					
masc. singular	пи́л	че́л	въ́рнал	живя́л	пи́сал	пра́л
fem. singular	пи́ла	че́ла	въ́рнала	живя́ла	пи́сала	пра́ла
neut. singular	пи́ло	че́ло	въ́рнало	живя́ло	пи́сало	пра́ло
plural	пи́ли	че́ли	въ́рнали	живе́ли	пи́сали	пра́ли

Past active participle - imperfect stem

	a-*conjugation*		и-*conjugation*		e-*conjugation*	
masc. singular	глéдал	отвáрял	нóсел	държáл	пúшел	четя́л
fem. singular	глéдала	отвáряла	нóсела	държáла	пúшела	четя́ла
neut. singular	глéдало	отвáряло	нóсело	държáло	пúшело	четя́ло
plural	глéдали	отвáряли	нóсели	държéли	пúшели	четéли

Past passive participle

	a-*conjugation*		и-*conjugation*		
masc. singular	глéдан	отвáрян	нóсен	жéнен	държáн
fem. singular	глéдана	отвáряна	нóсена	жéнена	държáна
neut. singular	глéдано	отвáряно	нóсено	жéнено	държáно
plural	глéдани	отвáряни	нóсени	жéнени	държáни

e-*conjugation*

masc. singular	пúт	чéтен	вър̀нат	взéт	пúсан	прáн
fem. singular	пúта	чéтена	вър̀ната	взéта	пúсана	прáна
neut. singular	пúто	чéтено	вър̀нато	взéто	пúсано	прáно
plural	пúти	чéтени	вър̀нати	взéти	пúсани	прáни

Present active participle

	a-*conjugation*	и-*conjugation*	e-*conjugation*
masc. singular	слéдващ	нóсещ	пúшещ
fem. singular	слéдваща	нóсеща	пúшеща
neut. singular	слéдващо	нóсещо	пúшещо
plural	слéдващи	нóсещи	пúшещи

Verbal adverb

a-*conjugation*	и-*conjugation*	e-*conjugation*
глéдайки	носéйки	четéйки

Verbal noun

a-*conjugation*	и-*conjugation*	e-*conjugation*
глéдане	нóсене	чéтене
		пúсане

CUMULATIVE GLOSSARY

INDEX

CUMULATIVE GLOSSARY

(PART 1)

Bulgarian - English

The following glossary contains all the Bulgarian words used in the first fifteen lessons of *Intensive Bulgarian*. Each entry is indexed to the lesson where the word or phrase first appeared. Most idioms or phrases are fully cross-referenced; for instance, the phrase **и́мам ну́жда от** "need, have need of" is glossed under **и́мам, ну́жда** and **от**.

All entries are accented. Accentual doublets are given where they are mentioned in all major dictionaries (such as **че́ло** or **чело́**); other accentual variants are not noted. Accepted accentual variations in the aorist and L-participle of unprefixed verbs are not noted, either in glossaries or in textual usage. Stress shifts onto the masculine definite article are noted: **ди́м, -ъ́т**.

Plural forms for nouns are given only when not predictable from grammar rules presented in the lessons. Thus, only plural forms in **-ове** where either ending syllable is stressed, plurals in **-и** of masculine monosyllables, feminine plural forms with shifted stress, or unpredictable neuter plural forms are specifically noted. Gender is noted only when not predictable: feminine nouns in a consonant other than in **-ост** are given with the article (**ве́чер, -та́**) and neuter nouns ending in other than **-о** or **-е** are given with the gender specified: **меню́** *(neuter)*.

Adjectives are given in the masculine singular indefinite form. The absence of a fleeting vowel is noted only when it is not predictable from rules presented in the lessons (thus **черве́н**, but **въ́лнен, -ена**). In the case of shifting vowels in the root (as in **ве́рен, вя́рна** or **ря́дък, ре́дки**), the non-masculine form is cross-referenced to the main entry.

Simplex imperfectives are given a single entry; all other verbs are given as aspect pairs with the imperfective listed first. All verbs are given in the standard 1st singular present form. The conjugation class of verbs whose stems end in **-ш, -ч** or **-ж**, or which is not predictable from the citation form, is noted: **пи́ша (-еш), пу́ша (-иш), къ́пя (-еш)**.

English glosses are given as simply as possible; for a larger range of meanings, the full Bulgarian-English dictionary (the source taken as standard for this glossary listing) should be consulted. When the English noun and adjective forms are homonymous, the notation *adj.* or an explanatory note such as [person] is added. Grammatical information such as *interrogative* or *relative conjunction* has been given in the relevant instances.

This glossary list consolidates and reproduces the fifteen separate glossary listings given at the end of each of the lessons. The form is slightly different, in that idioms and phrases are listed here under each of their major components (as opposed to alphabetically according to the first element in the phrase, as in the lessons). A somewhat fuller listing is given herein: certain definitions are more detailed, and certain phrases are given here which were omitted from the lesson glossaries.

а [1] and
абони́рам [11] subscribe
а́вгуст [5] August
автенти́чен [13] authentic
автобу́с [2] bus
автогра́ф [13] autograph
а́вторски [12] author's ; а́вторско пра́во [12] copyright
адвока́т (ка) [2] lawyer
адре́с [9] address
аеро́бика [8] aerobics
а́з [1] I ; а́з се ка́звам my name is
ако [4] if ; ако оби́чате [4] if you please
актьо́р [14] actor
албу́м [9] album, picture-book
алкохо́л [2] alcohol
а́ло [12] hello (on the phone)
ама [12] but
америка́нец [3] American (male)
америка́нка [3] American (female)
америка́нски [8] American (adj.)
ами́ [7] but, well
англи́йски [2] English (language)
англича́нин [3] Englishman, English person
англича́нка [3] Englishwoman
апара́т [5] [piece of] apparatus, equipment
апартаме́нт [8] apartment
апети́т [9] appetite
апри́л [9] April
апропо́ [13] apropos, by the way
ара́бски [11] Arab (adj.)
арома́тен [10] aromatic
а́рмия [12] army
археоло́г [3] archaeologist
архитекту́ра [7] architecture
асансьо́р [11] elevator
аспири́н [12] aspirin
атмосфе́ра [3] atmosphere
аха́ [5] aha

ба́ба [8] grandmother
Ба́ба Ма́рта [11] Granny March (harbinger of spring)
ба́вен [3] slow
бага́ж [2] baggage, luggage
ба́й [1] uncle, old man (term of address)
балко́н [13] balcony
ба́ница [10] banitsa (baked pastry) ; ба́ница с късме́ти [10] banitsa filled with fortunes
банке́т [14] banquet
ба́нски [13] bathing; swimming suit ; по ба́нски [13] wearing swimsuits
ба́ня [3] bath, bathroom

баро́к [10] Baroque
баро́ков [9] baroque (adj.)
баща́ [8] father
бе [6] (vocative particle) ; ка́к се ка́зваш бе? [6] what's your name, fella?
бедро́ [12] thigh
без [6] without ; пе́т без де́сет [6] ten to five (4:50)
бе́з да [14] without (relative conjunction)
безме́сен [7] vegetarian (i.e. without meat)
беле́жа (-иш) [7] mark
беле́жка [7] note; remark
беле́жник [7] notebook, notepad
бе́ли [2] see бя́л
бера́ [12] pick, gather
бе́ше [6] was (2nd, 3rd singular)
библиоте́ка [5] library
биле́т [11] ticket
би́ра [4] beer
благода́рност [9] thanks, gratitude ; де́н на благодарността́ [9] Thanksgiving Day
благодаря́ [10] thank, pay gratitude
благодаря́ [2] thank you
бле́д [11] pale
бли́зък [10] close (adj.) ; бли́зки са [10] they are very close friends
бло́к [8] apartment building
бо́б [10] beans
бо́г [9] god, God ; сла́ва Бо́гу [9] thank God ; Бо́же [9] oh God, oh my God
бога́т [7] rich
бо́дър [13] lively, cheerful
Бо́же see бог
боклу́к [14] rubbish, garbage
боледу́вам [10] be ill
бо́лен [2] sick, ill ; бо́лен от гри́п [13] down with the flu
боли́ (3rd person only) [12] hurt ; боли́ ме глава́та [12] I have a headache ; боля́т ме очи́те [12] my eyes hurt ; боле́ше [13] was hurting
бо́лка [12] pain
бо́лница [6] hospital
бонбо́н [10] candy
бо́с [13] barefoot ; хо́дя бо́с [13] go barefoot
ботани́чески [13] botanical ; ботани́ческа гради́на [13] botanical garden
боя́ [10] paint
боя́ се [8] fear ; не се́ бо́й [8] don't be afraid
бояджи́я, -и́йка [10] house painter; paint or dye merchant
боя́дисвам [10] paint, color; dye

бра́во [10] bravo
брада́ (*also* бради́чка) [12] chin
брада́ [12] beard; chin
брак [10] marriage
брат (*plural* бра́тя) [8] brother
братовче́д (ка) [2] cousin
бри́дж [14] bridge (card game)
броя́ [3] count
БСП (*pron.* бе́сепе) [14] BSP (Bulgarian
    Socialist Party)
бу́за [12] cheek
бу́ква [8] letter (of alphabet) ; чета́ до
    после́дната бу́ква [8] read every last
    word
бу́лка [10] bride
бурка́н [6] jar, can
бу́там [6] push, shove
бъ́да [7] be
бъ́дещ [9] future (*adj.*) ; бъ́деще вре́ме
    [9] future tense
Бъ́дни ве́чер [10] Christmas Eve
бъ́лгарин [3] Bulgarian (male)
бъ́лгарка [3] Bulgarian (female)
бъ́лгарски [1] Bulgarian; Bulgarian
    language
бъ́лгарче [13] young Bulgarian
бърз [6] fast, quick; urgent ; ста́ва бъ́рзо
    [6] it's quick, it goes quickly
бъ́рзам [4] hurry, be in a hurry
бъ́рша (-еш) [13] wipe, rub
бял, бе́ли [2] white ; бял дроб [12]
    lung (*see also* дроб)
бях [6] was (*1st singular*)
бя́ха [6] were (*3rd plural*)
бя́хме [6] were (*1st plural*)
бя́хте [6] were (*2nd plural*)

в [1] [6] in, into, on, at
ваго́н [6] wagon, car
ва́жен [8] important
вака́нция [6] vacation
вали́ (*3rd person only*) [12] rain, etc.
    (precipitation) ; вали́ (дъжд) [12] it's
    raining ; вали́ сняг [12] it's snowing
    ; вали́ град [12] it's hailing ;
    валя́т си́лни дъждове́ [12] it's raining
    heavily ; вали́ като из ведро́ [12]
    it's raining buckets
варя́ [3] boil, cook
вас [10] you (*plural/polite; direct object
    pronoun*)
ваш [8] your, yours (*plural/polite*)
вди́гам / вди́гна [6] raise, lift ; вди́гам
    шум [6] make noise
вдя́сно [11] on the right
вегетериа́нец [3] vegetarian (male)

вегетериа́нка [3] vegetarian (female)
ведна́га [4] immediately, at once
веднъ́ж [7] once
ведро́ [12] bucket ; вали́ като из ведро́
    [12] it's raining buckets
ве́жда [12] eyebrow
век, -ъ́т (*plural* векове́) [12] century
велосипе́д [14] bicycle
ве́рен, вя́рна [10] true, faithful ; вя́рно
    е, че [10] it's true that
ве́сел [9] happy, gay, lively
ве́стник [6] newspaper
ветрове́ *see* вя́тър
ве́че [3] already, by now
ве́чер, -та́ [9] evening ; до́бър ве́чер
    [9] good evening (*fixed phrase*) ;
    ве́чер, вечерта́ [9] in the evening ;
    та́зи ве́чер [9] this evening ; у́тре
    ве́чер [9] tomorrow evening
вече́рен [9] evening (*adj.*)
вече́рям [9] eat dinner
взи́мам (*or* взе́мам) / взе́ма [4] take;
    begin, take to ; вземи́ мо́ливите! [4]
    pick up the pencils! ; взе́мам си
    дови́ждане [13] make one's farewells
ви [5] you (*plural/polite, direct object
    pronoun*)
ви [7] (to) you (*plural/polite, indirect
    object pronoun*)
вид, -ъ́т [12] aspect, view, appearance ;
    (не)свъ́ршен вид [12] (im)perfective
    aspect
видеока́мера [5] videocamera
ви́деокасета [12] video cassette
ви́е [1] you (*plural/polite subject pronoun*)
ви́ждам / ви́дя [3] [4] see ; виж какво́
    [12] look, well (*topic focuser in
    conversation*)
византи́йски [8] Byzantine
ви́кам [12] shout, yell ; ви́кам на во́ля
    [12] shout to one's heart's content
ви́ла [10] pitchfork
ви́лица [10] fork
ви́наги [4] always
ви́но [2] wine
висо́к [5] tall, high; elevated ; loud
виц [12] joke ; разпра́вям виц [12]
    tell a joke
вка́рвам / вка́рам [12] push in, drive in ;
    вка́рвам гол [12] score [a goal]
включвам / включа (-иш) [14] include
вкус, -ъ́т [7] taste ; по вкуса́ на все́ки
    чове́к [7] to everyone's taste
вку́сен [6] tasty, delicious
вкъ́щи [6] home, at home
влак [2] train ; пъту́вам с влак [2]
    travel by train
вли́зам / вля́за [4] enter, go in

влю́бен [14] in love
вля́во [11] on the left
внима́вам [6] pay attention ;
  внима́вайте, бу́тате чове́ка [6]
  careful, you're pushing someone
внима́ние [14] attention ; внима́нието
  му се притъпи́ [14] his attention
  wandered
внима́телен [14] attentive
внук [10] grandson
вну́чка [10] granddaughter
вода́ [4] water
во́дя [8] lead, take
война́ [7] war
войни́к [7] soldier
во́ля [12] will, desire ; ви́кам на во́ля
  [12] shout to one's heart's content
врат [12] back of the neck
врата́ [2] door
вратовръ́зка [13] necktie
вре́ме (plural времена́) [2] [9] time;
  weather; season ; вре́мето е то́пло [2]
  the weather is warm ; в после́дно
  вре́ме [6] recently ; по това́ вре́ме
  [7] at about that time ; годи́шните
  времена́ [9] seasons (of the year) ;
  добро́то ста́ро вре́ме [11] the good
  old days ; от вре́ме на вре́ме [14]
  from time to time
вре́ме [9] verbal tense ; сега́шно вре́ме
  [9] present tense ; бъ́деще вре́ме [9]
  future tense ; ми́нало свъ́ршено вре́ме
  [12] aorist tense ; ми́нало
  несвъ́ршено вре́ме [14] imperfect
  tense
връ́зка [13] tie, string, shoelace
връх, върхъ́т (plural върхове́) [11]
  summit; tip
връ́щам / въ́рна [5] return (transitive)
връ́щам се / въ́рна се [11] return, go
  back
вря́ [9] boil (intransitive)
все́ [10] always, constantly; surely ; все́
  ме ня́ма [10] I'm never there ;   все́
  о́ще избѝрам [10] I'm still looking ;
  все́ едно́ и съ́що [10] [it's] always the
  same thing
все́ки, вся́ка, вся́ко [6] every ; все́ки
  моме́нт [6] any minute ; на вся́ка
  цена́ [12] at any price, at all costs,
  absolutely
всѝчко [2] all, everything ; всѝчко шест
  [6] six in all ; всѝчко ху́баво [2]
  all the best
вто́ри [8] second ; вто́ра ма́йка [10]
  stepmother ; вто́ри баща́ [10]
  stepfather
вто́рник [9] Tuesday

ву́йчо (plural ву́йчовци) [10] uncle
  (mother's brother)
вход [8] entrance
вче́ра [9] yesterday ; вче́ра следо́бед
  [9] yesterday afternoon ; вче́ра
  сутринта́ [9] yesterday morning
вче́рашен [9] yesterday's
във = в [7] in, into, on, at
въ́здух [4] air
въ́зрастен [4] adult; elderly
въ́зрастни [4] grownups
възто́рг [10] delight, rapture ;
  предизви́квам възто́рг у [10]
  enrapture
вълк (plural въ́лци) [8] wolf
въ́лнен, -ена [13] wool (adj.), woolen
вълше́бник [11] magician, wizard
въ́н [11] out
въобще́ [11] in general; at all
въпро́с [11] question
вървя́ [3] walk, move, go ; вървя́ с
  [10] go well with ; вървя́ си [10]
  get going ; вървя́ под ръка́ [14]
  walk arm in arm ; дне́с ня́ма да ми
  върви́ [14] today's not going to be my
  day
въртя́ се [14] turn around, rotate; move
въ́тре [11] in, inside
вя́рвам [7] believe
вя́рно see ве́рен
вя́тър (plural ветрове́) [2] [7] wind ;
  и́ма си́лен вя́тър [2] there's a strong
  wind, it's very windy

г. = годи́на [9]
га́ра [5] station (train or bus)
гарниту́ра [4] garnish ; пържо́ла с
  гарниту́ра [4] steak with the
  trimmings
ГДР (pron. гедере́) [14] GDR (DDR;
  former East Germany)
герда́н [14] necklace, collar
герма́нски [14] German
ги [5] them (direct object pronoun)
гимна́зия [3] academically oriented high
  school
глава́ [12] head
гла́вен [9] main, chief
гла́вно [9] mainly
глад [7] hunger
гла́ден [2] hungry
глас, -ъ́т (plural гласове́) [12] voice
гле́дам [4] [9] look at; look after
гле́зен [12] ankle
глъ́твам / глъ́тна [7] (take a) swallow
глъ́тка [3] swallow, gulp

334

гнездо́ [13] nest

гну́с ме е [12] feel nauseated

го [5] him, it (direct object pronoun)

гово́ря [3] speak, talk

годени́к [10] fiancé

годени́ца [10] fiancée

годи́на [3] year ; през 1975 г. [9] in 1975

годи́шен [9] yearly, annual ; годи́шните времена́ [9] seasons (of the year)

годи́шнина [10] anniversary

го́зба [5] dish

го́л [12] goal (in sports) ; вка́рвам го́л [12] score [a goal] ; изпу́скам го́л [12] miss [a goal]

голя́м, голе́ми [2] large, big ; голе́мите [4] big ones, adults ; голя́мо движе́ние [12] lots of traffic

гора́ [3] woods, forest

го́ре [11] up ; го́ре-до́лу [11] more or less

горе́щ [11] hot

горя́ [11] burn

господа́ [3] gentlemen ; да́ми и господа́ [3] ladies and gentlemen (vocative)

господи́н [1] Sir, Mr.

госпожа́ (plural госпо́жи) [1] Ma'am, Mrs.

госпо́жица [1] Miss

го́ст (plural го́сти) [5] [8] guest ; и́двам на го́сти [5] come/go over to visit

готва́рски [7] cooking, culinary ; готва́рска кни́га [7] cookbook

го́твя [4] prepare, cook

го́твя се [9] prepare, get ready

гото́в [6] prepared, ready

гра́д [12] hail

гра́д, -ъ́т (plural градове́) [6] [7] town, city

гради́на [3] garden

греша́ (-и́ш) [7] sin, err

гре́шка [3] mistake

гре́я [9] warm, heat (up); shine ; слъ́нцето гре́е [9] the sun is shining

гри́п [13] influenza, flu ; бо́лен от гри́п [13] down with the flu

гро́зде [9] grapes (collective)

гро́здов [2] [made] of grapes

гръ́б, гърбъ́т (plural гърбове́) [12] back

гръ́д, -та́ (or гърди́) [12] chest

гръ́к, гъркъ́т (plural гъ́рци) [6] Greek (male)

гу́бя [14] lose

гу́ша [12] neck, throat

гъ́ба [4] mushroom ; омле́т с гъ́би [4] mushroom omelet

гъ́лтам [8] swallow ; гъ́лтам лека́рство [8] take medicine

гърда́ [12] breast, bosom

гъ́рло [12] throat

гъ́рци see гръ́к

да [5] (subordinating/modal conjunction) ; и́скам да до́йда [5] I want to come ; не мо́га да до́йда [5] I can't come ; ако и да [9] even though ; да сте жи́ви и здра́ви [11] here's to your life and health ; и то́й да до́йде [13] he should come too

да́ [1] yes

да́вам / да́м (даде́ш) [9] give; allow ; да́й, да́йте [4] give (imperative) ; да́вам под на́ем [12] rent out ; да́вам на за́ем [12] loan

да́же [11] even

да́й see да́вам

дале́че (and дале́ч) [4] far, far away

дали́ [11] whether, if (relative/question particle) ; дали́ и́ма сми́съл? [11] does it make any sense? ; не зна́я дали́ и́ма сми́съл [11] I don't know whether it makes any sense

да́ма [3] lady ; да́ми и господа́ [3] ladies and gentlemen (vocative)

дано́ [10] let's wish, if only, I hope ; дано́ присти́гне навре́ме [10] let's hope it gets there on time

два́ [6] two (masculine)

два́йсет [6] twenty

два́ма [6] two (masculine animate)

двана́йсет [6] twelve

две́ [2] [6] two (feminine, neuter; in counting)

две́ста [9] two hundred

дви́жа се (-иш) [14] move, go

движе́ние [12] movement; traffic ; голя́мо движе́ние [12] lots of traffic ; правила́ на пъ́тното движе́ние [12] traffic laws, rules of the road

дво́йка [10] [13] pair; "2" (failing mark in school)

дво́йкаджия, -ийка [10] high school dropout

дво́р [11] yard ; игра́я на дво́ра [11] play in the yard

двуцве́тен [13] two-colored

де [10] (intensifying particle) ; земе́те де! [10] so take [some] already!

де́вет [6] nine

деветдесéт [6] ninety

девéти [8] ninth

деветнáйсет [6] nineteen

дéветстотин [9] nine hundred

дежýрен [10] on duty

дежýрство [10] duty

декéмври [9] December

деклами́рам [7] declaim, recite

демократи́чески [14] democratic

демокрáция [13] democracy

дéн, -ят (plural дни́, quantified form дéна or дéня) [4] [6] day ; рождéн дéн [5] birthday ; дóбър дéн (fixed accent) ; [6] hello, good day ; днéшен дéн [9] this very day ; дрýги дéн [9] the day after tomorrow ; óнзи дéн [9] the day before yesterday ; през деня́ [9] in the daytime ; Ден на благодарносттá [9] Thanksgiving Day

дерá [12] skin, fleece, tear, scratch

дéсен, дя́сна [11] right (as opposed to left)

десéрт [6] dessert

дéсет [6] ten

детé (plural децá) [1] [3] child ; от детé [12] since childhood

дети́нски [13] children's ; дети́нски рáботи [13] kid's stuff

джи́нси [13] jeans

дикту́вам [14] dictate

ди́м, -ът [4] smoke

дирéктен [8] direct

дирéктор (ка) [13] director

длáн [12] palm of the hand

днéвник [10] diary

днéс [1] today

днéшен [9] today's ; днéшен дéн [9] this very day

до [2] [5] [6] by, near, next to; [up] to; until ; тó е до вратáта [2] it's by the door

добрé [2] well, fine; O.K. ; добрé дошли́! [2] welcome! ; добрé ли си сегá? [3] are you O.K. now?

дóбър [2] good ; дóбър вéчер [9] good evening (fixed phrase) ; дóбър дéн (fixed accent) [6] hello, good day ; добрó ýтро [9] good morning ; добрóто стáро врéме [11] the good old days

довéчера [9] this evening

дови́ждане [8] goodbye ; взéмам си дови́ждане [13] make one's farewells

довóлен [6] pleased, satisfied

догоди́на [7] next year

дóйда see дохóждам

докáрвам / докáрам [10] drive to, bring to

докáто [9] while, until

докáто не [13] until

доклáд [12] report, (scholarly) paper

доли́там / долетя́ [13] come flying, fly up to

дóлу [11] down ; гóре-дóлу [11] more or less

дóм, -ът (plural домовé) [7] home, house ; у домá [10] at home

домáт [6] tomato

домáшен [2] [7] homemade; home (adj.)

домáшно [8] homework

донáсям / донесá [7] bring

допълнéние [8] addition, supplement

дори́ [8] even

досегá [6] until now

досмешáва ме / досмешéе ме (3rd person only) [13] [I] feel like laughing

досрамя́ва ме / досрамéе ме (3rd person only) [13] [I] feel ashamed

достáтъчен [7] enough

дохóждам / дóйда [5] come, arrive

дочу́ване [12] goodbye (on the phone)

дошъ́л, дошлá, дошли́ [11] come (active participle) ; добрé дошъ́л [11] welcome (to a male friend) ; добрé дошлá [11] welcome (to a female friend) ; добрé дошли́! [11] welcome (to group or formal acquaintance)

дрáг [2] [3] dear ; Дрáги Бóб, [2] Dear Bob, (beginning of a letter)

дрéха [10] article of clothing ; дрéхи [10] clothes

дрóб, -ът (plural дрóбове or дробовé) [12] lung (see also бя́л дрóб) ; чéрен дрóб [12] liver

дрýг [2] [7] other, another; next ; на дрýгата спи́рка [7] at the next stop ; дрýги дéн [9] the day after tomorrow ; дрýгата нóщ [9] tomorrow night

другáр (ка) [1] comrade

другáрче [13] playfellow, playmate

дýма [7] word ; за каквó стáва дýма? [11] what's the matter? what's it about?

дýхам blow ; дýха [1] it's blowing, there is air coming

дýши [6] people (counting form) ; кóлко дýши [6] how many people

дъжд, -ът (plural дъждовé) [12] rain ; валя́т си́лни дъждовé [12] it's raining heavily

дъ́лго [8] [for] a long time

дъ́лг [2] long

дъ́рвен (-ена) [13] wood (adj.), wooden
дърво́ (plural дърве́та) [7] tree
дърво́ (plural дърва́) [11] wood
държа́ (-и́ш) [11] hold, keep
дъ́х [8] breath, wind ; поéмам [си] дъх [8] catch one's breath
дъщеря́ [10] daughter
дя́до (plural дя́довци) [8] [10] grandfather ; Дя́до Мра́з [10] Jack Frost ; Дя́до Ко́леда [10] Santa Claus
дя́сна see де́сен

е [1] is (3rd singular) ; see съм
европе́йски [8] European
éвтин [9] cheap, inexpensive
еди́н [2] [3] one, a (masculine) ; еди́н и съ́щ [10] the same, one and the same
едина́йсет [6] eleven
еди́нствен, -ена [11] single, only
една́ [3] one (feminine) ; в една́ ста́я с [10] in the same room as
едно́ [2] [3] one (neuter; in counting)
едновре́менен [11] simultaneous
éдър [9] large, robust ; на éдро [9] wholesale
éзеро [3] lake, pond
ези́к [3] language, tongue
éй! [1] hey, oh
екзо́тика [7] exotica, exoticism
екзоти́чен [5] exotic
екску́рзия [8] excursion
ела́ [5] come (imperative of до́йда) ела́ да ти поле́я [13] come let me pour water [over your hands]
елега́нтен [5] elegant
еле́н [8] deer, stag
елха́ [13] fir tree ; новогоди́шна елха́ [13] New Year's tree
éра [9] era ; преди́ н.е. [9] B.C. ; от н.е. [9] A.D.
ерге́н [11] bachelor
éсен, -та́ [9] fall, autumn
ета́ж [0] floor (of a multi-story building)
éто [2] here (pointing)
ефе́ктен [5] effective
ефе́нди [1] effendi, sir (archaic term of address)

жа́ден [2] thirsty
жа́лко [11] too bad, pity
жела́ние [14] wish, desire

жела́я [7] wish, desire
жена́ [2] woman, wife
же́нен, -ена [10] married
же́ня [11] marry off
же́ня се [11] get married
жи́в [11] live, living; lively ; жи́в да го опла́чеш [11] it makes your heart bleed to see him ; да сте жи́ви и здра́ви [11] here's to your life and health
живе́я [3] live
живо́т [9] life
живо́ти́нче [13] little animal
живо́тно [8] animal ; права́ на живо́тните [12] animal rights
жиле́тка [12] waistcoat, cardigan sweater
жи́лищен [8] residential ; жи́лищен компле́кс [8] housing development, block of apartments
журнали́ст (ка) [5] journalist
жъ́лт [8] yellow

за [1] [6] [10] [11] for, to; about; here's to ; за къде́ пъту́вате? [1] where are you traveling to? ; за съжале́ние [1] unfortunately ; за две́ се́дмици [6] for two weeks ; кажи́ ни за тя́х [10] tell us about them ; зна́я за не́го [10] I know about him ; за мно́го годи́ни [11] many happy returns ; за какво́ ста́ва ду́ма? [11] what's it about? what's the matter?
за да [11] in order to (conjunction of purpose) ; за да не ста́ва тече́ние [11] so there won't be a draft
заба́вен [11] amusing, fun
забеля́звам / забеле́жа (-иш) [5] notice, spot
забо́ждам / забода́ [13] stick, pin
заболя́ва (ме) / заболи́ (ме) (3rd person only) [12] start to hurt
заболя́вам / заболе́я [12] get sick
забра́вям / забра́вя [7] forget
завали́ва / завали́ (3rd person only) [12] begin to precipitate [rain, unless otherwise specified]
заве́ждам / заведа́ [10] take somewhere, lead
зави́вам / зави́я [6] turn, bend, wrap
зави́ся [14] depend ; зави́си от ва́с [14] it depends on you ; зави́си то́й какво́ ще ка́же [14] it depends on what he will say
завъ́рзвам / завъ́ржа (-еш) [13] tie ; завъ́рзвам връ́зките на обу́вки [13] tie [one's] shoelaces

заглáвие [13] title

зад [13] behind, beyond ; зад ъ́гъла [14] around the corner

зáден [14] back, rear (adj.)

зáдник [12] behind, rear end

задýшен [4] stuffy

зáедно [5] together

заéмам / заéма [12] take up, occupy

заéт [7] busy, occupied

закáчвам / закачá (-и́ш) [13] hang, suspend

заклю́чвам / заклю́ча (-иш) [8] lock

закрáтко [11] for a short while

закýсвам / закýся [11] eat breakfast

закýска [10] breakfast

закъснéние [14] delay; tardiness ; с мáлко закъснéние [14] a little late

закъсня́вам / закъсне́я [7] be late

зáла [12] hall ; все́ еднó си в зáлата [12] it's just like being in the concert hall

заля́звам / заля́за [9] set (of the sun)

заминáвам / зами́на [9] leave, depart

занáсям / занесá [7] carry, take to

занимáвам [11] interest, occupy

занимáвам се (с) [11] be occupied (with)

зáпис [13] recording

запови́двам / запови́дам [5] command, order ; запови́дай [5] help yourself

запознáвам / запознáя [14] acquaint [someone] with

запознáвам се / запознáя се [10] meet, get acquainted

запóмням / запóмня [9] remember

запóчвам / запóчна [6] begin

зарáдвам се [12] cheer up

заради [13] for the sake of, because of

засегá [9] at present, for now

заслужáвам / заслýжа (-иш) [11] deserve, be worthy of

заспи́вам / заспя́ [14] fall asleep

затвáрям / затвóря [3] [4] close ; затвáрям вратáта под носá [на] [13] shut the door in [someone's] face

затвóрен, -ена [2] closed

затовá [5] therefore, thus

затрýпвам / затрýпам [11] cover up, bury under; pile up ; затрýпвам с въпрóси [11] burden with questions

зáхар, -тá [12] sugar

защи́та [12] defense

защó [3] why

защóто [3] because

звучá (-и́ш) [12] sound, resound ; звучи́ добрé [12] that sounds good

звънéц [5] bell

звъня́ [5] ring ; звъня́ по телефóна [10] telephone

здрáв [2] healthy, lasting, strong

здрáве [2] health ; полéзно за здрáвето [8] good for you [for one's health]

здравéй [6] hi

зéле [4] cabbage ; салáта от зéле [4] cabbage salad

зелéн [8] green

зеленчýк [7] vegetable

зи́ма [9] winter

зи́мен [11] winter (adj.) ; зи́мен курóрт [11] ski resort

зимóрничав [11] sensitive to the cold

злáтен [9] golden

злé [13] bad, badly

знáк [9] sign

знáм [4] see зня́я

знамени́т [14] famous, renowned

знáчи [1] that means, so, thus

значéние [9] meaning ; ня́ма значéние [9] it doesn't matter

зня́я [3] know

зрéя [9] ripen

зъб, -ъ́т (plural зъби) [6] [8] tooth

зъболéкар [12] dentist

и [1] and, also ; и áз [1] me too ; и то [11] at that

й [7] [to] her (indirect object pronoun)

и ... и [8] both...and

игрá [14] play, game

игрáя [5] play ; игрáя на двóра [11] play in the yard ; игрáя си [11] play around

и́да [5] come, go ; иди́ за хля́б [5] go get some bread

и́двам [5] come

идеáлен [5] ideal

идéя [5] idea

идили́чен [3] idyllic

иди́лия [7] idyll

из [11] around, throughout; out of ; пътýване из Бългáрия [11] a trip throughout Bulgaria ; разхóдка из градá [11] city tour ; из кы́щи [11] around the house (fixed phrase)

изби́рам / изберá [4] choose, select

и́збор [7] selection, choice

избы́рсвам / избы́рша (-еш) [13] wipe, dry

извáждам / извáдя [14] take/bring out, produce, extract

изведнъ́ж [5] suddenly

извéждам / изведá [9] take out, lead away ; извéждам кýчето на разхóдка [9] walk the dog

338

извѝквам / извѝкам [13] cry, call out

извинѐние [13] excuse, pardon

извинявам / извиня [5] pardon, excuse ;
извинѐте [2] excuse me

извън [10] out of, outside

изгарям / изгоря [14] get burned, burn
up

изглеждам [4] look, appear, seem ;
изглежда [6] it seems

издокарвам се / издокарам се [14] dress
up

издържам / издържа (-йш) [7] stand,
endure

иззвънявам / иззвъня [14] ring (out)

изкипявам / изкипя [14] boil over

изкъпвам се / изкъпя се (-еш) [14]
bathe, take a bath

ѝзлет [3] excursion

излѝзам / изляза [4] leave, go

измѝвам / измѝя [13] wash up

измѝслям / измѝсля [12] think up,
invent

измокрям / измокря [12] drench, soak ;
измокрям се до кости [12] get
soaked to the skin

изненада [12] surprise ; по
изненадите съм [14] I like surprises

изобщо [8] in general, at all ; те
изобщо не могат да чакат [8] they
can't wait at all

изпѝвам / изпѝя [5] drink up

изпѝрам / изперà [12] do laundry, wash

ѝзпит [5] exam, test

изплѝтам / изплета [12] knit, twist

изплъзвам се / изплъзна се [14] slip
out, slip through

изпращам / изпратя [8] send off, see
off, accompany

изпускам / изпусна [7] drop, let go;
miss

изпявам / изпея [11] sing (to the end)

изстѝвам / изстѝна [8] grow/become
cold

изтръпвам / изтръпна [14] fall asleep (of
a body part) ; изтръпвам от ужас
[14] freeze with terror

изумѝтелен [13] amazing, astounding

изучавам / изуча (-иш) [2] [4] study,
make a study of

изчезвам / изчезна [10] disappear

изчиствам / изчистя [14] clean up, clean
out

изяждам / изям (-ядеш) [9] eat up

изяснявам / изясня [14] clear up ;
след като нещата се изяснят [14]
when things get clarified

или [3] or

или ... или [8] either...or

им [7] [to] them (indirect object pronoun)

ѝма [2] there is, there are ; какво ѝма
в чантата? [2] what is there in the
bag? ; ѝма малко време [2] there's
not [very] much time ; ѝма още много
работа [2] there's still a lot of work
[to do] ; ѝма силен вятър [2] it's
very windy; there's a strong wind ; ѝма
смисъл [11] it makes sense

ѝмам [2] [3] have ; ѝмам нужда от
[4] need, have need of

ѝме (plural именà) [6] name

инженѐр [14] engineer

интерѐс [7] interest ; проявявам
интерес към [8] take an interest in

интерѐсен [2] interesting

интерѐсно [1] interesting ; много
интересно [1] that's very
interesting ; интересно, ти как си
[3] I wonder how you are

интересувам [8] interest (transitive)

интересувам се от [11] be interested in

ѝскам [5] want

ѝстина [1] truth

ѝстински [8] real, true

ѝстория [7] history, story

кабинѐт [4] office (e.g. doctor's)

кавгà [10] quarrel, dispute

кавгаджѝя, -ийка [10] quarrelsome
person, brawler

казвам / кажа (-еш) [1] [4] say

казвам се [1] my name is ; казва се
[1] his/her name is ; как се казвате?
[1] what is your name?

каймà [6] ground meat

как [1] how ; как се казвате? [1]
what is your name? ; как такà? [11]
how is it that, how can that be? ; как
не те е срам! [12] you should be
ashamed!

каквò [1] [4] what, what for ; какво е
"течение"? [1] what's a "течение",
what does течение mean? ; какво е
това? [3] what's this? ; какво
гледаш толкова в... ? [4] why are you
so absorbed in... ? ; какво работите?
[5] what [kind of] work do you do? ;
какво ще кажеш [7] what do you
think ; какво ли не [12] whatever,
whatnot

каквòто [12] whatever

както [9] as

какъв [3] what kind of, what ; какъв е
той? [3] what [work] does he do?;
каквà хубава къща [3] what a nice

house ; какъ́в ли е то́й [5] what's
he like, I wonder

ка́ня [10] invite

ка́ня се [11] plan, intend

капри́зен [13] capricious

ка́пя (-еш) [11] drip, dribble

ка́рам [6] drive, ride, push ; ка́рам кола́
[6] drive a car

ка́рам се [11] scold, quarrel

карнава́лен [12] carnival (adj.)

ка́рта [5] card; map, chart

карти́нка [3] small picture

ка́ртичка [11] postcard

касетофо́н [5] cassette player; tape recorder

като́ [3] like, as; when ; а́з пра́вя като́
ле́лята [3] I'm doing [just] like
auntie ; като́ бя́х [6] when I was ;
като́ ма́лък [11] when he was little

като́ че ли́ [14] as if, apparently ; като́
че ли́ се сме́еше [14] he appeared to
be laughing

кафе́ [5] coffee, cup of coffee

кафе́ен, -е́йна [6] coffee (adj.) ; ка́фена
лъжи́чка [6] coffee spoon

ка́чвам / кача́ (-и́ш) [7] carry up, take up

ка́чвам се / кача́ се (-и́ш) [7] ascend, get
on

кашкава́л [4] kashkaval (yellow cheese) ;
омле́т с кашкава́л [4] cheese omelet

кварта́л [9] district, living area

варти́ра [14] apartment, quarters

кеба́п [13] grilled or stewed meat

кеба́пче [6] kebab

килогра́м [6] kilogram

ки́но [5] cinema, movies

ки́р [1] sir (archaic term of address)

ки́ра [1] ma'am (archaic term of address)

ки́сел [6] sour ; ки́село зе́ле [6]
sauerkraut ; ки́село мля́ко [6]
yogurt

ки́тка [12] wrist

ки́хам (or ки́хвам) / ки́хна [14] sneeze

клас, -ъ́т [7] class, grade in school ; от
класа́ [7] from the same [school] class

класи́чески [3] classical

кли́мат [11] climate

клюн [13] beak

ключ [7] key

кни́га [2] book

княз (plural князе́) [8] prince

кни́жка [10] booklet; driver's license

кога́ [6] when (interrogative)

кога́то [11] when (relative conjunction)

кого́ [8] whom (interrogative)

ко́жа [12] skin; hide, fur

кой, коя́, кое́, кои́ [3] [5] who, which
(interrogative)

ко́кал [12] bone

коко́шка [11] hen, fowl ; коко́шка с
ки́село зе́ле [11] chicken and
sauerkraut casserole

кола́ [4] car, automobile ; ка́рам кола́
[6] drive a car

коле́га [10] colleague

Ко́леда [10] Christmas

ко́леден [10] Christmas (adj.)

коле́жка [10] female colleague

коле́кция [7] collection

колело́ [14] wheel; bicycle

коле́т [5] parcel, package

коли́чка [7] pushcart

ко́лко [4] [6] how much, how many ;
ко́лко стру́ва това́? [4] how much
does this cost? ; ко́лко стру́ва? [4]
how much is it? ; ко́лко ду́ши сме?
[6] how many of us are there? ; на
ко́лко сте годи́ни? [6] how old are
you?; ко́лко е часъ́т? [6] what time
is it? ; в ко́лко часа́? [6] when, at
what time?

коля́но (plural колена́ or колене́) [12]
knee

командиро́вка [10] business trip

коме́дия [11] comedy

коми́н [13] chimney

компа́кт ди́ск [12] compact disk

компле́кс [8] complex ; жи́лищен
компле́кс [8] block of apartments

кон, -ят (plural коне́) [8] horse

конду́ктор (ка) [5] conductor

консерви́рам [6] preserve, can

консерви́ран [6] preserved, canned

контро́лен [8] control (adj.) ; контро́лна
ра́бота [8] exam, quiz

контро́лно [8] exam, quiz

конфере́нция [12] conference

копа́я [10] dig

ко́пие [13] copy ; пъ́лно ко́пие [14]
exact replica

ко́пър [6] dill

коре́м [12] abdomen, belly

коридо́р [2] corridor, passageway; entryway

коса́ [12] hair

кост, -та́ [12] bone ; измо́крям се до
ко́сти [12] get soaked to the skin

костену́рка [9] turtle

костю́м [14] suit

ко́тка [10] cat

ко́фа [14] pail, bucket ; ко́фа за боклу́к
[14] garbage can

кошма́р [6] nightmare

край [7] edge, end

край (plural кра́ища) [8] district

крак, -ъ́т (plural крака́) [8] leg ; на
крак [12] hastily

крал, -ят (plural крале́) [8] king

кра́ставица [6] cucumber
кра́тък [9] short
кри́в [3] crooked
кро́тък [13] gentle
кръ́в, -та́ (plural кърви) [12] blood
кръг, -ъ́т [10] circle ; те́сен семе́ен
  кръг [10] immediate family
кръ́гъл [10] round, circular ; кръ́гла
  годи́шнина [10] decade anniversary
кръстосло́вица [8] crossword puzzle ;
  реша́вам кръстосло́вица [8] do a
  crossword puzzle
куби́нски [8] Cuban
ку́кла [13] doll, puppet
култу́ра [9] culture
култу́рен [12] cultural
кум, -ъ́т [14] godfather
кума́ [14] godmother
купе́ [2] compartment ; купе́ № 7 [2]
  compartment No. 7 ; купе́то е тя́сно
  [2] the compartment is cramped
купу́вам / ку́пя [5] buy, purchase
куро́рт [11] resort ; зи́мен куро́рт [11]
  ski resort
кути́я [10] box ; по́щенска кути́я [10]
  mailbox
ку́хня [5] [7] kitchen; cuisine
ку́фар [2] suitcase
ку́че [4] dog
къде́ [1] where (interrogative)
към [8] toward
къ́пя (-еш) [3] bathe
къ́рпа [13] cloth, towel
къс [12] short
къ́сен [4] late
късме́т [10] fortune, luck ; ба́ница с
  късме́ти [10] banitsa with fortunes
къ́ща [2] house
къ́щичка [7] little house

ла́кът, ла́кътят (plural ла́кти) [8] elbow
ла́я [11] bark
лев [4] lev (Bulgarian currency) ; 120
  ле́ва [4] 120 levs (or leva)
ле́ви see ляв
легло́ [4] bed
ле́гна see ля́гам
ле́ден, -ена [8] ice (adj.), frozen
лежа́ (-и́ш) [4] lie, be lying
лек [9] light, easy ; ле́ка нощ [9]
  good night
ле́кар (ка) [1] doctor, physician
лека́рство [8] medicine ; гъ́лтам
  лека́рство [8] take medicine
ле́кция [6] lecture, class
ле́ля [3] aunt (father's sister); "auntie"

ле́сен [6] easy
ли [1] [5] (question particle) ; от Ва́рна
  ли сте? [1] are you from Varna? ;
  какъ́в ли е то́зи чове́к [5] what is this
  person like, I wonder ; какво́ ли не́
  [12] all sorts of [things]
лист [4] sheet of paper
лист (plural листа́) [6] leaf
лице́ [12] face
ловя́ [9] catch ; ловя́ ри́ба [9] fish,
  catch fish
логи́чен [12] logical
лоза́ [6] vine
ло́зе (plural лозя́) [10] vineyard
ло́зов [6] grape, vine (adj.) ; ло́зови
  листа́ [6] grape leaves
лош [3] bad
лук [6] onion
луна́ [9] moon
лъжи́ца [6] spoon, spoonful
лъжи́чка [6] teaspoon, teaspoonful
лъ́скав [10] shining, bright
любя́ [13] love, be in love with
любе́зен [2] kind
люби́м [8] favorite
люби́тел [8] lover, fan
ляв (plural ле́ви) [11] left, Left
ля́гам / ле́гна [4] lie down, go to bed
ля́гам си / ле́гна си [8] go to bed
ля́то (plural лета́) [9] summer

магази́н [5] store
май [9] May
май [12] it seems, in all probability ;
  май оста́ва да оти́дем та́м [12] I
  guess we have to go there
ма́йка [2] mother
мака́р [14] at least; although
мака́р че [14] although, even though
мали́на [3] raspberry
ма́лко [1] [2] a little, [very] little ; той е
  ма́лко бо́лен [2] he's a bit under the
  weather
ма́лък [2] small ; ма́лко вре́ме [2]
  not much time ; ма́лките [4] small
  ones, children ; като ма́лък [11]
  when he was little ; от ма́лък [13]
  since he was little/a child ; с ма́лко
  закъсне́ние [14] a little late
ма́ма [2] Mom ; ма́мо [2] Mom
  (when addressed) ; а ни́е, ма́мо? [2]
  and what about us, Mom?
манасти́р [8] monastery
март [1] March
ма́ртеница [13] entwined red and
  white tassels worn as a sign of spring

мáртеничка [13] small martenitsa
мáса [7] table
мáсичка [13] little table
матýра [8] matriculation [exam]
мáхам [14] wave
мáч [12] [sports] match, game
мáщеха [10] stepmother
ме [4] [5] me (direct object pronoun)
между [12] between, among
мéк [15] soft, mild
мéн [12] (same as мéне)
мéне [10] me (direct object pronoun)
меню́ (neuter) [4] menu
мéсец [9] month
месó [6] meat
местá [6] see мя́сто
мéтър [15] meter
мечé [11] bear cub
Мéчо Пýх [11] Winnie the Pooh
ми [7] [to] me (indirect object pronoun)
мúгла [12] eyelash
мúл [4] dear ; добрé, мúло [4] all
    right, darling
милéя [13] hold dear, care for
минáвам / мúна [5] pass
мúнал [9] past ; мúналата нóщ [9]
    last night ; мúнало свъ́ршено врéме
    [12] aorist tense ; мúнало
    несвъ́ршено врéме [14] imperfect
    tense
министéрство [14] ministry
минýта [6] minute
миризмá [11] smell, scent
мúсля [5] think
мúшка [11] mouse
мúя [8] wash
млáд [7] young
младожéнец [10] bridegroom, newlywed
младожéнка [10] bride, newlywed
млéчност [10] milkiness
мля́ко (plural млекá) [6] milk
мнóго [1] [2] very; much; many ; мнóго
    рáбота [2] a lot of work ; мнóго
    интерéсно [1] very interesting
мóга (-жеш) [4] can, be able
мóден [13] fashionable ; мóдно ревю́
    [13] fashion show
мóже [4] [11] possible, OK; it's possible ;
    бúра мóже [4] OK, I can [have a]
    beer
мóже би [9] maybe
мóзък (plural мóзъци) [12] brain
мóй [8] my, mine
мóлив [2] pencil
мóля [4] please ; мóля ви се,
    госпóдине [4] please, sir ; мóля!
    [4] at your service

момéнт [5] moment ; в тóзи момéнт
    [5] then, at that point in time ; в
    момéнта [10] at the moment
момúче [1] girl
момчé [1] boy
мóмък (plural момцú) [13] young man
монéта [10] coin
морáвски [8] Moravian
морé [6] sea ; на морéто [6] at the
    [Black] Sea
мóрков [4] carrot ; салáта от мóркови
    [4] carrot salad
мóрски [15] sea (adj.) ; мóрското
    равнúще [15] sea level
мóст (plural мостóве) [6] bridge
мóтам се (or мотáя се) [14] fool around
мрáз [10] frost, chill ; Дя́до Мрáз [10]
    Jack Frost
мръ́сен [9] dirty
му [7] [to] him/it (indirect object pronoun)
мýзика [5] music
мýскул [12] muscle
мустáци (plural) [14] mustache
мъ́ж, -ът (plural мъжé) [8] man, husband
мъ́жки [8] male, masculine
мълчá (-úш) [10] be silent, fall silent
мъ́чен [13] hard, difficult ; стáна ми
    мъ́чно [13] I had a hard time
мя́сто [2] place, seat ; мя́стото е
    свобóдно [2] the seat is not taken

н.е. = новáта éра [9]
на [1] [2] [3] [7] of; in, on, at; per; for
    (indirect object) ; тú си на № 2 [2]
    you've got No. 2 ; на сéло [3] in the
    village ; на бъ́лгарски [3] in
    Bulgarian ; на [...] годúни [6] [...]
    years old ; на кóлко сте годúни? [6]
    how old are you? ; на éдро [9]
    wholesale ; на телефóна [12]
    speaking! [on the phone] ; по три пъ́ти
    на дéн [13] three times a day
наблúзо [4] nearby
навечéрие [10] the eve of; vigil
нáвик [11] habit
наврéме [5] on time ; съвсéм наврéме
    [5] at exactly the right moment
навъ́н [11] outside (directional)
навъ́тре [11] inside (directional)
навя́рно [14] probably
нагóре [11] up (directional)
награ́да [13] reward, prize
над [15] above
надéжда [8] hope
надóлу [11] down (directional)
нáдпис [14] inscription

342

надя́сно [11] to the right

на́ем [12] rent ; да́вам под на́ем [12] rent out

нае́сен [9] in the fall

наза́ем [12] loan ; да́вам наза́ем [12] loan

наздра́ве [11] cheers, to your health! *(toast)*

наизу́ст [4] by heart, verbatim ; а́з зна́м меню́то наизу́ст [4] I can recite the menu by heart

найстина [2] really, truly

най- [10] most... *(superlative degree particle)* ; най-по́сле [1] finally ; най-мно́го [10] the most ; най-разли́чни неща́ [10] all sorts of things

накра́тко [10] in short, briefly

накъде́ [11] to where

нали́ [3] *(added to form negative question)* ; нали́ ви́ждаш [3] don't you see ; нали́ зна́еш, че а́з съм... [3] you know, don't you, that I'm... ; голя́м е, нали? [3] it's big, isn't it?

наля́во [11] to the left

нами́рам / наме́ря [5] find

намръ́щен (-ена) [13] sullen, gloomy

нани́звам / нани́жа (-еш) [14] string together

нао́коло [9] around, round about

напи́свам / напи́ша (-еш) [5] write, write down, finish writing

напи́тка [4] beverage, drink

напосле́дък [8] lately

напра́вям / напра́вя [6] do, make ; напра́вя мя́сто на то́зи чове́к [6] make room for this man

напре́д [14] ahead, forwards

напре́дък [9] progress, gain

напреже́ние [14] pressure, tension

наприме́р [8] for example

напро́лет [9] in the spring

наре́д [7] in order ; вси́чко е наре́д [7] everything's O.K.

наре́ждам / наредя́ [6] set up, arrange

нари́чам / нарека́ (-че́ш) [13] call, name

наро́д [7] people, folk

наро́ден [5] national, folk

на́с [8] [10] us *(direct object pronoun)*

настъ́пвам / настъ́пя [13] come on, set in, occur; step on; advance

науча́вам / науча́ (-иш) [6] [9] learn; teach

науча́вам се / науча́ се (-иш) [14] learn to, learn about; get used to

нахра́нвам / нахра́ня [11] feed

нача́лен [3] beginning, elementary ; нача́лно образова́ние [3] elementary education

на́чин [6] way, manner; по то́зи на́чин [6] in this way

на́ш [8] our, ours

найждам се / найм се (-яде́ш) [9] eat one's fill, gorge on

не [1] not ; не те́ е сра́м! [12] shame on you!

не́ [3] [5] no; *(contrastive negation)* ; не́ та́м [5] not there [but somewhere else]

небце́ [12] palate (roof of mouth)

не́го [10] him, it *(direct object pronoun)*

не́гов [8] his

неде́ля [6] Sunday

не́ин, не́йна [8] her, hers

непозна́т [5] unknown

непреме́нен [13] indispensable, necessary

непреме́нно [13] by all means

несвъ́ршен [12] incomplete, imperfect ; несвъ́ршен ви́д [12] imperfective aspect ; ми́нало несвъ́ршено вре́ме [14] imperfect tense

неспоко́ен [4] uneasy, restless

несравни́м [11] incomparable

нестина́р [11] fire-dancer

нестина́рство [11] fire-dancing, fire-walking

нетърпе́ние [8] impatience ; ча́кам с нетърпе́ние [8] await eagerly

неудо́бен [13] inconvenient, uncomfortable

нече́тен [11] odd-numbered

не́що [5] something

не́я [10] her *(direct object pronoun)*

ни [5] us *(direct object pronoun)*

ни [7] [to] us *(indirect object pronoun)*

ни [8] not, neither

ни ... ни [8] neither...nor

ни́ва [10] [corn]field

ни́е [1] we

ни́жа (-еш) [14] thread, string together

ни́как [8] not at all

ни́какъв [8] none, no kind of

ни́кога [8] never

ни́кой [8] no one

ни́кого [8] no one *(object)*

ни́къде [8] nowhere

ни́то [8] not, neither ; ни́то една́ ду́ма [8] not a single word

ни́що [8] nothing ; ни́що, че ня́ма [10] no matter that there isn't [any]

но [2] but

но́в [7] new ; Но́ва годи́на [10] New Year's

новина́ [5] [a piece of] news

новогоди́шен [11] New Year's *(adj.)* ; новогоди́шна честитка [11] New

Year's greeting ; новогоди́шна елха́ [13] New Year's tree
нога́ [12] leg (dialectal, poetic)
ное́мври [9] November
но́ж (plural ножо́ве) [7] knife
но́жче [13] [razor] blade
но́кът, но́кътят (plural но́кти) [8] nail (on finger or toe)
но́мер (plural номера́) [2] [3] number; size ; пра́вя номера́ на [8] play dirty tricks on
но́с, -ъ́т (plural носове́) [11] nose ; затва́рям врата́та под но́с [13] shut the door in [someone's] face
но́ся [3] carry; wear
но́щ, -та́ [9] night ; през нощта́ [9] at night ; та́зи но́щ [9] tonight
но́щен [9] night (adj.) ; но́щно вре́ме [9] nighttime
ну́жда [2] need ; ня́ма ну́жда [2] there's no need, it's not necessary ; и́маме ну́жда от въ́здух [4] we need air ; и́мате ну́жда от пре́глед [4] you need to be examined
ня́как [8] somehow
ня́какъв [8] some sort
ня́кога [8] sometime
ня́кой [8] someone
ня́колко [6] several
ня́къде [8] somewhere
ня́ма [2] there isn't/aren't any ; ня́ма ну́жда [2] there's no need, it's not necessary ; ня́ма мя́сто за па́ника [3] there's no need to worry ; ня́ма значе́ние [9] it doesn't matter ; ня́ма ни́що стра́шно [11] there's nothing to be afraid of
ня́ма да [7] won't (negative future particle) ; ня́маше да [16] wasn't/weren't going to
ня́мам [2] [3] not have

оба́ждам се / оба́дя се [10] [12] call, get in touch; come to the phone ; оба́ждам се по телефо́на [11] call on the phone ; мо́же ли да се оба́ди [12] can s/he come to the phone
оба́че [7] however
о́бед (or обя́д) [8] lunch
о́беден [9] lunch, noon (adjective) ; о́бедно вре́ме [9] lunch time
обеща́вам / обеща́я [10] promise
оби́да [14] insult ; пона́сям оби́да [14] bear/sustain an insult
обикнове́н [8] usual
обикнове́но [2] usually

оби́рам / обера́ [8] plunder, pick
обича́ен, -а́йна [14] customary
обича́й [13] custom, convention
оби́чам [2] [3] like, love
обле́чен, -ена [14] dressed
обли́чам / облека́ (-че́ш) [13] dress [someone]
обли́чам се / облека́ се (-че́ш) [13] put on, don ; обли́чам се спо́ртно [13] wear/put on casual clothing
образова́ние [3] education
обръ́щам се / объ́рна се [14] turn
обу́вам / обу́я [13] put someone's shoes, stockings, etc. on
обу́вам се / обу́я се [13] put on shoes, stockings, etc.
обу́вка [3] shoe
обу́ща [13] footwear
о́бщ [7] general, common
общество́ [12] society
обя́д [9] (see also о́бед) lunch, noon ; след обя́д [9] afternoon, after lunch
огладня́вам / огладне́я [4] get hungry
огледа́ло [11] mirror
огле́ждам / огле́дам [14] survey, examine
огле́ждам се / огле́дам се [14] look at one's reflection
о́гън (plural огньо́ве) [7] fire
оже́нвам / оже́ня [11] marry (transitive)
оже́нвам се / оже́ня се [11] get married
оки́чвам / оки́ча (-иш) [13] adorn, decorate
око́ (plural очи́) [12] eye
окто́мври [6] October
окъ́пвам се / окъ́пя се (-еш) [14] bathe
о́лио [6] cooking oil
оме́квам / оме́кна [11] soften, grow milder
омле́т [4] omelet
омръ́звам / омръ́зна [12] tire, bore ; омръ́зва ми [12] I'm bored
она́зи [8] that (feminine)
она́я [11] that (variant of она́зи)
оне́зи [8] those
о́нзи [8] that (masculine) ; о́нзи де́н [9] the day before yesterday
они́я [11] those (variant of оне́зи)
онова́ [8] that (neuter)
ону́й [11] that (variant of онова́)
о́ня [11] that (variant of о́нзи)
опа́сен [4] dangerous
опа́шка [11] tail; line, queue ; ча́кам на опа́шка [11] wait in/on line
о́пера [12] opera
опи́свам / опи́ша (-еш) [7] describe
опла́квам / опла́ча (-еш) [11] mourn, lament, weep ; жи́в да го опла́чеш

[11] it makes your heart bleed to see him

оплаквам се / оплача се (-еш) [11] complain, grumble

опознавам / опозная [7] recognize, get to know

опомням се / опомня се [12] come to [one's] senses ; опомни се! [12] snap out of it!

организирам [12] organize

орех [6] walnut

ориз [6] rice

освен [4] except [for]; in addition to ; освен това [4] besides, in addition

осем [6] eight

осемдесет [6] eighty

осемнайсет [6] eighteen

осемнайсети [8] eighteenth

осемстотин [9] eight hundred

осми [8] eighth

особен [10] special, particular

особено [8] especially

оставам / остана [3] [4] remain, stay ; остава още малко [3] there's still a little left

останал [9] remained; remaining, left, left-over

оставям / оставя [8] leave (transitive)

от [1] [4] [6] [8] from; of; since (time); than ; салата от зеле [4] cabbage salad ; имам нужда от [4] need, have need of ; от всички страни [6] from/on all sides ; от един час само [6] for only an hour ; от н.е. [9] A.D. ; от дете [12] since childhood ; от ваша страна [15] on your part

отбор [12] team

отварям / отворя [2] [3] [4] open

отворен, -ена [2] open

отвън [11] from outside

отвътре [9] from within

отговарям / отговоря [10] answer

отговор [7] answer

отгоре [11] from above

отдавна [6] long ago ; отдавна вече [6] for a long time now

отделен [3] separate

отделно [2] separately, under separate cover

отдолу [11] from below

отдясно [11] from the right

отзад [3] in back, in the rear, behind

отивам / отида [5] go

отказвам / откажа (-еш) [13] cancel, refuse

откакто [10] [ever] since

отколкото [10] than, in as much

открито [13] openly, above board, without hiding

откъде [1] whence, from where (interrogative)

отляво [11] from the left

отминавам / отмина [14] pass by, leave behind

отначало [14] at the beginning

отново [2] again, once more

отопление [11] heating

отпуска [2] break, time off, vacation ; в отпуска [2] on a break, on vacation

отпътувам [7] set off for, depart

отскоро [11] [since] quite recently ; женени сме съвсем отскоро [11] we've just gotten married

отстъпвам / отстъпя [8] step back, yield, give up

оттам [3] from there

оттука, оттук [5] from here

охлюв [14] snail shell

очаквам [7] await, expect

очи see око

очила (plural) [11] eyeglasses

още [2] still, yet ; още много [2] a lot more, still a lot ; още не говоря [3] but I don't/can't speak yet ; тя още не чете [3] she doesn't [know how to] read yet ; още не [5] not yet

падам / падна [7] fall ; пада голям сняг [7] it's snowing heavily

пазя [8] guard, preserve

пак [9] again

палец [12] thumb, big toe

палто [13] coat

паника [3] panic, worry ; няма място за паника [3] there's no need to worry

панталон (or панталони) [14] pants

папагал [9] parrot

пара [11] coin

парен [11] steam (adj.) ; парно отопление [11] central heating

пари [11] money ; пет пари не давам [14] I don't give a damn

партия [14] party

парцал [14] rag

пациент (ка) [4] [medical] patient

певец [10] singer

пейзаж [3] landscape, natural scene

пейка [3] bench

пека (-чеш) [13] bake, roast

пека се на слънце [13] sunbathe

пера [12] wash

перо́н [7] (railway) platform

пе́сен, -та́ (plural пе́сни) [9] song

пе́т [6] five ; пе́т пари́ не да́вам [14] I don't give a damn

пета́ [12] heel

петдесе́т [6] fifty

пети́ма [6] five (masculine animate)

пе́ти [8] fifth

пети́ца [10] "5" (next to top mark in school)

петна́йсет [6] fifteen

петно́ [14] spot

пе́тстотин [9] five hundred

пе́тък [9] Friday

пеша́ [9] on foot ; хо́дя пеша́ [9] go for a walk, walk (not ride)

пе́я [11] sing

пие́са [12] play (theater)

пи́пам / пи́пна [9] touch, handle

писа́тел (ка) [10] writer

пискю́л [13] tassel, pendant

писмо́ [8] letter

пи́там [4] ask

пи́ша (-еш) [3] write

пи́я [3] drink

пия́ница [10] drunkard

пла́ж [14] beach

пла́н [7] plan

планина́ [3] mountain

пла́ша (-иш) [9] frighten

пла́ша се (-иш) [11] be frightened, fear

пла́щам / пла́тя [4] pay

пле́менник [10] nephew

пле́менница [10] niece

пло́д (plural плодове́) [7] fruit

пло́ча [7] [13] tile, slab; phonograph record

пло́чка [3] tile

плу́вам [9] swim

по [3] [5] [7] each; along, down; according to, in the manner of; about ; ха́йде по една́ глъ́тка [3] let's each have a drink ; по коридо́ра [5] down the corridor ; преподава́тел по бъ́лгарски [5] teacher of Bulgarian ; по това́ вре́ме [7] at about that time

по́- [8] [10] more... (comparative degree particle) ; по́-ху́бав [8] nicer, prettier ; по́-голя́м [10] older ; по́-ма́лък [10] younger ; по́-ра́но [14] before, earlier; "used to..."

побъ́рзвам / побъ́рзам [7] hurry up

по́вече [7] more ; по́вечето [11] the majority

пови́квам / пови́кам [13] call, call out

по́вод [13] occasion, cause ; по по́вод [13] regarding, in connection with

повта́рям / повто́ря [12] repeat

повторе́ние [12] repeat, replay

повя́рвам [8] believe, give credence to

погле́ждам / погле́дна [14] have/take a look, look at ; погледни́ [14] look! look over there!

погово́рвам / поговоря́ [12] talk for a bit

погри́жвам се / погри́жа се (-иш) [11] take care of, look after

под [3] under, below ; затва́рям врата́та под но́с [13] shut the door in [someone's] face

по́д [4] floor

пода́вам / пода́м (-даде́ш) [11] hand, pass, reach

пода́рък [7] present, gift

подаря́вам / подаря́ [9] give (away), give a present

подго́твям / подго́твя [12] prepare, make ready

подгото́вка [5] preparation ; подгото́вката върви́ [5] the preparation's coming along

подна́сям / поднеса́ [6] present, offer, serve

подо́бен [8] similar ; ни́що подо́бно [8] nothing of the sort

подози́рам / подозра́ [14] suspect, be suspicious

подпи́рам / подпра́ [14] prop up, support ; подпи́рам си бради́чката [14] [sit] with chin in hand

подпра́вка [6] spice (cooking)

подро́бен [13] detailed

подро́бно [13] in detail

подсе́щам / подсе́тя [4] remind, call to mind ; това́ ме подсе́ща [4] that reminds me

подска́звам / подска́жа (-еш) [13] hint, prompt

пое́мам / пое́ма [8] take, take up ; пое́мам [си] дъ́х [8] catch one's breath

пожела́вам / пожела́я [8] wish ; пожела́вам от сърце́ [10] send heartfelt wishes

позволя́вам / позволя́ [6] allow

позвъня́вам / позвъня́ [9] call

по́здрав [2] greeting

позна́вам [3] know, be acquainted with

позна́вам / позна́я [1] [3] [7] know; guess ; позна́вам по очи́те [7] tell by [some]one's eyes ; позна́вам число́ [14] pick/guess a number

позна́йник [13] acquaintance

позна́йница [13] female acquaintance

позна́т [8] acquaintance

поигра́вам / поигра́я [10] play for a while

по́исквам / по́искам [12] want, wish, ask for

пока́звам / пока́жа (-еш) [7] show

пока́нвам / пока́ня [10] invite

покрай [10] because of

по́крив [3] roof

поле́ [15] field, plain ; софи́йското поле́ [15] the plain around Sofia

поле́зен [8] useful ; поле́зно за здра́вето [8] good for you [for one's health] ; мо́га ли с не́що да бъ́да поле́зен? [13] can I help in some way?

по́лза [12] use, advantage ; каква́ е по́лзата [12] what's the use

поли́вам / поле́я [13] pour ; ела́ да ти поле́я [13] let me pour water over your hands ; поли́вам цветя́та [13] water the flowers

полови́н(а) [6] half

полуно́щ [9] midnight

получа́вам / полу́ча (-иш) [8] receive, get

пома́гам / помо́гна [7] help

поми́слям / поми́сля [12] think about

помо́лвам / помо́ля [13] beg, ask

по́мня [13] remember

по́мощ, -та́ [9] help

понася́м / понеса́ [14] carry off; sustain, endure ; понася́м оби́да [14] bear/sustain an insult

поне́ [9] at least

понеде́лник [9] Monday

поня́кога [8] sometimes

попи́твам / попи́там [14] ask, inquire

попи́твам се / попи́там се [13] ask oneself, wonder

поприка́звам [11] have a chat

популя́рен [12] popular

попя́вам / попе́я [11] sing a little

поразхо́ждам / поразхо́дя [11] take for a brief stroll

пора́ствам / пора́сна [14] grow up

портока́л [10] orange

портока́лов [10] orange (adj.)

по́рция [7] portion, serving

поръ́чвам / поръ́чам [4] order

поса́ждам / посадя́ [8] seat, plant

посеща́вам / посетя́ [11] visit

по́сле [2] [6] later, afterwards; then

после́ден [6] last ; в после́дно вре́ме [6] lately ; чета́ до после́дната бу́ква [8] read every last word

посо́ка [6] direction ; пи́там за посо́ката [6] ask directions

посоля́вам / посоля́ [9] salt

посре́щам / посре́щна [5] meet, greet, entertain

по́ст [10] Lent; fast

по́стен [10] Lenten, pertaining to fasting

постоя́нен [10] constant

постоя́нно [10] constantly

постя́гам / посте́гна [11] tighten, fasten; prepare, fix up

поти́чам / потека́ (-че́ш) [12] start flowing

потъ́рсвам / потъ́рся [7] look for, seek

поча́квам / поча́кам [7] wait

по́чвам / по́чна [10] begin, start, commence

почэ́рпвам / почэ́рпя [6] treat someone to ; почэ́рпвам вси́чки с по две́ [6] treat everyone to two each

почи́вам / почи́на [3] [4] rest, go on holiday

почи́вам си / почи́на си [8] rest

почи́вен [8] rest (adj.) ; почи́вен де́н [8] day off, holiday

почи́вка [3] vacation trip, rest

почи́на [8] die

почи́там / почета́ [11] read for a bit

почти́ [8] almost

почу́вствувам (or почу́вствам) [14] have the feeling, realize, become aware

по́ща [3] mail, post office

по́щаджия, -ийка [10] letter carrier, postman

по́щенски [10] postal ; по́щенска кути́я [10] mailbox

появя́вам се / появя́ се [14] appear

пра́в [4] straight, upright ; стоя́ пра́в [4] stand, remain standing

пра́вило [12] rule ; правила́ на пъ́тното движе́ние [12] traffic laws, rules of the road

пра́во [12] [legal] right ; и́мам пра́во [12] have the right ; а́вторско пра́во [12] copyright ; права́та на живо́тните [12] animal rights

правосла́вен [8] Orthodox [religion] (adj.)

пра́вя [3] do, make ; пра́вя и́злет [3] go on an excursion ; пра́вя номера́ на [8] play dirty tricks on

пра́зен [6] empty

пра́зник [10] holiday; feast

празну́вам [10] celebrate

пра́щам / пра́тя [2] [3] [4] send

преброя́вам / преброя́ [6] count out

пре́вод [14] translation

пре́глед [4] examination (medical) ; и́мате ну́жда от пре́глед [4] you need to be examined

прегле́ждам / прегле́дам [8] examine

пре́ден [10] front, anterior

347

преди [6] ago

преди́ [6] before; previously ; преди́
н.е. [9] B.C. ; преди́ Р.Хр. [9]
B.C.

преди́ да [14] before (relative conjunction)

предизви́квам / предизви́кам [10]
provoke, defy; cause, evoke, induce

преди́мно [9] primarily

преди́шен [9] previous

предла́гам / предло́жа (-иш) [8] proffer,
propose

предложе́ние [9] proposition, suggestion

предпочи́там / предпочета́ [4] prefer

представи́телен [14] representative;
personable, distinguished

представя́м / предста́вя [13] present,
offer

представя́м си / предста́вя си [13]
imagine

предстоя́щ [9] forthcoming, impending

през [4] [8] [9] during; through; at intervals
; гле́дам през прозо́реца [6] look
out the window ; през се́дмица [8]
every other week ; през деня́ [9] in
the daytime ; през нощта́ [9] at
night

прекале́н [13] excessive, unconscionable ;
прекале́но голя́м [13] way too big

прека́рвам / прека́рам [7] spend

препи́свам / препи́ша (-еш) [13] rewrite,
copy

преподава́тел (ка) [1] teacher (university
level)

пре́сен, пря́сна [8] fresh

пресе́чка [11] intersection

прехвъ́рлям се / прехвъ́рля се [12]
transfer; shift

пре́ча (-иш) [8] bother

при [7] at, by

приби́рам / прибера́ [8] gather, collect

приби́рам се / прибера́ се [8] arrive
home

приближа́вам / приближа́ (-и́ш) [14]
approach

привли́чам / привлека́ (-че́ш) [9] attract,
draw

привъ́рзан [11] tied, bound, attached

приго́твям / приго́твя [10] prepare, make
ready

прие́мам / прие́ма [10] accept, adopt

прика́звам [9] talk, converse; say

при́казка [12] tale, story; chat, talking

приключе́ние [14] adventure

прили́чам [10] look like, resemble

приро́да [7] nature

присти́гам / присти́гна [6] arrive

притесня́вам / притесня́ [8] worry, cause
concern to, embarrass

притесня́вам се / притесня́ се [7]
worry ; не се́ притесня́вай [7] don't
worry

притъпя́вам / притъпя́ [14] blunt, dull ;
внима́нието му се притъпи́ [14] his
attention wandered

приче́ска [12] haircut, hair style

прия́тел (ка) [1] friend

прия́тен [9] pleasant

проверя́вам / проверя́ [13] check, verify,
test

програ́ма [8] program

прода́вам / прода́м (-даде́ш) [6] sell

продава́ч (ка) [7] salesperson

продължа́вам / продължа́ (-и́ш) [5]
continue

прозо́рец (plural прозо́рци) [3] window

прозо́рче [13] small window

про́лет, -та́ [9] spring

проле́тен [13] spring (adj.) ; проле́тно
равноде́нствие [13] vernal equinox

проме́ням / променя́ [11] change, alter

проме́ням се / променя́ се [11] change

промя́на (plural проме́ни) [13] change

пропаст, -та́ [11] abyss, cavern

пропу́скам / пропу́сна [10] skip, let pass;
miss

прости́рам / простра́ [12] stretch out ;
прости́рам дре́хи [12] hang clothes
out to dry

просту́да [2] cold (illness)

профе́сор [13] professor

прохла́ден [15] cool

прочи́там / прочета́ [5] read (to
completion)

проявя́вам / проявя́ [8] appear, show ;
проявя́вам интере́с към [8] take an
interest in

пръст (plural пръ́сти) [12] finger, toe

пря́сна see пре́сен

пти́ца [7] bird

пу́блика [10] public

пу́канка (singular rare) [9] popcorn

пу́скам / пу́сна [10] let, allow; drop ;
пу́скам писмо́ [10] mail a letter

пуст [10] empty; wretched, damned

пу́ша (-иш) [4] smoke

пу́шене [4] smoking

пък [11] but, yet, and, while

пъ́лен [5] full; plump ; пъ́лно ко́пие
[14] exact replica

пъ́лня [6] fill

първенство́ [10] championship

пъ́рви [4] first

пъ́ржа (-иш) [6] fry

пъ́ржен, -ена [14] fried ; пъ́ржени
фили́йки [14] French toast

пържо́ла [4] chop, steak ; пържо́ла с
гарни́тура [4] steak with the
trimmings

пъстъ́рва [9] trout

път (*plural* пъти) [4] [6] time *(instance)* ;
за пъ́рви път съм ту́ка [4] this is the
first time I've been here

път, -ят (*plural* пъ́тища) [6] [8] way,
path, road ; дъ́лъг път [6] a long
way [to go] ; и́мам 6 ча́са път [6]
have 6 hours to go ; по пъ́тя [8]
along the way

пъте́ка [11] [foot]path

пъ́тен [12] road *(adj.)*, traveling ;
правила́ на пъ́тното движе́ние [12]
traffic laws, rules of the road

пътеше́ствие [11] trip

пъ́тник [7] traveler

пъту́вам [1] [3] travel

пъту́ване [7] travels, trip

ра́бота [2] [11] work, job ; на ра́бота
съм [4] be at work ; ще свъ́рши
ра́бота [11] it'll do the job ; и́мам
си ра́бота [14] have things to do

рабо́тен [6] work *(adj.)* ; рабо́тно
вре́ме [6] office hours, hours of
operation

работоспосо́бен [9] efficient, productive

рабо́тя [4] [11] work, be in operation ;
какво́ рабо́тите? [5] what [kind of]
work do you do? ; не рабо́ти [11]
it's out of order

ра́вен [15] even, flat; equal

равни́ще [15] level, standard, plain ;
мо́рското равни́ще [15] sea level

равноде́нствие [13] equinox

ра́двам се [5] rejoice, be happy

ра́дио [14] radio ; съобща́вам по
ра́диото [14] announce on the radio

ра́дост [10] joy, pleasure

ра́достен [5] happy, joyful

ра́ждам / родя́ [10] bear, give birth to, be
fruitful

разби́рам / разбера́ [1] [3] [4] understand

разби́рам се / разбера́ се [12] come to an
understanding, agree ; разби́ра се [3]
of course

разби́ране [12] understanding ; широ́ко
разби́ране [12] liberal interpretation

развале́н [11] spoiled, rotten

развлече́ние [12] amusement

разгле́ждам / разгле́дам [4] examine,
study

разгова́рям [10] converse

разда́вам / разда́м (-даде́ш) [8] give out,
distribute

ра́зказ [14] story

разка́звам / разка́жа (-еш) [8] relate, tell

разли́чен [10] different, various ; най-
разли́чни неща́ [10] all sorts of
things

размина́вам се / разми́на се [15] pass
each other, blow over

разпла́квам се / разпла́ча се (-еш) [14]
burst into tears

разпозна́вам / разпозна́я [8] distinguish,
discern

разпра́вям / разпра́вя [12] tell, relate ;
разпра́вям ви́ц [12] tell a joke

разреше́ние [13] permission

разсми́вам се / разсмея́ се [14] burst out
laughing

разсъ́рдвам се / разсъ́рдя се [14] get
angry

разу́мен [13] sensible, rational

разхо́дка [9] walk, stroll ; изве́ждам
ку́чето на разхо́дка [9] walk the
dog ; разхо́дка из града́ [11] city
tour

разхо́ждам / разхо́дя [10] take for a walk

разхо́ждам се / разхо́дя се [8] walk
around, take a walk

разчи́там [12] rely on, count [on] ;
мо́жеш да разчи́таш на ме́не [12]
you can count on me

раки́я [2] rakia (strong brandy from fruits)

ра́мо (*plural* рамена́ *or* рамене́) [12]
shoulder

ра́нен [13] early

ра́но [9] early ; ра́но-ра́но [14] very
early ; по́-ра́но [14] before, earlier;
"used to..."

реванши́рам се [5] make up, return a
favor ; с не́що да се реванши́рам [5]
make [it] up with/by doing something

реве́р [13] lapel

ревю́ *(neuter)* [13] revue, show ; мо́дно
ревю́ [13] fashion show

ре́дки *see* ря́дък

редо́вен [13] regular; in order

редо́вно [13] at regular intervals, regularly

редя́ [12] arrange, put in order ; редя́ се
на опа́шка [12] get/wait in line

ре́жа (-еш) [12] cut, slice

режисьо́р [12] director

река́ (-че́ш) [7] say, utter

река́ [9] river

ремонти́рам [2] redo, make repairs

репу́блика [14] republic

рестора́нт [4] restaurant

реце́пта [6] recipe

ре́чник [7] dictionary

ре́ша (-еш) [13] comb

реша́вам, реша́ (-и́ш) [8] [11] solve; decide ; реша́вам кръстосло́вица [8] do a crossword puzzle ; твъ́рдо реша́вам [11] firmly resolve

ри́ба [9] fish ; ловя́ ри́ба [9] fish, catch fish ; хо́дя за ри́ба [9] go fishing

ри́за [13] shirt, chemise

ри́лски [8] Rila (adj.)

рису́вам [3] draw

рису́нка [3] drawing

ро́ден [11] one's own, native ; ро́дно мя́сто [11] birthplace

роди́тел [9] parent

роднина́ [10] relative

родя́ see ра́ждам

рожде́н [5] birth (adj.) ; рожде́н де́н [5] birthday

рождество́ [9] Christmas ; Рождество́ Христо́во [9] Christmas ; преди́ Р.Хр. [9] B.C. ; след Р.Хр. [9] A.D.

ро́кля [12] dress

рома́н [3] novel

ръка́ (plural ръце́) [12] hand, arm

ръкави́ца [9] glove

ря́дък, ре́дки [10] rare

ря́дко [10] rarely

с [2] [9] with; by ; пъту́вам с вла́к [2] travel by train ; с вси́чки си́ли [9] with all one's strength, full tilt ; с една́ ду́ма [9] in a word ; с часове́ [9] for hours (on end) ; с ма́лко закъсне́ние [14] a little late

са [1] are (3rd plural) ; see съм

сако́ [13] jacket

сала́м [11] sausage

сала́та [4] salad

са́м, сама́, само́, сами́ [12] alone, [the] very, by oneself ; сами́ят а́з [12] I myself

са́мо [1] only

самоле́т [11] airplane

са́ндвич [9] sandwich

сарми́ [6] stuffed cabbage or vine leaves

са́тира [5] satire

СА́Щ = Съедине́ните америка́нски ща́ти [1] USA (United States of America)

сбо́рник [12] collection

сваря́вам / сваря́ [5] cook, boil

сва́т (or сва́тя) [10] in-law

сва́тба [10] wedding

сва́тбен, -ена [11] wedding (adj.) ; сва́тбено пътеше́ствие [11] honeymoon

све́кър [10] father-in-law (to bride)

свекъ́рва [9] mother-in-law (to bride)

свето́вен [10] world (adj.)

све́тъл [10] light (adj.)

сви́вам / сви́я [13] bend, fold, roll ; сви́вам гнездо́ [13] build a nest

сви́квам / сви́кна [15] get used to, grow accustomed to

свобода́ [7] freedom

свобо́ден [2] free ; мя́стото е свобо́дно [2] the seat is not taken ; свобо́ден съм сега́ [2] I'm free [not busy] now

сво́й [10] own (adj.)

свъ́ршвам / свъ́рша (-иш) [6] complete, finish ; ще свъ́рши ра́бота [11] it'll do the job

свъ́ршен, -ена [12] complete, perfect ; ми́нало свъ́ршено вре́ме [12] aorist tense ; свъ́ршен ви́д [12] perfective aspect

сго́твям / сго́твя [5] cook, make

СДС (pron. седесе́) [14] SDS (UDF, Union of Democratic Forces)

се [1] verbal particle

се [5] oneself (direct object pronoun)

се [7] oneself, themselves, itself, etc.

се́бе си [11] oneself (reflexive object form)

сега́ [1] now ; сега́ изли́зам [4] I'll go out right away

сега́шен [9] present-day, current ; сега́шно вре́ме [9] present tense

се́дем [2] seven

седемдесе́т [6] seventy

седемна́йсет [6] seventeen

се́демстотин [9] seven hundred

се́дми [8] seventh

се́дмица [6] week

се́дна see ся́дам

седя́ [4] sit, be seated ; седя́ на тече́ние [4] sit in a drafty place

сека́ (-че́ш) [9] cut

секрета́р (ка) [1] secretary

се́ло [2] village

семе́ен [10] family, domestic ; те́сен семе́ен кръг [10] immediate family

семе́йство [11] family

септе́мври [5] September

серви́рам [4] serve, have available ; не зна́м какво́ серви́рат ту́ка [4] I don't know what they have here

сервитьо́р (ка) [4] waiter

сестра́ [10] sister

се́щам се / се́тя се [11] recall, come to mind, think of, remember

си [1] are (2nd singular); see съм

си [5] [7] to oneself *(indirect object pronoun)* ; ка́звам си [5] say to oneself
си́гурен [6] sure, certain
си́гурно [9] surely, certainly
си́ла [7] strength, force
си́лен [2] strong ; и́ма си́лен вя́тър [2] it's very windy, there's a strong wind ; валя́т си́лни дъждове́ [12] it's raining heavily
син (си́ня, си́ньо, си́ни) [8] blue
син, -ъ́т (*plural* синове́) [9] son
си́рене [7] white cheese
скала́ [14] rock, cliff
ска́чам / ско́ча (-иш) [9] jump
ско́ро [1] soon
ско́рост [19] speed
ско́ча *see* ска́чам
скри́вам / скри́я [13] hide
ску́чен [13] boring
скъ́сан [14] torn
слаб [14] weak, thin
сла́ва [9] glory ; сла́ва Бо́гу [9] thank God
сла́гам / сло́жа (-иш) [4] put ; сла́гам да ле́гне [5] put [someone] to bed
сладоле́д [6] ice cream
сладка́рница [14] sweet shop
сла́дко [3] thick sweet preserves
сла́дък [3] sweet
след [6] after ; след 15 мину́ти [6] in 15 minutes ; след обя́д [9] afternoon, after lunch ; след Р.Хр. [9] A.D.
сле́д като [14] after *(relative conjunction)*
сле́дващ [8] next, following
следо́бед [4] afternoon ; следо́бед съм на ра́бота [4] I have to work this afternoon
следо́беден [9] afternoon *(adj.)*
сли́вица [12] tonsil
сли́зам / сля́за [7] get off, go down, descend
сло́жен [5] difficult, complex
слу́жба [14] service, position ; в слу́жбата [14] at work
случа́ен, -айна [12] accidental, chance
случа́йно [12] by chance, accidentally
слу́чай [12] instance; chance ; в такъ́в слу́чай [12] in that case
слу́шам [4] listen, obey
слъ́нце [9] sun ; слъ́нцето гре́е [9] the sun is shining
слъ́нчев [10] sunny
сме [1] are *(1st plural)* ; *see* съм
сме́ням / сменя́ [3] [4] change, replace
сме́шен [13] funny, humorous
смея́ се [13] laugh

сми́съл [11] sense, meaning ; и́ма сми́съл [11] it makes sense
смуща́вам се / смутя́ се [13] get confused, be embarrassed
смъ́ртен [4] mortal
смя́там / сме́тна [13] reckon, count; смя́там (за) [13] consider (to be)
смях, смехъ́т (*plural* смехове́) [11] laughter ; уми́рам от смя́х [11] burst one's sides/die laughing
снегове́ [7] *see* сня́г
сне́жен [11] snow *(adj.)* ; сне́жен чове́к [11] snowman
снежи́нка [10] snowflake
сни́мка [6] photograph
сно́щен [9] last night's
сно́щи [9] yesterday evening, last night
сня́г, снегъ́т (*plural* снегове́) [3] [7] snow ; бя́л като сня́г [3] white as snow
со́бствен, -ена [12] one's own ; ви́ждам със со́бствените си очи́ [12] see with one's own eyes
со́к [7] juice
со́л, -та́ [9] salt
соле́н [9] salted
солни́ца [9] salt shaker
софи́йски [8] of Sofia ; софи́йското поле́ [15] the plain around Sofia
софия́нец [14] Sofia resident (male)
софия́нка [14] Sofia resident (female)
социалисти́чески [14] socialist
специа́лен [9] special
спече́лвам / спече́ля [14] win, gain, earn
спи́рам / спра́ [11] stop
спи́рка [7] bus/tram stop ; на дру́гата спи́рка [7] at the next stop
списа́ние [8] magazine, journal
спо́мням си / спо́мня си [8] recall
спо́ртен [9] sports *(adj.)*
спо́ря [13] dispute, contend ; не спори́ [13] don't argue
спя́ [4] sleep
срам, -ъ́т (*plural* сра́мове *or* срамове́) [12] shame, modesty ; срам ме е [12] I'm ashamed, I'm too shy ; не те́ е срам! [12] you should be ashamed ; ка́к не те́ е срам [12] shame on you
среда́ [2] middle
сре́ден [3] middle *(adj.)*
сре́дище [9] center
средновеко́вен [9] medieval
средновеко́вие [8] Middle Ages
сре́ща [9] meeting, appointment
сре́щам / сре́щна [10] meet
срещу́ [12] against, opposite; across from
сря́да [9] Wednesday

ста́вам / ста́на   [1] [4] [10]   get up, stand up; become, happen; be ;   ста́ва тече́ние [1]   there's a draft ;   ста́ваме мно́го [10]   there gets to be a lot of us ;   синъ́т им ста́на на че́тири   [10]   their son has turned four ;   ще ти ста́не то́пло   [11]   you'll be/get [too] hot ;   за какво́ ста́ва ду́ма?   [11]   what's it about? ;   ста́на ми мъ́чно   [13]   I had a hard time

стадио́н   [12]   stadium

ста́р   [7]   old ;   добро́то ста́ро вре́ме [11]   the good old days

ста́я   [9]   room

сте   [1]   are (2nd plural) ;   see съм

сти́га   [3]   enough, that's enough ;   сти́га с то́зи прозо́рец   [3]   enough about that window ;   сти́га то́лкова   [10]   that's enough

сти́гам / сти́гна   [13]   reach, arrive at

стихотворе́ние   [3]   poem

сто́   [5]   (a) hundred

сто́ка   [9]   goods, commodity

стома́х   [12]   stomach

сто́л   [4]   chair

сто́п   [10]   stop-sign, hitchhiking

сто́паджия, -ийка   [10]   hitchhiker

стоя́   [4] [11]   stand, be standing; stay (in one place) ;   стоя́ пра́в   [4]   stand, remain standing

страна́   [6] [7] [15]   side; country; part ;   от вси́чки страни́   [6]   from/on all sides ;   от ва́ша страна́   [15]   on your part

страни́ца   [3]   page

страхо́тен   [5]   horrible, dreadful, terrifying ;   страхо́тна иде́я   [5]   [a] terrific idea

стра́х, -ъ́т (plural страхове́)   [12]   fear, dread ;   стра́х ме е (от)   [12]   I'm afraid (of)

страху́вам се   [14]   fear, be afraid of

стра́шен   [9]   terrible, fearful ;   ня́ма ни́що стра́шно   [11]   there's nothing to be afraid of

стру́вам   [4]   cost ;   това́ ко́лко стру́ва? [4]   how much does this cost? ;   ко́лко стру́ва?   [4]   how much is it?

стря́скам / стре́сна   [11]   startle, scare

стря́скам се / стре́сна се   [11]   be startled, take fright

сту́д, -ъ́т (plural студове́)   [7]   cold, chill

студе́н   [4]   cold

студенина́   cold, frigidity

студе́нт (ка)   [1]   university student

стъ́лба   [11]   step, ladder ;   ка́чвам се по стъ́лбите   [11]   climb the stairs

стъпа́ло   [12]   sole (of the foot)

сурвака́р   [10]   survakar (New Year's wassailer)

суро́в   [11]   severe

су́трин, -та́   [9]   morning ;   су́трин, сутринта́   [9]   in the morning ;   у́тре сутринта́   [9]   tomorrow morning

суше́н   [10]   dried

счу́пен, -ена   [11]   broken

съби́рам / събера́   [3] [4]   gather, collect

събли́чам / съблека́ (-че́ш)   [13]   undress [someone]

събли́чам се / съблека́ се (-че́ш)   [13] undress, get undressed

съ́бота   [8]   Saturday

събу́вам / събу́я   [13]   take [something] off [someone's] foot

събу́вам се / събу́я се   [13]   take [something] off one's foot

събу́ждам / събу́дя   [11]   wake

събу́ждам се / събу́дя се   [11]   wake up, awaken

съве́т   [10]   advice

съве́твам   [5]   advise

съвпа́дам / съвпа́дна   [10]   coincide, concur

съвсе́м   [5]   completely ;   съвсе́м навре́ме [5]   at exactly the right moment ;   же́нени сме съвсе́м отско́ро   [11] we've just gotten married

съгла́сен   [12]   in agreement

съжале́ние   [1]   pity ;   за съжале́ние [1]   unfortunately

съжаля́вам / съжаля́   [8]   regret, be sorry

съкро́вище   [13]   treasure

сълза́ (plural сълзи́ or сълзи́)   [12]   tear (from the eye)

съм   [1]   am (1st singular); to be (citation form)

съ́н (plural съ́нища)   [8]   dream

съ́н, -я́т   [8]   sleep

съну́вам   [6]   dream ;   съну́вам кошма́ри [6]   have nightmares

съобща́вам / съобщя́   [5]   announce, inform

съобще́ние   [5]   announcement ;   съобще́ние за коле́т   [5]   postal notice (for a package)

съпру́г, съпру́га   [3] [10]   spouse

сърби́ (3rd person only)   [12]   itch

сърде́чен   [2]   hearty

сърна́   [8]   deer, doe

сърце́   [10]   heart ;   пожела́вам от сърце́ [10]   send heartfelt wishes

със = с   [7]   with

съсе́д (ка)   [5]   neighbor

състоя́ се   [14]   consist of; take place

съ́щ   [3]   same ;   съ́щото   [4]   the same thing

също [1] also
съюз [14] union
сядам / седна [4] sit down, take a seat ;
    седнете, господине! [4] have a seat,
    sir!

та [13] and; so that
тази [3] this (feminine)
така [4] that way, like that ; как така
    [11] how is it that; how can that be
такси (neuter) [14] taxi
такъв (такава, такова, такива) [11]
    such ; такива неща [11] such
    things
там [4] there
таралеж [9] hedgehog
таратор [6] yogurt and cucumber soup
татко (plural татковци) [10] Dad
тача (-иш) [13] respect
тая [11] this (variant of тази)
твой [8] your, yours (singular)
твърд [11] hard, firm, steadfast
твърдо [11] firmly, staunchly ; твърдо
    решавам [11] firmly resolve
те [5] you (direct object pronoun)
те [1] they
театър (plural театри) [6] theater
тебе [10] you (direct object pronoun)
тежък [2] heavy
тези [3] these
тека (-чеш) [9] flow
телевизия [6] television
телефон [5] telephone ; на телефона
    съм [5] be [talking] on the phone
телефонен [13] telephone (adj.)
тенджера [6] (cooking) pot
тенис [13] tennis
тесен, тясна [2] tight, cramped, narrow ;
    тесен семеен кръг [10] immediate
    family
тетрадка [7] notebook
техен, тяхна [8] their, theirs
техника [12] technology
техникум [3] technical high school
течение [1] current, draft ; става
    течение [1] there's a draft
ти [1] you (singular, familiar)
ти [7] [to] you (indirect object pronoun)
тип [7] type
типичен [3] typical
тичам [8] run
тия [11] these (variant of тези)
то [11] then (particle) ; и то [11] at
    that
то [1] it (rarely, he or she)

това [2] [3] this (neuter) ; това не е
    ли шише? [2] isn't that a bottle? ;
    това е [13] that's that
тогава [4] then, in that case; at that
    point ; пий една бира тогава [4]
    have a beer, then
този [3] this (masculine)
той [1] he, it
току-що [14] just now
толкова (or толкоз) [4] so much, so
    many, to such a degree
топка [8] ball
топъл [2] warm
торба [11] bag, sack
тото [14] lottery, pool
точен [6] exact, precise
точно [6] [12] just, exactly
тоя [11] this (variant of този)
тракам [13] rattle
трамваен, -айна [7] tram (adj.)
трамвай [2] tram
треса [12] shake ; тресе ме [12]
    I've got the shakes; I've got a fever
трети [8] third
третирам [8] treat
три [2] three
трийсет (or тридесет) [6] thirty
трима [6] three (masculine animate)
тринайсет [6] thirteen
триста [9] three hundred
тротоар [14] sidewalk
труден [5] difficult
тръгвам / тръгна [1] [4] set out, leave ;
    тръгвам на училище [5] start school
трябва (3rd person only) [12] must,
    should ; той трябва да дойде [12]
    he needs to come
трябвам [12] be necessary to ; трябва
    му адвокат [12] he needs a lawyer
туй [11] this (variant form of това)
тук (or тука) [2] here (location)
турист [8] tourist
турци [6] Turks (plural of турчин)
туршия [10] pickles; pickled vegetables
тъй [11] thus (variant of така)
тъкмо [10] just, exactly; only ; тъкмо
    сега [10] just this minute
търговец [9] merchant
търпелив [3] patient (adj.)
търся [7] seek, look for
тъст [10] father-in-law (to husband)
тъща [10] mother-in-law (to husband)
тя [1] she, it
тях [10] them (direct object pronoun)

353

у [10] at the home of ; у дома́ [10] at home, at one's house

убежда́вам / убедя́ [11] persuade ; убежда́вам [14] try to convince

убедя́ [14] succeed in convincing

удо́бен [11] convenient, comfortable

у́жас [14] horror

ужа́сен [12] terrible

у́лица [3] street

у́мен [10] smart, intelligent

уми́рам / умра́ [11] die ; уми́рам от смя́х [11] die laughing, die from laughter

уморе́н [8] tired

уморя́вам се / уморя́ се [12] get tired, become exhausted

университе́т [7] university

университе́тски [12] university (adj.)

уре́ждам / уредя́ [9] arrange, settle

уро́к [5] lesson

уси́лено [3] intensively

успе́х [5] success ; успе́х на и́зпита [5] good luck on the test

успя́вам / успе́я [8] succeed, manage to

уста́ [12] mouth

у́стна [12] lip

устро́йвам / устроя́ [13] arrange, organize

у́тре [4] tomorrow ; у́тре ве́чер [9] tomorrow evening ; у́тре сутринта́ [9] tomorrow morning

у́трешен [9] tomorrow's

у́тринен [9] morning (adj.)

у́тро [9] morning ; добро́ у́тро [9] good morning

ухо́ (plural уши́) [12] ear

у́ча (-иш) [5] learn, teach

уче́бник [2] textbook, manual

учени́к [7] student, pupil

учени́чка [7] female student or pupil

учи́лище (plural учи́лища) [5] [6] school ; тръ́гвам на учи́лище [5] start school

учи́лищен [10] school (adj.) ; учи́лищен звъне́ц [10] school bell

учи́тел (ка) [1] teacher (up to 12th grade)

уши́ see ухо́

фане́лка (or флане́лка) [14] sweatshirt, T-shirt

февруа́ри [9] February

фестива́л [5] festival

фили́йка [14] little slice ; пъ́ржени фили́йки [14] French toast

филия́ [14] slice

филм (plural фи́лми) [8] film, movie

флане́лка see фане́лка

фотоапара́т [5] camera

фуро́р [13] furor ; предизви́квам фуро́р [13] cause a ruckus

фу́тбол [10] soccer

хазя́йка [15] landlady

ха́йде [3] come on, let's ; ха́йде по една́ глъ́тка! [3] [come on,] let's each have a drink! ; ха́йде да се чу́кнем [11] let's have a toast

ха́мстер [9] hamster

ха́пвам / ха́пна [15] eat, have a bite

харе́свам / харе́сам [7] [12] like

хартия́ [8] paper

хва́щам / хва́на [9] grasp, seize, catch

хе́м (хем ... хем) [12] and; both... and...; not only..., but...

хиля́да (plural хи́ляди) [9] thousand

хлади́лник [7] refrigerator

хлапа́к [14] kid ; но се появи́ о́нзи хлапа́к [14] and then this kid appeared

хляб [5] bread ; иди́ за хля́б! [5] go buy some bread!

хо́дя [6] go ; хо́дя на ки́но [6] go to the movies ; хо́дя на учи́лище [6] go to school ; хо́дя за ри́ба [9] go fishing ; хо́дя пеша́ [9] go on foot, walk (not ride) ; хо́дя бо́с [13] go barefoot

хо́ра [4] people

хоте́л [9] hotel

хра́ня [8] feed, nourish

христо́в [9] Christ's ; Рождество́ Христо́во [9] Christmas ; преди́ Р.Хр. [9] B.C.

ху́бав [2] fine, nice, beautiful, pretty ; вси́чко ху́баво [2] all the best

хубави́ца [5] beauty

ху́мор [5] humor

ца́р, -я́т (plural царе́) [8] tsar, emperor

цве́те (plural цветя́) [6] flower

цве́тен [3] colored

целу́вам / целу́на [5] kiss

цена́ [12] price ; на вся́ка цена́ [12] at any price, at all costs, absolutely

центра́лен [12] central

це́нтър (plural це́нтрове) [7] center

цига́ра [4] cigarette

цирк [6] circus

цъ́рква [3] church

цъфтя́ [9] bloom

цял, це́ли [7] whole, entire

ч. = часъ́т, часа́ [9]
чадъ́р (*plural* чадъ́ри) [12] umbrella
ча́ен, ча́ена (*or* ча́йна) [7] tea (*adj.*)
ча́й (*plural* ча́еве) [7] tea
ча́йник [7] teapot
чака́лня [15] waiting room
ча́кам [3] await, wait, wait for
ча́нта [2] bag, briefcase
ча́с, -ъ́т, 2 ча́са (*plural* часове́) [6] [7]
  hour; class ; ко́лко е часъ́т? [6]
  what time is it? ; в ко́лко часа́? [6]
  at what time? ; в 1 ч. [6] at 1:00
часо́вник [7] watch, clock
ча́ша [3] glass, cup
че [3] that (*subordinate conjunction*)
че́йндж [10] currency exchange office
че́йнчаджия, -ийка [10] unofficial money
  changer
че́ло (*or* чело́) [12] forehead
червен [3] red
черво́ [12] intestine
че́рен [11] black ; че́рен дро́б [12]
  liver
чере́ша [12] cherry
че́рпя [4] treat ; у́тре че́рпя а́з [4]
  it's my treat tomorrow
че́ст [3] frequent
че́стен [12] honorable, honest ; че́стна
  ду́ма [12] word of honor
чести́т [10] happy (*in greeting*) ;
  чести́то [11] congratulations! ;
  чести́та Но́ва Годи́на [10] happy
  New Year ; чести́т пра́зник [11]
  happy holiday ; чести́т рожде́н де́н
  [11] happy birthday
чести́тка [10] greeting card
че́сто [3] often
че́сън [6] garlic
чета́ [3] read
че́твърт, -та́ [11] quarter
четвъ́рти [8] fourth
четвъ́ртък [9] Thursday
че́тен [11] even-numbered
че́тири [6] four
чети́ридесет *or* четири́йсет [6] forty
четирина́йсет [6] fourteen
четири́ма [6] four (*masculine animate*)
че́тиристотин [9] four hundred
чи́й, чия́, чие́, чий [8] whose
  (*interrogative*)
число́ [14] number ; позна́вам число́
  [14] pick/guess a number
чи́ст [4] clean, pure
чи́чко [6] uncle (*diminutive*)
чи́чо (*plural* чи́човци) [10] uncle (father's
  brother)
чове́к [4] man, person
чове́че [13] dwarf

чу́вам / чу́я [10] hear, listen
чу́вствувам се (*or* чу́вствам се) [13] feel
чуде́сен [2] marvelous, wonderful
чу́дя се [5] wonder
чужби́на [12] abroad ; вси́чки са по
  чужби́на [12] they've all gone abroad
чу́жд [8] foreign, alien
чужде́нец [3] foreigner, stranger
чужде́нка́ [3] foreigner, stranger (female)
чу́квам / чу́кна [11] knock, clink (once) ;
  чу́кам на дърво́ [11] knock on wood
чу́кам се / чу́кна се [11] clink glasses,
  toast to ; ха́йде да се чу́кнем [11]
  let's have a toast
чу́шка [6] pepper (vegetable)

шампа́нско [11] champagne
ша́пка [5] hat
шейсе́т (*or* шестдесе́т) [6] sixty
ше́ст [6] six
ше́ствие [12] procession, train
шестдесе́т *or* шейсе́т [6] sixty
ше́сти [8] sixth
шести́ма [6] six (*masculine animate*)
шести́ца [10] "6" (top mark in school)
шестна́йсет [6] sixteen
ше́стстотин [9] six hundred
ше́там [10] do housework; be active
широ́к [12] wide, broad ; широ́ко
  разби́ране [12] liberal interpretation
шише́ [2] bottle
ши́я [12] neck
шка́ф [6] cupboard
шно́ркел [14] snorkel
шокола́д [5] chocolate
шо́пски [4] of the "Shope" area near
  Sofia ; шо́пска сала́та [4] "Shope
  salad"
шу́м [6] noise ; вди́гам шу́м [6]
  make noise
шу́мен [10] noisy
шу́нка [4] ham ; омле́т с шу́нка [4]
  ham omelet

ща́ [7] want ; ще́ не ще́ [7] whether
  one wants or not
ща́т [1] state ; Ща́тите [1] the States
щастли́в [12] happy
ще [7] will (*future particle*)
що́ [8] what
що́м [11] as soon as, since, as, if, once
щъ́ркел [13] stork

ъгъл (*plural* ъгли) [14] corner ; зад
    ъгъла [14] around the corner

юг [13] south
юли [2] July
юмрук [12] fist
юни [9] June

я [5] her (*object pronoun*)
я [6] (*imperative particle*) ; я направете
    място [6] come on, make space
ябълка [6] apple
явен [11] open, obvious
явно [11] clearly
ягода [11] strawberry
яд [12] anger ; яд ме е (на) [12] I'm
    angry (at)
ядене [9] food, meal; dish
яйце (*plural* яйца) [11] egg
яке [13] jacket
ям (ядеш) [9] eat
януари [8] January
ясен [11] clear ; ясно ми е [11]
    I get it, it's clear

CUMULATIVE GLOSSARY

(PART 2)

English - Bulgarian

The following pages contain a brief English-Bulgarian glossary. All words contained in the lesson glossaries are to be found here, indexed to the lesson in which the word appears in a glossary listing. Very few idioms are included in this glossary, however.

Grammatical information in this listing is likewise limited: only the part of speech is denoted (noun, verb, adjective and the like). Information necessary for correct usage in Bulgarian (conjugation type, plural formation, gender, etc.) is found in the Bulgarian-English glossary and in the lessons themselves. The purpose of this glossary is to aid the student in locating the section of the textbook where the word in question is introduced.

Neither of the two glossaries in this book is meant to function as a dictionary, as they are limited only to words used in volume 1 of this textbook (in very exceptional cases, words introduced in volume 2 of this textbook have been included). Students should acquire a standard dictionary as soon as they are able, and learn to use it.

A.D. от н.е. [9] ; след Р.Хр. [9]

abdomen корем [12]

abroad чужбина [12]

about по [7] ; наоколо [9] ; за [10]

above над [15] ; (from) above отгоре [11]

absolutely [at all costs] на всяка цена [12] ; [by all means] непременно [13]

abyss пропаст [11]

accept приемам / приема [10]

accidental случаен [12]

accompany изпращам / изпратя [8]

according to по [5]

acquaint with запознавам / запозная [14]

acquaintance познат [8] ; познайник, познайница [13]

across from срещу [12]

actor актьор [14]

addition допълнение [8]

address (n.) адрес [9]

adorn окичвам / окича [13]

adult възрастен [4] ; adults големите [4]

advantage полза [12]

adventure приключение [14]

advice съвет [10]

advise съветвам [5]

aerobics аеробика [8]

after след [6] ; след като [14]

afternoon следобед [4]

afternoon (adj.) следобеден [9]

afterwards после [2]

again отново [2] ; пак [9]

against срещу [12]

ago преди [6]

agree разбирам се / разбера се [12] ; in agreement съгласен [12]

aha аха [5]

ahead напред [14]

air въздух [4]

airplane самолет [11]

album албум [9]

alcohol алкохол [2]

alien чужд [8]

alive жив [11]

all, in all всичко [2] [6] ; all the best всичко хубаво [2] ; all sorts (of things) най-различни (неща) [10]

allow позволявам / позволя [6] ; пускам / пусна [10]

almost почти [8]

alone сам, сама, само, сами [12]

along по [5]

already вече [3]

also и [1] ; също [1]

although макар че [14]

always винаги [4] ; все [10]

am съм [1]

amazing изумителен [13]

American [person] американец [3] ; американка [3]

American (adj.) американски [8]

among между [12]

amusement развлечение [12]

amusing забавен [11]

and а [1] ; и [1] ; пък [11] ; та [13]

anger яд [12]

animal животно [8] ; small animal животинче [13]

animal rights правата на животните [12]

ankle глезен [12]

anniversary годишнина [10]

announce съобщавам / съобщя [5]

announcement съобщение [5]

annual годишен [9]

another друг [2]

answer (n.) отговор [7]

answer (v.) отговарям / отговоря [10]

anterior преден [10]

aorist [tense] минало свършено време [12]

apartment апартамент [8] ; квартира [14]

apartment building блок [8]

apparatus апарат [5]

apparently като че ли [14]

appear изглеждам [4] ; проявявам / проявя [8] ; появявам се / появя се [14]

appearance вид [11]

appetite апетит [9]

apple ябълка [6]

appointment среща [9]

approach (v.) приближавам / приближа [14]

April април [9]

apropos апропо [13]

Arab (adj.) арабски [11]

archaeologist археолог [3]

architecture архитектура [7]

are си [1] (2sg) ; сме [1] (1pl) ; сте [1] (2pl) ; са [1] (3pl)

aromatic ароматен [10]

around из [11]

arrange нареждам / наредя [6] ; уреждам / уредя [9] ; устройвам / устроя [13] ; put in order редя [12]

arrive пристигам / пристигна [6] ; стигам / стигна [13]

arrive home прибирам се / прибера се [8]

arm ръка [12]

army армия [12]

as като [3] [6] ; както [9] ; щом [11]

as if като че ли [14]

as soon as щом [11]

ascend качвам се / кача се [7]

ask   пи́там [4] ;   помо́лвам / помо́ля
    [13] ;   попи́твам / попи́там [14]
ask for   пои́сквам / пои́скам [12]
ask oneself   попи́твам се / попи́там се [13]
aspect   вид [11]
aspirin   аспири́н [12]
astounding   изуми́телен [13]
at   на [2] [3] ;   при [7]
at all   изо́бщо [8]
at home   вкъ́щи [6] ;   у дома́ [10]
at least   поне́ [9] ;   мака́р [14]
at present   засега́ [9]
at that   и то [11]
at the beginning   отнача́ло [14]
at the home of   у [10]
atmosphere   атмосфе́ра [3]
attached   привъ́рзан [11]
attend, pay attention   внима́вам [6]
attention   внима́ние [14]
attentive   внима́телен [14]
attract   привли́чам / привлека́ [9]
August   а́вгуст [5]
aunt   ле́ля [3]
authentic   автенти́чен 13]
author   а́втор [23]
author's   а́вторски [12]
automobile   кола́ [4]
autograph   автогра́ф [13]
autumn   е́сен [9]
await   оча́квам [7]
awaken   събу́ждам се / събу́дя се [11]

B.C.   преди́ н.е. [9] ;   преди́ Р.Хр. [9]
bachelor   ерге́н [11]
back (n.)   гръб [12]
back (adj.)   за́ден [14]
bad   лош [3] ;   зле́ [13]
badly   зле́ [13]
bag   ча́нта [2] ;   торба́ [11]
baggage   бага́ж [2]
bake   пека́ [13]
balcony   балко́н [13]
banitsa   ба́ница [10]
banquet   банке́т [14]
barefoot   бос [13]
bark (v.)   ла́я [11]
Baroque   баро́к [10]
baroque (adj.)   баро́ков [9]
bath   ба́ня [3]
bathe   къ́пя [3] ;   изкъ́пвам се / изкъ́пя
    се [14] ;   окъ́пвам се / окъ́пя се [14]
bathing (adj.)   ба́нски [13]
bathroom   ба́ня [3]
be   съм [1] ;   бъ́да [7]

be afraid   боя́ се [8] ;   be frightened
    пла́ша се [11] ;   be afraid of
    страху́вам се [14]
be concerned/occupied with   занима́вам се
    [11]
be embarrassed   смуща́вам се / смутя́ се
    [13]
be ill   боледу́вам [10]
be interested in   интересу́вам се от [11]
be necessary   тря́бвам [12]
be reflected   огле́ждам се / огле́дам се
    [14]
be silent   мълча́ [10]
be worth   заслужа́вам / заслу́жа [11]
beach   пляж [14]
beak   клюн [13]
bean   боб [10]
bear (n.)   ме́чка [29]
bear (v.)   ра́ждам / родя́ [10]
bear cub   мече́ [11]
beard   брада́ [12]
beautiful   ху́бав [2]
beauty   хубави́ца [5] ;   красота́ [18]
because   защо́то [3]
because of   покра́й [10]
become   ста́вам / ста́на [10]
become aware   почу́вствувам [14]
bed   легло́ [4]
beer   би́ра [4]
before   преди́ [6] ;   по́-ра́но [14] ;
    преди́ да [14]
beg   помо́лвам / помо́ля [13]
begin   запо́чвам / запо́чна [6] ;   почвам /
    почна [10]
begin to hurt   заболя́ва / заболи́ [12]
beginning (adj.)   нача́лен [3]
behind (n.)   за́дник [12]
behind (in back)   отза́д [3]
behind   зад [13]
believe   вя́рвам [7] ;   повя́рвам [8]
bell   звъне́ц [5]
belly   коре́м [12]
below   под [3] ;   [from] below   отдо́лу
    [11]
bench   пе́йка [3]
bend   зави́вам / завия́ [6] ;   сви́вам /
    свия́ [13]
besides, in addition   освен това́ [4]
between   между́ [12]
beverage   напи́тка [4]
bicycle   велосипе́д [14] ;   колело́ [14]
big   голя́м [2]
bird   пти́ца [7]
birth (adj.)   роде́н [5]
birthday   роде́н ден [5]
birthplace   ро́дно мя́сто [11]
black   че́рен [11]
blade   но́жче [13]

blood кръв [12]
bloom (v.) цъфтя́ [9]
blow ду́хам [1]
blow over размина́вам се / размина се [15]
blue си́н [8]
blunt (v.) притъ́пвам / притъ́пя [14]
boil варя́ [3] ; сваря́вам / сваря́ [5] ; вря́ [9]
boil over изкипя́вам / изкипя́ [14]
bone ко́ст [12]
book кни́га [2]
booklet кни́жка [10]
bore (v.) омръ́звам / омръ́зна [12]
boring ску́чен [13]
bosom гърда́ [12]
botanical ботани́чески [13]
both (...and) и ... и [8] ; хе́м ... хе́м [12]
bother пре́ча [8]
bottle шише́ [2]
bound (adj.) привъ́рзан [11]
box кути́я [10]
boy момче́ [1]
brain мо́зък [12]
bravo бра́во [10]
brawler кавгаджи́я, -и́йка [10]
bread хля́б [5]
break (n.) о́тпуска [2]
breakfast заку́ска [10]
breast гърди́ [12]
breath дъ́х [8]
bride бу́лка 10] ; младоже́нка [10]
bridegroom младоже́нец [10]
bridge мо́ст [6]
bridge (card game) бри́дж [14]
briefcase ча́нта [2]
briefly накра́тко [10]
bright лъ́скав [10]
bring дона́сям / донеса́ [7]
bring out изва́ждам / изва́дя [14]
broad широ́к [12]
broken счу́пен [11]
brother бра́т [8]
bucket ко́фа [14]
build a nest сви́вам гнездо́ [13]
Bulgarian бъ́лгарски [1]
Bulgarian [person] бъ́лгарин [3] ; бъ́лгарка [3]
burden with questions затру́пвам с въпро́си [11]
burn горя́ [11]
burn up изга́рям / изгоря́ [14]
bury under затру́пвам / затру́пам [11]
bus автобу́с [2]
business ра́бота [14]
business trip командиро́вка [10]
but но [2] ; пъ́к [11] ; ама [12]
buy купу́вам [5]

by с [2] ; при [7]
by chance случа́йно [12]
Byzantine византи́йски [8]

cabbage зе́ле [4]
call (v.) позвъня́вам / позвъня́ [9] ; оба́ждам се / оба́дя се [10] ; оба́ждам се по телефо́на [11] ; пови́квам / пови́кам [13]
call, name нари́чам / нарека́ [13]
call out изви́квам / изви́кам [13] ; пови́квам / пови́кам [13]
camera фотоапара́т [5]
can (n.) буркан [6]
can (v.) консерви́рам [6]
can, be able мо́га [4] [5]
cancel отка́звам / отка́жа [13]
candy бонбо́н [10]
canned консерви́ран [6]
capricious капри́зен [13]
car кола́ [4]
car (in a train) ваго́н [6]
card ка́рта [5]
cardigan жиле́тка [12]
care for миле́я [13]
carnival (adj.) карнава́лен [12]
carrot мо́рков [4]
carry но́ся [3] ; зана́сям / занеса́ [7]
carry up ка́чвам / кача́ [7]
cause (n.) по́вод [13]
cat ко́тка [10]
catch хва́щам / хва́на [9] ; ловя́ [9]
catch one's breath пое́мам [си] дъ́х [8]
cavern про́паст [11]
celebrate празну́вам [10]
center це́нтър [7] ; сре́дище [9]
central центра́лен [12]
central heating па́рно отопле́ние [11]
century ве́к [12]
certain си́гурен [6]
certainly си́гурно [9]
chair сто́л [4]
champagne шампа́нско [11]
championship пъ́рвенство [10]
chance (adj.) случа́ен [12]
change (n.) промя́на [13]
change (v.) сме́ням / сменя́ [3] [4] ; проме́ням / променя́ [11]
chat поприка́звам [11]
cheap е́фтин [9]
check (v.) проверя́вам / проверя́ [13]
cheek бу́за [12]
cheer up зара́двам се [12]
cheerful бо́дър [13]
cheese [hard yellow] кашкава́л [4] ; [soft white] си́рене [7]

cherry черéша [12]

chest грѣд [12] ; гърдѝ [12]

chief глáвен [9]

child детé [1] ; мáлко [4]

children децá [3]

children's детѝнски [13]

chill (n.) стýд [7] ; мрáз [10]

chimney комѝн [13]

chin брадá [12] ; брадѝчка [12]

chocolate шоколáд [5]

choice ѝзбор [7]

choose избѝрам / изберá [4]

chop [of meat] пържóла [4]

Christ's Христóв [9]

Christmas Кóледа [10] ; Рождествó Христóва [9]

Christmas (adj.) кóледен [10]

Christmas Eve Бѣдни вéчер [10]

church цѣрква [3]

cigarette цигáра [4]

circle крѣг [10]

circular крѣгъл [10]

circus цѝрк [6]

city грáд [6] [7]

class [grade in school] клáс [7]

class урóк [5] ; лéкция [6]

classical класѝчески [3]

clean (adj.) чѝст [4]

clean up, clean out изчѝствам / изчѝстя [14]

clear (adj.) я́вен [11]

clear up изясня́вам / изясня́ [14]

clearly я́вно [11]

climate клѝмат [11]

climb the stairs кáчвам се по стѣлбите [11]

cliff скалá [14]

clink чýкам / чýкна [11] ; clink glasses чýкам се / чýкна се [11]

clock часóвник [7]

close (v.) затвáрям / затвóря [3] [4]

close (adj.) блѝзък [10]

closed затвóрен [2]

cloth кѣрпа [13]

clothing дрéхи [10]

coat палтó [13]

coffee кафé [5]

coffee (adj.) кафéен [6]

coffee spoon кáфена лъжѝчка [6]

coin монéта [10] ; парá [11]

coincide съвпáдам / съвпáдна [10]

cold (n.) стýд [7]

cold [illness] простýда [2]

cold (adj.) студéн [4] ; get/grow cold изстѝвам / изстѝна [8]

colleague колéга [10] ; колéжка [10]

collect събѝрам / съберá [3] [4] ; прибѝрам / приберá [8]

collection колéкция [7] ; сбóрник [12]

color (n.) цвя́т [21]

color (v.) боядѝсвам [10]

colored цвéтен [3]

comb (v.) рéша [13]

come дохóждам / дóйда [5] ; ѝда [5] ; ѝдвам [5] ; дошѣл [11]

come, come on настѣпвам / настѣпя [13]

come to an agreement/understanding разбѝрам се / разберá се [12]

come to [one's] senses опóмняам се / опóмня се [12]

come to the phone обáждам се / обáдя се [12]

comedy комéдия [11]

comfortable удóбен [11]

command (v.) заповя́двам / заповя́дам [5]

commodity стóка [9]

common óбщ [7]

compact disk компáкт дѝск [12]

compartment купé [2]

complain оплáквам се / оплáча се [11]

complete (v.) свѣршвам / свѣрша [6]

complete (adj.) свѣршен [12]

completely съвсéм [5]

complex (n.) комплéкс [8]

complex (adj.) слóжен [5]

comrade дрýгар (ка) [1]

concur съвпáдам / съвпáдна [10]

conductor кондýктор (ка) [5]

conference конферéнция [12]

congratulations честѝто [11]

consider смя́там [13]

consist of състоя́ се [14]

constant постоя́нен [10]

constantly всé [10] ; постоя́нно [10]

contend спóря [13]

continue продължáвам / продължá [5]

control (adj.) контрóлен [8]

convenient удóбен [11]

convention обичáй [13]

converse (v.) приказвам [9] ; разговáрям [10]

convince убедя́ [14]

cook (v.) варя́ [3] ; гóтвя [4] ; сваря́вам / сваря́ [5] ; сгóтвям / сгóтвя [5]

cooking (adj.) готвáрски [7]

cool (adj.) прохлáден [15]

copy (n.) кóпие [13]

copy (v.) препѝсвам / препѝша [13]

copyright áвторско прáво [12]

corner (n.) ѣгъл [14] ; around the corner зад ѣгъла [14]

cornfield нѝва [10]

corridor коридóр [2]

cost (v.) стрýвам [4]

count (v.) броя́ [3] ; преброя́вам /
    преброя́ [6] ; смя́там / сме́тна [13]
count, count on разчи́там [12]
country страна́ [7]
cousin братовче́д (ка) [2]
cover up затру́пвам / затру́пам [11]
cramped те́сен [2]
crooked крив [3]
crossword puzzle кръстосло́вица [8]
cry пла́ча [16] ; burst into tears
    разпла́квам се / разпла́ча се [14]
cry, cry out изви́квам / изви́кам [13]
Cuban куби́нски [8]
cucumber кра́ставица
cuisine ку́хня [7]
culinary готва́рски [7]
cultural култу́рен [12]
culture култу́ра [9]
cup ча́ша [3]
cupboard шкаф [6]
currency exchange office че́йндж [10]
current сега́шен [9]
custom обича́й [13]
customary обича́ен [14]
cut сека́ [9] ; ре́жа [12]

dad та́тко [10]
dangerous опа́сен [4]
darling (form of address) ми́ло [4]
daughter дъщеря́ [10]
day ден [4] [6]
day after tomorrow дру́ги ден
day before yesterday о́нзи ден [9]
day off почи́вен ден [8]
dear (adj.) драг [2] [3] ; мил [4]
December деке́мври [9]
decide реша́вам / реша́ [11]
declaim деклами́рам [7]
decorate оки́чвам / оки́ча [13]
deer еле́н [8] ; сърна́ [8]
defense защи́та [12]
defy предизви́квам / предизви́кам [10]
delay (n.) закъсне́ние [14]
delicious вку́сен [6]
delight възто́рг [10]
democracy демокра́ция [13]
democratic демократи́чески [14]
dentist зъболе́кар [12]
depart отпъту́вам [7] ; замина́вам /
    зами́на [9]
depend зави́ся [14]
descend сли́зам / сля́за [7]
describe опи́свам / опи́ша [7]
deserve заслужа́вам / заслу́жа [11]
desire (n.) во́ля [12] ; жела́ние [14]
desire (v.) жела́я [7]

dessert десе́рт [6]
detailed подро́бен [13]
diary дне́вник [10]
dictate дикту́вам [14]
dictionary ре́чник [7]
die почи́на [8] ; уми́рам / умра́ [11]
different разли́чен [10]
difficult сло́жен [5] ; тру́ден [5] ;
    мъчен [13]
dig (v.) копа́я [10]
dill ко́пър [6]
direct (adj.) дире́ктен [8]
direction посо́ка [6]
director режисьо́р [12] ; дире́ктор [13]
dirty мръсен [9]
disappear изче́звам / изче́зна [10]
discern разпозна́вам / разпозна́я [8]
dish (n.) го́зба [5]
distinguish разпозна́вам / разпозна́я [8]
distinguished представи́телен [14]
dispute (n.) кавга́ [10]
dispute (v.) спо́ря [13]
distribute разда́вам / разда́м [8]
district край [8] ; кварта́л [9]
do пра́вя [3] ; напра́вям / напра́вя [6]
do (housework) busily ше́там [10]
do laundry изпи́рам / изпера́ [12]
doctor ле́кар [1]
doe сърна́ [8]
dog ку́че [4]
doll ку́кла [13]
domestic семе́ен [10]
door врата́ [2]
down до́лу [11] ; надо́лу [11]
down, along по [5]
draft (n.) тече́ние [1] ; there's getting to
    be a draft ста́ва тече́ние [1]
draw рису́вам [3] ; привли́чам /
    привлека́ [9]
drawing рису́нка [3]
dread (n.) страх [12]
dreadful страхо́тен [5]
dream (n.) сън [8]
dream (v.) сънувам
drench измо́крям / измо́кря [12]
dress (n.) ро́кля [12]
dress (v.) обли́чам / облека́ [13] ;
    обли́чам се / облека́ се [13]
dress up издока́рвам се / издока́рам се
    [14]
dressed обле́чен [14]
dried сушен [10]
drink (n.) напи́тка [4]
drink (v.) пи́я [3]
drink up изпи́вам / изпи́я [5]
drip (v.) ка́пя [10]
drive ка́рам [6]
drive in вка́рвам / вка́рам [12]

driver's license книжка [10]
drop *(v.)* изпускам / изпусна [7] ;
    пускам / пусна [10]
drunkard пияница [10]
dry *(v.)* избърсвам / избърша [13]
dull *(v.)* притъпявам / притъпя [14]
during през [4]
duty дежурство [10]
dwarf човече [13]
dye боядисвам [10]

each *(distributive)* по [3]
ear ухо [12]
earlier по-рано [14]
early *(adj.)* ранен [13]
early *(adv.)* рано [9]
earn спечелвам / спечеля [14]
easy лесен [6] ; лек [9]
eat ям [9] ; изяждам / изям [9] ;
    хапвам / хапна [15]
eat breakfast закусвам / закуся [11]
eat dinner вечерям [9]
eat lunch обядвам [17]
eat one's fill наяждам се / наям се [9]
education образование [3]
effective ефектен [5]
effendi [sir] ефенди [1]
efficient работоспособен [9]
egg яйце [11]
eight осем [6]
eight hundred осемстотин [9]
eighteen осемнайсет [6]
eighteenth осемнайсети [8]
eighth осми [8]
eighty осемдесет [6]
either...or или ... или [8]
elbow лакът [8]
elegant елегантен [5]
elementary начален [3]
elevator асансьор [11]
eleven единайсет [6]
embarrass притеснявам / притесня [8]
emperor цар [8]
empty *(adj.)* празен [6] ; пуст [10]
end *(n.)* край [7]
endure издържам / издържа [7] ;
    понасям / понеса [14]
engineer инженер [14]
English английски [2]
Englishman англичанин [3]
Englishwoman англичанка [3]
enough, that's enough стига [3]
enough *(adj.)* достатъчен [7]
enrapture предизвиквам възторг у [10
enter влизам / вляза [4]
entertain посрещам / посрещна [5]

entire цял [7]
entrance вход [8]
entryway коридор [2]
equinox равноденствие [13]
equipment апарат [5]
era ера [9]
err греша [7]
especially особено [8]
European европеец [8]
eve of навечерие [10]
even *(adj.)* равен [15]
even дори [8] ; даже [11]
even numbered четен [11]
even though макар че [14]
evening вечер [9]
evening *(adj.)* вечерен [9]
every всеки, всяка, всяко [6]
every other през [8]
everything всичко [2]
exact точен [6]
exactly тъкмо [10]
examination [school] изпит [5] ;
    контролна работа [8] ; контролно
    [8] ; matriculation exam матура [8]
examination [medical] преглед [4]
examine разглеждам / разгледам [4] ;
    преглеждам / прегледам [8] ;
    оглеждам / огледам [14]
example пример [18] ; for example
    например [8]
except, except for освен [4]
excessive прекален [13]
excursion излет [3] ; екскурзия [8]
excuse *(n.)* извинение [13]
excuse *(v.)* извинявам / извиня [5]
exit изход [20]
exotic екзотичен [5]
exotica, exoticism екзотика [7]
expect очаквам [7]
extract изваждам / извадя [14]
eye око [12]
eyebrow вежда [12]
eyeglasses очила [11]

face лице [12]
faithful верен [10]
fall *(n.)* есен [9] ; in the fall наесен [9]
fall *(v.)* падам / падна [7]
fall asleep заспивам / заспя [14] ; (of
    body part) изтръпвам / изтръпна [14]
fall silent мълча [10]
family семейство [11]
family *(adj.)* семеен [10]
famous знаменит [14]
fan *(n.)* любител [8]
far, far away далече [4]

fashion мо́да [21]
fashion show мо́дно ревю́ [13]
fashionable мо́ден [13]
fast (n.) по́ст [10]
fast (adj.) бъ́рз [6] ; по́стен [10]
fasten постя́гам / посте́гна [11]
father баща́ [8]
father-in-law свѐкър [10] ; тъ́ст [10]
favorite (adj.) люби́м [8]
fear (n.) стра́х [12]
fear, be afraid боя́ се [8] ; пла́ша се
    [11] ; страху́вам се [14]
fearful стра́шен [9]
February февруа́ри [9]
feed (v.) храня́ [8] ; нахра́нвам /
    нахра́ня [11]
feel чу́вствувам се (also чу́вствам се) [13]
feel ashamed досрамя́ва ме / досраме́е ме
    [13]
feel like laughing досмешя́ва ме /
    досмеше́е ме [13]
feel nauseated гнус ме е [12]
festival фестива́л [5]
fiancé годени́к [10] ; годени́ца [10]
field (n.) ни́ва [10] ; поле́ [15]
fifteen петна́йсет [6]
fifth пе́ти [8]
fifty петдесе́т [6]
fill пъ́лня [6]
film (n.) фи́лм [8]
finally най-по́сле [1]
find (v.) нами́рам / наме́ря [5]
fine (adj.) ху́бав [2]
fine (adv.) добре́ [2]
finger пръ́ст [12]
finish свъ́ршвам / свъ́рша [6]
fir елха́ [13]
fire о́гън [7]
fire dancer нестина́р [11]
fire dancing нестина́рство [11]
firm твъ́рд [11]
first пъ́рви [4]
fish (n.) ри́ба [9]
fish (v.) ловя́ ри́ба [9]
fist юмру́к [12]
five пе́т [6] ; пети́ма [6]
five hundred пе́тстотин [9]
fix up постя́гам / посте́гна [11]
flat (adj.) ра́вен [15]
fleece (v.) дера́ [12]
floor по́д [4] ; [of multi-story building]
    ета́ж [8]
flow (v.) тека́ [9]
flower (n.) цве́те [6]
flu гри́п [13]
fly, fly up to доли́там / долетя́ [13]
fold (v.) сви́вам / сви́я [13]
folk наро́д [7]

folk (adj.) наро́ден [5]
food я́дене [9]
fool around мо́там се (or мотая́ се) [14]
footwear обу́ща [13]
for за [1] [6] ; от [6] ; на [7]
for, for a short while закра́тко [11]
for now засега́ [9]
for the sake of заради́ [13]
forehead чело́ [12]
foreign чу́жд [8]
foreigner чужденѐц [3] ; чужденка́ [3]
forest гора́ [3]
forget забра́вям / забра́вя [7]
fork (n.) ви́лица [10]
forthcoming предстоя́щ [9]
fortune късме́т [10]
forty четири́десет, четири́йсет [6]
forwards напре́д [14]
four че́тири [6] ; четири́ма [6]
four hundred че́тиристотин [9]
fourteen четирина́йсет [6]
fourth четвъ́рти [8]
fowl коко́шка [11]
free свобо́ден [2]
freedom свобода́ [7]
freeze [with terror] изтръ́пвам от стра́х
    [14]
French toast пъ́ржени фили́йки [14]
frequent че́ст [3]
fresh пре́сен [8]
Friday пе́тък [9]
friend прия́тел (ка) [1]
frighten пла́ша [9]
from от [1]
from within отвъ́тре [9]
front (adj.) пре́ден [10]
frozen ле́ден [8]
fruit пло́д [7]
fry пъ́ржа [6]
full пъ́лен [5]
fun заба́вен [11]
funny сме́шен [13]
furor фуро́р [13]
future (adj.) бъ́дещ [9]

gain (n.) напре́дък [9]
gain (v.) спече́лвам / спече́ля [14]
game игра́ [14] ; ма́ч [12]
garbage боклу́к [14]
garbage can ко́фа за боклу́к [14]
garden (n.) гради́на [3]
garlic че́сън [6]
garnish (n.) гарниту́ра [4]
gather събира́м / събера́ [3] [4] ;
    прибира́м / прибера́ [8] ; бера́ [12]
gay, lively ве́сел [9]

general *(adj.)* общ [7] ; in general изобщо [8]

gentle кротък [13]

Gentlemen господа [3]

German *(adj.)* германски [14]

get получавам / получа [8]

get acquainted запознавам се / запозная се [10]

get angry разсърдвам се / разсърдя се [14]

get burned изгарям / изгоря [14]

get confused смущавам се / смутя се [13]

get dressed обличам се / облека се [13]

get in line редя се на опашка [12]

get in touch with обаждам се / обадя се [10]

get married женя се [11] ; оженвам се / оженя се [11]

get off слизам / сляза [7]

get on качвам се / кача се [7]

get ready готвя се [9]

get sick заболявам / заболея [12]

get tired уморявам се / уморя се [12]

get to be ставам / стана [10]

get to know опознавам / опозная [7]

get up ставам / стана [4]

get used to свиквам / свикна [15]

gift подарък [7]

girl момиче [1]

give дай [4] ; давам / дам [9] ; [a present] подарявам / подаря [9]

give birth to раждам / родя [10]

give out раздавам / раздам [8]

give up отстъпвам / отстъпя [8]

glass чаша [3]

gloomy намръщен [13]

glory слава [9]

glove ръкавица [9]

go вървя [3] ; ида [5] ; отивам / отида [5] ; ходя [6] ; движа се [14]

go back връщам се / върна се [11

go down слизам / сляза [7]

go in влизам / вляза [4]

go out излизам / изляза [4]

go to bed лягам си / легна си [8]

goal цел [16]

goal [sports] гол [12]

God, god бог [9]

godfather кум [14]

godmother кума [14]

golden златен [9]

good *(adj.)* добър [2]

good night лека нощ [9]

good old days доброто старо време [11]

goodbye довиждане [8] ; дочуване [12]

goods стока [9]

gorge *(v.)* наяждам се / наям се [9]

grade [in school] клас [7]

granddaughter внучка [10]

grandfather дядо [10]

grandmother баба [8]

grandson внук [10]

Granny March Баба Марта [11]

grape *(adj.)* гроздов [2] ; лозов [6]

grapes грозде [9]

grasp *(v.)* хващам / хвана [9]

Greeks гърци [6]

green зелен [13]

greeting поздрав [2]

greeting card честитка [10]

grow milder омеквам / омекна [11]

grow up пораствам / порасна [14]

grownups възрастни [4]

grumble оплаквам се / оплача се [11]

guard *(v.)* пазя [8]

guess познавам / позная [7]

guest гост [8]

habit навик [11]

half половин(а) [6]

hail *(n.)* град [12]

hail *(v.)* вали град [12]

hair коса [12]

haircut прическа [12]

hall зала [12]

ham шунка [4]

hamster хамстер [9]

hand *(n.)* ръка [12]

hand to подавам / подам [11]

handle пипам [9]

hang закачам / закача [13]

hang clothes out to dry простирам дрехи [12]

happen ставам / стана [4]

happy радостен [5] ; весел [9] ; [in greeting] честит [10]

Happy New Year честита Нова Година [10]

hard твърд [11] ; мъчен [13]

hastily на крак [12]

hat шапка [5]

have имам [2] [3]

have a bite хапвам / хапна [15]

he той [1] ; то [1]

head *(n.)* глава [12]

health здраве [2]

healthy здрав [2]

hear чувам / чуя [10]

heart сърце [10] ; by heart наизуст [4] ; send heartfelt wishes пожелавам от сърце [10]

hearty сърдечен [2]

heat, heat up грея [9]

heating отоплéние [11]
heavy тéжък [2]
hedgehog таралéж [9]
heel (n.) петá [12]
hello дóбър дéн [6] ; здравéй [6] ; алó [12]
help (n.) пóмощ [9]
help (v.) помáгам / помóгна [7] ; help yourself заповя́дай [5]
hen кокóшка [11]
hence, from here оттýка [5]
her (direct object) я [5] ; нéя [10]
her (indirect object) ѝ [7] ; на нéя [10]
her, hers нéин [8]
here éто [2] (pointing) ; тýк(а) [2] (location)
hey! éй [1]
hi здравéй [6]
hide (v.) скрѝвам / скрѝя [13]
high висóк [5]
high school гимнáзия [3] (academically oriented) ; тéхникум [3] (technical)
high school dropout двóйкаджия, -ка [10]
him (direct object) го [5] ; нéго [7]
him (indir. object) му [7] ; на нéго [10]
hint (v.) подскáзвам / подскáжа [13]
his нéгов [8]
history истóрия [7]
hitch-hiker стóпаджия, -ийка [10]
hitch-hiking стóп [10]
hold (v.) държá [11]
hold dear милéя [13]
holiday почѝвен ден [8] ; прáзник [10]
home (n.) дóм [7]
home, at home вкъ́щи [6]
home (adj.) домáшен [7]
homemade домáшен [2]
homework домáшно [8]
honest чéстен [12]
honeymoon свáтбено пътешéствие [11]
honorable чéстен [12]
hope (n.) надéжда [8]
hope (v.) надя́вам се [19]
horrible страхóтен [5]
horror ýжас [14]
horse кóн [8]
hospital бóлница [6]
hot горéщ [11]
hotel хотéл [9]
hour чáс [6] [7]
hours of operation рабóтно врéме [6]
house къ́ща [2] ; дóм [7] ; small house къ́щичка [7]
how кáк [1]
how many кóлко [4]
how much кóлко [4]
however обáче [7]
humor хýмор [5]

humorous смéшен [13]
hundred стó [5]
hunger глáд [7]
hungry глáден [2] ; get hungry огладня́вам / огладнéя [4]
hurry бъ́рзам [4] ; побъ́рзвам / побъ́рзам [7]
hurt (v.) болѝ [12]
husband съпрýг [3] ; мъ́ж [8]

I áз [1]
ice (adj.), icy лéден [8]
ice cream сладолéд [6]
idea идéя [5]
ideal идеáлен [5]
idyll идѝлия [7]
idyllic идилѝчен [3]
if акó [4] ; далѝ [11] ; щом [11]
if only данó [10]
imagine престáвям си / представя́ си [13]
immediate family тéсен семéен кръг [10]
immediately веднáга [4]
impatience нетърпéние [8]
impending предстоя́щ [9]
imperfect несвъ́ршен [12]
imperfect (tense) мѝнало несвъ́ршено врéме [14]
imperfective aspect несвъ́ршен вѝд [12]
important вáжен [8]
in в [1] ; на [2] [3] ; след [6] ; във [7]
in, inside въ́тре [11]
in general въобщé [11]
in-law свáт, свáтя [10]
in love влюбен [14]
in order редóвен [13]
in order to за да [11]
in short накрáтко [10]
include включвам / включа [14]
incomparable несравнѝм [11]
incomplete несвъ́ршен [12]
inconvenient неудóбен [13]
indispensable необходѝм [13]
inexpensive éфтин [9]
influenza грѝп [13]
inform съобщáвам / съобщя́ [5]
inquire попѝтвам / попѝтам [14]
inscription нáдпис [14]
inside въ́тре [11] ; (to the) inside навъ́тре [11]
instance пъ́т [6] ; слýчай [12]
insult (n.) обѝда [14]
intelligent ýмен [10]
intend кáня се [11]
intensively усѝлено [3]
interest (n.) интерéс [7]

interest (v.) интересу́вам [8] ; занима́вам [11]
interesting интере́сно [1] ; интере́сен [2]
intersection пресе́чка [11]
intestine черво́ [12]
invent изми́слям / изми́сля [12]
invite ка́ня [10] ; пока́нвам / пока́ня [10]
is е [1] (3sg.) ; isn't it? нали́ [3]
it то́ [1] ; тя́ [2] ; то́й [2]
itch сърби́ [12]

Jack Frost Дя́до Мра́з [10]
jacket сако́ [13] ; я́ке [13]
January януа́ри [8]
jar буркан́ [6]
jeans джи́нси [13]
job ра́бота [4] [11]
joke (n.) ви́ц [12]
journalist журнали́ст (ка) [5]
joy ра́дост [10]
joyful ра́достен [5]
juice (n.) со́к [7]
July ю́ли [2]
jump (v.) ска́чам / ско́ча [9]
June ю́ни [9]
just тъ́кмо [10] ; то́чно [12]
just now току́-що [14]
just this moment тъ́кмо сега́ [10]

kebab кеба́бче [6]
keep (v.) държа́ [11]
key (n.) клю́ч [7]
kid (young person) хлапа́к [14]
kilogram килогра́м [6]
kind (adj.) любе́зен [2]
king кра́л [8]
kiss (v.) целу́вам / целу́на [5]
kitchen ку́хня [5]
knee (n.) коля́но [12]
knife (n.) но́ж [7]
knit изпли́там / изплета́ [12]
knock чу́кам / чу́кна [11]
know позна́вам / позна́я [1] [3] [7] ; зна́я [3] ; зна́м [4]

ladder стъ́лба [11]
lady да́ма [3]
lake е́зеро [3]
lament (v.) опла́квам / опла́ча [11]
landlady хаза́йка [15]
landscape пейза́ж [3]

lapel реве́р [13]
large голя́м [2] ; е́дър [9]
last (adj.) после́ден [6]
last night ми́налата но́щ [9] ; сно́щи [9]
last night's сно́щен [9]
late къ́сен [4] ; be late закъсня́вам / закъсне́я [7]
lately в после́дно вре́ме [6] ; напосле́дък [8]
later по́сле [2]
laugh (v.) сме́я се [13] ; burst out laughing разсми́вам се / разсме́я се [14]
laughter смя́х [11]
lawyer адвока́т (ка) [2]
lead (v.) во́дя [8] ; заве́ждам / заведа́ [10]
lead away изве́ждам / изведа́ [9]
leaf (n.) ли́ст [6]
leak (v.) ка́пя [10]
learn у́ча [5] ; науча́вам / науча́ [9] ; науча́вам се / науча́ се [14]
leave (v.) изли́зам / изля́за [4] ; тръ́гвам / тръ́гна [4] ; оста́вям / оста́вя [8] ; замина́вам / замина́ [9]
leave behind отмина́вам / отмина́ [14]
lecture (n.) ле́кция [6]
left (adj.) ля́в [11] ; [to the] left наля́во [11] ; [from the] left отля́во [11]
left over оста́нало [9]
leg кра́к [8] ; нога́ (dialectal, poetic) [12]
Lent по́ст [10]
Lenten по́стен [10]
lesson уро́к [5]
let пу́скам / пу́сна [10]
let go изпу́скам / изпу́сна [7]
let pass пропу́скам / пропу́сна [10]
let's ха́йде [3]
let's hope дано́ [10]
letter писмо́ [8]
letter [of alphabet] бу́ква [8]
letter carrier пощаджи́я, -и́йка [10]
lev (currency) ле́в [4]
level (n.) равни́ще [15]
library библиоте́ка [5]
lie, be lying down лежа́ [4]
lie down ля́гам / ле́гна [4]
life живо́т [9]
lift (v.) вди́гам / вди́гна [6]
light (adj.) ле́к [9] ; све́тъл [10]
like (v.) оби́чам [2] [3] ; харе́свам / харе́сам [7] [12]
like като́ [3] [6]
line опа́шка [11]
lip у́стна [12]
listen слу́шам [4]
little ма́лко [1] [2]
live живе́я [3]

live (adj.) жив [11]
lively бодър [13]
liver черен дроб [12]
living жив [11]
loan (n.) заем [12]
loan (v.) давам на заем [12]
lock (v.) заключвам / заключа [8]
logical логичен [12]
long (adj.) дълъг [2] ; a long time
   дълго [8]
long ago отдавна [6]
look (v.) изглеждам [4] ; поглеждам /
   погледна [14]
look, look at гледам [4]
look after гледам [9] ; погрижвам се /
   погрижа се [11]
look around оглеждам се / огледам се
   [14]
look at one's reflection оглеждам се /
   огледам се [14]
look for търся [7]
look like приличам [10]
lottery тото [14]
lose губя [14]
love (v.) обичам [3] ; любя [13]
lover любител [8]
luck късмет [10]
lunch (n.) обед [8] ; обяд [9]
lunch (adj.) обеден [9]
lunchtime обедно време [9]
lung (бял) дроб [12]

Ma'am госпожа [1] ; кира [1] (archaic)
magazine списание [8]
magician вълшебник [11]
make правя [3] ; сготвям / сготвя
   (prepare food) [5] ; направям /
   направя [6]
make up [to someone, for something]
   реваншѝрам се [5]
mail (n.) поща [3]
mail [a letter] пускам [писмо] [10]
mailbox пощенска кутия [10]
main (adj.) главен [9]
mainly главно [9]
majority повечето [11]
male (adj.) мъжки [8]
man човек [4] ; мъж [8] ; young man
   момък [13]
manual учебник [2]
manner начин [6]
many много [1], [2]
many happy returns за много години [11]
map (n.) карта [5]
March март [1]
mark (v.) бележа [7]

marriage брак [10]
married женен [10]
marry женя [11] ; женя се [11] ;
   оженвам се / оженя се [11] ;
   оженвам / оженя [11]
marvelous чудесен [2]
masculine мъжки [8]
match [sports] мач [12]
matriculation exam матура [8]
matter (n.) работа [11]
May май [9]
maybe може би [9]
me (direct object) ме [4] [5] ; мене [10]
me (indirect object) ми [7] ; на мене
   [10]
meal ядене [9]
mean (v.) знача [1]
meaning значение [9]; смисъл [11]
meat месо [6]
meat (ground) кайма [6] ; (grilled/stewed)
   кебап [13]
medicine лекарство [8]
medieval средновековен [9]
meet (v.) посрещам / посрещна [5] ;
   запознавам се / запозная се [10] ;
   срещам / срещна [10]
meeting среща [9]
menu меню [4]
merchant търговец [9]
meter (n.) метър [15]
middle (n.) среда [2]
middle (adj.) среден [3]
Middle Ages средновековие [8]
midnight полунощ [9]
mild мек [15]
milk (n.) мляко [6]
milkiness млечност [10]
mine мой [8]
ministry министерство [14]
minute (n.) минута [6]
mirror (n.) огледало [11]
Miss госпожица [1]
miss (v.) изпускам / изпусна [7]
mistake (n.) грешка [3]
modesty срам [12]
Mom мама [2]
moment момент [5]
monastery манастир [8]
Monday понеделник [9]
money пари [11]
moneychanger [unofficial] чейнджаджия,
   -ийка [10]
month месец [9]
moon луна [9]
Moravian моравски [8]
more повече [7] ; once more отново
   [2]
more (comparative degree) по- [10]

more or less го́ре-до́лу [11]
morning (n.) су́трин [9] ; у́тро [9]
morning (adj.) у́тринен [9]
mortal (adj.) смъ́ртен [4]
most (superlative degree) на́й- [10] ; the
    most на́й-мно́го [10]
mother ма́йка [2]
mother-in-law свекъ́рва [9] ; тъ́ща [10]
mountain планина́ [3]
mourn опла́квам / опла́ча [11]
mouse ми́шка [11]
mouth (n.) уста́ [12]
move (v.) вървя́ [3] ; дви́жа се [14]
movement движе́ние [12]
movie фи́лм [8]
Mr. господи́н [1]
Mrs. госпожа́ [1]
much мно́го [2]
muscle му́скул [12]
mushroom гъ́ба [4]
music му́зика [5]
must тря́бва [12]
mustache муста́ци [14]
my мо́й [8]

nail [finger or toe] но́кът [8]
name (n.) и́ме [6] ; my name is а́з се
    ка́звам [1]
name (v.) нари́чам / нареќа́ [13]
narrow те́сен [2]
national наро́ден [5]
native (adj.) ро́ден [11]
nature приро́да [7]
near до [2]
nearby бли́зо [4]
necessary необходи́м [13] ; it's not
    necessary ня́ма ну́жда [2]
neck ши́я [12] ; neck, back of the neck
    вра́т [12] ; гу́ша [12]
necklace герда́н [14]
necktie вратовръ́зка [13]
need (n.) ну́жда [2]
need (v.) и́мам ну́жда от [4] ; тра́бва
    [12]
neighbor съсе́д (ка) [5]
neither ни́то [8] ; neither...nor ни ... ни
    [8] ; ни [8]
nephew племе́нник [10]
nest (n.) гнездо́ [13]
never ни́кога [8]
new но́в [7]
New Year's но́ва годи́на [10]
New Year's (adj.) новогоди́шен [11]
New Year's greeting новогоди́шна
    чести́тка [11]

newlywed младоже́нец [10] ;
    младоже́нка [10]
news [a piece of] новина́ [5]
newspaper ве́стник [6]
next (adj.) дру́г [7] ; сле́дващ [8]
next (adv.) по́сле [6]
next year догоди́на [7]
nice ху́бав [2]
niece племе́нница [10]
night (n.) но́щ [9]
night (adj.) но́щен [9]
nightmare кошма́р [6]
nine де́вет [6]
nine hundred де́ветстотин [9]
nineteen деветна́йсет [6]
ninety деветдесе́т [6]
ninth деве́ти [8]
no не́ [3]
no one (subject) ни́кой [8]
no one (object) ни́кого [8]
noise шу́м [6] ; make noise вди́гам
    шу́м [6]
noisy шу́мен [10]
none, no kind of ни́какъв [8]
noon (n.) обя́д [9]
noon (adj.) о́беден [9]
nose но́с [11]
not не [1] ; not yet о́ще не [3] ; not
    a one ни́то еди́н [8]
not at all ни́как [8]
not have ня́мам [2]
not only...but хе́м ... хе́м [12]
note (n.) беле́жка [7]
notebook тетра́дка [7]
nothing ни́що [8] ; nothing of the sort
    ни́що подо́бно [8]
notice (v.) забеля́звам / забеле́жа [5]
nourish хра́ня [8]
novel (n.) рома́н [3]
November ное́мври [9]
now сега́ [1]
nowhere ни́къде [8]
number (n.) но́мер [2] [3] [8] ; число́
    [14]

obey слу́шам [4]
obvious я́вен [11]
occasion (n.) по́вод [13]
occupy занима́вам [11] ; зае́мам / зае́ма
    [12]
occur настъ́пвам / настъ́пя [13] ;
    случвам се / слу́ча се [20]
October окто́мври [6]
odd numbered нече́тен [11]
of на [1] ; от [4]
of course разби́ра се [3]

offer (v.) поднасям / поднеса [6] ;
    представям / представя [13]
office кабинет [4]
often често [3]
oil [cooking] олио [6]
OK може [4] ; наред [7] ; добре [3]
old стар [7] ; how old are you? на
    колко сте години? [6]
older по-голям [10]
omelet омлет [4]
on на [2]
on duty дежурен [10]
on foot пеша [9]
on the left вляво [11]
on the right вдясно [11]
once (adv.) веднъж [7]
once (conjunction) щом [11]
one един [2] [3] ; едно [2] [3] ; една
    [3]
oneself сам, сама, само, сами [12]
oneself (direct object) се [5] ; себе си
    [11]
oneself (indirect object) си [5] [7] ; себе
    си [11]
onion лук [6]
only (adj.) единствен [11]
only (adv.) само [1]
open (v.) отварям / отворя [2] [3] [4]
open (adj.) отворен [2] ; явен [11]
openly открито [13]
opera опера [12]
opposite срещу [12]
or или [3]
orange (adj.) портокалов [10]
order (v.) поръчвам / поръчам [4] ;
    заповядвам / заповядам [5]
organize организирам [12] ; устройвам /
    устроя [13]
Orthodox [religion] (adj.) православен [8]
other друг [2]
our, ours наш [8]
out вън [11]
out of извън [10]
outside извън [10], навън [11] ; to the
    outside навън [11]
own (adj.) свой [10] ; собствен [12]

page (n.) страница [3]
pail кофа [14]
pain (n.) болка [12]
paint (n.) боя [10]
paint (v.) боядисвам [10]
painter, paint merchant бояджия [10]
pair (n.) двойка [13]
palate небце [12]
pale (adj.) блед [11]

palm [of the hand] длан [12]
panic (n.) паника [3]
pants панталон(и) [14]
paper хартия [8]
parcel пакет [5]
pardon (n.) извинение [13]
pardon (v.) извинявам / извиня [5]
parent родител [9]
parrot папагал [9]
part страна [15]
particular особен [10]
party партия [14]
pass (v.) минавам / мина [5] ; подавам /
    подам [11]
pass by отминавам / отмина [14]
pass one another разминавам се / размина
    се [15]
past (adj.) минал [9]
path път [8] ; пътека [11]
patient (n.) пациент (ка) [4]
patient (adj.) търпелив [3]
pay (v.) плащам / платя [4]
pay attention внимавам [6]
pencil молив [2]
pendant пискюл [13]
people хора [4] ; души [6] ; народ [7]
pepper (vegetable) чушка [6]
perfective aspect свършен вид [12]
permission разрешение [13]
person човек [4]
personable представителен [14]
persuade убеждавам / убедя [11]
photograph (n.) снимка [6]
physician лекар [1]
pick (v.) обирам / обера [8] ; бера [12]
pick a number познавам число [14]
pickles, pickled vegetables туршия [10]
picture-book албум [9]
pile up затрупвам / затрупам [11]
pin (v.) забождам / забода [13]
pitchfork вила [10]
pity (n.) съжаление [1] ; жалко [11]
place (n.) място [2]
plain (n.) поле [15] ; равнище [15]
plan (n.) план [7]
plan (v.) каня се [11]
plant (v.) посаждам / посадя [8]
platform перон [7]
play (n.) пиеса [12] ; игра [14]
play (v.) играя [5]
play around играя си [11]
play for a while поигравам / поиграя [10]
play tricks on правя номера на [8]
playing (n.) игра [14]
playmate, playfellow другарче [13]
pleasant приятен [9]
please моля [4]
pleased доволен [6]

plunder обѝрам / оберá [8]
poem стихотворéние [3]
pond éзеро [3]
pool (lottery) тóто [14]
popcorn пýканки [9]
popular популя́рен [12]
portion пóрция [7]
position (job) слýжба [14]
(it is) possible мóже [4]
post office пóща [3]
postal пóщенски [10]
postcard ка́ртичка [3]
postman пощаджѝя, -ѝйка [10]
pot тéнджера [6]
pour полѝвам / полéя [13]
precise тóчен [6]
prefer предпочѝтам / предпочетá [4]
preparation подготóвка [5]
prepare гóтвя [4] ; гóтвя се [9] ;
    приготвям / приготвя [10] ;
    постя́гам / постéгна [11] ;
    подгóтвям / подгóтвя [12]
prepared готóв [6]
present (n.) пода́рък [7]
present (v.) поднáсям / поднесá [6] ;
    представям / представя [13]
present-day сегáшен [9]
preserve консервѝрам [6]
preserved консервѝран [6]
preserves [thick sweet] слáдко [3]
pressure (n.) напрежéние [14]
pretty хýбав [2]
previous предѝшен [9]
price ценá [12]
primarily предѝмно [9]
prince кня́з [8]
prize (n.) награ́да [13]
probably мáй [12] ; навя́рно [14]
procession шéствие [12]
produce (v.) изва́ждам / изва́дя [14]
productive работоспосóбен [9]
professor профéсор [13]
program прогрáма [8]
progress напрéдък [9]
promise (v.) обещáвам / обещáя [10]
prompt подскáзвам / подскáжа [13]
prop up подпѝрам / подпрá [14]
propose предлáгам / предлóжа [8]
proposition предложéние [9]
protect пáзя [8]
provoke предизвѝквам / предизвѝкам
    [10]
public пýблика [10]
puppet кýкла [13]
purchase (v.) купýвам [5]
push бýтам [6] ; кáрам [6]
push in вкáрвам / вкáрам [12]
pushcart колѝчка [7]

put слáгам / слóжа [4] ; put to bed
    слáгам да лéгне [5]
put in order редя́ [12]
put on [clothing] облѝчам / облекá [13] ;
    облѝчам се / облекá се [13] [footwear]
    обýвам се / обýя се [13] ; обýвам /
    обýя [13]

quarrel (n.) кавгá [10]
quarrel (v.) кáрам се [11]
quarrelsome person кавгаджѝя, -ѝйка [10]
quarter (n.) чéтвърт [11]
quarters кварти́ра [14]
question (n.) въпрóс [11]
queue опáшка [11]
quick бъ́рз [6]
quiz (n.) контрóлна рáбота [8] ;
    контрóлно [8]

radio рáдио [14]
rag парцáл [14]
rain (n.) дъ́жд [12]
rain (v.) валѝ [12] ; валѝ дъ́жд [12]
raise (v.) вдѝгам / вдѝгна [6]
rakia ракѝя [2]
rapture (n.) възтóрг [10]
rare ря́дък [10]
rarely ря́дко [10]
raspberry малѝна [3]
rational разýмен [13]
rattle (v.) трáкам [13]
razorblade нóжче [13]
reach подáвам / подáм [11] ; стѝгам /
    стѝгна [13]
read четá [3] ; прочѝтам / прочетá [5]
read for a bit почѝтам / почетá [11]
ready (adj.) готóв [6]
real ѝстински [8]
really наѝстина [2]
rear (adj.) зáден [14]
rear end зáдник [12]
recall спóмням си / спóмня си [8] ;
    сéщам се / сéтя се [11]
recently отскóро (since recently) [11]
receive получáвам / полýча [8]
recipe рецéпта [6]
recite деклами́рам [7]
reckon смя́там / смéтна [13]
recognize опознáвам / опознáя [7]
record [phonograph] (n.) плóча [13]
recording зáпис [13]
red червéн [3]
redo, repair ремонти́рам [2]
refrigerator хладѝлник [7]

371

refuse (v.) отказвам / откажа [13]
regarding по повод [13]
regret (v.) съжалявам / съжаля [8]
regular редовен [13]
rejoice радвам се [5]
relate разказвам / разкажа [8] ;
    разправям / разправя [12]
relative (n.) роднина [10]
rely on разчитам [12]
remain оставам / остана [3] [4]
remaining останало [9]
remember помня [13] ; запомням /
    запомня [9] ; сещам се / сетя се
    [11]
remind подсещам / подсетя [4]
renowned знаменит [14]
rent (n.) наем [12]
rent out давам под наем [12]
repeat, replay (n.) повторение [12]
repeat (v.) повтарям / повторя [12]
replace (v.) сменям / сменя [3] [4]
report (n.) доклад [12]
republic република [14]
resemble приличам [10]
residential жилищен [8] ; residential
    district жилищен комплекс [8]
resort (n.) курорт [11]
respect уважавам [20] ; តача [13]
rest (n.) почивка [3]
rest (v.) почивам си / почина си [8]
rest, go on holiday почивам / почина [4]
rest (adj.) почивен [8]
restaurant ресторант [4]
restless неспокоен [4]
return връщам / върна [5] ; връщам
    се / върна се [11]
return a favor реваншрам се [5]
revue ревю [13]
reward (n.) награда [13]
rewrite преписвам / препиша [13]
rice ориз [6]
rich богат [7]
right (n.) право [12]
right (adj.) десен [11] ; right, to the right
    надясно [11] ; right, from the right
    отдясно [11]
Rila (adj.) рилски [8]
ring (v.) звъня [5]
ring out иззвънявам / иззвъня [14]
ripen зрея [9]
river река [9]
road (n.) път [6]
road (adj.) пътен [12]
rock (n.) камък [21] ; скала [14]
roll (v.) свивам / свия [13]
room стая [9]
rotate въртя се [14]
rotten развален [11]

round (adj.) кръгъл [10]
round about наоколо [9]
rub (v.) бърша [13]
rubbish боклук [14]
rule (n.) правило [12]
run (v.) тичам [8]

sack (n.) торба [11]
salad салата [4]
salesperson продавач (ка) [7]
salt (n.) сол [9]
salt (v.) посолявам / посоля [9]
salt shaker солница [9]
same същ [3] ; the same thing същото
    [4] ; one and the same един и същ
    [10]
sandwich сандвич [9]
Santa Claus Дядо Коледа [10]
satire сатира [5]
satisfied доволен [6]
Saturday събота [8]
sauerkraut кисело зеле [6]
sausage салам [11]
say казвам / кажа [1] [4] ; река [7]
scare (v.) стряскам / стресна [11] ;
    стряскам се / стресна се [11]
scent (n.) миризма [11]
school (n.) училище [5] [6]
school (adj.) училищен [10]
school bell училищен звънец [10]
scold карам се [11]
score a goal вкарвам гол [12]
scratch (v.) дера [12]
sea (n.) море
sea (adj.) морски [15]
sea level морското равнище [15]
seasons [of the year] годишните времена
    [9]
seat (n.) място [2]
seat (v.) посаждам / посадя [8]
second (adj.) втори [8]
secretary секретар (ка) [1]
see виждам / видя [3] [4]
see off, send off изпращам / изпратя [8]
seek търся [7] ; потърсвам / потърся
    [7]
seem изглеждам [4] [6]
seize хващам / хвана [9]
select (v.) избирам / избера [4]
selection избор [7]
sell продавам / продам [6]
send пращам / пратя [2] [3] [4]
sense (n.) смисъл [11]
sensible разумен [13]
sensitive to the cold зиморничав [11]
separate (adj.) отделен [3]

separately отде́лно [2]
September септе́мври [5]
serve серви́рам [4] ; подна́сям / поднеса́ [6]
service слу́жба [14]
serving по́рция [7]
set (v.) [of the sun] заля́звам / заля́за [9]
set in настъ́пвам / настъ́пя [13]
set out тръ́гвам / тръ́гна [4]
set up наре́ждам / наредя́ [6]
settle уре́ждам / уредя́ [9]
seven се́дем [2]
seven hundred се́демстотин [9]
seventeen седемна́йсет [6]
seventh се́дми [8]
seventy седемдесе́т [6]
several ня́колко [6]
severe су́ров [11]
shake треса́ [12]
shame (n.) сра́м [12]
she тя́ [1] ; то́ [1]
sheet [of paper] ли́ст [4]
shell [of a snail] о́хлюв [14]
shift (v.) прехвъ́рлям се / прехвъ́рля се [12]
shining лъ́скав [10]
shirt ри́за [13]
shoe обу́вка [3]
shoes обу́ща [13]
shoelace връ́зка [13]
Shope (adj., of the region) шо́пски [4]
short кра́тък [9] ; къ́с [12]
should тря́бва [12]
shoulder (n.) ра́мо [12]
shout (v.) ви́кам [12]
shove (v.) бу́там [6]
show (n.) ревю́ [13]
show (v.) пока́звам / пока́жа [7] ; проявя́вам / проявя́ [8]
sick бо́лен [2]
side (n.) страна́ [6] [15]
sidewalk тротоа́р [14]
sign (n.) зна́к [9]
similar подо́бен [8]
sin (v.) греша́ [7]
since от [6] ; отка́кто [10] ; щом [11]
sing пе́я [11] ; изпя́вам / изпе́я [11] ; sing a little попя́вам / попе́я [11]
singer певе́ц
single еди́нствен [11]
Sir господи́н [1] ; кир [1] (archaic)
sister сестра́ [10]
sit седя́ [4]
sit down ся́дам / се́дна [4]
six ше́ст [6] ; шести́ма [6]
six hundred ше́стстотин [9]
sixteen шестна́йсет [6]
sixth ше́сти [8]

sixty шестдесе́т, шейсе́т [6]
size но́мер [8]
ski resort зи́мен куро́рт [11]
skin (n.) ко́жа [12]
skin (v.) дера́ [12]
skip (v.) пропу́скам / пропу́сна [10]
slab пло́ча [7]
sleep (n.) съ́н [8]
sleep (v.) спя́ [4]
slice (n.) фили́я [14] ; small slice фили́йка [14]
slice (v.) ре́жа [12]
slip out, slip through изплъ́звам се / изплъ́зна се [14]
slow ба́вен [3]
small ма́лък [2]
smart (adj.) у́мен [10]
smell (n.) миризма́ [11]
smoke (n.) ди́м [4]
smoke (v.) пу́ша [4]
smoking пу́шене [4]
sneeze (v.) ки́хам (or ки́хвам) / ки́хна [14]
snorkel (n.) шно́рхел [14]
snow (n.) сня́г [3] [7]
snow (v.) вали́ сня́г [12]
snow (adj.) сне́жен [11]
snowflake снежи́нка [10]
snowman сне́жен чове́к [11]
so many то́лкова [4]
so much то́лкова [4]
so that та [13]
soak измо́крям / измо́кря [12]
soccer фу́тбол [10]
socialist социалисти́чески [14]
society общество́ [12]
Sofia resident софиа́нец, софиа́нка [14]
Sofia (adj.) софи́йски [8]
soft ме́к [15]
soften оме́квам / оме́кна [11]
soldier войни́к [7]
sole [of the foot] стъпа́ло [12]
solve реша́вам / реша́ [8]
some sort ня́какъв [8]
somehow ня́как [8]
someone ня́кой [8]
something не́що [5]
sometime ня́кога [8]
sometimes поня́кога [8]
somewhere ня́къде [8]
son си́н [9]
song пе́сен [9]
soon ско́ро [1]
sound (v.) звуча́ [12]
sour ки́сел [6]
south юг [13]
speak гово́ря [3]
special специа́лен [9] ; осо́бен [10]
spend [time] прека́рвам / прека́рам [7]

spice (n.) подпра́вка [6]
spoiled разва́лен [11]
spoon (n.) лъжи́ца [6]
spoonful лъжи́ца [6]
sports (adj.) спо́ртен [9]
spot петно́ [14]
spouse съпру́г [3] [10] ; съпру́га [10]
spring (n.) про́лет [9] ; in the spring
  напро́лет [9]
spring (adj.) проле́тен [13]
stadium стадио́н [12]
stag еле́н [8]
stand стоя́ [4]
stand, endure издъ́ржам / издъ́ржа [7]
stand up ста́вам / ста́на [4]
standard (n.) равни́ще [15]
start по́чвам / по́чна [10]
start flowing поти́чам / потека́ [12]
start to rain (or other precipitation)
  заваля́ва / завали́ [12]
startle стря́скам / стре́сна [11] ;
  стря́скам се / стре́сна се [11]
state [political] щат [1]
station (bus, train) га́ра [5]
stay оста́вам / оста́на [3] [4]
stay in one place стоя́ [11]
steadfast твъ́рд [11]
steak пържо́ла [4]
steam (adj.) па́рен [11]
step (n.) стъ́лба [11]
step back отстъ́пвам / отстъ́пя [8]
stepfather вто́ри баща́ [10]
stepmother вто́ра ма́йка [10] ; ма́щеха
  [10]
stick (v.) забо́ждам / забода́ [13]
still о́ще [2]
stomach стома́х [12]
stop sign стоп [10]
stop [bus or tram] (n.) спи́рка [7]
stop (v.) спи́рам / спра́ [11]
store (n.) магази́н [5]
stork щъ́ркел [13]
story при́казка [12] ; ра́зказ [14]
straight (adj.) прав [4]
stranger чужде́нец [3] ; чужденка́ [3]
strawberry я́года [11]
street у́лица [3]
strength си́ла [7]
stretch out прости́рам / простра́ [12]
string (n.) връ́зка [13]
string together ни́жа [14] ; нани́звам /
  нани́жа [14]
stroll (n.) разхо́дка [9]
strong си́лен [2]
student [university level] студе́нт (ка) [1]
student [elementary or secondary] учени́к,
  учени́чка [7]

study, examine разгле́ждам / разгле́дам
  [4]
study, make a study of изуча́вам / изуча́
  [4]
stuffy заду́шен [4]
subscribe абони́рам [11]
succeed успя́вам / успе́я [8]
success успе́х [5]
such такъ́в, така́ва, такова́, таки́ва [11]
suddenly изведнъ́ж [5]
sugar за́хар [12]
suggestion предложе́ние [9]
suit (n.) костю́м [14]
suitcase ку́фар [2]
sullen намръ́щен [13]
summer ля́то [9]
summit връх [11]
sun слъ́нце [9]
sunbathe пека́ се (на слъ́нце) [13]
Sunday неде́ля [6]
sunny слъ́нчев [10]
supplement (n.) допълне́ние [8]
support (v.) подпи́рам / подпра́ [14]
sure си́гурен [6]
surely си́гурно [9]
surprise (n.) изнена́да [12]
survey (v.) огле́ждам / огле́дам [14]
suspect (v.) подози́рам / подозра́ [14]
suspend зака́чам / закача́ [13]
sustain поня́сям / понеса́ [14]
swallow (n.) глъ́тка [3]
swallow (v.) глъ́твам / глъ́тна [7] ;
  гъ́лтам [8]
sweater жиле́тка [12] ; пуло́вер [12]
sweet (adj.) сла́дък [3]
sweet shop сладка́рница [14]
swim плу́вам
swim suit ба́нски [13]

T-shirt фане́лка (or флане́лка) [14]
table ма́са [7] ; small table ма́сичка
  [13]
tail (n.) опа́шка [11]
take взи́мам (or взе́мам) / взе́ма [4] ;
  во́дя [8] ; пое́мам / пое́ма [8] ; take
  somewhere заве́ждам / заведа́ [10]
take a bath изкъ́пвам се / изкъ́пя се [14]
take an interest in проявя́вам интере́с към
  [8]
take a look погле́ждам / погле́дна [14]
take a walk разхо́ждам се / разхо́дя се [8]
take care of погри́жвам се / погри́жа се
  [11]
take for a brief stroll поразхо́ждам [11]
take for a walk разхо́ждам / разхо́дя [10]

take off [clothing] събли́чам / съблека́
[13] ; събли́чам се / съблека́ се [13] ;
[footwear] събу́вам / събу́я [13] ;
събу́вам се / събу́я се [13]

take out изве́ждам / изведа́ [9] ;
изва́ждам / изва́дя [14]

take place състоя́ се [14]

take to занáсям / занеса́ [7]

take up ка́чвам / кача́ [7] ; пое́мам /
пое́ма [8] ; зае́мам / зае́ма [12]

tale при́казка [12]

talk (v.) гово́ря [3] ; прика́звам [9]

talk for a bit поговóрвам / поговóря [12]

tall висо́к [5]

tape recorder [cassette] касетофóн [5]

tardiness [state of being late] закъсне́ние
[14]

tassel пискю́л [13]

taste (n.) вку́с [7]

tasty вку́сен [6]

taxi такси́ [14]

tea (n.) ча́й [7]

tea (adj.) ча́ен [7]

teach у́ча [5] ; научáвам / науча́ [6]

teacher [university level] преподава́тел (ка)
[1] ; [elementary or secondary]
учи́тел (ка) [1]

team отбóр [12]

teapot ча́йник [7]

tear [in eye] сълза́ [12]

tear (v.) дера́ [12]

teaspoon лъжи́чка [6]

teaspoonful лъжи́чка [6]

technology те́хника [12]

telephone (n.) телефóн [5]

telephone (v.) звъня́ по телефóна [10]

telephone (adj.) телефóнен [13]

television телеви́зия [6]

tell разка́звам / разка́жа [8] ;
разпра́вям / разпра́вя [12]

ten де́сет [6]

tennis те́нис [13]

tense [verbal] вре́ме [9]

tension напреже́ние [14]

terrible стра́шен [9] ; ужа́сен [12]

terrifying страхóтен [5]

test (n.) и́зпит [5]

test (v.) проверя́вам / проверя́ [13]

textbook уче́бник [2]

than от [8] ; откóлкото [10]

thank благодаря́ [10]

thank God сла́ва Бóгу [9]

thank you благодаря́ [2]

thanks, thankfulness благода́рност [9]

Thanksgiving Day Де́н на благодарността́
[9]

that това́ [2] ; она́зи [8] ; óнзи [8]
онова́ [8] ; она́я [11] ; ону́й [11] ;
óня [11]

that (conjunction) че [3] ; та [13]

that way така́ [4]

that's that това́ е [13]

theater теа́тър [6]

their, theirs те́хен [8]

them (direct object) ги [5] ; тя́х [10]

them (indirect object) им [7] ; на тя́х
[10]

then, in that case тога́ва [4] ; то [11]

then, next пóсле [6]

thence, from there отта́м [3]

there та́м [4]

there is/are и́ма [2] ; there isn't/aren't
ня́ма [2]

therefore затова́ [5]

these те́зи [3] ; ти́я [11]

they те́ [1]

thigh бедрó [12]

thin сла́б [14]

think ми́сля [5]

think about поми́слям / поми́сля [12]

think of се́щам се / се́тя се [11]

think up изми́слям / изми́сля [12]

third тре́ти [8]

thirsty жа́ден [2]

thirteen трина́йсет [6]

thirty три́йсет [6]

this това́ [2] ; та́зи [3] ; тóзи [3] ;
ту́й [11] ; тóя [11] ; та́я [11]

this evening довéчера [9]

those онéзи [8] ; они́я [11]

thousand хиля́да [9]

thread together ни́жа [14]

three три́ [2] ; три́ма [6]

three hundred три́ста [9]

throat гъ́рло [12] ; гу́ша [12]

through през [6]

throughout из [11]

thumb па́лец [12]

Thursday четвъ́ртък [9]

thus затова́ [5] ; thus, that way така́
[4] ; тъ́й [11]

ticket биле́т [11]

tie (n.) връ́зка [13]

tie (v.) завръ́звам / завъ́ржа [13]

tied привъ́рзан [11]

tight те́сен [2]

tighten постя́гам / посте́гна [11]

tile плóчка [3] ; плóча [7]

time вре́ме [2] ; on time навре́ме [5]

time [instance] пъ́т [4] [6]

time off óтпуска [2]

tip (n.) връ́х [11]

tire (v.) омръ́звам / омръ́зна [12]

tired уморе́н [8]

title заглáвие [13]
to (preposition) за [1] ; до [5] ; на [7]
to (subordinating conjunction) да [5]
toast (v.) чýкам се / чýкна се [11]
today днéс [1]
today's днéшен [9]
toe прьст [12] ; big toe пáлец [12]
together зáедно [5]
tomato домáт [6]
tomorrow ýтре [4]
tomorrow's ýтрешен [9]
tonight тáзи нóщ [9]
tonsil слúвица [12]
too bad жáлко [11]
too much прекалéно [13]
tooth зьб [6] [8]
torn скьсан [14]
touch (v.) пúпам [9]
tour of a city разхóдка из градá [11]
tourist турúст [8]
toward кьм [8]
towel кьрпа [13]
town грáд [6]
traffic движéние [12]
traffic laws правилá на пьтното движéние [12]
train (n.) влáк [2]
tram трамвáй [2]
tram (adj.) трамвáен [7]
transfer прехвьрлям се / прехвьрля се [12]
translation прéвод [14]
travel (v.) пътýвам [1] [3]
traveler пьтник [7]
traveling (adj.) пьтен [12]
travels пътýване [7]
treasure (n.) съкрóвище [13]
treat (v.) чéрпя [4] ; почéрпвам / почéрпя [6] ; третúрам [8]
tree дървó [7]
trip (n.) пътýване [7] ; пътешéствие [11]
trout пъстьрва [9]
true úстински [8] ; вéрен [10]
truly наúстина [2]
truth úстина [1]
try to convince убеждáвам [14]
tsar цáр [8]
Tuesday втóрник [9]
Turks тýрци [6]
turn (v.) завúвам / завúя [6] ; обрьщам се / обьрна се [14]
turn around въртя̀ се [14]
turtle костенýрка [9]
twelve дванáйсет [6]
twenty двáйсет [6]
twist (v.) изплúтам / изплетá [12]
two двé [2] [6] ; двá [6] ; двáма [6]

two-colored двуцвéтен [13]
two hundred двéста [9]
type (n.) тúп [7]
typical типúчен [3]

umbrella чадьр [12]
uncle чúчко [6] ; вýйчо [10] ; чúчо [10]
unconscionable прекалéн [13]
under под [3]
understand разбúрам [1] [3] [4]
understanding разбúране [12]
undress (v.) съблúчам / съблекá [13] ; съблúчам се / съблекá се [13]
uneasy неспокóен [4]
unfortunately за съжалéние [1]
union (n.) съю́з [14]
United States of America Съединéните америкáнски щáти [1]
university (n.) университéт [7]
university (adj.) университéтски [12]
unknown непознáт [5]
until до [6] ; докáто [9] ; докáто не [13]
until now досегá [6]
up гóре [11] ; нагóре [11]
up to до [5]
upright прáв [4]
USA САЩ [1]
us (direct object) ни [5] ; нáс [10]
us (indirect object) ни [7]] ; на нáс [10]
use (n.) пóлза [12]
useful полéзен [8]
usual обикновéн [8]
usually обикновéно [2]
utter рекá [7]

vacation óтпуска [2] ; почúвка [3] ; вакáнция [6]
various разлúчен [10]
vegetable зеленчýк [7]
vegetarian (n.) [person] вегетериáнец [3] ; вегетериáнка [3]
vegetarian (adj.) [of food] безмéсен [7]
verbatim наизýст [4]
verify проверя́вам / проверя̀ [13]
very мнóго [1]
[the] very сáм, самá, самó, самú [12]
videocamera видеокáмера [5]
videocassette вúдеокасета [12]
view (n.) вúд [11]
vigil навечéрие [10]
village сéло [2]
vine (n.) лозá [6]

vine *(adj.)* ло́зов [6]
vineyard ло́зе [10]
visit *(v.)* и́двам на го́сти [5] ; посеща́вам / посетя́ [11]
voice *(n.)* глас [12]

wagon ваго́н [6]
waistcoat жиле́тка [12]
wait *(v.)* поча́квам / поча́кам [7]
wait, wait for ча́кам [3]
wait in line редя́ се на опа́шка [12]
waiter сервитьо́р (ка) [4]
waiting room чака́лня [15]
wake събу́ждам / събу́дя [11]
wake up събу́ждам се / събу́дя се [11]
walk *(n.)* разхо́дка [9]
walk *(v.)* вървя́ [3] ; разхо́ждам се / разхо́дя се [8]
walk the dog изве́ждам ку́чето на разхо́дка [9]
walnut о́рех [6]
want *(v.)* и́скам [5] ; ща [7] ; пои́сквам / пои́скам [12]
war *(n.)* война́ [7]
warm *(v.)* гре́я [9]
warm *(adj.)* то́пъл [2]
was бе́ше [6] *(2-3sg)* ; бях [6] *(1sg)*
wash *(v.)* ми́я [8] ; пера́ [12] ; изпи́рам / изпера́ [12] ; изми́вам / измия [13]
wassailer сурвака́р [10]
watch *(n.)* часо́вник [7]
water *(n.)* вода́ [4]
water *(v.)* поли́вам / поле́я [13]
wave *(v.)* ма́хам [14]
way на́чин [6]
way, road път [6] [8]
we ни́е [1]
weak слаб [14]
wear *(v.)* но́ся [3]
weather *(n.)* вре́ме [2]
wedding *(n.)* сва́тба [10]
wedding *(adj.)* сва́тбен [11]
Wednesday сря́да [9]
week се́дмица [6]
welcome добре́ дошли́ [2] [11] ; добре́ дошла́ [11] ; добре́ дошъ́л [11]
well добре́ [2]
well *(hesitation sound)* ами́ [7]
were бя́ха [6] *(3pl)* ; бя́хме [6] *(1pl)* ; бя́хте [6] *(2pl)*
what какво́ [1] [4] ; какъ́в [3] ; what is your name? ка́к се ка́звате? [1] ; what kind of какъ́в [3] ; що́ [8] ; what's it about? за какво́ ста́ва ду́ма? [11]

whatever какво́ ли не [12] ; какво́то [12]
wheel колело́ [14]
when кога́ [6] ; when, at what time в ко́лко часа́ [6] ; като [6]
whence, from where откъде́ [1]
where къде́ [1]
whether дали́ [11]
which ко́й, коя́, кое́, кои́ [5]
while докато [9] ; пък [11]
white бял [2]
who ко́й [3] ; коя́, кое́, кои́ [5]
whole *(adj.)* цял [7]
wholesale на е́дро [9]
whom кого́ [8]
whose чий, чия́, чие́, чии́ [8]
why защо́ [3] ; какво́ [4]
wide широ́к [12]
wife жена́ [2]
will *(n.)* во́ля [12]
will (v., future tense) ще [7]
win *(v.)* спече́лвам / спече́ля [14]
wind вя́тър [2] [7]
window прозо́рец [3] ; small window прозо́рче [13]
wine ви́но [2]
Winnie the Pooh Ме́чо Пу́х [11]
winter зи́ма [9]
winter *(adj.)* зи́мен [11]
wipe бъ́рша [13] ; избъ́рсвам / избъ́рша [13]
wish *(n.)* жела́ние [14]
wish *(v.)* желая́ [7] ; пожела́вам / пожела́я [8]] ; пои́сквам / пои́скам [12]
with с [2] ; със [7]
within, in [time] за [6]
without без [6] ; без да [14]
wizard вълше́бник [11]
wolf вълк [8]
woman жена́ [2]
wonder *(v.)* чу́дя се [5] ; попи́твам се / попи́там се [13]
wonderful чуде́сен [2]
won't ня́ма да [7]
wood *(n.)* дърво́ [11]
wood, wooden дъ́рвен [13]
woods гора́ [3]
wool *(n.)* вълна́ [21]
wool, woolen вълнен [13]
word ду́ма [7] ; word of honor че́стна ду́ма [12]
work *(n.)* ра́бота [2] [4] [14]
work *(v.)* рабо́тя [4] [11]
work *(adj.)* рабо́тен [6]
world *(n.)* свят [18]
world *(adj.)* свето́вен [10]

worry *(v.)* притеснявам / притесня́ [8]
worry, be worried притеснявам се /
    притесня́ се [7]
wrap *(v.)* зави́вам / зави́я [6]
wrist ки́тка [12]
write пи́ша [3] ; напи́свам / напи́ша [5]
writer писа́тел (ка) [10]

yard дво́р [11]
year годи́на [3]
yearly годи́шен [9]
yell ви́кам [12]
yes да́ [1]
yesterday вче́ра [9]
yesterday evening сно́щи [9]

yesterday's вче́рашен [9]
yet о́ще [2] ; пъ́к [11]
yield *(v.)* отстъ́пвам / отстъ́пя [8]
yogurt ки́село мля́ко [6]
you *(subject)* ви́е [1] *(pl.; sg. polite)* ; ти́
    [1] *(sg., familiar)*
you *(direct object)* ви [5] *(pl.; sg. polite)* ;
    ва́с [10] *(pl.; sg. polite)* ; те [5]; те́бе
    [10] *(sg., familiar)*
you *(indirect object)* ви [7] *(pl.; sg. polite)* ;
    на ва́с [10] *(pl.; sg. polite)* ; ти [7]
    (sg., familiar) ; на те́бе [10] *(sg.,
    familiar)*
young мла́д [7]
younger по́-ма́лък [10]
your, yours ва́ш [8] *(pl.; sg. polite)* ; тво́й
    [8] *(sg., familiar)*

Courtyard of house in eastern Bulgarian seaside town

INDEX

Note: alphabetic ordering in Cyrillic lists is as in Cyrillic.

Adverbs

      general form: 50
      directional (навън, отгоре, etc.): 223-224
      indefinite (някога, някъде, etc.): 147
      interrogative (кога, къде, etc.): 147
      of location (вътре, вън, etc.): 223-224
      negative (никога, никъде, etc.): 147
      of time: 174
      usage: 55

Agreement

      adjectives and nouns: 33-34
      adjectives with neuter plural nouns: 104
      definite articles and nouns: 33
      in conjoined adjectives: 161
      pronouns referring to nouns: 32
      "rhyming" principle: 34, 57, 199
      of past active participles: 172-173
      of verbs in да-phrases: 81
      вие with singular meaning: 41

Aorist tense

      general: 102
      and aspect: 245-246, 256
      meaning: 103
      of a-verbs (type питам, отварям): 102
      of e-verbs
            (type стана, пиша, пия, взема): 194-195
            (type къпя, копая): 202, 227
            (type живея, умра): 219-220
            (type лая, позная): 227
            (type пера, разбера): 245
      of и-verbs
            (type ходя, броя): 170
            (type вървя, видя): 219
            спя: 227
            боли: 248
      in -ox
            (type чета, дам, дойда, отида): 171
            (type сека): 180
      of съм: 102
      contrast of aorist and imperfect tenses: 293-294, 301
      relationship between aorist and present tense forms: 253-255
      usage of aorist: 245-246

Article, *see* **Definiteness**

Aspect

      general review: 316
      general: 64, 132-133, 302-303
      in да-phrases: 82-83
      and the aorist: 245-246, 256
      and conjunctions: 274
      and the future tense: 122-123
      and the imperative: 65, 70, 273
      and the imperfect tense: 302-303
      derivation of imperfectives: 132
      meaning of imperfective aspect: 69

Professor Eric Hamp in the courtyard of Bachkovo Monastery in the northern Rhodope Mountains